A PRODIGAL
SAINT

The Penn State Series in Lived Religious Experience
Judith Van Herik, General Editor

The series publishes books that interpret religions by studying personal experience in its historical, geographical, social, and cultural settings.

Lee Hoinacki, *El Camino: Walking to Santiago de Compostela*

Suzanne Selinger, *Charlotte von Kirschbaum and Karl Barth: A Study in Biography and the History of Theology*

Lee Hoinacki, *Stumbling Toward Justice: Stories of Place*

Nadieszda Kizenko, *A Prodigal Saint: Father John of Kronstadt and the Russian People*

NADIESZDA KIZENKO

A PRODIGAL SAINT

Father John of Kronstadt
and the
Russian People

The Pennsylvania State University Press
University Park, Pennsylvania

Studies of the Harriman Institute, Columbia University

The Harriman Institute, Columbia University, sponsors the Studies of the Harriman Institute in the belief that their publication contributes to scholarly research and public understanding. In this way, the Institute, while not necessarily endorsing their conclusions, is pleased to make available the results of some of the research conducted under its auspices. A list of the Studies appears on page 377 of the book.

Library of Congress Cataloging-in-Publication Data

Kizenko, Nadieszda, 1961–
  A prodigal saint : Father John of Kronstadt and the Russian people / Nadieszda Kizenko.
    p. cm. — (Penn State series in lived religious experience) (Studies of the Harriman Institute)
  Includes bibliographical references and index.
  ISBN 0-271-01975-1 (cloth : alk. paper)
  ISBN 0-271-01976-X (pbk. : alk. paper)
  1. John of Kronstadt, Saint, 1829–1909. 2. Christian saints—Russia—Biography.   I. Title. II. Series.
  BX597.S4K58 2000
  281.9´092—dc21
  [B]   99-28363
                                                                        CIP

Second printing, 2003

Copyright © 2000 The Pennsylvania State University
All rights reserved
Printed in the United States of America
Published by The Pennsylvania State University Press,
University Park, PA 16802-1003

It is the policy of The Pennsylvania State University Press to use acid-free paper for the first printing of all clothbound books. Publications on uncoated stock satisfy the minimum requirements of American National Standard for Information Sciences—Permanence of Paper for Printed Library Materials, ANSI Z39.48-1992.

to
Boris and Tamara Kizenko,
my favorite Batiushka and Matushka

Contents

	Acknowledgments	ix
	List of Illustrations	xiii
	Introduction	1
1	Priestly Formation	9
2	Liturgical Innovations	39
3	Apostolicity, Charity, and the Move Toward Sanctity	67
4	Letters as Examples of Religious Mentalities	97
5	Contemporary Representations and Their Role in Spreading Saintly Celebrity	151
6	The "Ioannites" and the Limits of Veneration	197
7	The Politics of Orthodoxy, Autocracy, and the Revolutionary Movement	233
8	Posthumous Legacy	261
	Conclusion	281
	Notes	287
	Bibliography	335
	Index	365

Acknowledgments

For their contribution to the research and writing of this book, I am grateful to many institutions and individuals. Grants from the Joint Committee on the Soviet Union and Its Successor States of the Social Science Research Council, the American Council of Learned Societies, with funds provided by the State Department under the Russian, Eurasian, and East European Training Program (Title VIII), the International Research and Exchanges Board (IREX), with funds provided by the National Endowment for the Humanities, the United States Information Agency, and the W. Averell Harriman Institute for the Advanced Study of the Soviet Union, Columbia University, have made work on this project possible.

Librarians at the following institutions facilitated my research: the Bakhmeteff Archive and Butler Library of Columbia University; the Library of Congress; Holy Trinity Seminary; the St. John of Kronstadt Memorial Fund; Widener Library of Harvard University; the Russian National Library (formerly Lenin Library) in Moscow; the Saltykov-Shchedrin Public Library and the Library of the Academy of Sciences in St. Petersburg; the New York Public Library; Princeton University; the St. Petersburg Theological Academy; St. Vladimir's Seminary; and the University at Albany.

My archival research in Russia was assisted by the staffs of the following archives: the Central State Historical Archive of St. Petersburg, the Central State Archive of Cine- and Photo-Documents, the Oral History Archive of the Russian State University for the Humanities, the Russian Federation State Archive of St. Petersburg, The Russian State Archive of Literature and Art, The Russian State Historical Archive, The Russian State Historical Archive of the City of Moscow; the Russian National Library, Manuscript Section; the State Archive of the Russian Federation, and the State Museum of Ethnography.

Acknowledgments

In the course of a decade researching and writing this book, I have benefited from the encouragement and assistance of many friends and colleagues. Catherine Bortoli Doucet, Igor Harlamov, Jennifer Hails Hedda, Edward Kasinec, Scott Kenworthy, Eve Levin, Laurie Manchester, Anastasia Pettit, Maria Plishevsky, and Aleksandr Polunov helped find references. Natalia A. Chekmareva at the Central State Historical Archive of St. Petersburg and Serafima I. Varekova at the Russian State Historical Archive went far beyond the call of duty in helping me not only with research, photocopies, and deciphering handwriting but also provided much-needed consolation when my St. Petersburg flat was burgled of everything on Christmas Eve, down to olive oil and slippers. Caroline Bynum, Michael Flier, Protoierei Boris and Tamara Kizenko, Gregory Freeze, and Elizabeth Priebe have shared generously their encyclopedic knowledge of things holy. Leopold Haimson, Irina Itina, Edward Kasinec, Isaac Lambertsen, Marina Ledkovsky, John Monfasani, Marc Raeff, Anastasia Schatiloff, Ivan Semyanko, Mark Von Hagen, and Richard Wortman have read sections of the manuscript; Eve Levin and Valentine Vronsky, to whom particular thanks are due, have read it in its entirety. They have helped me sharpen arguments and correct errors of fact and interpretation. Richard Hamm, Ann Withington, Dan White, Joseph Zacek, and my other colleagues at the University at Albany performed the vexing—and invaluable—function of regularly asking me when I was going to finish.

In a larger sense, intellectual debts go back much further. In Syracuse, Maria Pavlovna Nikitina, Monk Nestor (Levitin), and my late grandmother, Evgen'ia Dmitrievna, were my first contact with rigorous Russian pedagogy. Archbishop Averkii (Taushev), Archbishop Nektarii (Kontsevich), and the Reverend Moses Tarasevich were living examples of the continuity between émigré and pre-revolutionary theological thought. The monastic communities of Jordanville, Gethsemane, and Karpovka, especially the late Hieromonk Ignatii (Trepachko), Archimandrites Vladimir (Sukhobok) and Sergii (Romberg), and Nun Nadezhda, gave a window onto Father John's world. At Harvard, Cathy Frierson, William Fuller, Beth Holmgren, Edward Keenan, Steve Nielsen, Richard Pipes, Simon Schama, Vsevolod Setchkareff, and Jurij Striedter taught me that, Aksakov notwithstanding, there was more to Russian history than the lives of the saints; Maria Belaeff, Mark Eckenwiler, Geoffrey Featherstone, Peter Fekula, James Goldstein, Charles Hanson, Mary Kirk, Vladimir Klimenko, William Li, James Sheppe, David Wolff, Andrew Wachtel, and Lena Zezulin created a community as congenial as possible. In New York, Alison Frazier,

Acknowledgments

Steven Gordon, Andrei Holodny, Tory Lord, David Powell, Nicolas Schidlovsky, George Skok, and Robert Somerville made it possible to talk about saints in every context imaginable. Most recently, participants in the "Lived Orthodoxy in the Russian Historical Experience, 988–1999" workshop organized by Valerie Kivelson, especially Gregory Bruess, Jane Burbank, Laura Downs, Laura Engelstein, John Fine, Susan Juster, Daniel Rowland, Tatiana Senkevitch, Isolde Thŷret, William Wagner, and Christine Worobec, have given last-minute insights and perspectives. I am grateful to all of them.

Most of all, I would like to thank Pierre Frugier. He has served as a repository of knowledge, contributed to the conceptual framework, read and re-read chapter drafts, found references in places as far-flung as Nice, corrected theological lapses, and sought to purge the book of some passing trends, all in the face of my surliness. Any shortcomings that remain are entirely my responsibility.

Parts of Chapters 1 and 6 have appeared in print as "Ioann of Kronstadt and the Reception of Sanctity," *The Russian Review* 57 (July 1998): 325–44. All dates before 1918 are given according to the Julian Calendar, which was twelve days behind the Gregorian in the nineteenth century, and thirteen days behind in the twentieth. I have transliterated the Russian according to the Library of Congress system, with a few exceptions: the name of the subject of this book is given as John, rather than as Ioann Il'ich, and I have used the anglicized versions of well-known names and places.

List of Illustrations

Fig. 1	Father John in the late 1880s	xiv
Fig. 2	St. Andrew's Cathedral in Kronstadt where Father John served	14
Fig. 3	Father John in the early 1880s	101
Fig. 4	Matushka Elizaveta Konstantinovna Sergieva	147
Fig. 5	Father John with his sisters	165
Fig. 6	Tourist postcard of Father John visiting his homeland	169
Fig. 7	Father John and Elizaveta Konstantinovna with his godchild's family	182
Fig. 8	Father John in the company of colleagues and friends	203
Fig. 9	Father John surrounded by seekers	208
Fig. 10	Cover of *Pulemet*, 1905. Satirical depiction of Father John's leaving Kronstadt during the sailors' rebellion	253
Fig. 11	Postcard of Father John returning to Kronstadt from St. Petersburg across the ice at night	254
Fig. 12	Father John's funeral procession, St. Petersburg, December 1908	263
Fig. 13	The St. John Convent on the Karpovka river in St. Petersburg	264
Fig. 14	Icon of Saint John of Kronstadt made by the nuns of the St. John Convent in St. Petersburg, 1992	279

Fig. 1 Father John in the late 1880s. Photo courtesy of the Central State Archive of Cine- and Photo-Documents.

Introduction

All Russian history reads like the lives of the saints.—Konstantin Aksakov

Saints are literally living icons. They are both emanations of the Divine on earth and representations to followers of what their community most cherishes and idealizes. As religiosity evolves over time, however, a saint's initial identification may no longer correspond to the needs of new generations of followers. A saint's fierce qualities that suited an age of turbulence might seem overly aggressive in later, more placid, times. If living saints throw in their lot with a political faction and the other side triumphs, they also run the risk of becoming an anachronistic embarrassment, and the Church has either to ignore or to mask their more volatile qualities.[1]

This problem is especially acute for the Church hierarchy. People's devotion can wax or wane over the centuries, allegiances and the lighting of votive candles may change from Saint Anne or Saint George to Blessed Xenia or Serafim of Sarov—but the canonization of saints and their depiction in text and image show both the faithful and the outside world where the saints officially stand with respect to the Church. If the discrepancy in the correspondence between current sensibilities and liturgical expression becomes too great, even canonical texts on saints can be altered. Under the pressure of the political and social changes of the twentieth century, the Russian Orthodox Church stopped raising prayers for the health of the emperor and for victory over his enemies, the Roman Catholic Church dropped such saints as Christopher from the roster and eliminated phrases perceived as anti-Semitic, and Protestant denominations rendered particular hymns and carols nonsexist. For popular saints to maintain their place in people's hearts and minds as well as in the liturgy, they must appeal on a level that transcends that of their original context.

Of all the saints who have walked together with their societies, Father John Sergiev (Ioann Il'ich) of Kronstadt (1829–1908) occupies a unique niche. He was born on October 19, 1829, into the family of a poor sacristan in the remote village of Sura in Russia's northern province of Arkhangelsk. He was so frail that his parents had him baptized immediately, thinking he would not live till the morning. He was not initially a strong student, but through hard work and fervent prayers he eventually performed so well that he could go to seminary, and then to the elite Theological Academy in St. Petersburg in 1850.

Just at the point when Father John was ordained in 1855, both state and church authorities embarked on the "Great Reforms" that sought to address peoples' concerns and engage them more directly in society. Father John was part of this movement outward, becoming involved in giving to the poor, creating shelters, developing employment programs, and participating in the temperance movement. He exemplified the active social consciousness of the Reform-era Orthodox Church. Yet he went beyond these practical measures. He served ecstatically, exhorting the faithful to the chalice. People sought him out so much that the Church hierarchy allowed him to introduce mass public confessions. Although some authorities tried to rein in Father John, people spread the word that his prayers worked.

At first, Father John's reputation was local. Then, in 1883, the St. Petersburg newspaper *New Time* ran an open letter from grateful recipients testifying to their healing at his hands. This brought him national fame and established Kronstadt as one of the leading pilgrimage sites in Russia. People came by the shipload; those who could not travel inundated the post office with their pleas. He became the first modern Russian religious celebrity, with his image on souvenir scarves, mugs, placards, and postcards; in effect, all of Russia was his parish. In 1894, when he was asked to minister to the dying emperor Alexander III, his fame became international, attracting correspondents from Europe and the United States.

Introduction

To this point, Father John's successful combination of social service, liturgical revival, charismatic prayer, and healing seemed to embody the answer of the Orthodox Church to the challenges of secularism, urbanism, and sectarianism. With the rise of terrorism and the revolutionary movement, however, Father John allied himself increasingly with the politics of the far right. He called for the killing of all revolutionaries, as Moses had done with the rebels at Mount Sinai, accepted honorary membership in a number of monarchist organizations, and blessed the banners of the radical-right Union of the Russian People. These pronouncements were, to paraphrase the Futurist poet Vladimir Mayakovsky, a slap in the face of public taste. Neutrality about Father John was no longer possible: liberals squirmed, rightists hailed him as a prophet, and radicals branded him as being everything they hated about the Orthodox Church. He became a kind of litmus test: how one felt about him immediately identified where one stood on relations between Church and state, Tsar and revolution, priests and people, men and women.

This barometric quality only increased after Father John's death at the end of 1908. The revolution of 1917, official Soviet atheism, the émigré experience, perestroika, the millennium of Christianity in Russia in 1988, the jockeying for hegemony within the Church and the country afterward—all of these forces created new versions of Father John that corresponded to new social and political conditions. Although the process of altering *vitae* to suit historical circumstances is as old as hagiography itself, the pace of change in the nineteenth and twentieth centuries makes his case unique.

This book examines the dialectical relation between Father John of Kronstadt and modern Russian society. It explores his relation to currents in Church policy and examines his contribution to them. It identifies the notions of holiness that preceded him to see how much he fulfilled them, using his career to identify patterns—such as the importance of class and gender—in Russian religiosity. It traces Father John's social and political role, particularly his charitable work and his involvement in the politics of the far right. The book also links him to larger trends in religiosity, such as the importance of the priest in piety and politics and the importance of media and publicity in modern saints' careers. It questions what, if anything, is specific to modern sanctity. Finally, this book considers Father John's posthumous reputation and representations—and their creators—to see what has proven most lasting in his legacy and how the struggle to use him persists to this day.

Introduction

Three introductory comments may be helpful. While I have tried to do justice to a figure as complex as Father John, this is not a hagiography: it is a life, not a *vita* written for an exclusively Orthodox or exclusively Russian audience, and I hope those seeking one will understand the difference. Because I intend this book both for readers with a general interest in the history of Russia and in the history of Christianity, I have provided background material for both groups. Finally, I am well aware that Father John still sparks intense reactions, as do many saints who take a political stand. I can say only that I have tried to convey this intensity, both devout and hostile, and the reasons for it.

Historiography

Father John brings several discussions into the forefront: the role of the Orthodox Church in Late Imperial Russia, the notions of popular piety and lived religion as paradigms for analysis, the importance of gender in religiosity, the interrelation between saints and their cults, and the connection between religious figures and politics. Of these, the relation between the church and society in nineteenth-century Russia has enjoyed a recent renaissance. Gregory Freeze is the father of the study of parish clergy, inspiring research ranging from clerical mentalité to pastoral social activism. Brenda Meehan's and Adele Lindenmeyr's work also situates Father John within his social and political context, in two important aspects of his service—charity and the support of women's monasticism.[2]

Paradoxically, the notion of popular piety is not useful for describing Father John, even though his contemporaries referred to him as "the most popular man in Russia." The term "popular" itself is problematic for a host of reasons, beginning with an artificial distinction, neither clear nor absolute, between "high" and "low."[3] As used in the Russian case, "popular" has been taken to imply "rural," "peasant," even "proletarian," as opposed to "urban" or "elite."[4] Scholars working outside the Russian field have proposed a variety of alternatives to "popular": William Christian prefers "local"; Eamon Duffy suggests "traditional"; Leonard Boyle, using liturgical practice as the point of departure, opts for such categories as "semi-liturgical" or "para-liturgical" to express piety.[5]

None of these terms, however, is adequate in the case of a saint. Father John influenced the practice and perception of religion among people from *all* social classes, from workers to aristocrats, and attracted

Americans as well as Tatars. The notion of a "popular" piety, removed from that of the elite or the hierarchy, therefore does not apply in wide-ranging saints' cults. Because Father John's cult cuts across the conventional lines of class, geography, gender, and occasionally even religious denomination, a change of paradigm is called for. This book uses the practice-based approach of "lived religion."[6] It sees continuities rather than posing a dichotomy between "high" and "low"; it acknowledges the role of normative perspectives on practice instead of trying to displace them.

Two additional approaches to the case of Father John are necessary. The first approach is the idea of, to paraphrase Ernst Kantorowicz, the tension between the saint's two bodies: the body private, dealing with personal salvation and the relation between saint and God; and the body public, dealing with Father John's sacramental role as a priest and his responsibility to his parish. As Father John's life shows, the two bodies clashed almost as often as they complemented one another.[7] The second is the idea of ever-expanding growth, with the saint's cult acquiring its own momentum and influence, even prompting the saint to unexpected actions.[8] In Father John's case, the transition from local to imperial figure proved to have political implications. Above all, this book explores the many overlapping, sometimes even contradictory, meanings a symbolic figure embodies.

This book also addresses the importance of gender in evaluating religious experience. While this is a truism for Europe and North America, it is less so for Late Imperial Russia. For various reasons, Soviet and "first-generation" feminist scholars of nineteenth- and twentieth-century Russia either ignored or distorted women's religiosity. Father John's life, however, shows how important he and religion were in women's lives—and it does so through their own words. By examining the letters thousands of women wrote to him, their reminiscences, and the way in which both were represented, this book presents voices and experiences that have been largely ignored.[9]

Of all the scholarly fields Father John crosses, the institutional Church-State framework has been apparently the best served. But, as with gender and modern sanctity, the involvement of the Orthodox Church and its clergymen in the politics of Late Imperial Russia has been ideologically charged. For decades, it was commonplace in both Western and Soviet scholarship to assert that the Orthodox Church was "the handmaiden of the state."[10] More nuanced treatments of the Russian Church-State relationship appeared from the 1970s, and scholars now largely accept that the Church pursued its own aims, which only partially coincided with those of the state.[11] While this research is a welcome development, there is a grain of apology in its assumption that independence for the Church is the most desirable condition. Father John is interesting precisely because such a paradigm was alien to him: his life illustrates just how thoroughly intertwined "official" ideology and "personal" convictions were, and how great a role members of the clergy played in actively supporting the ideas of the Tsar for Russia, and Russia for the Russians. While the study of lived religion tends to favor resistance to official structures, people such as Father John of Kronstadt remind us that lived religion is not always dissent, and that charismatics can support, not only subvert, structures of legitimation and power.[12]

The interrelation between saints and their cults is a huge field, but nineteenth- and twentieth-century Russian saints have been woefully neglected. The Revolution of 1917 cut short the burgeoning fields of hagiographical study within Russia, and scholars outside Russia had limited access to materials. It was difficult, to put it mildly, to study lived religion in a context where religion was discouraged at best and persecuted at worst. With the encouragement of religious expression and the wave of new canonizations in Russia after 1988, however, the study of Russian saints and their cults is a rich, largely unexplored field of inquiry. By studying one of the most political of modern saints, this book seeks to reintegrate Russian sanctity into its universal context and provide a framework for further study.

Sources

Father John has been the subject of many biographies, many of which were published during his lifetime and immediately after his death. Most of these, however, are hagiographical and were written at least partially with the aim of providing material and proofs for his eventual canonization. While these works provide much useful biographical information and are valuable for an analysis of his reception, they approach him from a largely edifying point of view; his social and political roles are passed over lightly.[13]

Virtually every literary contemporary of Father John's, from Aleksandr Amfiteatrov to Zinaida Gippius, commented on him; they provide a secular, less devotional perspective. Memoirs about Father John published during and immediately after his life provide a wide range of biographical material, but tend to be either accounts as unequivocally

Introduction

positive as the budding hagiographies or radical attacks hostile to the point of caricature.[14] Most Western accounts tend to repeat uncritically the radicals' comments.[15] In Soviet publications until 1990, Father John appears only as one of the minor stock villains in the revolutionary drama until, in a sudden about-face, the rebuilding of the Commonwealth of Independent States (CIS) and his canonization in 1990 spurred an apologetic reading and a wave of new publications. Outside the Soviet Union, the first person to compile materials on Father John was I. K. Surskii (Il'iashevich), in a two-volume study published in Belgrade in the 1930s. Because of its advocacy, however, it must be used with caution.[16] In the 1950s and the 1960s, Father John's memory was fostered by publications of the Holy Trinity Monastery in Jordanville, New York, and the St. John of Kronstadt Memorial Fund in Utica, New York. The monographs of Bishop Alexander (Semenoff-Tian-Shanskii) and Alla Selawry are the most important scholarly contributions,[17] though they had to be written without the benefit of archival material and do not cover the developments in Father John's cult after his death. He is discussed briefly in isolated articles or in more balanced studies of modern Russian religiosity, but mention of him is not comprehensive.[18] This book draws on all of these sources, for the changing representations of a saint shows how new audiences shape a saint's life to suit their own needs.

Above all, this book draws on primary sources. It is the first study of Father John to use the diaries he kept from his ordination in 1856 until his death in 1908, the letters to him, and other archival material, including the files of the Department of Police. All the diaries except for the last one, which is in the Central State Historical Archive of St. Petersburg (Tsentral'nyi Gosudarstvennyi Istoricheskii Arkhiv Sankt-Peterburga), are located in the State Archive of the Russian Federation (Gosudarstvennyi Arkhiv Rossiiskoi Federatsii), formerly known as the Central State Archive of the October Revolution (Tsentral'nyi Gosudarstvennyi Arkhiv Oktiabr'skoi Revoliutsii).

An examination of Father John's diaries is crucial to understanding the tension between the public and private life of a figure whom society regards as holy. As a chronicle of the evolution of a saintly figure, they complement the official version of Father John's *vita* by concentrating on the events of his private life. They depict the gradual outward movement of his religiosity, from scriptural meditation to a private asceticism modeled on the example of the Desert Fathers, and finally to his identification with the priestly role and his concentration on the salvation of his people.

Introduction

The chief difficulty lies in discerning from the purpose the diaries served in the life of Father John any information that would be of interest to the historian. The diaries are scanty on events and experiences that are not of a specifically religious nature; the entries are not consistently dated; there is little on Father John's involvement in politics. But these deficiencies recede when one considers the nature of these documents, which is a matter of genre. Virtually everything about the diaries—their concentration on religious themes, their overwhelmingly self-critical and negative tone, which depicts the author as a selfish and willful tyrant, their tireless chronicling of every lapse on his part—becomes comprehensible if they are not treated as diaries in the classic sense but as the spiritual chronicle that every Orthodox priest in Russia was encouraged to keep of both his own progress and that of his parishioners.[19] Neither do John's diaries constitute a fully formed retrospective religious autobiography, such as that of Saint Augustine, Saint Teresa of Avila, or the Old Believer priest Avvakum. Instead, Father John's diary notes express the developing nature of his needs and characteristics; they go from being private meditations on scripture to a chronicle of never-ending appointments and visits. As the topics covered vary in topic and his tone changes, his evolving relation with the Divine and with society become more clear.

Most letters to Father John are housed in the Central State Historical Archive of St. Petersburg. Their quantity and range are unique even for a modern saint. He had the equivalent of a separate postal code, and bushels of letters to him arrived every day. Of these, approximately ten thousand survive in Russian archives,[20] a fraction of all the mail received, as after 1900 *outgoing* donations from Father John's office averaged about fifteen thousand a year.[21] The letters reveal a great deal about public perceptions of Father John and responses to the phenomenon of living holiness, as well as religious mentality more broadly. While this study does not pretend to exhaust the letters' contents, the variety of requests are a window into turn-of-the-century Russia. They show that Father John was expected to offer help in virtually every incident that might befall people in the course of their lives, from business disputes and choosing winning numbers on lottery tickets to healing sick relatives and instructing nuns in the Jesus Prayer. They show, finally, that a saint is not all representation or projection. However much publicity or respect a saint may receive, if he or she does not actually help people on some level, people will ignore him or her in favor of others who can.

1

Priestly Formation

The Russian Milieu, 1830–1855

During the 1830s and the 1840s, John Sergiev's childhood years, the role of Russian priest was an ambiguous one. True, Russians were among the most religiously observant people in Europe. Their participation in religious rites remained high up to the Revolution of 1917.[1] But their observance did not necessarily carry with it a high valuation of the priest who performed those rites. The reforms of Peter I lowered the social status of priests, and even made them temporarily subject to corporal punishment.[2] Many of the most common religious traditions and customs, which ranged from going on pilgrimages or honoring local shrines, icons, and relics, were either independent of the priest or ancillary to him. Monasticism was still regarded by many as the most authentic version of the religious life. The high valuation of both monasticism and virginity led to the subtle devaluation of priests, who were almost invariably married. The priest was still of this world and tied to it; the wanderers, recluses, and monks had placed themselves outside and were, in the minds of most clergy and laity, closer to heaven.³

If priests lost out to unofficial ascetic figures in private charisma, they also lost out in official status—and wealth—to bishops, their superiors in the Church hierarchy. This anomalous position of the ubiquitous and neglected parish clergy was reflected in the roster of Russian Orthodox saints: by the nineteenth century, after nine hundred years of Christianity in Russia, virtually no priests had been canonized. Warriors, grand princes, and above all monks, bishops, and the occasional holy fool filled the *menaia*. By the mid-nineteenth century, sanctity in Imperial Russia was still something essentially other-worldly—or highly ranked.⁴

The marginalization of the priest in Russian piety was connected to the gradual marginalization of the sacrament that was supposed to be central to church life: the Eucharist. The relative neglect of partaking of the Eucharist had a long history in Russia and in Orthodox Christianity generally, stemming from the language of dread in referring to the sacrament dating back to Cyril of Jerusalem, and was reinforced by the thicket of rules surrounding it.⁵ Partaking of communion "unworthily" was accompanied by such formidable threats that, in some cases, people did not go to communion even after they had received absolution for their sins.⁶ As a result, the practice of taking communion only once a year was regarded as normal by the sixteenth century and persisted to the nineteenth century. The requirement by Russian law of communion for all Orthodox citizens, with entire government offices, guards regiments, and school classes partaking as a group on days designated by the various administrations, made its fulfillment as much a civic duty as an act of devotion.⁷

The development of Church architecture in Russia only exacerbated the tendency toward fear and mystery. In a tendency opposite to that in Roman Catholicism, where the Eucharist was displayed in monstrances and carried in public processions on the feast of Corpus Christi, the Orthodox icon-screen separating the altar from the body of worshippers grew higher over the centuries to the point where the sanctuary was completely hidden from view—and with it much of the liturgical action pertaining to the Eucharist, such as the consecration of the bread and wine. The icons and other tangible objects that could be venerated—holy water, blessed bread (and meat and fruit on the feasts of Easter and Transfiguration, respectively), holy oil, crosses, relics—came to seem more accessible than the intimidating Eucharist.⁸

The Great Reforms of Alexander II prompted Russian bishops to seek a wider range of measures to spread their message and change the behavior and attitudes of their people. These measures ranged from education at the elementary school level in both parish and state schools to preaching, medicine, and social leadership for priests. Along with the government, the Church began to publish periodicals, brochures, and pamphlets seeking at once to both encourage and direct religious devotion.[9] Cases of miracles that occurred during church services began to be reported in such journals as *Edifying Reading* (*Dushepoleznoe chtenie*), indicating a new emphasis on the salvific power of the liturgy.[10]

A fuller appreciation of the liturgy was manifest in other ways. Guides to church services were published to explain the meaning of liturgical actions and prayers that, religious writers acknowledged, remained obscure among the general public.[11] Lay people especially liked parish discussions, which included question-and-answer sessions and hymn-singing.[12] Bishops began to encourage more frequent communion. Metropolitan Filaret (Drozdov), for example, sought to increase the number of times received to four rather than once a year. Bishops and court composers alike stressed comprehension of the text rather than aesthetic abandon for those who came to church. They exhorted church singers to cast aside the Italianate music of the eighteenth century and perform "sacred melodies [that] must be without exception short and invariably fixed so that they become rooted in one's memory and not distract one's attention with either novelty or variety; they must be simple and inspired by heartwarming fire, inflaming the heart and elevating the spirit!"[13]

Bishops, then, pursued two goals simultaneously: to direct the focus of religious observance to the liturgy and to increase the pastoral role of the priest to include preaching and education. Finally, the movement outward to engage the masses found its most direct expression in the missionary work that was enthusiastically resumed in the nineteenth century.[14] Missionaries traveled to the farthest corners of the Russian Empire, the Theological Academy in Kazan devoted a special section to missionary studies, and the scriptures were translated into most of the empire's languages.[15]

By the time Father John began his career, currents initiated within both the church hierarchy and the laity were moving toward a common point. As in contemporary France, the emphases on preaching and education, more fervent private prayer, and pilgrimage attested to a religious impulse that expressed itself in an increasing range of forms.[16] Sectarianism and Old Belief also grew, forcing Orthodox Christians to more clearly articulate their beliefs.[17] Father John was both the product and a symbol of this evolution. His innovations must be placed in a context of lay diversity, as well as the hierarchy's wish to incorporate these trends in an Orthodox direction.

Father John's Early Life and Pastoral Career

John Sergiev was born on October 19, 1829, in the far north of Russia—in the village of Sura in Arkhangelsk province—to the sacristan (*diachok*) of the local church, Il'ia Mikhailovich Sergiev, and his wife, the illiterate Fedora Vlas'evna. As a child, he was sickly; his parents had him baptized immediately at home for fear that he would die, and once he nearly died of smallpox. In his autobiography, Father John described Il'ia Mikhailovich and Fedora Vlas'evna as being intensely devout and credits them with instilling in him a love of prayer and a deep religiosity.[18] Although the family was poor, they used their meager means to send John to the Arkhangelsk parish school at the age of ten. Unfortunately, for all his diligence, John showed no aptitude for learning at first, and was tormented by the thought that his parents were spending their last pennies on him. After nights of intense prayer, however, he suddenly understood his lessons clearly and became one of the school's best students. He continued on to seminary and finished first in his class in 1851, thereby earning a full scholarship to the St. Petersburg Theological Academy.

His father died in that same year, however, leaving his widow with no means of support. To help his mother, John offered to forgo the Academy and take a position immediately as a deacon or psalm-reader, but she refused to hear of it. Instead, John worked as a scribe and secretary for the Academy administration and sent his entire salary—ten rubles a month—home.

John's position entitled him to have a room of his own, and he appreciated the solitude. In the Academy, he studied philosophy, history, Latin, literature, physics, mathematics, and modern languages, as well as patristics and theology. Although he wrote little of this period, it was decisive in many ways. He received a broadly based education, came to love the writings of the Church Fathers, especially St. John Chrysostom and Metropolitan Filaret of Moscow, and began to feel an intense calling for the priesthood.[19] He had no close friends, preferring to spend his free time in the Academy garden in study and prayer. Years later, his classmates could recall only that "he kept talking about humility."

In his last year at the Academy, he fell into an inexplicable depression, and later said that he was only able to get out of it through long prayer.[20]

In his dreams, he once saw himself entering the apse of a large cathedral and going out through the south door (the reverse of a layperson's path). As it happens, the cathedral turned out to be the one in which he would later serve as a priest.[21] For although it is not clear at whose initiative, John married the daughter of Archpriest Konstantin Nesvitskii, who served at St. Andrew's Cathedral in Kronstadt—the church in his dreams. (Apparently, John only made the final decision to marry Elizaveta Konstantinovna when he visited Kronstadt and recognized the cathedral.) In rapid succession, he was married, ordained deacon, and then ordained priest by the end of 1855.[22]

Information about Father John's life during this period is laconic, and either retrospective or second-hand; it is only after his ordination that we become privy to his thoughts as they occurred. Just as Anthony the Great had encouraged monks to record their thoughts and deeds as a spiritual tool, so Russian seminarians were encouraged to keep diaries when they became priests, both to monitor their own spiritual lives and those of their parishioners.[23] In Father John's case, the idea was a godsend. His pattern of holiness was so unusual that it raises several questions. Was he consciously striving toward sanctity and, if so, did he see this as compatible with his priestly role? After all, holy men in his religious tradition had been overwhelmingly ascetic and monastic. How, then, did he reconcile the path toward spiritual perfection with married priestly service?

Father John's diaries show his path to holiness as an ever outward expansion of his private spirituality. The notion of a priest's two bodies is key to understanding this path. Like the medieval kings Ernst Kantorowicz described, the priest had two bodies to care for: a body private—his own salvation and holiness—and a body public—the souls and fates of his parishioners. The potential internal tension between these two personae was especially palpable for a priest seeking sanctity, as clerics from John Chrysostom onward have ruefully noted. Father John's diaries reflect this struggle.[24]

The first impression one gets in the diaries is that of immersion and apprenticeship. In the beginning of Father John's career, from his ordination in 1855 to about 1860, his journals consisted almost entirely of meditations and commentaries upon scripture; they were largely a means of internalizing the contents of the Bible. This is characteristic of the religious life in any tradition. One begins by studying the

Fig. 2 St. Andrew's Cathedral in Kronstadt, where Father John served.

Priestly Formation

tradition within which one intends to work, and then making it one's own, absorbing it fully before undertaking to create anything oneself. Given Father John's initial exclusive attention to biblical exegesis, it would seem that he perceived himself as a prospective theologian.[25]

A closer examination of his commentaries, however, reveals another inclination. In drawing on scripture, Father John's undertaking was neither scholarly nor strictly theological but deeply personal. He wanted to read the word of God in an immediate, intimate way, like some of the Desert Fathers—the difference being that he wrote down the results of his contemplation.[26] Unlike such monks as the Optina elders, who drew on their own monastic training and the living experience of the other elders, Father John pursued his course alone, with scripture and the immediate experience of God as his only guides. In a path most unusual within the Orthodox tradition, he had no "abba" or mentor himself.[27]

The absence in the diaries of quotation marks, or any other means of distinguishing the words of scripture from his own, reveals Father John's organic appropriation of scripture, rather than his having it remain an external object. What he looked for in scripture is telling as well. He sought to extract the essential and simplest moral lesson it contained, rather than distance himself from the text in any way or evaluate it and engage in analysis. His utilitarian approach to scripture is something like that of the novice artist approaching the works of his predecessors, with simultaneous reverence and desire for mastery. Almost all of the biblical passages he copied and commented upon, from Genesis to Isaiah, follow a similar pattern of paraphrase, distillation, and meditation. His commentary on the Tower of Babel is typical:

> See how your creature thanked you ... she was not able to sustain being worthy of you. Look at her origins: from earth, from dirt, from inanimate matter God created such a wonderful creature, consisting of such a beautiful body and an even more beautiful soul endowed with reason and freedom—and instead of living and blessing and thanking God and subjecting oneself to Him for this, man forgot himself in his beauty and his grandeur, the creature wanted herself to become Divinity ... so poorly and imperfectly did they understand. So little did they understand what is earth and what is heaven.[28]

Thus, certain themes that remain constant in his work and find public expression in sermons, such as God's inherent superiority over human beings and the misplaced pride and *hubris* of human beings in their refusal to accept their subordination, first appeared in the guise of scriptural commentary. Long meditations upon and copying out of scripture reinforced Father John's already intimate acquaintance with it. He was already thoroughly imbued with liturgical texts through attending services and reading the New Testament from early childhood.[29] After only a few months of daily copying out of scripture combined with serving the liturgy, it became second nature for Father John to think in liturgical and scriptural language. The exclamation "Thou, O Christ our God, who alone art the life of all, have mercy upon me!," for example, is as typical of his diary as it is of an Orthodox litany or canon. Similarly characteristic for him is the easy combination of liturgical and colloquial language. When he writes, "Glory to Thy power, O Lord!," he follows immediately with, "Glory to you, too, holy apostles, faithful servants of Christ, our God!" The familiar "you, *too*" has the effect of removing formality from the strictly liturgical, integrating it into everyday usage.[30]

The integration of the liturgical and the personal was central to Father John's early period and illustrates his aims in both his spiritual life and in his diaries. He wanted the personal and the scriptural to merge, wanted the line between them to disappear. He sought to become as transparent as possible in order to become a fit vessel for God. At this initial stage (1856–60), he still viewed himself largely as a willing learner of scripture who sought to understand and absorb its salvific message (and only that) as much as possible. He did not yet regard this quest as unique. As the first page of his first diary entered on December 14, 1856, declares:

> This book is not to be destroyed upon my death: perhaps someone like me in thoughts and feelings will appear who will express his profound sympathy for what is written in this book—even if not for all of it (which I dare not hope for, because if someone reads critically, mistakes may be found here as well), at least for some parts of it. Everything good and fair here I regard not as my own, but God's ... mine are only the mistakes and the shortcomings.[31]

Thus while Father John was not yet thinking in terms of a potential reading public in the first years of his keeping a diary, he had not ruled out the possibility of kindred spirits and may even have been consciously addressing them in his writings. This awareness of a potential reader may explain another quality of his early approach to scripture.

The Bible was not only something that he sought to internalize for the sake of his soul. He also used its events and descriptions as a code for events in his own life. In the early diaries, from 1856 to 1860, Father John quoted selections from scripture that seemed to him to parallel or reflect what he was experiencing in his own life rather than describe those events directly, as he would later.

This "encoding" worked in a way that is best understood by way of an example. Father John's biographers later described the beginning of his career as a time when both his clerical superiors and many of his parishioners harshly criticized him.[32] From 1862 onward, he referred explicitly to the ridicule he encountered and to how he responded with such phrases as "Rejoice when others mock you and belittle you: this is a sure sign that you are on the narrow path leading to eternal life."[33] In the earlier diaries, however, he cloaked the temptations he encountered in scriptural parallels. In commenting on Psalm 22, he wrote: "How painful it is for a person when his enemies rejoice at his unhappiness and how necessary is God's help against such enemies. But in order to obtain this help, lack of malice on our parts is required."[34]

Although Father John clearly identified here with the biblical writer crying to heaven against his foes, he steered clear of specifically mentioning his own struggles, striving for a detached tone of moral edification. Such distance, however, proved too difficult for him to maintain for long. Within a matter of weeks after beginning his diary, he adopted the Psalmist's indignation as his own. The first inkling that he thought of himself as a servant of God, whom others opposed precisely because he sought to be God's servant, emerged in his tone of identification with David:

> Psalm 42, 4 ... "My tears have been my food day and night, while they continually say unto me, Where is thy God?"—My God! So there were such godless ones among your chosen people, who would mock your servant every day, saying "Where is your God?" Oh, how difficult this is for the pious soul![35]

Thus as early as 1856, in his very first diary, Father John showed signs of identification with previous "servants of God" who he recognized as his predecessors. The same impulse to seek parallels to his own situation compelled him to compare his own temptations to those of Jesus Christ. This identification was necessarily of a different nature than his identification with the Psalmist. Although the Orthodox liturgy does refer to identifying oneself with Christ, particularly during the Paschal period, the general Orthodox tendency in both art and liturgy—in contrast to the Roman Catholic approach, particularly after the *devotio moderna*—is to emphasis Christ's divinity (and consequently His essential distance from human beings) rather than His humanity.[36] Father John's willingness to draw parallels between himself and Christ thus suggests a familiarity with the divine unusual for contemporary Russian Orthodoxy and something of the "boldness" before God that the Orthodox prize in the saints they venerate.

> As he was about to serve in the world, Jesus Christ was tempted by the devil. And so it is with every person, the greater his service, the more intensely is he initially subject to the devil's attack; because by doing so the devil attempts to destroy from the very start the beneficent influence which a person who takes upon himself service to society can have, in time.[37]

Father John's perception of his own role and position is covered with the thinnest of veils here. His intent to serve and convert society as a priest met obstacles and hostility in the very first year of his ordination. He is less concerned with describing the exact circumstances and nature of the obstacles than with marshaling his forces and not allowing himself to lose sight of his aim. He cites the example of Jesus in order to hearten himself: If someone as powerful as Christ could be tempted, surely he himself should be prepared to encounter ordeals as well. Similarly, Father John's discussions of the trials endured by Job, Ezekiel, and other biblical heroes are meant to encourage himself to persevere in the course of serving God and to ignore the resistance of his foes.

From his apprenticeship by mimesis, in which he sought to impress the words of Scripture upon himself as on a blank slate, Father John moved quickly to a more personal relation to both God and scripture. Bursts of lyrical effusion punctuated pages of literalness:

> On Psalm 23, The Lord is my shepherd and I shall not want.... How good I feel at the thought the Almighty and All-good Lord Himself is my shepherd in the green pastures; that he leads me on the path of righteousness—me, a great sinner. I almost feel that the words of David's psalm were composed just for me—they are so close to my heart, so appropriate to my condition. Oh, my kindest, sweetest shepherd, Jesus! Tend me in the green pastures; send [me] your sweetness, your peace in my heart, as you send

succulent grass to your sheep, so that without them I do not turn to the bitter herbs of passions and vices and kill my soul with them.[38]

This intensity of Father John's devotion reveals the nature of his relation to God. No other affective bond approached it. God to Father John was Father and Mother and Bridegroom in one; he felt alienation from God as keenly as a Romantic hero did from his lover. During such moments of desolation, his gropings back to God reached lyricism:

> Lord! Grant me to rest in the bosom of your love, as I once had the bliss of resting in it. Ah, I know reciprocally, my God, my Father, how sweet it is to be together with you in love. A small child is not as consoled in its mother's arms after its tears as those who are worthy of your love are consoled by it. Your love is soothing, peaceful, full of inexpressible joy which is holy and sublime ... the person who abides in your love fears nothing, even though the entire world might threaten him with innumerable calamities. Without you I am sad and burdened; my soul is disturbed and confused; my heart painfully pines and sorrows; I am completely not myself; I am as one cast out, as one who has lost his way. I am contemptible then in my own eyes; it is then as if your beautiful world does not exist for me. But when I rest in the arms of your divine love, then you are with me, and when I am together with you, then everything is with me: the holy and shining angels; all of the Fathers, my love for whom then makes them as close to me as brothers; and every creature, the entire visible world, heavenly and earthly. The world becomes your common house then, and it becomes my property as well, because then I am your son, and the property of the Father is also the property of the son.[39]

This longing for intimacy with God directed the turn Father John's religiosity would eventually take. He identified most with the ascetics who sought a similar closeness and his diary began to reflect his concern with forming a specifically ascetic identity. His lists of reading material to buy—Ephraim the Syrian, John Chrysostom (a favorite from his days at seminary and the Academy), Gregory of Nyssa, Bishop Filaret's *Teaching on the Fathers of the Church*—show his desire to master classics of asceticism, as well as the mechanics of the liturgy.[40] An entry from the early 1860s reflects his absorption of these classics:

I wish to be entirely an instrument of my God, as were the prophets and the apostles: I want to be a temple of God, I want my heart to be an altar of God, to have my word be the word of God, who lives in me; to have my hands to only those works which are pleasing to God. It is meet and right: I am entirely the Master's not my own;—yes, he acts through all of me.[41]

The most telling moment in this ascetic path came when Father John applied to himself the thirty steps to ascetic perfection that Saint John of the Ladder outlined in the prototypical monastic manual, *The Ladder of Divine Ascent*. This guide was so highly regarded in the Russian Orthodox tradition that people put off reading it until they felt prepared to dedicate themselves fully to their inner life; John's turning to it signaled his seriousness.[42] Although he was already preaching, helping the poor, and serving the liturgy in his public life during the late 1850s, his diary entries during this time speak almost exclusively of his inner struggles, his relation with God, and his drive for self-perfection. Here Father John appears to be following the classic ascetic pattern of withdrawal from the world in order to properly serve it later, with the obvious difference that as a priest he had to perform the liturgy and serve others even as he struggled to perfect himself. Precisely because so much of his later life was spent in public, this early period was important for laying the inner foundation for the outer activity and the private reserves that made the public life possible. It was inconceivable to Father John that he might only do good works and help others (although later reforming priests espoused precisely this): his relation to God was the measure of his outer activity, as well as primary justification. Because of this, his first diaries dwell largely on how he might perfect that relation, and refer as examples to the ascetics who best achieved it.[43]

The ascetic ideal is also striking in the people Father John cites admiringly as exemplars. They range from the prophet Elijah to the elder Savva of Solovki, and in the first years of his career Father John was more struck by their asceticism than any other aspect of their activity, whether preaching or prophecy. In enjoining himself to shun vanity, for example, he reminded himself of Elijah and Savva with: "They wore coarse robes; however, they were great spirits, for there were no external charms to them. Keep in mind your inner clothing."[44]

This emphasis on asceticism and self-denial, as manifested in his condemnatory attitude toward an excessive concern with clothing and vestments, is all the more striking because it is not mandatory for an

Orthodox saint, especially an ordained one, to be concerned with outward dress. Basil the Great normally dressed very simply but kept a mirror and comb in the altar vestry to use before serving liturgy—so as, he explained, to do justice to the Eucharist and the glory of God. Holy clerics are depicted iconographically in full vestments.[45]

In his quest for models, then, Father John did not have to restrict himself to the Desert Fathers or the hermit monks who were their heirs. That he did so in the beginning of his career shows that they were for him the most authentic examples of sanctity. He chose more homely examples of asceticism as well:

> Remember the incredibly difficult life of the wanderer Nikitushka: how he labored for the Lord and the kingdom of God, wearing heavy chains, never bathing, allowing a multitude of lice to eat him, not allowing himself satiety, good-tasting things, not the smallest bit of pride, subjecting himself to mockery and beatings,—and emulate his life as far as you are able. Compare your life with his: you live in softness, luxury, satiety.[46]

This admiration for wanderers shows that even as Father John became more accustomed to the comforts of his position, he reminded himself of who the truly desirable models were. His recognition of the extreme, chain-wearing form of mortification particular to Russia is also indicative that he was not choosing a theologian, or even one of the less harshly ascetic saints, as an exemplar.

Also noteworthy is that Father John perceived his current life as luxurious by his previous standards of poverty—he instinctively compared himself with the poor, who represented the norm for him against which the rest of society must be judged, rather than the middle or upper classes. When Father John compared himself to Nikitushka he was living modestly on the second story of a rectory that bore a striking resemblance to an army barracks. Compared to both his childhood and the lives of his heroes, however, his adult life seemed relatively luxurious to him. As he moved further away from the poor setting of his youth, he was all the more struck by the religious virtues it could impart: "Today I had a visitor, a collector-peasant from Riazan province. A wonderful man! Meek and humble, kind and simple-hearted, and a real faster: he has not eaten anything non-Lenten for the last eleven years, even on non-Lenten days. The grace of God visibly rests upon him. What dedication to God!"[47]

All of these models fostered his own asceticism, which took many forms. Father John's pessimistic perception of human nature surpassed that of many Desert Fathers, who had taught that all things, bad and good, could be found in the human heart. He wrote, "The heart is a sewer, a foul-smelling, impure pit: one must turn away from it and cleanse it with tears of repentance and thoughts of God."[48] Similarly, his concentration on God and self-improvement extended to all aspects of his life in ways that went beyond patristic and ascetic teachings. Unlike most of his clerical contemporaries, such as the saintly bishop Ignatii (Brianchianinov), and the Desert Fathers, who tended to mistrust or disregard dreams as snares of the Devil, Father John thought that

> [t]he life of the human being, the sinner, is full of abomination, both in reality and in one's sleep: it is visibly evident in reality, in one's actions; in one's sleep, it is evident in unclean visions, so that any person can see his shortcomings and his weak sides in dreams. Even a person who lives, as far as possible, in a holy way, but who has his weak sides which his self-esteem conceals from him in waking, can see them clearly in his sleep. One should not disregard or neglect dreams—our life is reflected in them as in a mirror.[49]

Father John examined his dreams more carefully than did most Orthodox saints, plumbing them for information about his spiritual life. When he saw himself gnawing at and eating silver coins in a dream, for example, he interpreted it as a sign of his miserliness.[50] In the late 1860s, after a dream in which "the enemy kept throwing me into high society balls and [then] to simple dinners: at the first I gawked and fussed and was vain; at the latter I greedily ate an abyss of food," he condemned his appetites.[51] During another night, he dreamed that a rabbit had been chased up a tree by a dog and that he had hoisted up the dog so that the two animals could have it out. "The bunny fought bravely but the foe grabbed it with its teeth and ripped it apart." When he later thought about the dream in his waking hours, Father John blamed himself for giving a weak creature to a strong one for the sake of a bloody spectacle—"that is, for his own amusement"—and drew the analogy that he was destroying his spiritual flock through his own laziness and inattention.[52]

While one might dispute Father John's interpretations of his dreams, his urge to blame himself for the bad actions he committed in them, to espy flaws in character on their basis and admonish himself to improve, provide a striking example of an essentially religious personality at work. His unconscious, as well as his conscious, activity is held up for equal scrutiny. The sense of responsibility for his unconscious life was exacerbated by how literally he took his dreams: to him, dreaming about something was virtually identical to experiencing it while awake and conscious, especially with regard to temptations of the flesh. Although Father John does not appear to have felt conscious sexual desire during his waking hours in the first years of his career, not referring to it at all while he minutely detailed others "falls" and temptations, he was not immune from physical desire in his sleep. He wrote in the mid-1860s, for example, "In general, dreaming is not time wasted for the Christian: it is the time for attacks on his chastity."[53] He held himself strictly accountable for such attacks. If he had a sensual dream, he would rise immediately to recite the "Prayer after Defilement," "... for the soul (although not the body) was defiled with fleshly passion."[54]

Such strict attention to physical and mental purity and asceticism was almost unheard-of for a priest. In effect, Father John was seeking to hold himself to the same ascetic standards as monks and nuns while being a married priest living in the world. This focus on ascetic subordination to the Divine was central to his religiosity. There was no room in his worldview for anything that was not religious; he subjected every aspect of his life to the eye of God. He scrutinized the most ordinary turns of phrase and found them wanting as not expressing the proper focus on the holy.

> People say to one another "Good night, pleasant dreams," but they do not say, "I wish you earnest prayer so that you may have good dreams," which would be much more proper (prayer as a necessary precondition for good sleep).... Our usual good wishes to one another should bear a Christian imprint, not merely a worldly one or a fleshly one. The spiritual must be put ahead of the fleshly, the emotional, at every point.[55]

Father John used the all-encompassing term "softness" to condemn too great an attachment to the most basic worldly comforts, striving for complete *apatheia*: "How can I know whether I am soft? If I react badly to foul odors rather than being indifferent to them (think of the holy father who kept a foul-smelling vessel in his cell), if I moan and moan while sick, if mosquito bites seem unbearable (or an ugly face)."[56] In short, like the ascetics, Father John focused all aspects of his life around the Divine and attempted to control any appetites or distractions that seemed to get in the way. He wrote in 1868, for example, "Use the system of compulsion on yourself more often."[57] His regarding compulsion as a "system" suggests his rigorous, typically monastic approach, where compelling himself to virtue was an end in itself. He would call himself to "extinguish" his passions and appetites in classic ascetic terms: "My life must every day be made an offering to God, a sacrifice.... I must with the help of the holy spirit reduce to ashes all of the passions which rise up in me."[58]

To accomplish this extinguishing of passions, Father John turned to ascetic practices borrowed from a variety of monastic sources. Some focused on religious imagery. In a practice that was used also by monks and nuns, for example, he would tell himself to look at the Cross and hit himself on the chest when looking at the Crucified One, saying, "The immortal one is dying for me; so I must eternally suffer and die according to the justice of God."[59] He drew on other Orthodox ascetic techniques as well. When he thanked God "for the gift of tears of repentance," for example, it was in keeping with the Orthodox tradition of seeing tears as a Divine gift, as well as an emotional state that one sought to induce in oneself using the same method as the ascetics.[60] In some respects, his wish to eliminate the personal even surpassed conventional ascetic practices in its inventiveness. "You like to walk in fresh air and breathe it with pleasure," he wrote, "[but] this is not enough, it is only good for the body: during your walk you must also meditate on God, the lives of the saints, on the Gospels, etc."[61]

The central feature of Father John's asceticism was his intense awareness of the effect of the physical on the spiritual. His borrowing from monks extended to mundane forms of bodily discipline. "Do not sleep underneath a very warm blanket so as not to relax the body and consequently the soul through excessive warmth," he wrote in 1867, "for the soul is intimately bound up with the body and any relaxation or contentment in the body is echoed by relaxation and contentment in the soul." (The solution was to "use only moderately warm blankets and certainly never duvets."[62]) In the first twenty years after Father John's ordination (1856–76), the central object of his physicality, as was typical for male and particularly female ascetics (and the hungry generally), was fasting and food, rather than erotic desire.[63] Indeed, during this period it was as if he experienced sensual desire only in terms of its connection to food and drink. He admired the restraint of Nikita the wanderer in eating only Lenten food. In the first decades of his own career, he felt food to be the most significant obstacle to purifying himself. He initially understood and described fasting in conventional Orthodox terms: "How great is the power of fasting and prayer! It is not difficult to understand why: when one fasts, the soul begins to rule over the lusts of the body, and generally subjects the body to itself ...with what did the Lord Himself defeat the devil? with prayer and fasting."[64]

Nevertheless, Father John felt the power of food over himself, and the causality between eating certain foods and his sinful responses, more strongly than mere ascetic convention would suggest. As someone who had grown up in poverty, he shared the infatuation with food that characterized contemporary works of literature and dinner-party menus.[65] His diary reveals his overwhelming obsession with food and the hold it had over him: he drew explicit connections between what he consumed and how he responded. Father John felt the effects of food so keenly that he blamed his insensitive reaction to a fire in Kronstadt on October 18, 1867, on his having consumed fish, tea, and black and white bread together.[66] On another occasion, he wrote, "Because of satiety on the eve of the holiday (I had buckwheat groats with almond milk), I was subjected to powerful temptation while serving Matins."[67] His notion of "temptation" covered a broad range of harmful spiritual states, from drowsiness to irritability; so eating or drinking the wrong things affected him acutely. There were other occasional culprits of bad spiritual reactions: marinated lampreys, green cheese ("and it makes the teeth hurt, too"), pies (especially with rice and fish and vegetable oil), sweet *kissel* ("it is worse than milk in inflaming desire"), beer on fasting days ("this is drunkenness"), fish ("it leads to fleshly temptation; must be used with caution"), an omelet made in meat juices, rich sabayon sauce (which he blamed for turning him into "a dog"), and good food generally.[68]

This connection between food and drink and a lack of spiritual vigilance led Father John to develop careful and elaborate rules for "using" food similar to those of the ascetics of the desert. The rules covered combinations of foods he considered bad ("No horseradish with vinegar!"), quantities consumed ("You may drink three little cups of coffee with cream after dinner, after about three hours; four [cups] is excessive and sinful. Or mixing tea and coffee—it won't do"), types of food ("buckwheat kasha is good, cream bad"). Finally, nearly in despair, he gave up the various careful rules he had devised and sought to reduce them to one terse rule, written in capital letters: "NEVER EAT SUPPER!"[69]

Father John's condemnation of gourmandise was connected to his initial rigorous condemnation of sensations that were not purely religious. The consumption of food was the area in which he felt most acutely his inclination to enjoy the immediate rather than concentrating on the

Divine. His being a priest only heightened the food requirements he set for himself, however. It is interesting to see his identity as a priest specifically, rather than as an ascetic struggler generally, first emerging in his notebooks in an ascetic context, connected with physical temperance:

> It does not do for a priest to use milk, butter, and especially meat (although doing so is not forbidden). What may suit a layperson does not suit a priest. It is particularly inappropriate for a priest to drink vodka—perhaps the smallest amount, if that—or to smoke or take snuff. All of this coddles our flesh, which we should crucify, and distracts him from his communion with God. Yes, the lips which are so often sanctified by partaking of the Divine Mysteries and serve as the gates for them must choose extremely carefully what else they allow in through themselves.[70]

This connection between food and purity is particularly important. While food and drink caused Father John a variety of temptations, the most dangerous temptation was their capacity to call forth other sorts of physical responses and desires. He wrote in 1866, for example, "I was a guest at someone's house and drank three cups of sweet tea, a shot of vodka, and two glasses of wine—Jerez and Malaga; ate game, bread, and butter; at home I had a glass of milk. *Because of this* at night there was defilement."[71] He felt the almost anthropomorphic connection between the consumer and the consumed and described it graphically: "It is better to avoid meat, which turns you into an animal." Father John described the symptoms he felt as clinically as possible. He warned himself to beware, for example, of

> the harm that comes from taking sweet tea (and its sweetness, stickiness): [it causes] weakening [of the body] and frequent emission of seed from the sexual organs. One should not drink sweet tea, during Lent in particular: whoever drinks sweet tea does no better than the person who eats non-Lenten food. Although tea does not burden the body in the same way as do meat, milk, and buttery foods, it does coddle the body awfully and causes one to sink into one's parts in the same way as do fornication and adultery. A trifling cause, it would seem—and yet how much harm it brings to our purity: if there were no sweet tea, there would not be such frequent nocturnal emissions; there would be less occasion for Satan to defile us with cards and voluptuousness.[72]

His interpretation of the connection between food and sensuality, although it is firmly rooted in the ascetic tradition, has rarely been described so concretely and in such detail.[73] A striking feature of Father John's inner life is the slow progression from temptation almost exclusively by food to sensual desires as a conscious and independent concern. The awakening of sexual desire is also linked to his fame and the appearance of female devotees, both of which are a post-1880s phenomenon and will be discussed below. More pertinent to the initial stages of Father John's asceticism, however, is his rejection of sexual relations with his wife.

This aspect of his asceticism appears the most perplexing upon examination. In sexuality as in food, Father John's ascetic behavior and ideals were very similar to monastic ones. But he differed from monks and nuns in one obvious respect: for them, chastity was an essential attribute, along with poverty and obedience; he was a married priest for whom physical relations with his wife were a similar given. Priests in the Orthodox tradition were all but required to marry rather than remaining celibate (as compared to Roman Catholic priests). Father John's having both virginity and marriage was an unusual blurring of distinct categories of Orthodox religious life that begs explanation.

Unfortunately, there is no reliable information that allows an explanation of his chastity. He was silent about the matter in his diaries for years. The only conclusive mention comes on October 19, 1866—ten years after his wedding and ordination—when he admits to thinking patronizingly of a colleague, "Well, after all, I am a virgin, not like you."[74] If it were not for this chance comment, one might question whether Father John had thought about the matter at all. He never acknowledged publicly that he had deliberately chosen chastity in his married life, going only so far in his brief official autobiography as to say, "I do not have and have not had any children."[75] And yet Father John's unusual ménage was apparently common knowledge, as his biographers assert. These suppositions remain conjectures, however, as they appear during the later period of his life, and are thus, at best, attempts to interpret backward. What then may be said of the circumstances of Father John's early chastity?

Part of the answer must be sought in Orthodox teaching on sexuality. The Fathers of the Church argued that sexuality was antithetical to the true state of human nature. Before the Fall, the original, perfect created being had no trace of sexuality.[76] Eve was meant to be Adam's companion and helper; their relation consisted only of spiritual love.[77]

Sexuality entered the world because of sin and was inextricably connected to sin. Because sexuality was a sign of the disruption of the original balance and perfection, the more closely one approached perfection, the less sexual one would be. Slavic clerical writers articulated this notion particularly clearly, stating that sexual impulses came exclusively from the Devil so that he might lead people away from God and their salvation. The notion that sexuality might be anything other than negative was entirely absent.[78]

For the individual who aspired to holiness, virginity as a way of life was by far preferable to marriage. This sentiment goes back to Saint Paul:

> It is good for a man not to touch a woman. Nevertheless, to avoid fornication, let every man have his own wife, and let every woman have her own husband.... The unmarried woman careth for the things of the Lord, that she may be holy both in body and in spirit: but she that is married careth for the things of the world, how she may please her husband. (I Corinthians 7:1–2, 34)

Monastic life was regarded as the optimal religious state, most approximating the angelic life. If one did wish to marry, it was regarded as best a concession to fallen human nature ("It is better to marry than to burn," [I Corinthians 7:9]).

The central notion here is that sexual activity was considered inherently tainted, even in marriage. This belief was remarkably tenacious. Pious seminarians describe in a host of memoirs hesitating to "defile" both themselves and their prospective wives; laypersons' confessions sent to Father John refer to sexual relations *within marriage* as a "lawful sin."[79] It is not surprising that saints' living without sexual intercourse even within lawful marriage (something occasionally referred to as "spiritual marriage") was highly regarded in both East and West.[80] The Orthodox clerical climate was so conducive to an aversion to sexual relations that Father John's attitude may have been the result of his religious background taken to its logical ends.

This is especially possible given the lack of an Orthodox theology of marriage in the mid-nineteenth century. Here Father John more clearly than anywhere else reflects both the tension between his two bodies and the mentality of his times. In his public, priestly body, he was the spiritual father of his parishioners, and potentially of every Orthodox Christian. But this religious responsibility did not extend to his family. There, in his private body as a married man, he had another spiritual responsibility: that of attaining mystical unity with his wife.[81] That the Orthodox Church understood the two responsibilities as separate is evident in the prohibition for priests to hear their wives' confessions. Father John thus had two different spiritual responsibilities—to his wife in his private body and to his flock in his public one. Because of the lack of models for pursuing sanctity as a sexually active spouse, however, he ignored the former, forcing himself to see his wife in the same terms as he did his parishioners.[82]

There was also a pragmatic factor in his abstinence. Celebrating the liturgy daily and partaking of the Eucharist were central to his religiosity. But the canons of the Orthodox Church forbade laypeople and clergy alike sexual relations on the eve of communion; priests in particular were enjoined to abstain before serving liturgy.[83] This sense that the lingering presence of sensuality would defile the Eucharist dates back to early Christianity, when the Council of Elvira ruled just before 303 that "bishops, priests, deacons and all members of the clergy connected with the liturgy must abstain from their wives."[84] Although by the mid-nineteenth century some city priests who served liturgy daily quietly ignored the restriction, it still retained much of its traditional force.[85] Given Father John's passionate devotion to the Eucharist and his literal acceptance of Church canons, it is highly unlikely that he would have transgressed them in this respect. Chastity was thus a matter of pragmatic necessity for someone who wished to serve liturgy daily, and it was no doubt the central reason for his virginity. Because he did not serve *every single* day, however, other factors clearly played roles as well.

For all the likely importance of Orthodox teaching and custom, Father John's silence on the subject of his sexual life prohibits anything beyond speculation. The absence of this element in his early diaries is at least partly a matter of chronology. From the very beginning of his priestly life (1856–58)—the time when he might have been most expected to take some notice of his young wife—his writings were devoted to biblical commentary. By the time personal elements crept into his diaries, the period of adjustment with his wife and her family would have ended. Neither Elizaveta Konstantinovna nor other family members left diaries or letters that would shed light, either. The matter remains a mystery.

One thing is clear, however: in his chastity, Father John stood the hagiographic tradition on its head. The phenomenon of married people either remaining chaste or choosing celibacy is not unknown in the lives of the saints, but it is usually initiated by the wife rather than the husband, and usually takes the form of persuasion rather than categorical refusal.[86] But Father John made the decision to remain chaste even before his marriage—a resolution of which his bride appears not to have been aware, given both the secondary references and the hints in his diaries.[87] How is one to understand this? However pragmatic the arrangements of clerical marriage may have been, with both parties understanding that the husband was to inherit the parish of his wife's father, the assumption that the husband and wife would have normal marital relations was not questioned. Given the weight of convention and the reasonable expectations of one's spouse, it is not enough to simply point to liturgical rules concerning communion. There are two separate matters here. If Father John did not intend to fulfill what was assumed of a married man, why did he marry at all rather than becoming an ordained monk? If he wanted to both have daily communion and serve in the world, inheriting the archpriest Konstantin Nesvitskii's position at St. Andrew's Cathedral in Kronstadt through marrying his daughter Elizaveta, surely he owed it to his fiancée to seek her consent before the wedding rather than presenting her with a *fait accompli*?

It is undeniable that if Father John wanted to serve in the world, to serve the poor, and to serve the liturgy itself, priesthood in the world—which, in nineteenth-century Russia, meant being married—was the only possible path. Hieromonks ministered largely to their communities; bishops' administrative responsibilities reduced their opportunities to minister over their lay flocks to a minimum—hence, the wish of Bishop Feofan (the Recluse) to withdraw into solitude in order to pursue his scholarly work as well as being a *directeur de conscience*. Except in the cases of such extraordinary men as Saint Tikhon of Zadonsk and Metropolitan Filaret (Drozdov), bishops' official responsibilities tended to overshadow those of spiritual ministry.[88] In a purely spiritual sense, then, a priest in his own parish often had much more contact with laypeople than either a bishop or a priest-monk. If contact with laypeople was what Father John wished for his priestly life, he could have sought the prior consent of his bride-to-be rather than assuming she could be persuaded after the wedding—or not warned her in advance precisely for fear that his proposal would be rejected. In the former case, word of his unusual request would have spread, making it difficult for him to find another bride and family who would agree to his terms. Once the marriage had occurred, on the other hand, it would have been much more difficult (while not impossible) for Elizaveta Konstantinovna to extricate herself and then to remarry.

It seems unlikely that Father John was so intent on pursuing his chosen path of salvation that he would have been willing to exploit his fiancée's trust to achieve his ends, although this is not impossible for a saintly figure for whom the relation with God overrode all others (think of Alexis, the man of God, abandoning his bride on their honeymoon).[89] It is more probable that Father John hinted at chastity to her before their marriage but that she did not understand or chose not to understand him, or perhaps even felt that she could change his mind. As her husband's diaries and her niece's reminiscences show, Elizaveta Konstantinovna genuinely loved Father John and respected his religious fervor. She may have either hoped that his intent to remain chaste was but a phase of youthful religious ardor or even believed that she might come to identify with it and share his quest. Her initial efforts to win him over, then resignation to her lot, then fury as he started to pay attention and spend time with other women, thus assume a new meaning.

Indeed, it is remarkable how little reflection on marriage and family relations Father John reveals in the first five years of his diaries. The only such mention is nearly illegible and reads simply: "In your dreams you see the amiable features of your beloved wife as if seeing her herself."[90] The disparity between the feelings of Father John for his wife and hers for him, however, was far more typical than this fleeting moment of tenderness. He noticed his wife's affection for him, but rather than being moved to respond in kind, he exhorted himself to draw spiritual lessons from her warmth. When he wrote in 1862, for example, "My wife's love for me is very touching," he followed immediately with "this is how I should love everyone, particularly paupers, even if there be unworthy among them."[91] This extrapolation is utterly characteristic.

The discrepancy between Elizaveta Konstantinovna's affection and desire for Father John and his coolness toward her quickly widened. One must exercise some caution in interpreting the diaries, however. Just as in evening prayers Christians recall their sins—not their accomplishments— of the previous day, so in his journals, which served a similar function, Father John accentuated the negative. As with the diaries of Tolstoy's wife, Sophia, written only in moments of difficulty, one must be careful not to assume that just because the good times do not appear, they are not there.[92] In this sense, Father John is to be commended for at least acknowledging his failings and seeking to correct them. He reproached himself for noticing all his wife's faults, for example, whereas she "does not notice my weakness and covers everything I do because of her love for me."[93] Here, also, however, he extrapolated from their relationship what most mattered—his relationship to God: "How fervidly your wife loves you, and how cold are you to her? How fervidly Christ loves you, and how cold are you to Him? If you do not love your wife, how can you love God?"[94]

In general, Father John trained himself to think of God as soon as he thought of his wife. This progression quickly became a reflex, almost instinctive: "How my wife protects me everywhere and with what love! *But how the Lord loves me*—it is unimaginable." "Accept your wife's advice with respect, as that of your friend and helper, and do not despise her or be saddened at her, and *generally treat every person with respect*, as being *the image of God* and having *an immortal soul*." The shift had the double benefit of lessening Father John's ties to his wife and increasing those to God. His ambivalence toward his wife was much more easily managed if it could be incorporated into, indeed fully absorbed by, his own relation to God. Once he mastered this transition, when he felt angry or impatient with his wife, he would berate himself by saying to himself, "First, she loves you; second, *she is the Lord's creation and the image of His Church*."[95] From this equation it was but a short step to depersonalize her, equating her with any Christian: "Protect the vessel of your wife, *if for no other reason* than that it is the dwelling-place of Divine food and drink—the body and blood of Christ. Moreover, it is the house of an immortal soul, created in the image and likeness of God, and the dwelling-place and the temple of the Holy Trinity."[96] One might argue that Father John was taking his wife as seriously as he was capable by incorporating her into his economy of salvation—that his denying her any importance other than that which he felt he owed any Orthodox Christian might even be construed as a backhanded compliment—but the end result was still to deny her the intimacy she desired.

In trying to decode their married life, one must also be careful to approach Father John and Elizaveta Konstantinovna on their own terms. Might emotional and spiritual intimacy have proved sufficient compensation for the absence of physical intimacy and the possibility of children? This is quite possible, given the utter absence of literature on the cult of physical pleasure when they were growing up in the reign of Nicholas I. The notion of sexual fulfillment was particularly alien to the environment of the clergy in which Elizaveta Konstantinovna was raised; that context stressed self-sacrifice and the bearing of mutual burdens, especially for girls and women.[97] Here the difference between Father John and Elizaveta Konstantinovna comes through most clearly. While he could not both yield to his wife's desire for children and remain virgin, he could have made her more of a partner in his private life and quest for salvation. At times, Elizaveta Konstantinovna seems to have sought precisely this, making repeated references to the role the family could play in one's—that is, his—private religiosity. Father John quotes her as saying in the 1860s, "One must love, caress, and protect everyone at home before everything else—and only then turn to others. Love your neighbor first of all at home, in this little Church. When you learn to love and respect those at home, then you will come to love and respect everyone."[98] It was incomprehensible to her that her own husband would relegate her to a marginal role in his economy of salvation.

Father John's diaries, however, show that he had little sense of himself as a partner in any kind of marriage or personal relation save that which he had with God; his conception of the religious life was essentially solitary. (It is hard to say whether this was *a priori* or whether it had anything specific to do with Elizaveta Konstantinovna.) He sought first to turn his relations with his wife into a detached moral lesson or admonition to all married men and then to an admonition to pray for his wife's moral improvement:

> Let your wife's love for you express itself in actions and do not be sad or angry at her because these actions are sometimes foolish, irksome, or tiresome; respect your wife's intention—that of showing you her love. Husbands: love your wives and do not be saddened by them. Do not disregard love, do not insult it with your own caprices: love scorned is jealous and vengeful, like a mother-bear enraged by the loss of her cubs. I must thank God for my wife's love and pray to Him to affirm her and to make her wise, reasonable, and pleasing to God.[99]

The reference to love scorned is a rare moment of nonreligious psychological acuity for Father John. More typically, he preferred to cloak his comments, as he had with earlier events in his life, in the guise of moralizing or a parable. As in the conflicts he had with his parishioners, he initially masked the tensions he felt for his wife and her relatives in the guise of analogy and commentary upon scripture and even the classics. He wrote in the late 1850s, for example, "Xanthippe was the Devil's weapon seeking to undermine Socrates, but God turned her into a weapon strengthening and raising him."[100] The extent to which this reference is a veiled commentary on his own wife becomes evident in the transition to scripture that follows:

"He who does not despise his mother, his wife," that is, one must despise their fleshly demands as one must despise the demands of one's own ancient, sinful flesh which resists the saving teaching of Christ. There were many parents of Christians, particularly in the first three centuries, and there are those now, who distract their sons and husbands with their fleshly demands, not heeding the way of cross taught by Christ. Who loves such parents and does not loathe them, or loves and does not loathe such a wife, cannot be a disciple of Christ.[101]

While this passage does not explicitly refer to the desire of Elizaveta Konstantinovna for normal marital relations, it does suggest the process of thought whereby Father John may have rationalized to himself his own position. Particularly interesting here is the connection he makes between the "fleshly demands" of one's mother and wife (and does not include "of father and son," although the text of Matthew 10:37, on which he comments, does) and that of "one's own ancient, sinful flesh." Father John was aware, of course, of the biblical and Church Fathers' teachings on women. He once wrote casually, for example, "To God, all women are like Eve: that is why before Him all of them are impure in their blood and from their birth." His novelty, however, lies in his extension of the sentiment. He goes on to say, "*And it is the same with men.* In sins, in iniquities, and in vile things—all [people] are the same before Thee."[102] This interpretation suggests that, although he shared the view of women as being more sinful and earthbound than men, he differed by occasionally removing some Church restrictions, such as that against not taking communion while menstruating, and by extrapolating, as here, from the accusations leveled against women to include the other sex. Father John's sense of duty to his family, moreover, as well as his emphasis on family virtues in a positive Christian sense, was unusual in contemporary Orthodox teaching. He used family imagery in his diary and his sermons applicable to both family and church: "The mother," he wrote in 1863, "teaches her children, and the child submits to her and does not doubt her lessons, being confident that the mother knows better than he what she is teaching."[103]

This element in Father John's writings should not be underrated. Both Orthodox and Roman Catholic Christian Fathers blamed "evil" women for talkativeness, their supposedly greater links to paganism, and their "innately greater" sexuality.[104] Father John's expression of relative equality was part of the reason women sought him out in such numbers. But while he was generous as regards women generally, not automatically associating them with "fleshliness" and consequent impurity, his attitude was more complicated with respect to his own wife. Elizaveta Konstantinovna may not have been a source of erotic temptation for Father John, but she was associated with the preparation and kind of food that he consumed. Given the importance food held in his ascetic struggles, this role was far from innocuous. At first he was indulgent: "Do not get upset when your wife cooks food that you do not like—it is not worth losing love and peace over it. Kill the flesh like the martyrs and ascetics."[105] Soon afterward, however, he began to perceive his wife's attempts to cater to him as threats to his spirituality: "Let not him who is married submit blindly to his wife as Adam did to Eve, for your wife just may slip you something like the forbidden fruit; she may, for example, offer your something sweet to eat or drink when it is not strictly necessary, and this will weigh you down in body and spirit. Watch out for this."[106]

This attitude became increasingly strained when it concerned the fasting rules of the Orthodox Church. In the absence of sexual relations, meal times and food became the arena in which husband and wife's struggles were played out and their marital tensions were most evident. As relations with his wife worsened over the years, Father John grew suspicious of her increasingly lax approach to fasting, seeing it as a challenge to his asceticism, religious identity, and authority. When he became angry at his wife for frying fish during Lent but ate it, he later felt his "genital member greatly strained" and a disposition to "sweet thirst." He exploded: "Now you see what comes of eating fish! That is why it is forbidden during the fasts!"[107] Father John began to transfer his suspicion of the food itself to the person who gave it to him: "*Never* have bouillon at night; it is poison for me—and my wife forces it on me! O, fleshly person! *O unreliable companion in the spiritual life!*"[108]

If one is to judge on the basis of Father John's diaries, the entire story of his relation with his wife is one of gradual deterioration. In typically patristic fashion, Elizaveta Konstantinovna finally came to represent for him the incarnation of the mundane, "fleshly" forces seeking to tie him to this life rather than to the next. This association had its origins in Father John's relation with his mother. In a pattern typical for sons of clergy, he equated the "fleshly demands" made by both mother and wife with distraction to sons and husbands.[109] Although biographers made much of his mother's piety, as evinced by her reputedly refusing to give her blessing to his eating non-Lenten food during a fast, in private Father John minimized the religiosity of both his parents as if to emphasize his sole responsibility for his religious formation. As he told himself in 1864, "Remember that you are the son of a sacristan, the son of poor parents *who did not distinguish themselves by their piety*."[110]

This brings up another matter. Father John's insecurity about his social origins became the most important factor in his intense ambivalence toward the poor. He was painfully conscious of the enormous distance between the poverty of his upbringing and the milieu in which he now found himself. His wife's urban, relatively cultured family intimidated and irritated him as much as his well-born parishioners did. He wrote testily of his sister-in-law's continued insistence on their social background:

> If she raves about counts and princes, do not get angry at her ... such a spirit is the result of her upbringing: her godfather is a Count, he lived with them; she went to school with the daughters of counts and princes ... how else can she act? When a tree was trained in one direction—not the way it should have been—how can it be corrected? So you must look through your fingers a bit and make allowances.[111]

Father John sought unsuccessfully to emphasize his identification with education and culture in order to compensate for his sense of inferiority, an attempt that crumbled when his mother came to live with his new family soon after his marriage. She was a perpetual reminder of where he had come from and what he had tried to escape. In the equation of the personal and the liturgical that was characteristic of his diaries, he sought to equate his discomfort at her lack of polish with the discomfort he felt at religious phenomena that disconcerted him, from badly painted icons to Christ Himself:

> Do you remember how the evil one led you by the nose and tormented you because of an icon of the Mother of God which was not painted to your taste—it inspired loathing and repugnance—as if holy faces painted improperly are unworthy!—and prayer would not come easily until you conquered him. It is the same with Mother: her rough form prevents me from praising her as worthily as she is due.[112]

> Mummy, with her simplicity, her humility, her lack of education, humbles my pride extremely. Do you not love Christ's dishonor, do

Priestly Formation

you not bear His defamations in [the person of] your mother in her simplicity and in the careless way she arranges her hair? Remember what Christ looked like during His trial and on the cross, how dishonorable his appearance was.[113]

When religious metaphors were not successful in moving Father John from his wish to distance himself from his mother and his origins, he tried to appeal to ordinary decency ("Look here: your Mum is a lonely person here, make her separation from her relatives and her homeland as imperceptible for her as possible").[114] Despite such attempts, however, Fedora Vlas'evna's looks, manners, and language repeatedly embarrassed Father John. Just when he felt that he had succeeded in putting his village past behind him, it stood before him in the form of his mother. Even as he enjoined himself to acknowledge his debt to her, he still wanted to act according to the urban forms of behavior he had adopted during his years away from the home and the village. When his mother came in to say goodnight, for example, Father John could not bring himself to kiss her hand as he had done years before, and lay awake in torment before he overcame himself and went back to her room to ask forgiveness.[115]

Language posed even more of a problem than did gestures or looks. When Father John's mother used such village expressions as "Hello, *ditiatko*" in greeting him, he could not respond with his former "Hello, *mamasha*" without forcing himself. He enjoined himself not to despise his mother's "village, crude, ungrammatical language, so unlike your own educated one; do not disdain it just as you do not disdain the Samoyed or Tatar languages."[116] Father John consciously equated the language of the village with alien tongues in order to stress the distance he now felt from it.

This sense of having broken the ties to his origins cannot be overstated in Father John, if only because it has been deliberately minimized in biographies. Although his intimate connection with the people was constantly stressed by his biographers, he clearly felt alienated from and ambivalent toward the uneducated poor people among whom he had grown up. Rather than seeing it as a possible source of company and comfort in the religious life, he perceived his family as a stumbling block if not an actual obstacle to his salvation.

When Father John was ordained in 1855, Russian priests were indispensable executors of the sacraments, but rarely were considered candidates for sanctity. His diaries and notebooks from the early years of his career (1856–69) reveal his attempts to harmonize the traditional ascetic ideals of saints with his role as a married priest living in a city. He lived the tension between the priest's two bodies: body private, struggling for its own salvation, and body public, the responsibility for others. Father John's relations with his wife, with whom he never consummated his marriage, reflect this tension. In his heart and in diaries, his family was incidental rather than central; the early period of his religiosity and asceticism remained a private rather than a collective endeavor.

2

Liturgical Innovations

As central as asceticism was to Father John's religious identity, it proved to be only one of several religious models that attracted him. His early concentration on restricting his physical appetites and his turning to the Desert Fathers and hermits as models gradually came to include a wider range of exemplars and qualities to emulate. These included apostolicity, liturgical fervor, mutual responsibility, and charity. In these ways, his religiosity quickly assumed both a public and a private face, and it was this public face—the second of the priest's two bodies—for which he would become most celebrated.

Part of the transition outward may be traced to the hostility Father John encountered toward his early forms of asceticism. His family was not alone in regarding him with exasperation; his parishioners and fellow clergy did as well. His attempts to pursue constant prayer, for example, led to his walking the streets of Kronstadt with his hands crossed over his chest and a far-off gaze that did not appear to recognize what was around him. While this was a direct borrowing from the monastery of Studion in Constantinople, whose rule Saint Feodosii borrowed for the Kievan Monastery of the Caves ("He who is walking must hold his hands clasped on his breast"), more than a few people regarded it as dubious for the same reason they looked askance at Father John's giving beggars the last of his coins and the boots off his feet. Holy foolishness (*iurodstvo*) was disapproved of in those who "ought to know better"—and was a violation of the Synod's rules.[1] His fellow clergy saw such behavior as ill-befitting the dignity of his clerical rank (and perhaps a reproach to their relative stinginess). After they decided to issue Father John's salary directly to his wife in an attempt to remind him of his financial responsibility, he started teaching at the local high school to fund his charitable impulses.[2] The part of Kronstadt society that was conscious of its social status as a Petersburg satellite and had grown accustomed to elegant priests, moreover, also disliked his "excessively" humble appearance and harsh, emotional manner of serving, dismissing him as a "village *pop*."[3]

Partly because of the lack of sympathy for his asceticism, Father John began to develop other forms of piety. Of these, mutual responsibility among Christians was key. This was not unique in contemporary Russian Orthodox thought. Aleksei Khomiakov's revival of the theology of *sobornost'* and Dostoyevsky's insistence that "all are responsible for all" were typical of the emphasis on spiritual community, especially as contrasted with the "overly individualistic" West. But many Slavophiles and Dostoyevsky thought of community and mutual responsibility as national traits and virtues with corresponding social manifestations; Father John regarded them as personal spiritual qualities to cultivate.[4]

Mutual responsibility had several aspects for Father John. The first aspect, a practical application of "Love thy neighbor as thyself," consisted of not making a fetish of one's own salvation at the possible expense of others. The potential tension between the two salvations emerged in an early incident when Father John loaned one of his favorite books and it was returned damaged. He was hurt and angry, but concluded:

> If someone borrows a book from you and returns it to you soiled, do not get irritated with him or say, "I will not let him take any more." By doing so, you betray your attachment—first, to things, and second, to surfaces. Is not the spiritual benefit to your brother more important than you book? If he has derived benefit from it, the book has accomplished its function. Give your soul-saving books to anyone who asks. If the books just stand in your book-case, they

will accuse you just as the rich person's gold and silver piled up in trunks accuse him or her.[5]

This sense of responsibility for others, and of sacrificing oneself for them, led Father John to value company as an end in itself. The positive value he assigned to sociability appeared to be a sharp departure from the monastic ideal Saint Serafim of Sarov had expressed famously as "Save yourself, and around you thousands will become saved."[6] Father John was one of the first religious figures in Russia not simply to accept the necessity of relations with other people but to appreciate their positive role in one's betterment. His was, in a sense, the lay version of the monastic cenobitic ideal. The advantage of pursuing the monastic life with the benefit of both the experience of others and the advice of a spiritual master had been recognized by Pachomius as more appropriate, and indeed safer, for most strugglers as long ago as the third century A.D. Basil the Great had also emphasized the resemblance of the cenobitic monastery to the early communal ideal of the apostles.[7] Even after a millennium of communal monasticism, however, a certain snobbery that regarded solitude as the purest form of holy life persisted, particularly in regard to women. While such elders as Feofan the Recluse often advised women to pursue their salvation by serving others, they tended to choose solitude for themselves, and indeed regarded solitude as the highest stage of the religious life.[8] Implicit in this point of view is that community is a beneficial interim state in the religious life, while being alone with God, the angels, and oneself was the highest. By contrast, Father John, like other priests of his day, came to regard sociability as a uniquely useful means to salvation—one that, moreover, was not a necessary lower state through which Christians had to pass merely to attain higher enlightenment, but one that would benefit them throughout their lives.

The value of sociability grew out of living in a family and from the contributions of family members. Sociability did not come easily to Father John, who tended to prefer solitude and reading and to think of his salvation largely in terms of himself and his relation with his flock. The effort initially required for him to engage in social relations emerges from such exhortations to himself, as one he wrote in 1872: "We should not disdain visiting guests: during their visit it becomes revealed how much we are obliged to one another and how much we respect one another: do not forget social intercourse, it is said.... In general our virtues and our passions become known through our relations with others."[9]

This appreciation of the positive role others played in his religiosity changed the pattern of Father John's life. He gradually began to spend more time in company, both entertaining in his own home and being a guest in the homes of others. The memoirs of those who knew him in Kronstadt in the 1870s speak of him as a frequent and welcome guest.[10] But he did not restrict his appreciation of sociability to practice; he raised it to the level of theory and incorporated it in his economy of salvation. As he elaborated this theme of fellowship and sociability as a means of increasing one's religious awareness and knowledge, he used similar language to praise the cenobitic life of the Desert Fathers:

> It is also good to go out as a guest in others' houses because this is a part of the work of Christian sociability. By observing others we appropriate each other's good qualities, noticing spiritual treasures and gathering them for ourselves: for left to our own devices, we are poor and weak and unskillful, in not only Christian life but social life generally. Nothing disposes one to virtue as much as good, living examples.[11]

Sociability was not merely a means of abstract edification, however. Father John was vividly aware of its immediate and tangible consolations. Believing himself prone to moroseness and glumness, he told himself, "Compel yourself to talkativeness: the word chases away the soul's depression; it calms and expands the inner depths of the soul; it enlightens and revives it."[12] In an insight that would be nearly impossible for someone living alone, he was particularly appreciative of the benefits of sociability with people outside one's home in lessening the strain of family life, saying, "One must have relations with people and go out to their houses: [in public,] even one's family suddenly and somehow becomes closer, more mild and candid, more cordial."[13]

This positive valuation of family and public life reflected the concern of such 1860s thinkers as Nikolai Dobroliubov, Vissarion Belinsky, and Nikolai Chernyshevsky with the material and the tangible over the abstract and the spiritual—or, more accurately, the infusion of the material with the importance formerly accorded to (and classified as) the realm of the spirit. The positive emphasis on human relations, however, is only one aspect of Father John's relation with others. Although he benefited from other people, he also saw relationships with others as being one of his priestly responsibilities. In the 1870s, Father John enjoined himself to pray "as fervently for others as you do for yourself, as did Moses, Samuel, Daniel, Elijah, Elisha, the divine Isaiah, Jeremiah;

Liturgical Innovations

Paul the Apostle, Peter, and John and the rest; Sergii [of Radonezh]; Dmitrii, the Chrysostom of Rostov; and Saint Tikhon, the newly glorified wonderworker."[14]

These figures Father John mentions are not the ascetic hermits or wanderers he had admired in the first stages of his priesthood, but people who acted in the world in the name of God for the benefit of others. Above all, to Father John, Jesus' twelve apostles were a metaphor for the ideal closeness to God and His people and the ideal form of mediating between the two. One senses in Father John's diaries a personal identification with their mission lacking in his description of the ascetic Desert Fathers. Nevertheless, he was most struck by the aspect of the apostles' careers that lent itself least to emulation: their capacity for performing miracles. He wrote, in his first months as a priest, commenting on Matthew 19:7–8:

> "Heal the sick ..." and so on. In these words the apostle saw God in the flesh, the Creator of all, to whom it was enough to say that a certain matter or a certain object ought to be, in order for it to be so. Can a person speak of such things in the same way now, however? Let us say that you were to say to me, "Heal the sick." I would say to you, "Give me the means to do so—for example, medicines, advice which I could give the sick person for his or her use, and so on. I myself do not have the power to do so, I cannot: how can I restore order in the body of the patient when I do not know well what disorder occurred in it, nor how to help order arise from a disordered organism. How will this marvelous machine listen to me? How could I, who am inexperienced, not ruin it?" That is what I would say to you.[15]

While this pragmatic approach would appear to question the possibility of the miraculous, it had the effect of impressing Father John all the more with the potency of the Divine. His own inability to perform miraculous exploits only reinforced their wondrous quality and the power of their source. It was the apostles' extraordinary closeness to the Divine that enabled them to work wonders:

> In the apostolic period described here in Matthew there is none of this resistance to the miraculous: the word is uttered; no one says a word: this means that it will happen. Whereas if you were to say to me, "Raise the dead," I would regard you as a madman and would not deem it necessary to continue to speak to you. I

would say to you only that God alone has the power to raise us from the dead, while people without an extraordinary gift from God cannot do this. If you were to say then, "Exorcise demons," I would say to you, "Why, are you stronger than demons?—for in order to exorcise these, one must be stronger than they. But because they are bodiless spirits, even though they are spirits of darkness and were once angels, they are without a doubt stronger than you, who are fleshly. If you overcome them, then either God is with you, or you are God yourself."[16]

Father John's characteristic literal-mindedness, whether in approaching scripture or his dreams, is evident here. Even as he is struck by the gulf that separates the apostolic period from his own and the gifts of the apostles from his, the distance for him is one of spirit rather than history. The gifts the apostles received might yet be given to others. If miracles happened before, there is no reason for them not to happen again. Unlike his secular contemporaries—and even some of his devout ones—Father John did not assume that the miraculous aspect of the apostolic period was unique to early Christianity and had been since irrevocably lost (albeit with other qualities to take its place—think of the Roman Catholic argument presenting the Church as possessing different qualities at different states of evolution: *ecclesia militans, ecclesia triumphans*, and so on).[17] He regarded the apostles as possessing and maintaining the ideal balance between heaven and earth. They represented the most desirable path, combining as they did love and service to God with love and service to men and women in God's name. Although his diaries emphasize the ascetic labor necessary to attain divine support, the element of apostolic mission to the world also emerges. As Father John wrote admiringly on May 9, 1856: "Grant unto me, too, O Lord, the unexalted station, sorrow, poverty and boldness in the face of the world of Thy apostles, that I, too, might have their fame, their joy, their wealth, their possession of everything necessary to my temporary happiness and my eternal salvation."[18]

For him, the closest contemporary equivalent of the apostle's calling was that of the priest. This might seem surprising to those influenced by the conception of the apostolic succession, who would be inclined to see the bishop as the apostles' heir. In Orthodoxy, as in Roman Catholicism, there is a tradition that regards bishops as the apostles' successors in theology and liturgy alike. The kontakion hymn to the holy bishop Saint Tikhon of Zadonsk, for example, declares in typical fashion, "O successor of the apostles, adornment of hierarchs, teacher of the

Orthodox Church." In the first centuries of the church, the presbyter was ordained "to share in the presbyterate and govern Thy people with a pure heart," but he had no liturgical functions that were uniquely his; the bishop had, in the words of Dom Gregory Dix, "almost a liturgical and sacramental monopoly as *high*-priest of the whole 'priestly' body, the church."[19]

Another early Christian tradition that emphasized the sacraments allowed a different interpretation of the roles of bishop and priest, however. In 115 A.D., Saint Ignatius spoke of the bishop as "enthroned as the type of God, and the presbyters as the type of the college of the apostles."[20] This sacramental potential in the priest, initially latent but hinted at by Ignatius, found its expression in the fourth century under the emperor Constantine, when the Church became a stable institution and integrated into the fabric of Byzantine church-state symphony. Conditions of peace and growth increased the numbers of believers to the point where it was difficult for bishops to act as the sole ministers of sacraments, and the presbyter also came to assume a liturgical, or truly "priestly," function.[21]

Father John's lofty conception of the priest stemmed from this sacramental emphasis upon priestly attributes. His association of the priest rather than the bishop with the sacramental aspect of the apostolic role also reflected the contemporary Russian condition with which he was most familiar. The bishop was so burdened with managing his subordinates and mediating between the clerical and governmental spheres that he was a remote figure in the eyes of not only the laity but even the lower clergy. He had little time to perform what in Father John's eyes was the one thing needful for a cleric: prayerful intercession for others and the performance of the sacraments. It is thus not surprising that Father John would associate the pastoral apostle who lived among the people with the priest rather than with the bishop and his chancelleries.[22]

His was a supremely collective and sacramental concept of the priesthood. Two ideas impelled Father John's pastoral practice: that of perishing humanity and the unique role of the priest in helping humanity gain its salvation. He wrote in his autobiography:

> [I]n pondering God's wondrous, love-filled economy (His providence) for the salvation of the human race, I shed copious and fervent tears, burning with the desire to help work towards the salvation of perishing humanity. And the Lord fulfilled my desire. Soon afterwards, upon finishing higher education, I was elevated to the height of the priestly rank.[23]

To him it was indeed a height. The priest, Father John wrote in *My Life in Christ*, "is a mediator between God and people; he is His close friend. It is as if he were a God for men, with the power to bind and to forgive their sins, to minister for them the life-giving and fearful sacraments and thereby to deify both himself and others."[24]

The ability to officiate the sacraments, particularly that of the Eucharist, raises the priest above the nonordained, whatever heights of sanctity the nonordained may reach independently:

> By means of the priesthood God accomplishes great and redeeming works among mankind: He purifies and sanctifies people, animals, and elements; He delivers people from the villainous works of the devil; He renews and strengthens; He converts bread and wine into the purest Body and Blood of the God-person Himself; He marries people and makes marriage honorable and the nuptial bed pure; He absolves sins, heals illness, converts earth into heaven, unites heaven with earth, the human being with Himself; He joins angels and people in one gathering ... what do they not lack, the people who have no priesthood! They are deprived of salvation. It is not in vain that the Lord, the Accomplisher of our salvation, is called the Chief Priest.[25]

Exclaiming "The priest is an angel, not a man!," Father John appropriated for the priesthood the traditional description of monasticism as the angelic life. He insisted upon the institutional, impersonal superiority of the priesthood. Although the nun may and must pray for the world, for example, the efficacy of her prayer rests on her personal sanctity. The priest, by contrast, has access to a constant stream of grace that comes directly from God through the sacraments. It is the sacraments, as a source of contained and objective grace, that allow the priest to represent God to other men and women—and allow him to plead their case before God: "The priest is sublime during the celebration of all the daily services and especially during the fulfillment of the sacrament when he is invested by God with the greatest authority; [then] he is all-powerful and can plead for the whole world."[26] Precisely because the source of the priest's goodness is not any virtue of his own but the grace of God, Father John equated priesthood with sanctity and priests with the saints as vessels through which the Divine flows to the human.

This role of priest as mediator, as the meeting-point between God and people, manifested itself in numerous ways. When first ordained,

Father John was filled with joy at finally performing the office to which he had aspired. He perceived his service to God above all as an act of praise:

> Then will I go unto the altar of God, unto God, my exceeding joy from my youth: yea, upon the harp will I praise thee.... O God, my God! I have the happiness of often going unto the altar of God and praising him—not upon the harp, but with my own voice and [through] the voices of those who sing and chant. Glory to Thee and thanks for Thine having granted me the happiness of David,—even surpassing his.[27]

Above all, Father John felt that all of a priest's activity must be directed outward toward his parishioners. If the priest, like the medieval king, had two bodies—body private and sacramental body public—there was no question which mattered more. It was not enough for the priest to pursue his own salvation; he must also constantly bear in mind the salvation of the flock entrusted to him. "It is sinful for a priest to pray only for himself," he declared, "prayer for his flock must always follow." Selfishness or self-absorption was a priest's greatest potential offense; the priest did not have the moral right to a private life. In his diary, Father John chided priests for reading but not passing along the results gained from it to their flocks. "And so, pastors of Christ's flock, read on—but then yourselves speak, yourselves write, be like bees.... Your life must be dedicated to the well-being of your flock, as the life of parents should be dedicated to their children."[28]

The priest's surest means of reaching the people and winning their salvation was his ability to perform the sacraments that constituted the basis of his spiritual authority. The most important of these, and the center of the spiritual life for Father John, was the Eucharist. Entries on the sacrament fill his diaries, as he speaks gladly of the force and joy he receives from it. To him, the Eucharist was life itself, and partaking of it every day meant being spiritually alive and together with God in an intensity he had never experienced ("O, greatest ecstasy, Holy Mysteries! O, Holy Mysteries, giving life! O, unutterable Divine love!").[29] He fully absorbed the prayers assigned to be read before and after communion, ascribing his physical as well as his spiritual health to his partaking of the Eucharist daily.[30] Just as earlier he had wondered about the miracle of the loaves and fishes, however, he now began to wonder about the transformation of the elements and how it was possible. He began by using analogies:

> What is surprising in the Lord's offering you His body and blood as your food and drink?... Just as previously as an infant you were fed by your mother and lived through her, through her milk, so now, having grown up and become a sinful person, you are fed by the blood of your Life-giver in order that you live and grow spiritually into a man of God, a holy man; more briefly: just as then you were your mother's son, so now you are the child of God, educated and nourished by His flesh and blood, and all the more by His Spirit (for His flesh and blood are spirit and life).[31]

But such analogies were not proofs, and Father John would occasionally become consumed by doubt. It is not surprising: accepting that bread and wine literally become the Divine Body and Blood is beyond all reason, so much so that theology seems almost to take a pleasure in acknowledging the leap of sheer faith the Eucharist requires. Eucharistic miracles, with bread and wine turning into flesh and blood, are testimony to both people's doubt and their wish to believe.[32] For a sincere priest, however, doubting the foundation of his faith was torment. Father John's relation to the Eucharist was a constant feat of faith. Thus on Holy Thursday (the day when the Orthodox commemorate the establishment of the Eucharist at the Mystical Supper) in 1860, he doubted the Lord's being completely present in every particle of communion—but his prayers to fight the Eucharistic doubts were answered; he overcame the doubt. It was not the only such occasion; almost every communion represented a victory of faith to Father John. Such statements as "I believe and I confess that the smallest piece of the Lamb [e.g., the bread used in communion] and the smallest drop of wine is His blood," must be understood as a response to and a means of overcoming other moments of hesitation. Assertion and exhortation merged: "Regardless of how many pieces there are, all of them are the spirit and the life of, or the complete, Christ, and all of them are from one bread.... So Christians, however many there are, are one body of Christ."[33]

Remarks of this kind appear only in the first years of Father John's priesthood. He ultimately concluded that there was no rational explanation for the conversion of bread and wine to the Body and Blood, and began to attach greater importance to the state of the communicant in the Eucharistic mystery. His subsequent meditations on the Eucharist combined empiricism—a minute recording of his reactions to communion—and practical ways of overcoming his doubt. He wrote, for example:

"He that eateth my flesh, and drinketh my blood, dwelleth in Me, and I in him." This is tangible and experience confirms it. Most blessed and most filled with life is the person who partakes of the holy Mysteries with faith and with heartfelt repentance of sins.— This truth is tangible; it is also clear from the obverse. When you approach the holy Chalice *without* sincere repentance of your sins or with doubt, then Satan enters into you and dwells in you, killing your soul; and this can be extraordinarily palpable.[34]

The note of simultaneous fear and threat in the last sentence—the dread of an unworthy communion that was to be echoed by the people who confided to him their religious concerns—was stated even more strongly later. "Whoever approaches the holy chalice with any passion whatever in his heart," Father John declared, "is a Judas, and comes to falsely kiss the Son of man."[35] He did not write such things to terrorize his parishioners; he felt *himself* to be a traitor after an "unworthy" communion and agonized over it for days. But how then, faced with the fear of betraying God, could he ever approach the chalice without dread? He devised methods that allowed him to partake of communion. One such technique, referring to the "I am who am" affirmation of Yahweh to Moses (Exodus 3:14), went as follows:

In order to partake of the Life-giving Mysteries with unwavering faith and to triumph over all the snares of the enemy and all his falsehoods, imagine that what you accept from the Chalice is "The Being," that is, the only One Who Is. When you have such a disposition of your thoughts and heart, then, from partaking of the Holy Mysteries, you will suddenly calm down, rejoice, and revive; you will know in your heart that the Lord abides in you truly and essentially, and in you in the Lord.—[via] experience.[36]

The terse word "experience" (*opyt*) is an example of Father John's willingness to draw on his own ordeals as a proof of Divine presence. It was precisely such appeals to experience, rather than a process of theological reasoning, that would endear him to contemporary Protestants, and allow him to use the Eucharist as a point of departure for other religious mysteries.[37] Rather than devote his energies to proving rationally that which required the greatest leap of faith, he began to use the miracle of the Eucharist as a point of comparison—and indeed as a proof—of other suprarational phenomena characteristic of the religious life:

Through the constant miracle of the transubstantiation of bread and wine into the true Body and Blood of Christ.... I see the miracle of the constant invigoration of the human being through divine breathing and his becoming a living soul. "And so," it is written, "the first man was made a living soul," while at the Holy Meal the bread and wine upon transubstantiation become not only a living soul, but also "a quickening spirit." And all of this takes place before my eyes; and I feel it with my soul and body; I feel it keenly. My God! What fearful Mysteries You work! Of what unutterable Mysteries have you made me a witness and a communicant. Glory to Thee, my Creator! Glory to Thee, Creator of the Body and Blood of Christ![38]

The fact of the transformation of bread and wine into the Body and Blood of Jesus Christ was so miraculous that other miracles paled next to it, or emerged from it logically, as it were: if one can believe that bread and wine are God's Body and Blood, then one can accept other supranatural phenomena as well. Father John's attitude toward the miraculous generally came from this initial moment of acceptance of the Eucharist. The Eucharist, the very foundation of Christian ritual, is suprarational, defying all natural laws. It is by definition an ever-repeating miracle. The potential for other miracles must therefore also be perpetually present among Christians, particularly when they are linked to communion, which unites the human being with God in the most immediate way possible. Father John described the miraculous potency of communion in a matter-of-fact fashion:

It is good for me to pray for people when I have taken communion worthily: then the Father and the Son and the Holy Spirit, my God, is within me, and I have great boldness before Him.—My King is within me then as in a dwelling: ask whatever you wish. "We will come unto him, and make our abode with him. Ye shall ask what ye will, and it shall be done unto you."[39]

The sense of God within would later give Father John the "boldness" to pray for the granting of others' requests and feel confident that the requests would be granted. In the largest sense, however, his mission as a priest meant transmitting something of his own devotional fervor to his flock. After less than five years of priesthood, he began to identify his spiritual life with responsibility for that of his flock, so much that he wanted them to share in the benefits he felt himself. He wrote in his diary in 1866, for example: "Today I united with the Lord in the sacrament of communion at early liturgy and I became the fullness of Him who filleth all things in everyone. O, if this were so always!—that is, *to fill everyone—all hearts*."[40] Sharing the Eucharist with his flock was the supreme expression of the priest's public body.

In his desire to fully share the liturgy, Father John transformed the way Russians experienced both it and the priest who served. The mid-century desire for the liturgy to be more immediate found in him its strongest advocate. His love for the Eucharist, combined with the sense of the priest's responsibility for his flock, impelled him to enter fully into performing the ritual of the Eucharist and to convey his own emotional experience of it to the people present. These efforts met with remarkable success. For both the clergy and people who served with him, Father John was almost literally a revelation.

Even his manner of serving was as different as could be from the traditional stylization almost invariably practiced by most Orthodox clergy. Aspiring priests and Psalm-readers were taught in seminaries and enjoined in the clerical press to eliminate as much of the personal from their serving and their way of reading liturgical texts as possible. The ideal was to provide as direct as possible a conveyance of the text, intoning all one's lines on one note without stressing one section of a phrase over another. The hierarchy's position was stated by Metropolitan Antonii (Khrapovitskii):

> Unhurried reading, the singing of the sacred canticles, reverent bows according to the established order, a correct, unhurried sign of the cross—all of this in itself takes away the soul from Earth and draws it to Heaven.... On the other hand, arbitrariness on the part of even a pious priest in public prayer gradually leads into prelest', that is, into spiritual self-delusion; it teaches him to interest the people not in the service but in his person; it makes him not the leader of prayer, but an actor.[41]

Against this background, Father John's intensely personal approach to serving could hardly have been more startling. He sought to engage everyone present. While Orthodox practice (and Roman Catholic practice before Vatican II) required the priest and deacon to recite their petitions facing the altar with their backs to the people, Father John would often turn to face his parishioners during such petitions as "Let us stand aright," "Let us lift up our hearts," and "We give thanks unto the Lord." Whenever the priest was to refer to people as "these" or "those" in prayers, Father John would gesture toward some, or pass his hand over all. It had been all too easy to detach oneself during the liturgy and assume that the main action was proceeding without one's participation. Suddenly facing Father John's eyes just before the Eucharist and hearing him say directly to oneself and one's neighbor, "Come, drink ye all of it," reminded those in the nave of the church that they, too, were expected to partake of the Eucharistic celebration.[42]

He did not only look directly at his parishioners. In contrast to the usual reedy tenor of a priest's petitions uttered on one deliberately passionless note, he wept, shouted, and cried out the words of the matins canons and the liturgy, smiled beatifically at references to the Mother of God and the saints and angrily shook his service-book while uttering the words "Satan" or "Devil."[43] His contagious fervor managed to jolt the congregation out of their customary passive reception. The poet-publicist Konstantin Fofanov, who stood in the altar on one occasion when Father John was serving, wrote: "He uttered the words [of the service] sharply, abruptly; it was as if he was convincing, commanding; rather, insisting upon his requests. "My power and sovereign! You are my light!" he exclaimed, raising his arms with tears in his voice and suddenly falling prone to the floor."[44] On another occasion, the last Ober-Procurator's assistant noted: "Suddenly, impetuously, during the singing of the canticle to the incarnation of Christ—"Only-begotten Son and Word of God"—he took the cross on the altar-table and kissed it, embraced it lovingly with both hands, looked at it so tenderly and ecstatically, kissed it again three, four times in a row, pressed it to his forehead."[45]

While these observers were favorably moved, the celebrated liberal lawyer Anatolii Koni was both more graphic and more negative:

> When he began to read the Gospel, his voice took on a harsh and commanding tone and he began to repeat the holy words with a kind of hysterical shriek: "If your brother asks you for bread," he exclaimed, "and you give him a stone—give him a stone!... A stone!—and if he ask you for you fish, and you give him a serpent ... give him a serpent!... a serpent!—give him a stone!..." and so on. This sort of serving did not inspire reverence but a kind of strange uneasiness, a kind of fearful feeling which communicated itself to others.[46]

While people responded differently to such a personal interpretation of the liturgy, the change Father John introduced in the perception of the priest was powerful. The priest moved from being the neutral, barely noticeable conduit of objective grace to a sort of lightning-rod who could affect those present with his own fervor. Even skeptics who came to see him realized immediately that Father John's expressions came from intense prayer and inner rigor that were the opposite of theatricality. As Priest Mikhail Paozerskii recalled the words of the priest's service-guide in 1897, watching Father John's face freeze into utter concentration at the beginning of the Cherubic hymn, "On him, you could read as in a book, 'No one attached to fleshly desires and sweetness dare approach.'"[47] Here may lie the deepest reason for his chastity: if Father John could reach such levels of spiritual intensity while serving, he may have feared that after relations with his wife, the intensity would diminish or vanish.

Father John's highly personal interpretation of the liturgy was not restricted to the manner in which he served. Even more sensational, particularly to his fellow clergy, was his free alteration of the text of the liturgy as he saw fit. In order to realize the shock this practice produced, it must be remembered that, unlike Protestant groups who emphasized the "gift of tongues" and speaking (or not) as one were inclined, the Orthodox Church celebrated religious services according to a strict rule and order, with even silent prayers and every swing of the censer prescribed by the service-book well-thumbed by every deacon and priest. Certain combinations of services reached baroque levels of complexity, compelling clerics to consult the Typicon, a guide to the structure of services listing virtually every possible scenario and combination of texts for any given day. In both the training and practice of clerics, the emphasis was on the art of determining the proper daily text to be used rather than on its execution.[48]

In this rigid context Father John allowed himself unusual liberties. He interjected his own phrases, even entire prayers, into the liturgy. At the moment before the creed, for example, when, after the petition "Let us love one another," the clergy in the altar is supposed to embrace each other with the words, "Christ is in our midst," he would add, "alive and active" (or "living and acting"). A visiting student who later became a clergyman wrote of his astonishment at hearing this interpolation:

> I stood stunned stock-still by these words and suddenly thought—yes, Christ the Savior is right here among us, and not somewhere far off in the distance, not dead, not some kind of detached, abstract doctrine, not simply as a familiar historical personality, but alive, "alive and active." He is among us. And even "acting." It

was eerie and terrifying; despite itself my soul began to quiver and quake. I was ready to fall right down before the altar-table.[49]

Other additions were more extensive. Perhaps because he had grown up in an area filled with Old Believers, Father John was ever concerned with bringing those outside the fold of the Orthodox Church into it. His impulse outward and concern with saving souls besides his own, evoking the missionary ambitions ascribed to him, emerges in the improvised prayer he would read during the Credo:

> Unite in this faith all the great Christian societies, woefully having fallen aside from the unity of the holy Orthodox catholic and apostolic church, which is Your body and whose Head art Thou and the Savior of the body ... grant unto their hearts to know the truth and salvific nature of Thy Church and to unite with it; link to Thy holy Church also those who are suffering from ignorance, delusion, and the stubbornness of schism.... Draw all nations populating the earth to this faith, that they may all glorify Thee, the only God of all, with one heart and one mouth.[50]

These additions, while not part of any canonical text, are nonetheless perfectly in keeping with Orthodox texts. Father John's use of Church Slavonic instead of Russian vernacular (*zhivyi i deistvuiai* versus *zhivushchii i deistvuiushchii*, for example) also contributed to the sense that the addition fit seamlessly, indeed properly belonged, in the customary text. Praying for those outside the Church *during a service*, while unusual, is not unheard-of, evoking as it did the prayers read at extraliturgical Orthodox supplicatory services (*molebens*) and baptisms. In more than a few instances, however, Father John used expressions that sounded not only distinctly modern but that seemed to contain a Protestant undertone as well. Just after taking communion, he would say, for example, "The Lord is in me *personally*, God and man, hypostatically, essentially, immutably, cleansing, enlightening, victoriously, deifingly, wondrously, *which I feel in myself as well*."[51] Despite the retention of such Orthodox theological terms as "hypostasis" and "essence," the explicit emphasis on personal apprehension and personal experience (even if taken to refer to the Divine rather than to Father John) spoken in vernacular Russian to heighten its immediacy, ran utterly counter to the rote delivery of other Orthodox priests.

Paradoxically, while he prayed for Protestants as being outside the true church and hoped for their conversion, in such instances as this one he used language similar to theirs. Certainly, the presence and activity of Protestant and post-Reformation Roman Catholics in St. Petersburg exposed Father John to their popularizing methods and their emphasis on the spirit. In 1873, for example, Father John mentions a conversation he had with an English pastor who criticized aspects of Orthodoxy relative to Protestantism ("he called holy wanderers fanatics, monks egoists who live only for themselves, and icons idols"). Nevertheless, although Father John knew of the "Protestant critique" and was able to discuss it with non-Orthodox clerics, his consistent criticism of Lutherans and Anglicans argues against conscious emulation.[52] A more likely source for his prayers was the tradition of composing one's own prayers for particular purposes. Not only saints, but ordinary women and men used prayers bordering on being spells for such purposes as ensuring the fidelity of a spouse, a good harvest, or winning someone's affections.[53] While the pre-Christian origin of the incantations is obvious, there are enough prayers that are perfectly Orthodox in spirit to suggest that a similar pious impulse may have prompted Father John in his liturgical worship.[54]

There was, of course, a difference between prayers for private use and those prescribed for the liturgy. Prayers used in private could take virtually any form; liturgical prayers required strict adherence to church canons. If every priest were as free with the set texts and motions as Father John was, the result would have meant a dangerous loss of consistency, perhaps even Orthodoxy.[55] It is surprising that he was able to proceed unchecked with his improvisation. The key, however, was that he insisted that any improvisation remain within the sacramental and dogmatic framework of the Orthodox Church. He believed that God was experienced "objectively" only in the sacraments of the Orthodox Church; seeking to revivify the relation of his parishioners and concelebrants to God was to him synonymous with the sacraments. Thus, for all that Father John sought to make his parishioners' experience of the sacraments more intimate and more frequent, he would never dispose of the sacraments altogether, as did contemporary Protestant sects. But he could and did change the circumstances under which one received the sacraments, and lessened the thickets of regulations surrounding them.

Before communion, for example, men and women were supposed to fast for a period ranging from a minimum of three days to a week and, if literate, read several prescribed canons and the special prayers before communion.[56] Women could not receive communion if they were menstruating regardless whether they had fulfilled the other conditions;

this taboo, moreover, was often taken to extend to such paraliturgical activity as venerating the icons and kissing the cross.[57] Father John's Orthodox contemporaries considered (as Orthodoxy still does) the physical notions of purity characteristic of Judaism, Islam, and early Christianity to be a necessary precondition of receiving communion. This was, in fact, one of the reasons why Russians communicated infrequently: the preparations were so elaborate that they required an active verb for their description; in order "to do it right" for fear of profaning the sacrament, one had to devote more time than may have been practicable on a regular (weekly, even monthly) basis.[58]

Father John sought to reduce the sense of intimidation and formality that surrounded communion. In his sermons, he linked spiritual health to the reception of the Eucharist.[59] He broke with tradition and contemporary practice, occasionally permitting menstruating women to the chalice and allowing both men and women whose lives he knew to communion with little or virtually no formal preparation. Given the weight of tradition, however, Father John had to use a good deal of discretion in this regard. He would not do something so un-Orthodox as to place all initiative for partaking of communion in the hands of parishioners. He still had the last word, as when he refused to allow, for example, obvious drunkards and adulterers, or young people who had not combed their hair.[60] While the greater access to communion was thus not as thoroughgoing a change as it might now seem, it was the first such instance in the Russian Church. Moreover, in an institution as deeply conservative as the Orthodox Church—when Father John began his career as a priest, the order of the Orthodox vespers, matins, and liturgy had not changed at all in over two hundred years—any change at all came as a revelation. Those whom he deemed ready for a certain amount of flexibility found it extraordinarily liberating.[61]

Encouraging people to more frequent communion, however, was an uphill battle. Father John felt the perfunctory performance by his parishioners of their "obligations" keenly and privately expressed his dismay: "How meagerly you take communion, and how necessary it is to partake more frequently! Your soul is parched with hunger and thirst for grace. Think of the Samaritan woman and Jesus Christ and know how to seek the living water of grace."[62]

He decried the discrepancy between his own perception of the sacraments, and that of both fellow priests and parishioners. This sense of indignation in God's name—which would later translate into political activity—the sense that he stands with God against the unfeeling world, appears in Father John from the start:

Liturgical Innovations

> What if You, my Lord and God Jesus Christ, would flash the light of Your Divinity from your Most Pure Mysteries when they rest on the holy altar—on the discos during the Liturgy or in the tabernacle or in the portable tabernacle (*daronositsa*) when Your priest carries them on his breast when going to or from a sick person?—from this light every one encountering them on the street or seeing them from his house would fall to the ground in terror, for even the Angels cover themselves from Thine unapproachable glory! And how indifferently withal some treat these most heavenly Mysteries![63]

The reverence for all things Divine, and the urge to have everyone share this reverence, had other aspects. Father John cared nearly as much about the singing of the choir and the chanting of the clergy as he did about the sacrament, for a prayerful atmosphere depended on them. In a brief autobiographical account submitted to the journal *The North* in 1888, he emphasized that from earliest childhood, he loved prayer and church services, especially good singing.[64] This attention to the technical level of music during a church service would also persist in John's later life. His diaries are full of such references to singing as:

> I served the liturgy with tender emotion, but during the Cherubic hymn the enemy all but deposed me, disturbing me with displeasure at the singers, the nuns of the Leushinskii convent, who were singing Lvov's arrangement of "Let us who mystically represent the cherubim," which I did not like one bit. I repented privately and entreated the Lord to grant me mercy and peace—sinful, willful, capricious me.[65]

Many others shared Father John's appreciation for good church singing, of course. Laypeople from all class backgrounds might prefer to attend a convent or monastery rather than their parish church for services just because the singing was better, and Old Believers occasionally returned to Orthodoxy because of "sweet singing" alone.[66] Similarly, foreign observers note the high technical appreciation Russian peasants evinced for music and especially singing.[67] But Father John's attention to the text and music during services was unusual. One eyewitness wrote:

> The choir begun to sing the verses "on the verses." During this time Father John had almost entirely vested himself to serve

liturgy. He had only to put on a robe. Quickly, impetuously, running rather than walking, he moved from the altar to the kliros, joined the singers, and began to sing together with them. He sang with ardor and with profound faith in each word, himself directing, repeatedly stressing individual words and slowing the tempo where it was necessary according to the logical meaning, the content of the text. The singers would guess these words, tempo, and beat by instinct, and harmonized with him with no small artistry and inspiration. The singing, initially not entirely harmonious, quickly became so, strong, resonant, powerful, inspirational; it poured forth throughout the entire church, filling the entire soul of those present. How touching it was to watch the singers during this time. It was as if one holy early Christian family with its father at the head was singing its victorious, sacred, great hymns.[68]

In short, Father John wanted the faithful to have a complete liturgical experience, in every sense. Making communion more deeply felt also meant affecting penance, and Father John transformed the rite of confession as well. This was important. Because preaching was still a rare phenomenon in the mid-nineteenth century, despite the clergy's efforts, the confession was the only vehicle for religious counsel in many cases, and parishioners valued highly the ability of a priest to respond attentively to their confessions.[69] In this respect Father John shone. He identified with the parishioner, noting that "repentance must be sincere and absolutely free, in no way pressured or constrained by time or custom or the person of the confessor."[70] He sought to make the experience of confession as favorable as possible, as when he increased the privacy of those who came to confess by having a special partition with gates made at the side of the church—something that would later be incorporated as a standard feature in church architecture—and sometimes waived the usual requirements of a week's prior prayer, church attendance, and fasting.[71] These efforts reflected his conviction that in order to work properly, the confession had to be "created" by both priest and supplicant. When the parishioner was either laconic or insouciant, the priest's task was all the harder: "Woe when dryness encounters dryness, when a priest at confession, wounded by the enemy [e.g., the devil], faces a spiritual child who has not prepared at all. And how many of them there are!"[72]

In the beginning of his pastoral career, Father John spent as much time as possible with each person. As one confessant recalled:

> He was not content with a simple, formal confession, but embarked on an entire education, testing, and examination of the feelings of the soul and of the penitent's religious knowledge. Sometimes he would spend hours with the penitent and, postponing the absolution, made him return and again. As the years went by the number of penitents grew tremendously.[73]

Over time, Father John's commitment to the sacrament gradually bore its fruits. A circle of people who went frequently to confession and communion began to form around him and gradually extended outside the area of Kronstadt and St. Petersburg. While he does not appear to have singled out women and young girls as part of a pastoral strategy, their participation in the sacraments (and their letters to him on their sacramental lives) far outnumbered that of men, as was the case with Jean-Marie Vianney of Ars, Father John's French contemporary.[74] The phenomenon of significant numbers of women moving to Kronstadt for the sole purpose of being able to have confession and communion from him regularly, moreover, had no male counterpart. This devotion to the sacraments and to Father John could reach significant proportions: one woman described her happiness at having lived "in such grace"—that is, going to him for regular communion—for seventeen years.[75]

The emphasis on the sacraments of Eucharist and confession as well as the person of the confessor was something new in Russian practice. While many charismatic elders and eldresses had followers, such followers came to the elders primarily for *counsel*, as opposed to *communion*, which Father John insisted upon. He sought always to link any visit, counsel, or act of prayer or healing with communion on the part of the subject, as did the curé of Ars.[76] Although the devotion to the Eucharist in some cases sprang initially from Father John's own charisma and power—a woman named Varvara wrote of "uniting myself twice to Christ's Mysteries *in order to be closer in spirit to you*"—the identification and then transfer of devotion from his person to the sacrament were so complete that devotion to the Eucharist persisted even after Father John's death.[77] A more regular and thoughtful observance of communion was perhaps his most significant contribution to Russian piety. Both the change in widely held standards of "proper" behavior, which previously had avoided frequent communion as leading to the possible diminishing of reverence for the sacrament, and the revival of Eucharistic theology in Russian Orthodoxy that has lasted to this day, may be traced to this quiet revolution.[78]

Father John was so eager to receive the confessions of his parishioners that, especially in the first years of his career, he welcomed them with open arms, not complaining to himself about their coming in the sporadic intervals and large numbers that Bishop Antonii had bemoaned. He wrote in 1859: "What a wonderful thing! I heard people's confessions yesterday from 4 to 11 P.M., and even though I was a little tired, I went to bed at midnight, and having gotten up at 4:30 A.M., felt brisk and healthy! How good it is to work for the Lord! How He strengthens one—it is marvelous!"[79]

For all of Father John's enthusiasm about Divine support, however, his encouragement of the sacraments became so successful that to hear properly the confession of everyone who wished to come to him became physically impossible. In 1882, just at the point when his reputation was beginning to extend beyond the borders of Kronstadt, he thanked God "for the grace of communion which enabled me to hear (while standing) the confessions of 243 people today, from three to ten-fifteen p.m."[80] This would have meant an average confession of less than two minutes per person. Three years later: "Four hundred people at communion today. Glory be to God!" When the numbers of supplicants reached the thousands and Father John had to listen to confessions through the night until morning, he took an unprecedented step: he began to hear confessions *en masse*.[81] By the late 1890s, confession at St. Andrew's in Kronstadt at "peak times" of the year had become a group event involving thousands of people crowded together, shrieking out their sins. Under Father John the Orthodox confession changed from being a private event virtually independent of the nearly anonymous confessor who asked questions by rote to a public one that rested primarily on the charisma of a celebrity. The very nature of the sacrament seemed to be transformed nearly beyond recognition.

In retrospect, it appears surprising that there was not more controversy among the hierarchy over whether or not such an innovation ought to be allowed. There were several factors at work. One was a post-Emancipation willingness to revive old forms or devise new ones if such adaptations were consistent with the spirit of Orthodoxy.[82] The confession had just such a precedent in early Christian practice: in the first centuries of Christianity, sinners were supposed to acknowledge their sins publicly, before the entire congregation, before being accepted back into the community of the Eucharist.[83]

But one did not have to return to the first centuries of Christianity to find a precedent for Father John's innovation: a specifically Russian and more modern variant of public confession also existed, albeit in nonsacramental guise. Dostoyevsky's repeated emphasis—Liza to Raskolnikov in *Crime and Punishment*, and Zosima to Alesha in *The Brothers Karamazov* being the most obvious cases—on the need to repent of one's sins and beg forgiveness publicly, before "all four corners of the earth" if no people were available, was only the most celebrated version of the belief that repentance had to be public in order to be valid. Throughout the Slavic Orthodox world, the ritual on Forgiveness Sunday before Lent included bowing to the ground and begging forgiveness before one's family at home and before the entire parish in church.[84]

There is, moreover, an abundant literature on the popular phenomenon of confessing to the earth, to which the liturgy itself contains references.[85] The phenomenon of public confession held in contexts that were not strictly religious as well: the punishment for an offense committed against the village commune, for example, was halved if the offender owned up and begged pardon.[86] In some districts of Russia, a couple with difficulties begetting children was supposed to ask the forgiveness of women neighbors.[87] Father John's innovation might thus seemed to have incorporated an element of pre-Christian practice into the sacraments of the Orthodox Church.

And yet there were several factors that distinguished the mass confession to Father John from these other versions of public repentance. In the cases when the penitent addressed the neighbors or the commune, she or he did so as an individual. In Father John's confessions, the process was reversed. Although each person still confessed his or her sins individually, the effect of hearing one's own voice as but one of thousands substantially altered the experience. It was the loss of private shame that other clergymen noticed and criticized most strongly, of which more will be said below. Next, Father John's deliberate omission of the external attributes of the priest during liturgy—full vestments, chasuble, mitre—had the effect of signaling a caesura or "time-out." His appearing only in cassock and stole (*epitrakhilion*) acted to reinforce the sense of a private confession, as this was the proper attire for a cleric performing the rite. Finally, as one devout observer commented, Father John began "without our usual words of introduction, 'in the name of the Father and the Son and the Holy Spirit.'"[88] The absence of this otherwise inevitable and invariable formula had the effect of heightening the immediacy of the moment, lifting it out of the usual boundaries people expected in a church service.

The rejection of such formulae was also typical of contemporary Protestants.[89] Although Father John's approach superficially seemed to have some elements in common with theirs, the end result—a liturgical sacrament administered by a priest—remained quite different. He began by addressing the crowds immediately with the words "Male and female sinners, who are like me!," which had the effect of emphasizing the link between priest and laypeople rather than the differences in their religious status. Similarly, Father John read the prayers before confession himself—an act usually performed by a lesser-ranking reader or even a layperson—with great emotion and with many of his own interjections. Doing so removed any sense of formulae and conveyed the tie he felt to those present. As the crowds of people listened to his shaking voice, they grew increasingly emotional. Their mood, in turn, passed itself to Father John. The dynamic between priest and people, with each party fueled by the other, created an atmosphere of ecstatic religious release. As an eyewitness wrote:

> Father John covered his face with his hands, but even behind them the large tears continued to fall down his face onto the cold floor of the church.... He cried, joining his tears with the tears of the people, like a true shepherd of Christ's flock; he grieved and rejoiced in his soul for his sheep. And these lost, sinning sheep, seeing the tears on the face of their beloved pastor and understanding the state of his soul in these minutes, were all the more ashamed of themselves and burst into even greater shrieks, moans, and lamentations, and a pure river of tears of repentance poured forth even more abundantly to the altar of God, cleansing the soiled souls in its stream. The huge cathedral was full of moans, shrieks, and howls; it seemed as if the whole church was shaking from the shattering wails of the people.[90]

Whether or not one approved of such a transformation of the confession depended as much on the nature of one's predilection for collective experiences as it did on any notion of canonicity. The Religious Consistory had resisted the introduction of mass confessions, regarding them as perilously close to the frenzies of the self-mutilating sect of the *khlysty*.[91] Others found positive qualities in the loss of self within the group. To describe the power and the appeal of the mass confessions, Father John's champions emphasized the merging of all social classes within a larger unity:

> In these minutes it was no longer a mass of individual people, but it was as one person, one body, one living organism moving this

way and that. Everything merged and united in this mass. There were no longer any divisions. The wealthy person and the poor one, the notable and the obscure, the educated and the uneducated, woman and man,—all were together, all had during these minutes one heart and one soul, like the early Christians.[92]

While such moments provided an extraordinary release for many of the faithful, they chilled to and repelled the more skeptical. A prominent atheist noted with repulsion:

> At the sight of Father John, the crowd reached a frenzy: everyone pushed forward, closer to the ambo. They shoved, they climbed up onto the benches, on the steps; they all but trampled the shroud used during Holy Week in order to see the elder. Thousands of hands stretched themselves out to him, thousands of mouths cried out his name....
> And then something awful began. Nothing is visible in the darkness, all is permitted. In the darkness the people's tongues were loosened. All the vileness of the human soul flooded out into the open. The holy fools began to wail and howl. The epileptics fell to the ground. Suddenly it emerged that everyone in the church was a criminal:
> "I stole!"
> "I burned my neighbor's house!"
> "Batiushka, forgive me—I am sleeping with my father-in-law!"
> Someone was already ripping her clothing, wailing about having aborted a child. Someone felt himself in Hades, crying, "Save me ... Fiery Gehenna ... Hell! hell! hell!" The well-dressed lady next to me was poking herself with a hat-pin.... Blood was pouring out of the mouth of my neighbor, a meshchanin: he had knocked out his teeth. If these lunatics had had knives, they would have sliced themselves to the point of senselessness.[93]

The impression the mass confessions made was uncannily similar. The descriptions of the devoted and the hostile alike coincide both in the individual details of chaos and in their recounting of Father John's magnetic hold over the crowd. The following account by a pious clergyman, for example, differs little from the preceding one by Serebrov:

> There was a fearful, unimaginable noise. Some wept, other fell to the floor, others stood stock-still in a frozen, wordless state....

"Repent, repent," Father John repeated from time to time. Suddenly he would look at a particular part of the church and everyone there felt his gaze upon them. Immediately the voices from that part of the church would sound louder, noticeably standing out from the general choir of sound and infecting the rest of the crowd even more.... How powerfully he held this whole mass of people—he was like a magician or a sorcerer. If during these minutes Father John were to tell the people to follow him, they would have followed their pastor anywhere.[94]

The line between Father John's charisma and the redeeming power of the sacrament as such appeared perilously finely drawn, to the possible detriment of the latter. People came in droves, so much so that on at least one occasion, when over eight thousand visitors came to Kronstadt for communion, over two thousand had to be turned away (it was impossible to prepare so many Gifts).[95] Certainly the potential for the abuse of the public confession as an excuse to avoid the more demanding, more revealing, and more potentially embarrassing private one was evident. A priest named Father Boris Nikolaev, for example, made the charge that many people preferred public confessions precisely because it absolved them of the responsibility of owning up to their actions alone in front of the priest. Other clerics felt that the cathartic mood and absence of personal accountability might have only a negligible effect on people's behavior once the ceremony was over.[96]

It is precisely these aspects of the mass confession, which spread quickly in the Soviet period, that would earn the most criticism. By 1926, Archpriest Valentin Sventitsky felt compelled to give a series of lectures on the abuse of the practice, explaining that "general confession" was utterly uncanonical and to be avoided at all costs. The question was then reasonably raised that if Father John had done something, had indeed introduced it, how bad could it be? But the point was that Father John, with his discernment, was not just any priest. In responding to would-be emulators, Father Valentin, as many émigré bishops after him, underscored Father John's uniqueness:

> The necessary condition for individual Confession—the obligation of the confessor to know the sins of the penitent—was fulfilled by Father John with Grace-given clairvoyance. Father John did not permit many to come the chalice without a preliminary questioning because *he could see the sin* on the soul of the person; *he knew* it even if he did not ask.... The general confession of Father John

of Kronstadt was a unique, unprecedented phenomenon. It is essentially inaccessible to us as an example to be imitated.[97]

Similarly, a contemporary priest admitted that, "in his mass confessions, the Kronstadt pastor achieves far greater fruits than I do in private confession, even if I were to talk for half an hour about repentance to each sinner," and also felt that Father John's grace was unique.[98] (On the other hand, as Bishop Alexander (Sememoff-Tian-Shanskii) pointed out, if Father John was indeed righteous, priests should look to him and his practices as an example.[99]) Because Father John left no discussion of the public confessions in his diaries, it is difficult to determine whether they were simply an *ad hoc* response to circumstances, as his biographers have it, or whether he assigned to them an independent, positive religious value. In either case, the mass confession appeared to be so convenient a solution to the problem of more supplicants than minutes in a day that it is difficult to imagine there being a less spectacular alternative.

Such an alternative did exist, however, in the example of Jean-Marie Vianney, the French Roman Catholic curé who was contemporary with Father John. Like Father John, Vianney was a parish priest who became the focus of the largest pilgrimage in mid–nineteenth-century France and who became, according to his *vita*, the "quintessential" priest. Like Father John, the curé of Ars became celebrated for his powers of healing and his emphasis on more frequent communion. Unlike Father John, however, Vianney abandoned an active apostolate in order to become an "immobile missionary" who became virtually imprisoned in his confessional, where he would spend fifteen hours a day year-round. While Father John spent the greater part of his day going from house to house or appointment to appointment, fulfilling the wide range of the services sought of Russian priests (particularly *molebens*, or services of intercession), Vianney reduced the nature of his pastoral function exclusively to hearing confessions and administering communion.[100]

It is a sign both of the multiplicity of functions required of an Orthodox priest relative to the Roman Catholic one and of Father John's wide range of activity that he appears never to have considered such a Eucharistically focused alternative. It also suggests that he did not change people's habits as much as might have liked. Father John's desire for more frequent communion on the part of his parishioners, and Orthodox Christians generally, came to mean in practice that the mass confessions were not a daily or even a weekly occurrence, but limited to the Lenten times of year when Russians had traditionally gone to confession and communion. Metropolitan Antonii (Khrapovitskii)'s hope that this habit might change, with confession and communion distributed more efficiently throughout the year, was only partially addressed in Kronstadt. Lay association of confession, fasting, and communion with traditional holy days proved stronger than either official *dicta* or individual charisma.

The interpenetration of lay expectations of the Russian priest and the strength of Father John's persona also emerged in the many extraliturgical services he was called to perform, especially the individual "commissioned" *moleben* services of prayer for healing, help, or thanksgiving. To give some sense of their relative proportion in his activity, Father John spent the morning (from 5 A.M. to approximately 11 A.M., depending on the number of people taking communion) at liturgy and the rest of day until midnight going from house to house or institution visiting the people who had either requested a private visit or who, after 1883, had come to Kronstadt on a pilgrimage in hopes of seeing him. Father John did not resist these extraliturgical requests, nor did he regard them as anything but a desirable manifestation of faith and piety—even when they threatened to cut into time spent in church, both at confession and at the chalice. It was during *molebens* and other private services that people expressed their most intimate and desperate wishes; both he and flock valued *molebens* too highly to imagine ever doing without them.

While asceticism represented the private aspect of his religiosity, Father John expressed his priestly role in public liturgical service. He loved the Eucharist so much he tried to partake of it daily and encouraged his parishioners to more frequent reception. His unusual fervor attracted so many that he was allowed to confess people *en masse*. Although both innovations found critics as well as champions, they have endured in Russian church practice. The other aspect of Father John's public, sacramental body was his charity.

3

Apostolicity, Charity, and the Move Toward Sanctity

Father John's conception of the ideal priest included the edification of his flock, charity, and social work, along with his liturgical responsibilities. These qualities were the logical extension and expression of his own religious turning outward, and contributed to his image as a social-minded, even "progressive," priest. His focus on active love was but one aspect of the public face of his piety. As important was the apostolic mission of edifying his flock in the broadest sense, through education, preaching, and denouncing the injustices and ills of society. In Father John's commitment to transforming society in order to make it conform to the Orthodox ideal, his early sermons anticipate the political turn he took in the last decade of his life. Because of his own class insecurity and the gap between his actual social standing and the one he believed he ought to have as a priest, this criticism would acquire an even sharper edge.

The literal approach to scripture that characterized Father John's asceticism guided his vision of society as well. His conception of what an ideal life in the world ought to be did not mean an idealization of what he saw around him in contemporary Russia but rather a wish to make Russia conform to his ideal of a Christian society. Extending to one's neighbor the same charity God showed us was central to this total vision. Father John took literally the most extreme statements in the Gospel concerning sharing one's goods with one's neighbor, from "If any man will sue thee at the law, and take away thy coat, let him have thy cloak also," to "If thou wilt be perfect, go and sell that thou hast, and give to the poor, and thou shalt have treasure in heaven" (Matthew 5:40; 19:21). He was struck by the unselfishness and sense of unity the sentiments of the Gospel presupposed. In describing the apostolic period, he wrote in his diary in 1861: "'Not one of them would declare anything to be his own, but they had everything in common.' Here is the character of Christian life! Unity in everything! Here are the words which serve as a beacon of light to our souls in the darkness of the passions of greed and avarice, of not wanting to hold anything in common, of miserliness!"[1]

This premise that the communal and the shared was good and the individual or the "selfish" was suspect had both private and social implications. In a social sense, one of the chief means of overcoming the alienation between the rich and the poor was to shrink the gulf that separated them. To accomplish this, charity on the part of the haves toward the have-nots was an indispensable part of Father John's total religious vision of society. His belief in charity affected him personally. He felt compelled to alleviate the misery he saw around him on an immediate, human level and could not justify to himself walking past someone who was asking for money.

But these impulses to charity were not easy to realize. Although Father John believed in principle that the Gospel injunction to share everything with one's neighbor must be taken literally, he found it difficult to do so. Had he been content to set aside a portion of his income for the poor, even half or most of it, and accept that reserving a certain amount for himself was not sinful, he might not have struggled so. He thought, however, that *everything* he owned ought properly to belong to those who had nothing, describing his money as a kind of public utility, like heating and plumbing: "The sea-water which comes into the house by a pipe—is it any the less sea-water only because it comes into *my* house? As the sea-water belongs to everyone, does not my money belong to everyone who is poor? What kind of blindness is it that I persist in regarding it as exclusively my property?"[2]

Father John willed himself not only to distribute his salary to those who needed his assistance, but to be endlessly hospitable as well. His pastoral commitment included charity and material help on a scale that went far beyond even the higher standard set by the post-Emancipation climate. There was no want of opportunity: Kronstadt was the bowery of St. Petersburg; it was the place where the capital's surplus vagrants were transported so as to preserve the elegant appearance of the imperial city.[3] Father John devoted himself to ministering to these *posadskie* from the time of his ordination, bringing eggs and medicine to hungry women with sick children and walking the streets from hovel to hovel late into the night, offering material and spiritual assistance. His rectory became an open house where virtually anyone who dropped by could expect hospitality and refreshment, and he soon came to be followed by crowds of beggars clamoring for money. A priest who gave, not asked for money, was so unusual that beggars shared news of their bounty with their needy friends, and poor people actually began to come to Kronstadt for the express purpose of getting help from Father John.[4]

This generosity is all the more remarkable because it did not come to Father John easily. A life spent in the grimmest childhood poverty and material hardship as a seminarian had taken its toll. Much as he believed that hospitality was something he owed every person who wished it, as that person was an image of God, it nearly killed Father John to give things away rather than saving them "for a rainy day." He could not keep from watching obsessively what each relative or passerby took on his or her plate, mutely begrudging every extra spoonful of sugar and hating himself for it.[5] In front of others, Father John shared generously the food of the household; in private, his diaries revealed the extent to which this enforced graciousness wore on him:

> Miser! When guests come, or when you see your relatives eating your bread, tell yourself, "It is not as if they are taking away your last piece from you!"[6]

> How to respond when one of your visitors eats an immoderate amount of your sweets which cost you dearly, and your heart constricts with criminal regret? Use this prayer.[7]

The struggle that Father John's charity actually represented cannot be appreciated adequately without examination of such entries from his diary. Every act of generosity, however small, represented willed effort to overcome nature. It was not that he was miserly; he simply had been very poor and knew what it was to live in dread of hunger and the coming day. Giving away everything rather than squirreling a bit for the future meant uprooting all his naturally frugal instincts. However often he enjoined himself to do so, it was not easy to imagine "that all of the food at the table are gifts from God, common for everyone; you are only the consignor."[8] Every meal and every teatime became an arena in which Father John sought to overcome his tendencies to hoard what little he had. It was a painful process that took years, even decades, to overcome.

The only things that made such giving bearable for Father John were the thought that he was fulfilling God's commandment of charity—and the connection that he began to observe between how much he gave and how much he was given. The relation between giving and receiving appeared to be almost directly proportional:

> Marvelously, palpably the Lord provides for those who do mercy: those who show mercy will themselves receive generous charity from people impelled to do so by God Himself. So, for instance, sinful I gave alms today to one poor old woman and two poor men.—And what do you think?—Upon coming home I see that I myself have been brought a gift from a kind person: a big pot of fresh milk, a pot of fresh farmers' cheese, and ten fresh eggs. Marvelous are Thy works, O Lord! Obvious is your right hand, All-Merciful, on me, a sinner.[9]

Such a literal understanding colored Father John's relation toward charity, and the principle of sharing one's goods generally, for the rest of his life. Almsgiving and hospitality were not only the tangible expressions of a generous nature but of a hard-won trust and faith in the Divine. If he obeyed the Gospel's exhortations to take all he had and give it to the poor, Father John believed, he would be rewarded for his faith and continually be given more.

Father John took this premise much further, however. Because he had to compel himself to give, he thought that others ought to do the same. This conviction was almost as startling as his approach to the liturgy. Previous generations of Orthodox clergy had interpreted the notion of sharing as an ideal and as something ultimately voluntary. Russian bishops and priests tended to enjoin each class to acquit itself properly in its own context—the poor to bear their lot without complaining, the rich to show "mercy." Even Saint Tikhon of Zadonsk, who wrote that "it is a sin to offend a man of wealth, but it is inhuman to offend a poor man," and criticized cheating by tradesmen, employers who withheld wages, and corrupt government officials, nonetheless emphasized the essential neutrality of money and being contented with what one had.[10]

A certain inequality between the various classes was accepted as part of the natural order of things, with Mark's "The poor you always have with you" (14:7) used as a justification. Father John's position was different. He believed that in Imperial Russia, which was supposed to be a Christian society, the enormous disparity that existed between its members was actually evil. The very presence of the poor made heinous the comforts of the well-to-do and rich.

These elements of early Christianity had been noted and appropriated by such contemporary socialists as Mikhail Bakunin, but even in the era of Alexander II's Great Reforms it was unusual to hear them coming from someone within the clergy.[11] Father John singled out businesspeople and anyone actively pursuing wealth for particular criticism. "The greatest injustices on earth," he wrote, "are committed by people who are wealthy or by those who want to become wealthy, who rake up riches in their paws using all possible measures, regardless of the suffering of the poor."[12] But he did not dwell on any distinction between inherited wealth and wealth acquired by "shady" business dealings. Wealth and inequality themselves were evil, not the excesses of capitalism specifically:

> The Lord created everything so that there would be enough for all creatures, with room to spare. But the rich, gathering up a great many of God's goods into their hands and trunks and keeping it to themselves like vultures, deprive thousands of people of food, drink, clothing, and work, and thus bury God's talents into the ground through their luxuries, furniture, and clothing.[13]

The idea that the rich used their money for luxuries while their neighbors shivered outraged Father John. By the mid-1860s, he became increasingly concerned with both giving to the poor himself and persuading others to give to the poor as well. The very force that he had to use on himself made him equally strict in his demands of others. Because he regarded every good thing in one's life as a gift from God, it seemed elementary to him that one ought to give as freely as one had received. As a result, Father John expected charity for the poor not only from gamblers or those who had inherited their money but also from those who labored for their bread "honestly." In diary notes that later became a sermon, he wrote in 1869 that

> [i]gnorant shop-keepers who trade in leather and textiles—how many poor people they could clothe and shoe!—while as it is one

cannot persuade them to part them with a single shirt, not one pair of shoes, not a single cloak—and so many goods lie in their shops without moving. O, if only they could regard it as their good fortune to dress one pauper, as if he or she were Jesus Christ Himself! O, if only they sought spiritual wisdom from the Lord, which would inspire them to regard that negligible cost as the greatest acquisition.[14]

Part of Father John's antipathy for the rich and the better-off stemmed from their wish to enjoy the pleasures money could buy rather than sharing their "surplus" with their poorer neighbors. Conspicuous consumption—which to him was any expression of one's earthly comfort—was an especially flagrant offense. He, the boy who had walked home barefoot hundreds of miles at the end of school terms to save wear on his boots, obviously had a different sense of life's necessities than did wealthy aristocrats. Father John's objection to the expenses of the wealthy stem not so much from a neo-Puritanical objection to luxury, however, as from the sense that every dinner party and every new frock represented so many loaves of bread or shirts for the poor. The obsession with elaborate hairstyles and clothing struck him as a disgraceful waste of time and money. "If we had Christian love," he exclaimed, "it would not allow such inequality in clothing and housing to persist: the rich would share with the poor, they would have less sumptuous meals, Christian love would force us to leave these destructive, parasitic habits (well-appointed furnishings, an abundant table, fashionable clothes, carriages)."[15]

Father John was also responding to specific trends in decorating and architecture. In the middle of the nineteenth century, an ever wider audience had come to associate luxury and opulence with good taste and bought furniture, a profusion of ornaments, and bric-a-brac as a means of expressing social status.[16] All of this, of course, ran against his ascetic ideal. (Interestingly—and not surprisingly—his radical contemporaries, especially those of clerical background, Soviet, and feminist historians also condemned these aspects of fashion in nearly the same terms.[17]) The construction boom that began mid-century in both St. Petersburg and Kronstadt fueled his anger as well:

Now more than at any other time the passion to build and to remodel—and often that which is not at all necessary to redo—has taken over people. Huge amounts (600 thousand for repairing the Arts Academy!) are spent for these constructions and alterations—

huge amounts which are often obtained through the sweat, blood, and tears of the people. This is a sign that the Lord's Second Coming is near: the Lord himself said, that before it, people will have a passion for building houses and gardens.... Why do engineers and architects bother to make unnecessary alterations to a building that has already been begun? Because [as the proverb has it] where logs are hewn, the splinters fly. And here the splinters are golden: many of them find their way into the pockets of architects and engineers. Wealthy people build and remodel because they have nowhere [else] to put their money.[18]

Here Father John also differed from most Orthodox clergy. Bishops had rarely gone so far as to state that the rich *had* to show mercy, *had* to share their wealth, in order to be saved. Father John linked salvation with charity. To him sharing with the poor was not only desirable, but mandatory: "Rich people! Redeem righteously your falsehoods and injustices: give your unrighteous profits to the lowly as alms: and then you may hope for salvation. *You will not be saved in any other way.*"[19] In short, Father John believed there was no such thing as a "righteous" profit or a Christian work ethic that did not include immediate re-distribution among the poor.[20] His use of the "reward" principle is an element that must be taken into account if Christianity is to be the basis of society: if one does not buy an insurance policy, one has to have good reason to believe that God, or one's fellow Christian, will provide instead. And Russian society was to Father John's mind not functioning as a Christian society; it was not providing for its poor.

With the same pragmatism he demonstrated with regard to his own charity, Father John sought to make his listeners aware that they were partners in a contract that was both social and religious. If one could not respond with genuine compassion for the poor, one might at least recognize in them a possible means to one's own salvation, if that were what it took to make one ease their lot. A Russian proverb described the compact: "People enter Heaven through holy almsgiving: the poor person is fed by the rich one, while the rich one is saved by the prayers of the poor one."[21] Indeed, according to the historian Vasilii Kliuchevskii, charity in pre-Petrine Russia was only comprehensible in this immediate, personal sense: "The benefactor had to see for himself the human need he was easing in order to obtain spiritual benefit; the needy person had to see his benefactor in order to know who to pray for."[22] In an appeal published in 1872, Father John sought to instill in his parishioners this sense of mutual responsibility:

Ants build anthills in which they are warm and sated even in winter; animals build lairs; bees build beehives; birds build nests; spiders—spiderwebs.... Similarly, because people are made to live in communities and because according to God's intent people must make up one body of whom individually they are its members, the strong must bear the burdens of the weak. One hand washes the other, and each finger another finger (*manus manum lavat, et digitus digitum*). With such a rich variety of talents in our society, with so many educated and artistic and practical people, it would be sinful before God and a disgrace before people to leave so many of our members (I have in mind our *meshchane* here) cut off and isolated from the social body and its well-being. Why not link them with the social organism by building them housing and giving each of them some kind of work, especially given that many of them know various trades—and, together with work, to give them bread and everything else necessary to live?... I appeal to you in the name of Christianity, in the name of loving mankind, in the name of humanity: let us help these shelterless poor, let us support them morally and materially, let us not deny our solidarity with them as with fellow human beings.... Will we allow ants and bees to have the advantage over us?[23]

The use of the phrase "social *body*" and its comparison to the animal world was typical for the radical social thought of the period, especially that of Nikolai Dobroliubov. One can also discern the Christian conception of the organism: the Church is the Body of Christ, with every Christian an element of the Body through the reception of His Body and Blood in the Eucharist.[24] Whatever the source of his thought, the growing conviction that one must think in terms of social rather than only individual virtue led Father John to seek a civic solution that would rest less on individual impulse and more on a structural change in society.[25] He believed that "Orthodox Russia" had much to learn from other forms of community, whether political or religious, in how to care for all its members. Unlike the Slavophiles, Father John found both Russia and the Orthodox Christians wanting in terms of social relations relative to the West and to other religions: "Look at societies abroad: see how they handle this problem. Look also at Jewish, Muslim, and schismatic communities [in Russia]: how much mutual aid and support they offer to one another! Whereas what selfishness, what reserve on the part of our wealthy as regards themselves!"[26]

In presenting his case for organized welfare and work assistance programs to both his parishioners and the city officials of Kronstadt, Father John felt that his religious and social functions had merged into one. His sense of society as a religious and political totality meant that he could express himself in what sounded like strictly civic terms and feel that he was serving God by doing so. God was served by serving others; one was a good citizen by being a true Christian:

> Every citizen, every member of society has the right to express his opinion concerning society for the good of society: this is why I, *first as a citizen, then* as a priest who knows well the crying need of a significant part of the local society's *meshchane*, have now decided to raise my voice for its benefit: a significant part of *meshchane* society has no place or shelter, while they must be accommodated somewhere. Its situation is unnatural: it is cut off from the rest of the urban population and abandoned to the whims of Fate, without any care on the part of the City Duma. It has no corner in which it can settle, no work by which it may feed itself, no money, no clothing. They are a black mark upon urban society.[27]

Strikingly, Father John believed so strongly in everyone's participation in creating a better society and in the responsibility of the civil authorities for alleviating poverty that he chose to emphasize his secular civic status rather than his priesthood in calling for change. His impulse to find shelter and comfort for the poor came from his own experience of the degradation of poverty. He was convinced that one had to address the material needs of the poor before one could, or in order that one could, talk to them about God: "What you need to give the have-nots is first and foremost a roof over their heads."[28] A shelter for the poor, accordingly, became his first priority.

It was not enough, however, to simply give enough for the poor for their daily bread; there ought be no more poor at all. In accordance with his vision of equal Christians in a unified society, Father John wanted the indigent to become useful members of society. He conceived of an establishment where everyone would be given food, clothing, and shelter—but also one where those who were capable of working would be taught a trade. He addressed the city Duma with a memorandum concerning the homelessness of the Kronstadt *meshchane* and his ideas of a workhouse as early as 1868, although the project he proposed was not realized until 1881.[29]

Father John conceived of a model workhouse, the House of Industry

(*Dom Trudoliubiia*), as providing both immediate, practical help for the poor and an outlet for the prosperous who wished to help the poor but wanted those to whom they gave working rather than being idle. The emphasis on work was particularly important. Father John was blamed on more than one occasion for increasing the amount of the poor rather than decreasing them: as word of his charity spread, critics including Georgii Gapon, the priest who led the march to the Winter Palace on Bloody Sunday, suggested that beggars actually migrated to Kronstadt in order to obtain a higher standard of living at Father John's expense.[30] In order to counter these accusations and appeal to those who wished to help the "deserving" poor, Father John stressed the productive aspects of his project in 1872:

> How good it would be to establish such a "House of Industry!" Then many people could turn to the center with a request to have this or that task performed or this or that object made, and our *meshchane* could live there, work, and thank God and their benefactors. Many would improve in a moral sense as well. Whereas if anyone healthy and able-bodied should not want to work, then out of town with him: Kronstadt is not a breeding-ground for parasites.[31]

The *Dom Trudoliubiia* became a prototype for other "houses of industry."[32] It began with providing simple work—gluing hat-brims, scutching hemp, and so on—for which the workers received food, a place to sleep, and a modest wage. It later increased in scope to include a workshop and shelter exclusively for women (Father John was particularly concerned with providing an economically feasible alternative to prostitution), training in other trades including shoe-making and carpentry, a free medical clinic, a library, a bookstore, public lectures, a public day school for children, and evening courses for adults. All in all, it was a model example of relief for an acute social problem, and attracted enthusiastic comment in the contemporary press.[33] Part of its success was due to Father John making it chic, so that it became one of the pet causes of such leading ladies of society as Lidiia Rimsky-Korsakov.[34]

Father John was concerned with providing for the religious needs of the house's clientele as well as for their material ones. In notes for a sermon, he wrote in 1881:

> It would be good to see to it that the *meshchane* who can work in— and some who can live in—the House of Industry could go to church

on Sundays and holidays, as members of the Church, and annually receive communion: for it is well-known that many of them have not been to communion for ten or more years because of their poverty and *not having decent clothing*.³⁵

The last comment came directly as a result of people writing him, saying that they could not go to church for being "improperly dressed."³⁶ While in some cases this may have been a tactic to get money, Father John had known such attitudes as a child and understood the poor's diffidence. And so the House of Industry included both a house church (attendance was not mandatory)—and the opportunity to attend it "decently." The House attracted so many who wished to use its services that providing a regular subsidy and income for it became a perpetual concern. In the earlier stages of his career Father John could not rely on his own means to fund the center and worried constantly about its maintenance. In one reverie, he wrote:

> When I was going with the Holy Mysteries to visit the sick, I stood for a long time in a prayerful mood looking at the DT [House of Industry], built according to my idea and my appeals in the printed word, praying to God for it—may He give this people-loving establishment material security as long as the city stands. Grant it, O God! ... O, if only I could see the realization of my wish in my lifetime! Whereas now we are in debt and have no fixed capital other than the annual 1600 ruble subsidy from the Sovereign, from the Grand Duke Mikh. Mikh., and the Duma (500 rubles).³⁷

To this end, he initiated a sophisticated program of fund-raising and development. He traveled on a regular basis to Moscow and other major cities to raise money for the House of Industry. He also sent appeals for support to individuals in high places.³⁸ The appeal sent by the House's board of trustees to the Synod Ober-Procurator Konstantin Pobedonostsev for a subsidy *in perpetuo*, for example, illustrates how well Father John knew what language to use and which points to emphasize. After describing the establishment and work of the center, from the children's shelter to the workshops to the hospital to the soup-kitchen, he wrote:

> We will need about five to six thousand rubles per year, of which three thousand can be raised in Kronstadt. We thus need to seek other regular sources of income. Because of this requirement, and *knowing that the Ministry of Finance does not reject opportunities*

for the development of trade knowledge and the productive forces of the people, and also *bearing in mind that the Committee for the Investigation of the Poor gets a subsidy from the State Treasury,* the St. Andrew Parish Board of Trustees humbly requests Your Excellency to grant us an annual subsidy in the amount of 1000 rubles per year for the support of the Kronstadt House of Industry in memory of the Unforgettable Tsar-Liberator. [signed] Chairman of the Board of Trustees, prot. I. Sergiev.[39]

The reference to Alexander II was not coincidental. After the assassination of the emperor, Father John had arranged a meeting at the governor's to have him intercede on their behalf to name the House of Industry the "House of the Emperor Alexander II." While he was genuinely shaken by the killing, he also realized that the imperial reference might manifest itself as material support and so wished to accomplish both an act of patriotic piety and one that might provide finances.[40]

Besides the House of Industry, for which he was the chief source of income, Father John supported a host of other causes and institutions: the Red Cross, temperance societies, wounded veterans' organizations, scholarships for seminarians in the St. Petersburg Theological Academy (his alma mater), orphanages, and the people from his old village.[41] He was on the mailing lists of virtually every charitable and religious organization in the Russian Empire, from hospitals, apiculture societies, and the Society for the Prevention of Cruelty to Animals to an association offering "Brotherly Aid to the Armenian Victims of the Turks."[42] In their letters to him, the organizations stressed the huge symbolic importance of his support: when Father John supported a cause, they wrote, this established its worthiness. People all over the Russian Empire who wanted to help their fellows but also wanted to know which causes were the most beneficial looked to his example. Thus his donation of one hundred or five hundred rubles or more actually translated into many times that amount.

The extent to which Father John was a lifeline for many causes emerges in the letters of grateful recipients. They illuminate the feature that set Father John apart from many professed "friends of the poor" on the other side of the political spectrum, such as Lev Tolstoy and the priest Georgii Petrov.[43] While Tolstoy, Petrov, and others spoke of the need of helping the poor, the letters to Father John claim that he was the only one who regularly did so. While this may have been a device the writers used with other possible funding sources, the specificity of the phrases suggests that most were quite sincere when they claimed that they had exhausted all their other resources. As K. M. Tatarinova, the chairman of the Voikin Sol'skii Red Cross, wrote to him in the famine of 1907:

> Our own dear breadwinner, it is difficult to imagine what we would do without you. We have opened up a soup kitchen where we feed 214 people daily.... I have written to many people asking for help, including the Committee for Labor Assistance, the Grand Duke Konstantin Konstantinovich, and the priest [Georgii] Petrov—I asked the latter to just give me some names to contact for help and got a rejection; not a word from the Grand Duke either. Can you give us some other names? You, you are the *only one* who has responded to this devastating misfortune. Our starving population is ready to kiss your feet for your good deed to them, especially given that no one else is responding to the enormous disaster which has struck them.[44]

While Father John began by concentrating on the poverty and social inequality he saw as being the effects of an imperfect realization of the Gospel, he did not neglect what he saw as the causes. The notion of the responsibility of the political authorities for their society was central to Father John, who proposed civic and political as well as religious solutions to social ills. This is because—unusually for a nineteenth-century clergyman—he did not believe that poverty was inescapable or the fault of the poor themselves; dubious government policies were responsible for creating the have-nots. By doing so, he promoted socialist solutions, but from the conservative position of scripture. He showed the concrete possibility of a socioeconomic redistribution different from those proposed by capitalism or Marxism. In the early 1900s, he put it still more forcefully, asking the Church and the state to climb the proverbial sycamore:

> The question of poverty in our city and in Russia in general must be posed directly to the Church and to the government. Poverty has greatly multiplied, it has nowhere to go, there is no demand for its labors—and we do not know what to do with it. It is overcoming us; it strikes in the eye on streets and at intersections, on the roads and highways. What can be done with it? We have a Duma, and the Duma needs to think about it, all the more so given that our poverty is its [the Duma's] adopted child. A positive

resolution of this matter is required [of us] by the Gospel, by the Church—the Lord Himself; the Head of the Church and the Sovereign, the Head of the government must act on this.... O, if only we had more Zaccheuses in our midst![45]

In another sign of his nationwide perspective, he attacked abuse of liquor on a state level, not merely on an individual one. He wrote in 1869:

> What must be done in Russia without delay? Restricting the sale of vodka (a certain amount per certain date) and to forbid its sale on Sundays and holidays.... The Sovereign Emperor needs to pay particular attention to this evil. Otherwise he will answer for his lack of attention at the Dread Judgment before the King of Kings and will not escape harsh censure for his remiss and negligent pastorhood.[46]

Father John thus perceived the role of the ruler as being pastoral—that is, explicitly religious—rather than simply providing the religious authorities with the practical means of implementing their goals. But everyone's role in society implied submission and religious duty, and at the head of this responsibility stood the priest.[47]

The Role of the Priest

The priest's responsibility for society had several aspects. Father John believed that in order for his parishioners to have the "conscious" spiritual life he desired for them, they would need to understand and be literally schooled in its mysteries. In keeping with the general Orthodox "outreach" of the Great Reforms era, he sought to make Church teachings comprehensible and logical. "Parishioners and pupils," he wrote in 1869, "must be shown the *meaning* of the Divine services, rites, prayers, the cross, icons, their relation to our life—and not be forced to learn by heart the litanies and prayers, which the Church repeats unceasingly without our help as it is."[48]

For someone as attached to the liturgy as Father John, this hint of impatience with the repetitive quality of Orthodox services shows how he understood the idea that the clergy must play a more active role rather than relying on tradition to hold its flock. In order to appreciate fully the Divine services, which, as he admits, can be mysterious and cryptic, simple attendance is not enough: their meaning must be learned—and taught. This requires an effort both on the part of the people—"[People] must prepare themselves for confession as a student for a lesson: analyze yourselves, think of various sides of yourself, your spiritual condition"[49]—and of the priest: "Set up readings of the Old Testament in the [church] hall—particularly acquaint the people with the prophets."[50]

These references to students are not coincidental. As well as serving at St. Andrew's, Father John also taught at the local secondary school from 1857–82 in order to have a salary he could distribute unimpeded to the poor. His teaching methods contrasted sharply with the more common rote methods characteristic of clerical and primary Russian education. Having spent the first years of his own education struggling in despair with bullies, apparently impenetrable texts, and brutish teaching methods, Father John sought to have both his students and his parishioners appreciate their material.[51] Although his growing reputation eventually made it necessary for him to leave his school position in order to devote himself to his priestly activities, his students regularly described him as being the only bright spot in their academic lives.[52]

As a result of his teaching experience, Father John learned to adjust the level of his instruction to the level of his audience. He stressed independent action and appropriation rather than passive acceptance (more characteristic in the case of the lower classes, he believed) or passive denial (more characteristic in the case of the upper classes). Thus he felt that he must "impress upon the learned and laypeople that *they must train their mind and heart to independent activity* at all times, and especially during prayer."[53] This appeal to the intellect and initiative contrasts sharply with the sinking into the liturgy, to the oblivion and loss of self, that was an ever-present risk with such elaborately ritualized religions as Orthodoxy.[54] Father John's call to sober reflection and concentration might be regarded as a "Protestantizing" tendency within Russian Orthodoxy, as Simon Dixon has suggested, but the suspicion against vague mystical transports was present in Orthodoxy itself. The Desert Fathers and a number of Russian Fathers repeatedly stressed the need for spiritual "sobriety," warning against excessive ecstasies and exaltation.[55] In calling for a personal, intellectual, and emotional internalization of Orthodoxy, Father John was both taking the edifying aims of the Great Reforms-era Orthodox Church to their logical end—and going beyond that end.

The key to understanding Father John's sense of responsibility for the education of his flock is realizing that it extended to guiding their behavior in the largest sense. He felt his responsibility as a priest so acutely that he could not conceive or admit of any compromise:

> At the Dread Judgment of our God I am responsible for you. I am not going to watch to see whether or not it is pleasant for you to listen to me, but am going to do my work. What kind of doctor would not seek to heal or to visit his patients? But what then is my calling, my having been chosen? Do I stand on my church pulpit? Am I not a teacher of faith? Am I not the shepherd of the sheep entrusted to me? Am I not the performer of the mysteries of the faith? No: let my right hand lose her cunning if she not write the words of truth upon the charter; let my tongue cleave to the roof of my mouth if it does not turn in my mouth towards the utterance of the rules of faith and piety!... May my heart fall apart if it grow cool towards the work of God! —No, as long as I have reason and memory, I will remember that woe is me if I do not speak the good word abroad, that the Heavenly pastor will exact from my hand the blood of those of my sheep who perish from my negligence and laziness.[56]

Education and Culture

As Father John came into ever greater contact with educated people through his pastoral and charitable work, the spheres of intellect and culture commanded an ever-increasing share of his attention. Even more than the familiar vices of hard-heartedness or avarice, intellect and culture threatened to upset his simple, ideal view of what earthly society ought to be like. Culture and education, Father John sensed, were together becoming a surrogate moral sphere, one that insisted on its autonomy, its independence of all laws save for its own—and one that had entered into direct competition with the Church. Because he saw the poor and their burdens every day, he turned against anyone who suggested that Russia's social injustice might be part of some mythical "progress":

> O marvelous progress! O sage progress! O progress drawing one near to the bottom of hell! —And what of the progress of living, heartfelt faith? what of the progress of Christian love?... Christian love not only in the most basic, immediate sense, but also the kind that fills the glaring, horrifying needs of others who do not

even have their daily bread, their necessary clothing and their shelter? Where are you, true progress? They have forgotten you, they have stolen your name away from you and applied it instead to this monstrous, satanic progress!—[57]

Worse yet, people who might otherwise have turned to the Church for moral guidance were now seeking such direction elsewhere. In the beginning of his career, Father John was inclined to be sympathetic to the intellectual seeking or the nonreligious diversions of his parishioners, regarding their casting about as the product of well-meaning ignorance.[58] At first he thought the problem might be solved through education, through such means as translating liturgical texts into the Russian vernacular for private reading, so that people would know them as well as they knew Western works of fiction and philosophy. Another course was for Christians to harmonize all aspects of their lives with Orthodox belief by reclaiming the arts: "Instead of worldly music, sing church songs or the psalms of David—play them on instruments if you like."[59] Father John's position was optimistic in the sense that it was militant: he believed that most of the problem lay in ignorance rather than in conscious opposition. If people were educated properly in Orthodoxy, secular culture would be less attractive to them.

But he also felt that people should look for their solace (and entertainment) in religion before seeking it elsewhere. Because of his commitment to a vision of total Orthodox culture and a totally Orthodox society, he was profoundly bothered by those aspects of Russian high culture that existed independently of religion. He mused in 1866, for example: "As regards the Karamzin celebrations—the world has its holidays, the Church has its own. It is a pity that the Christian world has its own, worldly holidays and that the church holidays are neglected. There is a whiff of the pagan about it."[60]

The opposition between the Christian and the pagan was central to Father John's worldview—"pagan" being anything, whether neoclassical or contemporary, not informed by Christian religious values. The producers of contemporary pagan culture were much more culpable than its consumers, for they deliberately ignored Orthodox Christianity and its teachings. Because he himself was consumed with religious faith and felt it as a burning, immediate presence, he could not forgive the neglect of religious themes in contemporary art and the press:

> Why do I loathe worldly theaters and journals? Because in them one never hears the name of the Father and the Son and the Holy

Spirit; they never talk about the great matter of our redemption from sin, death, and damnation—it is all worldly vanity, empty worldly words.[61]

Will you ever hear the name of Christ in the theater in any other context save that of a joke?—the words "create a pure heart in me, O Lord?" No. Why then do they call the theater moral, virtually Christian? It is paganism in Christianity: and it came to us from paganism.[62]

Although Father John felt the theater to be particularly harmful, virtually all spheres of secular culture fell under the same condemnation. In 1867, he anticipated Tolstoy's *Kreuzer Sonata* in condemning music that "arouses worldly thoughts and passions" instead of "calming one's soul, conscience, and one's relation with others."[63] His idea of paganism was not limited to high culture. Like the curé of Ars, he condemned as sinful nonreligious "popular" or "low" culture as well—as did, incidentally, some of the peasants and *meshchane* who were its consumers.[64] Just as he evaluated every aspect of his own life in religious terms, from eating habits to how he said goodnight, so Father John did not believe that nonreligious spheres or activities might be neutral in a religious sense. His own worldview was so all-encompassingly religious that he could scarcely imagine life in any other terms and rejected any other interpretation. Either an activity fostered one's Orthodoxy or it did not.[65] Nor did he regard himself as exempt from the principle that "innocent" amusements and pastimes were sinful merely because they were not actively spiritual, because they did not help in the all-important and only-important work of salvation:

> I sinned before the Lord: I was at a reindeer-race yesterday at a tobogganing hill.—Everything about our way of life is contrary to God: the [tobogganing] hills, and the reindeer- and horse-races, and the music they play there—and where are those who are concerned with saving their souls? . . . What is this short life given to us for, after all—for amusement?[66]

This last statement gets at the root of Father John's objections to contemporary society. As with fashion, an entire industry of entertainment was arising that was dedicated purely to people's leisure and amusement, ranging from operettas to summer gardens and carousels.[67] His objection to these contemporary forms of entertainment reveals a great deal about the elements in his religiosity that link him specifically to his time and place.

On first reading, his harshness appears to be but a contemporary variant of the ascetic objections to vanity and worldliness that have been a staple of Christian preaching from the earliest periods. Upon closer examination, however, Father John sounds a note in his religious criticism of society that is specifically tied to mid–nineteenth-century Russia, and even more specifically to Kronstadt and St. Petersburg. He became convinced by the late 1860s that the times in which Russia lived were particularly evil and began to single out particular vices to prove his point. It was precisely these elements of contemporaneity in combination with more perennially Orthodox pronouncements that gave Father John's sermons their potency and made him seem to many Russians to be a holy man sent specifically for the changing conditions in which they lived. He addressed the anxieties many of his listeners felt about the erosion of a more traditional and predictable way of life, and framed those anxieties in an Orthodox context that acquired greater immediacy as a result. He assigned contemporary causes to the ailments he sought to treat, and actually called down God's judgment and punishment on the perpetrators: "The officers of Kronstadt do not go to confession or to Communion. Here are the fruits of free-thinking! Here are the fruits of theaters, clubs, dinners, masquerades! What corruption of the soul! Send them evil, O Lord, send evil to them that are powerful upon the earth."[68]

This call for Divine vengeance against people who Father John believed to be corrupt would resurface with particular force with respect to Lev Tolstoy and the revolutionaries. But even before he became famous, his sense of priestly responsibility already extended to summoning God to act on his behalf. All purveyors of "corruption" were guilty, especially those who were undermining the common people. Whereas the common folk might have been a collective of unspoiled virtue in past times, they were now infected with the same malaise as the educated. Thus, *all* of Russian society was becoming more "pagan," and the Church hierarchy was ignoring it. He wrote in the late 1860s:

> The contemporary world, following the teaching of the evil one, is seeking to introduce, and has already introduced several corrupt customs from earlier times into the life of the common people. . . . They have taken off their bridle of the fear of God, the fear of the coming Judgment, of the eternal flames of Gehenna, and are giving way to drunkenness, dissipated merry-making—while the

Holy Synod and local bishops, *who know their flocks but little*, are not undertaking anything against this evil.[69]

By the late 1860s, Father John had singled out a culprit for the contemporary mores he bemoaned. The worst offenders, educated people, were the most significant obstacles to his vision of an ideal Christian society. To someone as steeped and schooled in Orthodoxy as Father John, the ignorance of religion he encountered among his educated flock was scandalous. In 1866, just a little over ten years into his career, he wrote of the upper classes: "They are dolls, soulless statues! It drives one to laugh and to cry to see how they are in church, especially at confession!"[70] However ignorant the uneducated might be of Orthodoxy, at least, he felt, they had a lively sense of sin and did not propose other models of an ideal society than that provided by Orthodox Christianity. The educated, however, resisted acknowledging even formally the primacy of Orthodoxy.

The separation of the educated public from religious life was a theme that Father John began developing in the late 1860s. When voices were raised in 1869 concerning the possibility of a new translation of the service books to make them more "accessible" to the general educated public—something he had mentioned himself—Father John was alarmed at the proposed choice of translator. He took this occasion to note the rift that existed between the educated public and the Church:

> Our irreligious, atheistic nature has had little in common with the Church in its development. When our writers and teachers left school or seminary and became involved in public activities, they forgot the "Our Father" and the Creed, and definitively broke with the Church. Some tenuous connection just barely lasted until the beginning of our century. From December 14 on it burst. Or it virtually does not exist. Where are they supposed to get a Biblical language from? Who in our "smart set" reads Godly books? Who concerns himself or herself with religious questions? What the clergy wrote, none of the best or the leading writers read (they mocked it because they were progressive), except perhaps for Gogol (more honor to him), but he (they say) perished from his connection with religion (*no*: religion revives; it does not destroy).... As a consequence of the estrangement of this (imaginary, self-willed, would-be) society from the Church, we did not deem it necessary to preserve even the half-dead Church language in our existing translation. What can we expect from such a

translator as Vadim? Vadim, who actually referred to himself as an atheist?[71]

Father John's singling out the date of December 14, the date of the Decembrist rebellion in 1825, as the date when the educated and the intelligentsia broke *with the Church* is telling. Although on the surface that uprising was a largely political event led by nobility in uniform, it was above all a rebellion of intellectuals.[72] To Father John, the Decembrist revolt represented not simply a desire for a new political order that left untouched Russia's religious traditions but also the first step on the part of the educated away from the old order as exemplified by the autocracy and Orthodoxy. It is the first instance of his unconscious equation of Orthodoxy and autocracy, one that would emerge again after the assassination of Alexander II in 1881. The gulf Father John perceived between the educated and the Church, however, was a perpetual leitmotiv in his writing from the 1860s onward. In emphasizing simplicity, he was one of the first clerics to suggest that the educated did not and could not speak for the people; it was the Church who had the real authority to do so. This emphasis on simplicity would be one of his most enduring legacies, in a negative sense as well as a positive one.[73]

The tension Father John felt with respect to the educated was personally charged. Just as his forcing himself to charity had made him more demanding of others, so his ruthless overcoming of his bouts of doubt made Father John intolerant of those who refused to wage a similar struggle in their relation to God. He had doubts, but he understood that he must struggle to overcome them. Why did not the educated do the same? Throughout the 1860s and 1870s, he developed the opposition between educated people and everyone else.

Father John thought that the educated suffered from many vices, beginning with the development of their minds at the expense of their other faculties. This Rousseau-esque objection toward intellect at the expense of morality and "wholeness" had been voiced by other Russians before him, from the eighteenth-century publisher and Freemason Nikolai Novikov to Saint Tikhon of Zadonsk.[74] Although Father John went further than did his predecessors in the condemnation of an improper education, he was only enlarging upon an existing tradition. Because of his poor origins, however, Father John added a note missing from his genteel predecessors. He linked appearance to education as something that allowed the privileged to set themselves apart. Here, as in the suspicion of sensual pleasure, he anticipated Tolstoy and the socialist realists—and won the hearts of the similarly socially resentful. In a sermon draft 1866, he wrote of the typical privileged person:

> The moment he gets a book education and puts on a student jacket or a bureaucrat's uniform, he imagines that he has become another person, as if another nature from the uneducated, crude simpletons, and regards himself as some kind of a divinity relative to them—but you are the same wretched sinner and mortal [as he]. The same concerns the woman in a silk or a velvet dress wearing gold and jewels in relation to beggars.[75]

This biting sense of class difference appealed to the many recent arrivals from the countryside, who felt out of place in both Kronstadt and St. Petersburg, and subscribed enthusiastically to the anti-elitist position expressed by both Father John and the *St. Petersburg Police Gazette*. In the 1860s, before such groups as The People's Will began their terrorist activity, Father John saw the chief sin of "liberals" in their defense of their narrow class interests and their refusal to work for the common good. Thus, to him, social selfishness and atheism were all of a piece, and it was education that was to blame:

> Where do liberals spring from, those monsters of cruelty, those people whose aim it is to live for themselves and for their own pleasure, not for the cause—those egotists, those who do not empathize with their brethren? They come about because the mind works in them without the heart. Their hearts are not warmed by love for God and man, and they deny the existence of God, the foundations and bases of our common holy life, the rules of morality. Here is your education, students! This is because of your stupid education, Messrs. pedagogues![76]

The central point for Father John—as, again, for Tolstoy and the radical intelligentsia of the 1860s—is the notion that talent is useless if it is not used for the spiritual benefit of one's people. There is one moral yardstick for all, and that is the only measuring unit that matters.[77] Because of this single standard, he could not tolerate the acclaim that such "suicides" as the poets Alexander Pushkin and Mikhail Lermontov, who had both been killed at duels, received; or the closeted homosexuality of a composer he abbreviated "Tch.". When "Tch.'s" widow told Father John in 1894 that "her husband did not live with her as a wife, but did so with one beautiful youth—lived with him as if he were his wife," he wrote in outrage: "Here is your glory, great people of the world! Of course, he did not become celebrated for this filth (but many people did know about this filth), but for his musical talent. But what is the point of talent if it is not used for the glory of God and the benefit of the soul—if he did not have spiritual talent within himself to accompany the worldly one?"

In short, the problem lay in the discrepancy between worldly ideals and religious ones. While Father John had believed earlier that the two might be reconciled, by the 1890s—ironically, precisely at the time when worldly culture began to explore the realm of the "spiritual"—his attitude to worldly culture had hardened into pure opposition. He especially resented the acclaim that the "immoral" Tchaikovsky and Tolstoy received:

> See whom the world glorifies—and how they glorify him—they simply adore him! He gets thousands of wreaths! They erect monuments costing hundreds of thousands [of rubles] with which many philanthropic and charitable institutions could be built!—What can these worldly public figures, so lawless and not having repented before God and awarded countless times by worldly people like themselves, expect from the Lord at His Judgment?[78]

It fell to the priest, Father John came to believe, to point out what was of spiritual benefit to the people and what was not. While he still thought that the revival of the sacraments was the foundation of a spiritual renewal, he also believed that the priest had a larger social role to play in the total society he envisioned. The priest was supposed to act as did the prophets of Israel, haranguing his flock until they improved.[79]

The key word for Father John's notion of the activity of the priest in public life was "denounce" (*oblichat'*). The priest could not close his eyes to the evil—or the erring people—he saw around him, but had to "denounce them mercilessly."[80] Even though they were too cowed by the rich and powerful to dare to object (a failing to which Father John himself confessed), they must struggle against it all the same:

> The priest must be higher than the lordly haughtiness of well-born and coddled and not cringe before or fawn upon this haughtiness; he must not lower himself, not be cowardly before the powerful of this world, but hold himself with an awareness of his clerical dignity, gravely, evenly, in a pastoral manner—and serve unhurriedly,

not so as to please people. He must denounce caprices, lordly arrogance, and any coldness to matters concerning the faith.[81]

In one such example of denunciation, Father John confronted mummers in an attempt to make them see the error of their ways, chasing the carriages of the more recalcitrant revelers down the street.[82] He grew more aggressive in his sermons and his published writings as well. His sense of opposition between himself as priest and the unyielding among his flock hardened into a sense of war. They clearly (he felt) thought he had no business interfering in their lives; he insisted otherwise. It is precisely in this stridency and aggressive opposition to contemporary failings that Father John differs most from the holy people closest to him chronologically. The saints Serafim of Sarov and Tikhon of Zadonsk, to name only the two most prominent, were revered for their gentleness and their mildness; the Optina elders Amvrosii and Makarii preferred to chastise individuals indirectly and in parable.[83] Father John, rather than concentrating on his own inner life or offering advice only when asked it, rather than seeing the role of the priest only as minister of the sacraments or comforter, believed that the priest had to be militant in seeking to change the world around him. In this sense, as with his anti-aesthetic utilitarianism, he had more in common with such radical socialist thinkers as Dobroliubov and Chernyshevskii—both, incidentally, of clerical origin—than with most contemporary Orthodox clerics.

Opposition

For all of his spirited intentions, however, Father John ran into resistance. As the third priest in St. Andrew's Cathedral, he was subordinate to both the dean of the cathedral (the *nastoiatel'*) and the second in command. While he could engage in charitable works independently and occasionally be assigned the sermon, his liturgical responsibilities were strictly defined, and his opportunities for introducing study groups or private pastoral visits within St. Andrew's Cathedral were limited by both his clerical superiors and the resistance of St. Andrew's parishioners, who did not appreciate his calling attention to their vices.

Father John's diaries are full of references to his being thwarted at every step by the hostility he perceived from the Metropolitan Isidor of St. Petersburg and from priests who out-ranked him. In both cases, his clerical superiors mistrusted what they regarded as his over-zealousness and departure from the priestly norm. They tried to chastise him in countless ways, everything from disparaging comments to making him wear the oldest and grimiest vestments on major feasts.[84] On the other hand, he was not immune from resentment himself. St. Andrew's Cathedral had the policy that priests would pool and divide evenly all the income they earned from extraliturgical services (*treby*). As the junior priest, most of these services fell to Father John—who then had watch the money go to the others. This was bad enough; but then he learned that one of the other priests kept back some of the common pool for himself.[85] Worst of all, he seemed to be the only one who was giving to the poor, while the other priests felt no such compulsion. He was exquisitely aware that he had no right to condemn others, but the raging inequality plagued him all the same:

> I envy my fellow clergy, seeing the honors and increased external prosperity they accrue—that is, the wealth that they get as a result of saving it and not giving it to the poor. I am vexed that I alone have to squander my small income obtained through my great efforts; that the brethren [i.e., fellow clergy] for whom I labor greatly and whose own wealth is increased through my efforts do not participate with me in alms-giving. The junior priest is particularly noxious: he gets the same amount that I do, with minimal and lazy work—and because of this, I am often indignant at the crying disproportion between compensation for work and giving to the poor, of whom there is no end. I am irritated and embittered at the senior priest, who accumulated tens of thousands of rubles and does not give any of it to anyone; he lives and serves calmly as if he were innocent, *as if his conscience were clean*.[86]

Similarly, Father John could run into trouble with his employers at the high school for his innovations and his religious zeal. He complained in 1865, "The school principal lets the pupils go to the theater, he organizes dances, he lets them eat non-Lenten food during Lent, but does not let me read them edifying books in class."[87] His colleagues did not always appreciate him, either. In 1869, he recorded being mortally offended that the art teacher greeted everyone except him at a pedagogical council meeting. This hurt him so much that he brooded over it for nearly two hours, finding momentary relief only when looked up at the icon of the Savior. But even that did not help enough: at the end of the meeting, he said good-bye to everyone except his hapless colleague.[88]

Father John's reaction to rebuffs like these was interesting. His relation to God was so intimate that he had no hesitation in enlisting Him to his side. Just as he would later pray for God to humble the "arrogant" Tolstoy and the minister of finance, Sergei Witte, so at the beginning of his career he called upon Him to punish—or at least enlighten—those who made his life difficult, especially if they had humiliated him publicly. When a drunken merchant insulted him before others, saying that priests were worthless and could not do anything without the Metropolitan's blessing, Father John prayed, for example, "May God send retribution, so that he learns not to blaspheme the sacerdotal rank"—and made a note to himself to denounce the behavior in a sermon beginning with the words, "In a certain town there was a rich merchant."[89] After another incident, he wrote:

> The principal saddened me greatly today with his proud and stupid claims concerning my pupils' reading a prayer upon my entry into class, saying that it was not done anywhere in the Petersburg high schools, and that he had asked the Administrator concerning it, who had also denied the need for such a custom—and said that reading prayers takes time away from class (takes time away! it takes half a minute, while he sometimes prattles on for as long as a quarter of an hour in the teachers' lounge).... *Lord, restrain the cunning of the principal; may his pride be changed to grief.* May it happen![90]

The sense of distance between the consciousness of a holy individual and that of his public, inevitable in virtually any context, was particularly acute in Father John's case, for he had consciously linked his own salvation to that of his flock. The priest's two bodies were in fact one and the same. His religiosity was not independent of his flock's: his apostolic, sacerdotal identity depended on how well he succeeded in converting the world around him. It was a symbiotic relation rather than one of two independent parties. This is not surprising. In a religious service, as in an artistic performance, there is a dynamic created between those who serve and those who stand and pray to which both parties contribute. If the priest or the chanters are indifferent to their tasks, it is difficult for the congregation to pray; but if those present are indifferent, it is also difficult for the priest to continue with the necessary concentration and fervor. On more than a few occasions, the sight of his flock in church helped Father John, fortifying him in his struggle against temptation and the demons.[91]

Resistance was more typical than a sense of support, however. One of the chief reasons for Father John's nervousness about addressing the vices of his parishioners was the status of the priest in the religious life of Russians. Even as he wished everyone to share his religious fervor, he found his own spiritual concentration affected by the response he received. The tension between his own perception of the dignity of his clerical rank and the position the priest actually occupied in Russian society manifested itself at every step. It typically emerged in such everyday matters as offering a blessing. According to Orthodox etiquette, the priest or bishop was to raise his hand, make the sign of benediction, and the close of the movement extend his hand outward slightly toward the lay recipient, expecting the hand to be kissed. Similarly, the layperson was expected to greet a priest or bishop by inclining the head, crossing the hands one over the other, and then kissing the cleric's proffered hand.

Although that is how the blessing was supposed to operate, in practice it had come to mean something very different by the nineteenth century. More than a few members of the upper classes and the intelligentsia, ostensibly Orthodox though they were, could not bring themselves to kiss the hand of someone they thought occupied an inferior position socially (or would not do so out of principle). Most priests had become resigned to this reluctance and tended to avoid giving a blessing unless asked, as Nikolai Leskov wittily depicted in the novella *Cathedral Folk*.[92] Father John, by contrast, tried to give almost everyone a blessing and became furious when it was rejected. On those occasions when the person did not kiss his hand and literally left it hanging mid-air, he perceived it both as a social snub and a sign of disrespect to his office. "The priest must know to whom to offer his hand, and especially not to offer it to high-minded young ladies," he wrote in his diary in 1867, "Let them learn to value the priestly right hand."[93] He grew so incensed at people's shunning his blessing that he composed an imprecation in Church Slavonic that was simultaneously curse and prayer, ending with the words, "Get ye hence, damned ones [those rejecting a blessing].—If you will not take a blessing, then have a curse."[94]

Such rebuffs contributed to Father John's feeling intimidated and crushed by his social "betters." When he began his priestly career during the era of the Great Reforms, and especially after the emancipation of serfs in 1861, both reforms and democratic rhetoric helped to create a sense of shifting social boundaries. In this unsteady atmosphere, it became less clear (but no less important) whom one recognized socially, and whom one "cut" publicly. With his combination of class insecurity and respect for his office, Father John responded badly to such things as a junker's insulting him on the street.[95] This was bad enough; when he felt awkward while serving in church, he was devastated. The presence of generals, bureaucrats, the wealthy, and well-dressed women made him cower:

> Why do I perform prayers and sacraments boldly and unhesitatingly before simple people and meekly, timorously, hesitantly in the presence of learned ones and bureaucrats?... Why do I doubt the truth of some expressions of prayers in their presence and do not doubt them in the presence of simple people? Why should I fear the learned and the eminent, who for the most part do not have spiritual wisdom? I become embarrassed by the words of the Lord and the words of our Mother Church; I become possessed by false shame and fear.[96]

The notion that he was "betraying" Jesus Christ and the Mother of God by shrinking inside himself during services when "archbishops, archpriests, various bureaucrats—worldly, military, and scholarly—, the rich and famous, and smartly dressed women" were present depressed Father John.[97] (It is striking but not surprising, incidentally, that high-ranking clergy had the same quashing effect on him as did high-ranking secular figures of authority. He never forgot that he was the son of a *diachok*, not that of an ordained deacon or priest, who stood far higher in the pecking order of the Orthodox clerical estate.[98]) He took literally the injunction that "He who is ashamed of Me now, of him will I be ashamed at the Judgment" and felt his class anxieties to be a sin and a disgrace. "Are they not all as worms before God?" Father John exclaimed to himself. "Ah, you of little faith! Raise your voice like a trumpet, especially where your stupid, frightened, hypochondriac heart tells you to remain silent." [99] Before simple people, he had "a simple, firm, heartfelt language," before the wealthy, he felt himself to be "sly, phony, doubtful at reading liturgical prayers."[100] This sense of inferiority could extend as far, for example, as believing that the presence of a certain general actually prevented him from calling down the Holy Spirit; or that two captains and a ship's pilot made him feel that some parts of the litanies were out of place.[101]

It was therefore a source of profound shame and rage for Father John that, for all of his recognition of the distance between himself and the privileged, he was nonetheless drawn to them rather than to the poor. Part of it was simply the material comforts the wealthy could provide.

One served in more attractive surroundings, one was rewarded more handsomely for one's efforts, one would likely be offered better food and wine afterwards. Father John was as susceptible to such temptations as any poor priest, but at least he felt badly about it. As he wrote guiltily in 1868, "When the wealthy summon you for a christening or a *moleben*, you hurry with pleasure, particularly if you anticipate a good savory pie served afterwards; but if a poor person asks you to baptize an infant in church after the liturgy, or to serve a *moleben* there, you are angry and irritated."[102] Even worse, he thought, was his being tempted to cut corners when asked by the poor to come and serve:

> You say to yourself, "Why administer extreme unction? The sacraments of confession and communion will be enough for them." ... When arriving at someone's home for performing a sacrament and seeing traces of poverty and destitution—crowding, messiness, dirt—there, do not say in your heart, "Everyone in here is poor, lowly, illiterate, and I can perform the sacrament more quickly and in more abbreviated form than usual, any old way—" remember, the Lord and the angels are there, God sees you.[103]

But Father John's shamed reaction went beyond creature comforts. His ambivalence toward the poor and the rich was more complicated than that caused by ordinary material reasons, and his class anxiety had deeper origins. Although his biographers would constantly stress his intimate connection with the *narod*, Father John clearly felt alienated from and ambivalent toward the uneducated poor people among whom he had grown up, beginning with his mother. The poor village environment in the far north in which he had grown up offered little in terms of either intellectual or physical sustenance. Moreover, the purely physical as well as the social gulf between the poor and the rich in the second half of the nineteenth century can hardly be appreciated by inhabitants of postmodern, postindustrial society who do not venture out of their ghettos of comfort. One's bearing and one's clothing instantly identified one as being either "white-boned" or unspeakable, but the difference was particularly palpable with respect to simple hygiene—whether and how often one bathed, whether one smelled of the perfumery or bodily effluvia, whether one had teeth, rotting stumps, or nothing at all in one's mouth. Precisely because he had grown up in squalor and sought in every way to escape it, Father John hated being thrust back into the world he had fled: in the early 1870s, he shuddered of the poor, "I am so put off by their rude and slovenly appearance, their crude language, their clothing, their manners, the way they walk!"[104]

In 1884, he referred to "the horribly foul smell of the mass of poor people gathered together during a *moleben*."[105] At the same time, he responded to the wealthy and those who could take care of their appearance in the same way he responded to physical beauty generally: with almost visceral pleasure (he wrote sternly to himself, "Wanting people to be attractive—soft, rosy, clever—is as much of a kind of sweet tooth as is food").[106] Although he understood that as a Christian he ought to treat all equally, he could not bring himself to feel neutral with regard to the people who approached him ("I resented bitterly the meek and humble, poor eldress Evfimiia for always coming up to me for a blessing: if she were rich, beautiful, and well-dressed, how eagerly I would have responded!").[107]

It is all the more remarkable, then, that Father John overcame his instinctive reactions. Through a combination of vigilant self-criticism and prayer, he succeeded in making every supplicant feel equally welcome. His weaknesses are not surprising; the extent to which he noticed them and fought them is. As with any form of mastery, others found his kindness and generosity to be effortless. Nevertheless, his path toward sanctity consisted of unflagging attention to others' needs—and his own flaws.

Father John's celebrated indifference toward the material condition of his supplicants was something hard-won rather than something that came naturally. Part of his striving toward social equality and equitable distribution of wealth, and razing of both social and economic barriers, came from the continual ambivalence he experienced toward both the poor and the rich. Nevertheless, the charity he showed to others, which began in individual acts of giving and culminated in the House of Industry, was one of the strongest examples of his religiosity's becoming focused ever outward, including others as well as himself. His sense of priestly responsibility for others also included education and the socially focused preaching that would anticipate his later criticism of Tolstoy and liberal politics.

4

Letters as Examples of Religious Mentalities

In the first twenty years of Father John's priesthood, the traits that would characterize the rest of his life emerged: an intense prayer life (both in private and in the liturgy), self-analysis in his diaries, charity to the needy, and a commitment to convert society through Christian ideals. But his influence remained local. He only became nationally famous, fittingly, thanks to the efforts of the laypeople he had been both trying to serve and to lead. His "service" aspects, significant as they were, paled next to the one that would most distinguish his career: the reputation that his prayers for others "worked." In the early 1880s, he crossed the line that separated ordinary goodness from the supernatural that, according to a contemporary historian of hagiography, set apart the chosen saint.[1] So far we have looked at Father John's path toward sanctity from his perspective and in his voice. Now his audience enters the scene, and his story becomes as much a story of broad attitudes and beliefs toward goodness and holiness as it does one of Father John himself.

The Move Toward Sanctity

In the beginning of Father John's career there was little difference between himself and any other priest in the area of prayer: when asked to perform a *moleben* for someone's recovery, he obliged without either party's having any expectations beyond the conventional. The turning point came when a woman from Kostroma, Paraskeva Kovrigina, insisted he pray specifically for her friends' recovery. As Father John later told a group of priests in Sarapul in 1904, he initially resisted the request:

> I began to pray, *committing the sick people into the hands of God*, asking that His will be done. But then unexpectedly the pious old woman insisted that I pray for the sick persons *in no terms other than for their recovery*. I remember that I was almost afraid to do it: 'How can I have such boldness?' I thought. But Paraskeva Ivanovna's relentless requests finally beat me, and I started to pray to God with firm conviction. God heard my prayers, even though they were unworthy, and the sick and infirm were healed. This cheered and encouraged me. I started to pray to God more and more often at people's request, and the Lord worked many wonders because of our prayers. In this I see a special obedience for me from God—to pray for all who ask God's mercy for themselves.[2]

There are two distinct moments in this description that would influence Father John's subsequent role as an intercessor for others: first, his conviction that God would not deny *anyone's* prayer; second, his coming to regard *himself* as an instrument chosen by God for the purpose of petition. Both would affect his prayers for others and, in turn, the nature of others' turning specifically to him rather than to any other priest. In other accounts, Father John's conception of his role in the process of praying for others emerges particularly clearly:

> The infants Pavel and Olga were healed from the spirit of illness which held them in its thrall, thanks to the boundless mercy of the Master and to the prayer of my sinfulness.... I went there to pray nine times with bold faith, hoping that my faith and hope would not be ashamed, that it would be opened to the one who knocks, that the Master would give me what I asked for because of my insistence alone; that if the unjust judge finally acquiesced to the

Letters as Examples of Religious Mentalities

woman who entreated him, then, all the more, would the most just Judge of all satisfy my sinful prayer for the blameless children; that He would look down on my labor and my effort, at my words of prayer and prostrations, at my boldness and my hope. And indeed so the Master did: he did not shame me, a sinner.—When I came for the tenth time, the babes were well.[3]

Most of Father John's subsequent fame as a holy man rests on this moment. His conviction that it was his unique calling to pray for others, and the intense, indeed demanding, quality of his prayers were conveyed to others. The first incident he recorded of his successful prayers was on February 19, 1867, when he wrote in his diary, "Lord! Thank You that through my prayer, through the laying on of my priestly hands, You healed the Kostylev child. O what approval, o what consolation for your unworthy servant!"[4] During the next several years, such incidents of Divine favor began to occur with greater frequency, but until the end of the 1870s they were still a novelty to both Father John and the recipients. He was careful to record every one in his diary, sometimes adding the comments of the person involved ("After a moleben served by me, the servant of God Melitina became better, as if someone had lifted off her sickness with his hands (her words), and she had been ill for a long time").[5] Divine favor did not limit itself to healing. On July 30, 1869, he recorded, "I cried unto the Lord with complete hope and faith for the cessation of a torrential rainstorm, and within five minutes the sky cleared."[6] By the end of the 1860s, then, at least some people began to experience the powers of his prayers.

As word began to spread that Father John's prayers were efficacious, he was approached by more and more people to pray on their behalf. At this stage there was little question of whether or not his prayers were miraculous, and for most people the question was irrelevant. What mattered was whether one's child or husband or sister recovered, not whether the recovery could be explained by natural or supernatural causes. A similarly functional approach had characterized lay attitudes to shrines of healing since antiquity and to such phenomena as relics or wonder-working icons in the Christian period.[7] All possible methods of treatment, ranging from contemporary medicine to the objects of religion, were seen as having a certain amount of power. None were foolproof, some were preferred to others for certain ailments, but all were considered.[8]

The dialectical nature of Father John's relationship with those who sought him out emerges with particular clarity in the letters he received. The language in which people addressed him, the things they asked of him, and the things they told him of their situations affected his sense of himself as their mediator before God. And the influence went both ways. People did not only appeal to Father John's authority; they also used him in their relationships with the imperial administration, the church hierarchy, and their immediate families. Their letters show to what extent his life was the product of a relationship between him as a priest growing toward holiness and a turbulent context that included political unrest, terrorism, imperialism, and industrialization—which, from the 1880s onward, went from being a purely local to an international one. The letters offer unique evidence for the mutual influence between a saint and his environment. The question may be posed very simply: in what ways did people believe Father John could help them and why? And what does this tell us about religious mentality in Late Imperial Russia?

Requests for Healing

In his classic *Old Russian Saints' Lives as a Historical Source*, Vasilii O. Kliuchevskii made an observation that would define nineteenth-century naturalistic and Soviet scholarly approaches to hagiography. He noted that, when stripped of their literary conventions, the saints' lives he examined yielded little of interest to the historian: only posthumous healing miracles recorded at the saints' tomb might be useful for the scholar of medicine and public health.[9] And indeed, if one follows Kliuchevskii, the range of ailments Father John was asked to cure can serve as a survey of the state of the empire. People asked him to pray for every illness imaginable: for diphtheria, for an office-worker's eyestrain, for a seamstress's deafness of fifteen years, for neurasthenia.[10] But there are other, and better, indices of public health in Late Imperial Russia.[11] The letters Father John received asking for healing are particularly informative as regards the powers people believed him to have and the connection that people identified between sins and sickness, body and soul.

First, and most important, people who wrote to Father John were convinced of his power to heal. In this respect, he was true to Christian expectations of holiness. Healing was a saint's function *par excellence*, and healing miracles were one of the most common "proofs" of posthumous sanctity.[12] While such other contemporary holy figures as the elders of Optina were famous mainly for their spiritual insight, healing was Father John's particular specialty, and people knew it. It was

Fig. 3　Father John in the early 1880s.

newspaper testimonies from the grateful healed, after all, that made his successes public. The volume of the correspondence is one of the strongest indicators that overwhelming numbers of people believed that he could help them. Nearly four thousand letters asking for his prayers in healing represent the highest single category of letters to Father John.[13] Those that are dated range from 1883 (the year when the first of many grateful testimonials appeared in *New Time*) to 1908, the year of his death. A slightly higher proportion (60 percent) come from women, who are usually asking on behalf of others, who were almost always relatives; more men than women report having what they call "sinful" diseases.

The writers provided specific information so that Father John would know exactly whom to pray for and why. People did not hesitate to give him the most intimate details of their condition. In an era when reproductive ailments were covered by the euphemism "women's diseases," for example, a woman wrote of her thirteen-year-old daughter Emily that "she passes a great deal of phlegm through her nose and her bottom, although she will only be thirteen in May and has not yet begun to menstruate." She knew that mentioning such details was scandalous, and apologized for it, but added that she felt Father John ought to know as much as possible. Because people were either puzzled by someone's condition or wanted to make sure that all the aspects of an illness were cured, they included all the symptoms they could.[14]

The most interesting letters for the purposes of religious mentality are those that combine requests for healing with other pleas. One pattern that emerges is the extent to which the people who wrote to Father John seem to have internalized Church teaching that body and soul are connected, and therefore that illness is in some way connected to previous sin.[15] Thus a man asked Father John to pray for his sins, "*for which the Lord has called me*, sending me sickness in my feet."[16] The barely literate Anna "Aliksievna" wrote on November 23, 1883, "Forgive me for the love of God in my unconcern I took little notice of my sins *so* I fell into sickness, I have been shivering from fever and chills for four days already pray for me, a sinner, that the Lord would help me get better."[17] Most people saw illness as a punishment sent by God, or at least as chastisement, especially those who believed, according to the Church and the scriptures, that certain illnesses were provoked by the sins of one's parents. The peasant Nikolai Shenarii, for example, wrote: "*For our sins,* the Lord God saw fit to visit me and my family with a great trial. For three years now, my seventeen year old daughter has had rheumatism, hysteria, and can no longer walk. She cannot stand any noises and curses all the time. Please ease our bitter burden and grant health to her; strength and hope to us."[18] Similarly, the connection several wives drew between illness and virtue impelled them to request that their husbands' characters change, "*and also* their health."[19]

One might be tempted to regard the linkage between sin and sickness as either a convention, with people's absorbing Church teaching, or a tactic deliberately used to win Father John's sympathy. The variety of the ways in which the sentiment was expressed, however, argues against the notion of automatic reproduction. Moreover, in some cases the conviction that one's sins brought about one illness led people to promise to change their behavior as a sign of gratitude for healing (although, pragmatically, few vowed to improve in advance). The Cossack Polikarp Litvintsev expounded on the notion of sickness as one's spiritual responsibility:

> My wife and I have been visited with the same sickness: digestive catarrh. I think that because of my sins, my sickness is the more fierce; it infected my wife.... I now have to walk around with a staff, treat myself with mineral water, and turn to the source of God's mercy with repentance—pray, Batiushka, for the forgiveness of sins and the healing of me and my wife Elena, *I believe and hope and promise to improve my life.*[20]

The promise to undertake a variety of grateful acts if one were healed was a sort of quid pro quo with the Almighty according to a scale of values one thought He (or Father John) cherished. While most people vowed simply to improve, others were more specific, promising concrete actions, especially pilgrimage. A woman named Akilina wrote in May 1898, for example, "If the Lord rescues me from my sickness through your prayers, Father John, I promise before God and you that I will go with my son to the Kiev-Pechersk shrine to bow down to the [icon of the] Dormition of the Mother of God and the holy saints."[21]

The connection Father John's writers made between body and soul emerges particularly strongly with respect to vows and curses. One peasant woman with a deaf-mute daughter of seventeen explained that her condition began at the age of four. When her daughter Pelagiia had called her names, she had cursed her by saying, "May you go deaf!" The girl then took ill and after her sickness could no longer hear or speak. Interestingly, the mother did not ask Father John for Pelagiia's cure, although she desired it: she simply wanted his advice on how to pray to God about it, because she felt responsible. Similarly, when Ekaterina's son Egor offended her with a swear-word, she cursed him back—and from that point on he fell ill. She writes Father John, "I recognize that I sinned before God in doing this. Please pray for me and my sick son Egor." This sentiment, acknowledged as it was by the clergy, was not limited to the uneducated. Even the highly literate Kapitolina feared that her cursing her children—sometimes in anger, sometimes as a bad habit—led to their dread diseases, and begged Father John to remove this burden from her.[22]

The connection between peoples' curses and their emotional disturbances emerges even more strongly than in the cases of cursing's leading to physical illness. Both those cursing and those being cursed believed that a chance word uttered in the heat of the moment could have lasting consequences. Thus a woman who had cursed her deaf-mute daughter in a rage with the words, "Be you anathema, damned by me!" felt as responsible as the mother who felt that she might have brought on her daughter's depression and contrariness by once saying in response to the child's disobedience, "Oh, you unblessed child!" (and children could use this against their parents: as the mother added ruefully, "she remembers this from time to time").[23]

Cursing was not the exclusive domain of the Russian, or the Orthodox, or the less literate. A well-educated Roman Catholic woman wrote to Father John pleading for the release of a family curse invoked by a relative who had been "ruined" by her great-grandfather. The girl had had three Masses served to have God revenge her lost innocence, and her relative was afraid of the effect the summoned revenge might have on the entire family.[24] Cursing, in short, was part of a broadly perceived contact with the spirit world, whether in the form of the work of demons or life beyond the grave. Although the better- and less-educated describe their brush with the shades in slightly different terms, there appears to be little functional difference between their experiences.[25]

Definitions of Health

Partly because of the notion that body and soul were intimately connected, health was a very elastic notion to Father John's correspondents. Letters from peasants often included information about every family member in need, showing both the pragmatic desire to have the letter go as far as possible and that Father John was believed to be able to help in the broadest possible sense. Thus, Aleksei wrote with his wife Nadezhda:

Pray for my family, all of it is sick. Our daughter Agafia suffers from seizures. Our son Nikolai suffers from hemorrhoids; he is a fisherman but not a successful one, he has only losses. Aleksandr, Fedor, and Akim drink heavily. Our son-in-law Ioann lives badly with his wife: he beats her, he frightened her and she is sick. I rely on God's mercy and your holy prayers, that the Lord will not leave me, full of many sins, will calm me, and that the Queen of Heaven will forgive me.[26]

In an example of how behavior labeled sinful was considered something to be cured, adolescent boys routinely asked for help battling masturbation, using the ecclesiastical term *malakia* rather than the more secular *onanizm*, perhaps because they were writing to a priest. Grown men asked to be "healed" of adultery.[27] The people who wrote to Father John, in short, did not distinguish between physical, psychological, and religious ills; all were part of the body-mind-spirit continuum that they drew.

Their perception of a continuum emerges particularly clearly with respect to mental illness, possession, and alcoholism. While both the Orthodox Church and the Russian language distinguished between the properly "spiritual" (pneumatic) *dukhovno* and the more generic "emotional-psychical" *dushevno*, most of the people who wrote to Father John did not draw so fine a distinction. To most of them, mental disease was even more connected to the life of the soul and the spirit than was physical disease. Because of this, they were more likely with mental disease than with physical ailments to draw connections between those actions they thought had brought about the current symptoms.

Requests for the cure of alcoholism are telling in this respect. Father John was one of the most active priests in the campaign against heavy drinking.[28] His well-publicized sermons against the abuse of alcohol, in fact, were widely reprinted and redistributed both immediately after his death and in the 1990s.[29] It is to be expected, then, that letters asking for the sobering of drinkers would figure prominently among letters to him. Nevertheless, the writers made no particular association between him and a cure for drinking; he was not yet like Saint Boniface, for whom curing alcoholics was a specialty. The patterns are predictable: over 90 percent of the letters were from wives or mothers writing on behalf of their husbands and sons, with four letters from alcoholics' children and only two from drinkers themselves. The letters recount the harmful behavior of heavy drinkers: bringing the family to ruin, beating wives and children, and so on.

What is most interesting in them, however, is the extent to which drinking, like other forms of sickness, is perceived and explained in religious terms. Even as women recognized the practical effects of their husbands' habits, and sometimes asked Father John to arrange work for them so that they could support themselves and their children, they expressed the most concern for the souls of their husbands and their families. Most forcefully, they consistently described the addictive nature of alcoholism as "possession." Aleksandra Timofeevna Konashkina was particularly explicit in a letter of August 3, 1901. While she was perfectly aware of the everyday misery her husband's drinking brought, she was terrified at the thought that he might be the servant of "the enemy":

> He never goes past the taverns, *as if he is drawn there by some unseen force*. When he comes home he always goes into his cursing, his foul songs, his dancing.... Please pray for us sinners not to perish in this abyss of sin, for the Lord to rescue my husband from this poison, from enemies and destroyers—but above all for the Lord to at least save him from a bad death—at least let the Lord give him death with repentance, as often when he drinks vodka he falls into some kind of delirium, saying *words that recall the unclean spirits*, for example: "get away from me, I don't owe you anything, I only owe you for the vodka and the tobacco."[30]

Less uniform than the letters on alcoholism are those on behalf of, or from, those classified as "spiritually [emotionally] ill" (*dushevnobol'nye*). The term encompasses a wide range of behavior, ranging from possession to simple contrariness, and seems to have been applied almost any time when behavior departed from the norm or when people cracked under the stress of their situation. In some cases, psychological illness was linked to alcoholism: as their relatives describe, more than a few wives snapped mentally because of their husbands' drinking and became the hysterical shriekers known as *klikushy*. For both men and women, one of the most universally recognized signs of spiritual illness was an excessive fear of everything. There was some variation according to sex, however. In a pattern similar to that of contemporary France, women tended to fear clergy, whereas men's fear most often expressed itself in thoughts of suicide, itself universally ascribed to the instigation of the Devil.[31]

Responses to the emotionally disturbed varied strikingly by sex as well. While people feared but tolerated disturbed men, women defined as disturbed, particularly those from the middle classes, were likely to be committed. This discrepancy came partly from people being more afraid of the damage men could do. Parents with disturbed sons, for example, told Father John that they were physically afraid to throw the young men out of the house, but were just as afraid of their sons' souls perishing, or their becoming vagrants. They asked him whether he counseled gentleness or strictness.[32] Parents showed far less hesitation with their daughters, however. One young woman whose fiancé betrayed her was put in a sanatorium for three years. Another wrote to Father John in 1899, claiming that her mother had wrongly committed her to an asylum two years before; she wanted to be released, saying that she feared that she had already lost her soul in the place. Yet another was sent to an asylum in Helsinki for having dabbled in spiritualism ("Please get me out of here," she writes, "I'm not crazy").[33] All of this suggests that, as in contemporary France, women in Late Imperial Russia who acted outside the narrow contemporary norms established for feminine behavior and whose families perceived them as bringing possible disgrace were far more likely than men to be institutionalized for being either depressed or hysterical.[34] What is remarkable is that, from the confines of their asylums, they regarded Father John as someone who could release them, as much because of his authority in the eyes of the clerical and governmental establishments as of his power of prayer. It is precisely in such requests for intervention and intercession that he emerges as an authority figure whom people could use *against* the established authorities and structures of power. His charisma was so widely acknowledged that it could be used to circumvent them.

Besides fear, another symptom of spiritual disturbance consisted of not going to communion or not going to church. These were sure signs to people that someone was far from both God and the community. Because, as Soviet writers later argued, showing panic at the sight of the chalice or the hearing of the Cherubic hymn were popularly accepted signs of possession, people who felt close to the brink may have unconsciously displayed those signs; it is difficult to say whether the symptom or the state came first.[35] In an extension of this principle (for not going to church or Communion was as characteristic of many sectarian groups as of the mentally disturbed), Orthodox Christians sometimes associated sectarianism not only with antisocial behavior but linked it explicitly with mental illness.[36] The parents of a twenty-three-year-old woman who had gone to Sarov to venerate the relics of Saint Serafim, for example, related how their daughter had been accosted by Old Believers who tried to discourage her from making the three-fingered sign of the cross and from venerating the newly canonized saint. The young woman was so shaken by this, according to her parents, that she became unhinged: in the three months after her return, she had been making nooses and exhibiting other signs of strange behavior. Her parents asked Father John to pray for her sins (and hence recovery).[37] Similarly, the wife of a man who had joined the flagellant *khlyst* sect, and was now in the hospital for insanity, linked her husband's sectarianism with his illness. She did not ask for her husband's healing but for his leaving the *khlysty* and becoming a son of the Orthodox Church, evidently assuming that once the sectarian allegiance was withdrawn the illness would depart as well.[38]

People also linked assault, especially sexual assault, with emotional disturbance. With a sensibility nearly alien to the current one, most did not blame the perpetrator: the damage was done, the victims may have brought it upon themselves, and only they and their families were left to pick up the pieces. The exhausted mother of an eleven-year-old girl, for example, described how her daughter had been literally scared out of her wits by a fifteen-year-old village boy who had attacked her in the dark. She wrote grimly in 1902:

> Now she spends all day and night on my lap and will not let me step away for an instant; she will not allow others to come near her either. Please pray either for her to die or for her to quiet down and let me go away from her for at least an hour or so. There are idiots in families—I can resign myself to that, and do not murmur at God. I am ready to bear any work, any penance, but just not this.[39]

In general, the extent to which people accept nerve-shattering situations with a stoic refusal to assign blame boggles the mind. While *snokhachestvo*, a peasant patriarch's pressing his daughter-in-law for sexual favors, was not normally considered a disease, it could lead to what people interpreted as severe mental disturbance. Remarkably, however, the erring father-in-law was almost invariably the last, or the least, blamed. A priest from the Kuban region, for example, described a situation in the family of his Cossack parishioners in which the son came back from military service to find his wife pregnant amid "evil rumors" that she had sinned with his father (not the reverse). Both relatives and strangers began to laugh and mock Stefan, which drove him to bitterness, which in turn manifested itself in his spending the night in empty houses and stopping confession and communion. His sickness, the priest continued, had now assumed an acute character: he saw demons everywhere, even in church. The priest hazarded that the condition was probably "something like possession." The most amazing thing of all, however, is that the priest was asked to write the letter asking for Father John's prayers by Stefan's parents, who felt sorry for their son. There is not a trace of compunction on the part of the father nor recrimination by the mother, nor any regret expressed about the young wife.[40] People who wrote to Father John, in short, perceived a rupture with confession and communion as ominous, antisocial behavior. Breaking with Orthodoxy was in itself a sign that something had gone amiss.

Doctors, Saints, and Medicine

If people perceived illness as part of a spiritual and physical continuum, how did they regard the process of healing? Their different approaches to medicine and to Father John are extremely instructive. Doctors, icons, and saints were part of a constellation of sources to which people turned for healing.[41] Physicians themselves (especially if they were women) might ask Father John to come to their dying patients.[42] In most cases, however, people turned to him only after despairing of medical help. It was extremely unusual for someone to avow that they believed medicine to be useless altogether and relied on faith alone. Letter after letter, from people of every class background, describes in detail how the petitioner sought medical help (the wealthier writers included the names of the specialists they consulted), but to no avail.[43] Thus the Countess Olga Murav'eva-Amurskaia begged Father John to pray for her five-year-old son, saying, "The doctors find his condition hopeless, but God can do everything, and through your mouth he will hear our prayer."[44] In one case where the writer consulted with "the eminent Professor Pavlov," she admitted that although her son was better, he still itched, and added, "I know that he will be healed more quickly through your holy prayers than through any medicines."[45] The attitude toward the relative efficacy of prayers and medicine, and the faith in pilgrimage, also emerges in this letter from Pavel Afanas'evskii in 1897:

> My son bashed his head when he fell over fifteen feet in the cellar. Ointments and medicines were no help. At that time the day was drawing near for my wife's departure to a monastery for the feast

of the Dormition of the Most Holy Mother of God. As her husband, I bade her go with God, and said if he gets worse I'll let you know, and, just imagine, Batiushka, today my wife leaves, and the next day my son gets up and his head is completely well. A doctor's help isn't even necessary. Only now his speech is not clear and he learns with great difficulty. Please pray for his becoming diligent in his studies.[46]

But it was not as tidy as medicine is useless; therefore, now to prayer and Divine assistance. When Averkii Samokhin asked Father John to heal his son on May 5, 1906, for example, he wrote without mentioning any doctors, "We have tried *everything*: we have served molebens, took holy water from the chalice, carried him up to the entry with the chalice in three different churches, but there is no change in the condition of this innocent martyr."[47] Here, "everything" refers to the arsenal of possible *Divine* sources. Calling one's son a martyr is also, of course, a sign of interpreting suffering in religious terms. The strongest illustrations of the faith people had in Father John's prayer come in the form of three telegrams, each relaying a similar instance: someone has died but the body is not showing any signs of decay. The relatives are telling Father John that the burials have been postponed in hopes that through his prayers, God may bring the reposed back to life (which had occurred at least once, according to *New Time*).[48]

Father John shared his correspondents' acceptance of medicine. The son of Mikhail Saltykov-Schedrin, the writer, recalled how his parents had tried to keep separate the visits of Father John and the celebrated doctor S. P. Botkin, to avoid offending the physician, and were amazed to have the two greet one another as old friends.[49] On one occasion, Father John told people not to consult doctors and crashed his fist down on tables with medicines; but, more typically, he not only recommended certain physicians but sent his own. He also accepted invitations to speak at the openings of both pharmacies and associations of homeopathic medicine. Ironically, Soviet writers in the period of official atheism attempted to use his own willingness to consult doctors against him, suggesting that this was hypocritical behavior on the part of a man of prayer.[50] But here, as in many other respects, Father John simply shared the beliefs of his flock: both medicine and prayer had their place in the Orthodox cosmology of Late Imperial Russia, as they did in late antiquity.[51] This may be why some people asked whether they should go to doctors, or to a holy place (if so, which one), or whether they should visit Father John himself.[52] The most striking testimony to people's faith in his powers came from those who decided on their own that no medical help was necessary. This occurred most often, surprisingly, not with peasants or the barely literate, but with educated urban women who used good-quality paper and ink. A wealthy matron wrote:

> We have heard so much about your universal help and decided to ask for your holy prayers and healing, and I wrote you for the first time in July. At that time my husband was going to Moscow for business and wanted to seek counsel with doctors again while he was there, but I dissuaded him because I had sent you a letter. And because I was so hoping for your healing, because I believed in it so much, I waited for my husband's return in complete confidence to see him completely well. But what sadness I was in when I learned that he still could not hear! Batiushka! Our only hope is in God! I implore you, pray for him.... I will be very, very grateful to you.[53]

The last turn of phrase is typical of the highly educated and wealthy, for whom expressing gratitude was both a convention and a sign of self-worth. The poor and the less educated, whose speech was not automatically sprinkled with such phrases as *"Budu vam priznatel'na,"* tended to tell Father John that "I will pray for *you*, too."

Their use of this phrase suggests a number of things. First, the poor and less educated were far more keenly aware than the wealthy that no one's services came free, certainly not a priest's. Most tried to include at least a token amount, such as the peasant man who, after describing his illness and diagnosing it as punishment for a youth spent in "drinking, dissolution, and other pernicious deeds," enclosed his "feasible mite" of one ruble. Those who could not manage even this could at least offer their prayers.[54] But there is another, larger implication. In the eyes of most people who wrote to him, Father John was not an isolated beacon of holiness, but part of the general constellation of Orthodox sanctity, of which they were also a part. The priest or the holy man did not exist in a charmed universe outside the reach of ordinary mortals. He may have been closer along the continuum to God than they were, but his correspondents recognized that they and he were traveling on the same path, one which had been traveled previously by now-established holy people. This is why they emphasized their praying for Father John, or closed their letters with such phrases as "The Queen of Heaven save you." While he was "pleasing to God," he was still a mortal, still as subject—perhaps even more subject—to the assaults of the enemy as they. By telling him that they would pray for him, they were affirming their active role in the economy of salvation. They were not simply passive receptacles, or an audience waiting for the successful performance of a magician.[55]

This perception of Father John as perhaps the best living representative of, but nonetheless part of the broad constellation of, Orthodoxy, is why so many people tried to help him in his own quest. As well as praying for him, they also offered him the same tangible repositories of grace that they would to a family member or a valued friend. One woman sent him a blessed *prosphora* and part of a relic from the holy bishop Mitrofan; another passed along holy water from Saint Feodosii of Chernigov and oil from Saint Barbara.[56] Finally, because he was a priest, people asked not only for his holy prayers but also asked him to pray to other saints—not only to the Savior, but to the Tikhvin icon of the Mother of God, to Nicholas the Wonder-Worker, to Panteleimon for health, and so on.[57]

Attitude Toward Father John and Divine Intervention: Who Heals?

This brings us to the question of precisely how people perceived Father John's role in the praying and healing process. They show a remarkable, and Orthodox, consistency. The lack of success of their own prayers was proof that both their prayers and their faith were weak. Father John, by contrast, was a more effective means of access to God's grace; those who sought him out believed that he had a more direct connection to God than ordinary mortals. When asking for the recovery of her sister's children from scarlet fever in 1898, for example, the Baroness Lieven expressed her wish by saying, "I believe that God is all-powerful *and* that the pure, earnest prayer of people who are pleasing to him works wonders."[58] Because of this sense of hierarchy, when the desired effect was reached, the credit went first to God, and only then to Father John's prayers.

What, then, of those occasions where despite everything, his prayers seemed to have failed? Here the joint responsibility of saint and subject emerges particularly clearly. If sin led to sickness, the connection between faith and healing was just as crucial. Father John repeatedly told those who approached him that they would receive according to their faith, which may be why so many writers emphasized their own piety. But, as one mailman from Torzhok who had unsuccessfully sought his help wrote on November 17, 1890:

Batiushka, when I came up to you in the altar after liturgy and asked for your prayers, you asked me in detail about my previous visit to you five years ago, and said that I had not been cured because I had little faith. But, Batiushka, I am an unparalleled sinner, a layperson, and one who lives in a veritable sinners' manger—the post office—and not once in my life have I had anything happen to me that would confirm me in faith. Of all the things I have asked the Lord God for, I have not received a single one. And I have tried asking the holy intercessors: I asked the holy martyr Panteleimon to heal me, and so far that has not happened. I have also asked other holy favorites of God to heal me and to help me in my needs and shortcomings which have almost eaten me up—but, alas, having this joy in my life is not meant to be....

So please pray for my healing and also for me to become confirmed in faith, which I think will be confirmed if you heal me. This will be a fact for my whole life, and will destroy all my heretical thoughts. Batiushka, Saint Panteleimon himself became confirmed in faith after he brought someone back to life from the dead—then how are we sinners supposed to reach this grace if you, most holy pastor and living intercessor for us before God do not reward us?[59]

Thus, in admitting their apparent lack of faith, Father John's supplicants pointed out very reasonably that this faith would be confirmed by the fulfillment of their request. This is not necessarily manipulation; it is an acceptance of the rules and a wish to achieve what they wanted in Orthodox terms.

Requests for Visits

While people believed that Father John's prayers would work at a distance, most still preferred a personal audience. By the 1890s, however, so many people wished to see him that personal visits became harder to come by. Moreover, he had hired a staff of screeners to manage his appointment schedule. In practice, this meant that access to him was now limited to those who could afford to pay for it. As a result, in the letters from the 1890s onward, poor people seem to have nearly given up on getting Father John to come visit, with the bulk of visit requests coming from those secure in their wealth or social status, such as the titled aristocracy from the environs of St. Petersburg. Their letters, moreover, only began to arrive in significant numbers after 1894, when Father John had been asked to minister to the dying Alexander III. This suggests that most of the highest nobility waited for a sign of Imperial favor before they turned to Father John, although, once attracted, they made a powerful constituency.

There is hardly a well-known aristocratic family that did not request a visit: Volkonskii, Gagarin, Sheremetev, Apraksin, Kropotkin, Lanskoi, Shakhovskoi, Tatishchev, Kutuzov, Rimsky-Korsakov, Sviatopolk-Mirskii, Obolenskii, Bagration, Lobanov-Rostovskii, Trubetskoi, Murav'ev, Ol'denburgskii, Tiesenhausen, Kulomzin, Cherkasskii, Tolstoy, Ukhtomskii, Orlov, Golitsyn, Taneev, and so on. The importance they attached to their emotions is also evident. In a manner decidedly unlike that of people from other class backgrounds, who clearly felt some diffidence in addressing Father John and wrote laconically, the titled aristocracy often mentioned its feelings in even the shortest telegrams, such as one sent in 1895 by Prince Bariatinskii that ended, "Please visit her as soon as possible—for the love of God, go, all of us are in despair!"[60] Even at their most desperate, their feelings mattered, and they assumed those feelings should matter to Father John as well.

The Tsar's family also wrote to Father John. Nicholas II sent a telegram expressing his happiness at Father John's recovery, Alexandra Feodorovna asked him to bless three icons, and the Dowager Empress Marie thanked him for his prayers and his blessing her work with deaf-mutes. Father John was also invited to serve at the wedding and coronation of Nicholas II and the christenings of several of his children.[61] Because of these contacts, it is surprising that the Emperor and Empress seem never to have considered inviting Father John to court to pray over Tsarevich Alexei after the Heir's first bout of bleeding in 1904. After all, they consulted everyone from French quacks to the mentally challenged to Rasputin; why not a bona fide Orthodox healer who was just around the corner?[62]

This lacuna is striking particularly if one considers the repeated—and utterly unfounded—assertion that it was no one other than Father John who had chosen Rasputin as his own successor and even introduced Rasputin to the Imperial Family in 1903.[63] Repeating the common mistaken notion that it was Father John *Sergiev* of Kronstadt, rather than Protopresbyter Ioann *Ianyshev*, who was the actual confessor of the Imperial family, later Western writers present an improbable scenario: that, just at the moment when Father John held up the chalice and pronounced the words, "With the fear of God, draw near," he suddenly cried, "Stop!," picked the ragged Rasputin out of the crowd,

Letters as Examples of Religious Mentalities

and told him to approach. Not only did he bless Rasputin, but asked to be blessed in return.[64] Father John then "advised the Empress to have a talk with the devout peasant."[65] Similarly fanciful are the assertions that Father John warned Rasputin that his name (meaning "dissolute") was destiny, or that Father John had also introduced to the Imperial family the French "doctor," Nizier Anthelme Philippe.[66]

Admittedly, the sources for these assertions are not the most serious scholarly works. Nevertheless, their content continues to dominate the perception many have of Father John. There are several separate questions here: Was Father John close to the Imperial family? Did he have any contact with Rasputin? If not, where and why did the myth spring up?

First, Father John was not particularly close to the Imperial family. He held them in reverence and the invitation to pray at the bedside of the dying Alexander III was one of the high points of his life, but that was the only truly personal contact with them he had. With all his attention to rank and honors, and his minute recording of any contact with members of the Royal House, he would certainly have mentioned any such incidents in his diaries or letters. The strongest personal contacts he describes are Nicholas's donating a 300-desiatine grove to the Sura convent at his request and his telephoning to inquire after Father John's health at the House of Industry.[67] Father John knew his place painfully well. His casually suggesting to the Empress that she have a talk with any peasant is inconceivable.

Almost as unlikely is the story of his blessing of Rasputin. Father John, who spent the Eucharistic canon in a state of exaltation at the thought of union with God, would not have stopped the sacrament for anyone (after all, we are speaking of someone who continued giving Holy Communion after a woman seeking to approach the chalice was crushed to death by the impatient crowd).[68] Moreover, the high regard for his priestly rank he expressed repeatedly militates against his asking for a blessing from anyone unordained.[69] Even if, for the sake of argument, he had done anything so extraordinary, such an act would have found its way into his diaries; it is not there. Finally, and most seriously, there is no contemporary supporting evidence for the assertion, for the simple reason that no contemporary would have believed it. The most plausible account of Rasputin's rise to fame is that of his own secretary, Aron Simanovich, who denies that Father John played any role, and ascribes the introduction of Rasputin to Alexandra to the Montenegrin princesses Militsa and Anastasia, as does Nicholas II himself, although other contemporaries argue that it was Bishop Feofan or the Countess Ignatiev.[70]

Why, then, the later repeated assertion that it was Father John who introduced Rasputin? For many writers, Rasputin may be the Lee Harvey Oswald of Russian history. It is difficult to believe that he made his way into the court alone, without the protection or good offices of the established religious authorities. Because Father John was both official enough and original enough to serve such a hypothetical role, and because he was often confused with Father Ioann Ianyshev, he may have seemed to later writers to be a logical source. More insidious is the implicit suggestion that Father John was somehow passing on the mantle of "Russia's spiritual father" to Rasputin—something that would reflect only badly on him.

The question needs to be stood on its head. Why, when faced first with the lack of a male heir and then with a hemophiliac son, did Nicholas and Alexandra *not* seek out the help of such a prominent Orthodox figure with a reputation for healing as Father John? Arguing for the absence of something is always tenuous, but some causes may be advanced. First, and most likely, is that on the single occasion when the Imperial family had previously sought out his prayers in hopes of his power to heal—when Alexander III was dying in Livadia in 1894— those prayers did not work; Alexander died anyway. If Father John had not succeeded once, he could fail again. Other "healers" at least had the virtue of being untested. Another possibility is the eclectic character of Alexandra's religiosity. For whatever reason, the Empress seems to have been drawn not to pillars of Orthodoxy, but to holy fools, spiritualists, and "psycho-physiologists."[71] In any case, whether because he had not succeeded with Alexander III or he was too conventional, Father John was not sought out by either Nicholas or Alexandra. Only the Empress's sister, the Grand Duchess Elisaveta Feodorovna (Ella), showed signs of greater than conventional warmth. It was she who advised Nicholas to consult with Father John when seeking Alexandra's hand and it was on her behalf that Nadezhda Arsen'eva wrote in October 1907, "The Grand Duchess greatly thanks you for the holy bread [*prosphora*] you sent her—she loves you so much, honors you so, and so treasures your prayers that she was overjoyed and glad to know that you pray both for her and the repose of the soul of her husband, the Grand Duke Sergei Aleksandrovich."[72]

Requests for Material Assistance

Next to requests for healing, letters for material assistance constitute the other large category of letters to Father John. People wrote to ask him for everything imaginable: a daughter's dowry, money for a return ticket, their next meal. Their letters demonstrate how, in the absence of insurance policies or social security, a double illness in a family could spell utter ruin. As a result, people who asked for healing sometimes asked for money as well, particularly the families of sick breadwinners with small children to feed and clothe. In such an environment, Father John often seemed to be people's only resource. "You are the only one I can turn to," "You are the only kind person in the whole world," appear in almost every letter. The phrases are more than formulae, however. As one police officer wrote:

> After my wife's and mother's illnesses, I am seven thousand rubles in debt. Everything has been pawned, including my clothing, underwear, coat, and boots. Because of the lack of clothing, I cannot even go to work, and have to pretend to be sick. Our friends and relatives have given up on helping us a long time ago—they think they will never get their own back. If you don't help me, no one on earth will.
>
> Please ask one of your supporters to cover at least half my debts —three thousand rubles—save me, I am perishing. I can't even afford to buy bread.[73]

Whatever the appeal for help, Father John was supposed to act as a substitute benevolent and rational parent—and classic holy patron, righting wrongs and restoring a sense of both cosmic and social rightness. The educated women who wrote to him stand out as a category, striking exasperated and manipulative notes. While both men and women thought of God as an actor in their lives, educated women reacted to Him more personally, especially if they felt their hopes had been betrayed. It is as if, having fulfilled their part of their bargain, they became incensed when God seemed to not have done the same— a tendency, incidentally, noted by contemporary clerics.[74] In this respect, educated women differed both from educated men and from uneducated women who, even at their most desperate, did not presume to think God owed them anything. The educated women, moreover, were not shy about manipulating either saint or symbol, even as they tried to remain within an Orthodox framework. Any subtlety vanishes as they try to stoke Father John's ego, suggesting what better opportunity for God's (and his own) might to manifest itself than to grant their wish? Note the if-then constructions and the almost comical contrast between the holy names invoked and the goal sought in a letter of January 1891:

If you are a kind Father and close to God and the Almighty is accessible to you—you have to—your heart has to—feel compassion for me. How many tears, how many torments of the heart have fallen onto my unfortunate lot. O, Lord, enough already!

Otherwise the Lord is vicious, and not merciful. I prayed to Him, prayed to the point of losing consciousness, but He does not hear me. Holy Father! The Lord hears your prayers and fulfills them. I implore you by the Queen of Heaven, by all the saints, by the Lord Jesus Christ our Savior; I conjure you through the power and might of the Life-giving Cross, the Unfathomable Holiness of the Lord's Body and Blood; I conjure you by the Holy Creed; and beg you to pray for me, may the Lord hear and fulfill my small and modest wish: I have a single lottery ticket: let it win! This will give me the possibility of being farther away from people's squabbles and filth. [If I win,] I will put more than a tenth into your disposal, worthy Father.

If the Lord and his inscrutable Mysteries exist, if your prayers are valid, then my wish and my request will be granted, and faith will grow stronger in my soul, and I will glorify the name of the Lord, and yours, too, spiritual father.... I conjure you one more time: from the depth of my heart, I conjure you by the Holy Gifts of Communion: pray sincerely for my request, which is so possible for the Lord—let Him show his Merciful Mightiness and the Wonder and the Power and the Might of the prayers of the Righteous man who is pleasing to Him.[75]

The misguided woman, alas, did not know that Father John detested all games of chance. At least she tried to sound pious. Others implied that their bitterness was so extreme that they could no longer muster the signs of belonging to the Orthodox community. They seemed to think that, by threatening the loss of their souls, they could bully Father John into submission. Varvara, for example, deliberately used the lower case in referring to God, except when referring to her formerly faithful state:

You have been sent by god to all of us who sorrow, now listen to me and my woe, ask god for me for him to help me. I have gone through and am going through so much that my patience is coming to an end.... People have taken away all my fortune after a whole series of sufferings. All I have left is one nobles' lottery ticket and a three thousand ruble debt of honor. You can ask god for me and He will do it for you: you yourself say, "Just believe and pray and God will give you whatever you ask for." Well, I *have* prayed, to the point of frenzy, to the point of anguish.... As I prayed, I believed that there is a God and that He hears me—well, those were just thoughts. There is no happiness for me, but when you look around, you see people, there they go, living and being happy. Is it a sin to want the kind of happiness and life you should have, in the circle you come from?

I haven't gone to confession or communion for—soon it will be three years, and I just can't. If I become fortunate—then and only then will I go to church.[76]

The frequent references to lottery tickets as solutions for financial woes attest to more than the spread of lotteries in Late Imperial Russia.[77] Their interest for religious mentality lies in their being a new avenue merging desperation and pious hopes. If such people as Varvara needed money to pay for something they knew Father John disapproved of (a gambling debt, for example), it seemed more appropriate to ask him to pray for a winning number than asking for the money outright: he would still be helping, but without incurring any financial loss.[78]

Noblewomen with children were far more successful when they stressed both their class humiliation and their position as mothers in pleading on their families' behalf. While mothers of all economic backgrounds asked on behalf of their children, only those from the nobility saw motherhood as giving them a kind of privileged position. By having done everything right, by having fulfilled the obligations of their sex and class and expressing such appropriate attitudes as that of Christian submission, they now felt they had the moral *right* to get help. As Princess Vera Shakhovskaia wrote:

You served *molebens* at our house more than once—but then I was rich. And every time you served at our house, God gave us happiness and good fortune. But now all that is changed. My husband has died, leaving me penniless with three sons.... Now I beg you on my knees, as the mother of her children. Do you have any idea of what it is like when children who were brought up in luxury cry, 'Mama, give us some bread!' Now everything is pawned, there is no money to get it back.... For you some hundred and fifty rubles is not worth thinking about, for me it is a question of life or death. If this sum should seem too great for any reason, please help us as much as you find possible.

PS. I hope that your heart will respond to my hopeless situation. *I am bearing a frightful cross, but am bearing it like a good Christian woman* and do not have the right to pass it along to my children.

You are the first person I am turning to. You will understand me and your responsive heart will say its own word on my behalf, kind Batiushka.[79]

Such requests, emphasizing as they did that one had remained within the traditional parameters of Christian womanly virtue, and flattering Father John with intimacy, were effective. Whether because of his attraction to the noble and the beautiful or simply because of pity, Father John responded quickly, as attests another letter on mourning stationery he received from Princess Nadezhda Obolenskaia almost immediately after he did Shakhovskaia's:

You are our Shrine, your prayers reach the Almighty. I have just buried my brother Boris (Prince Golitsyn), and this has affected my dear son's health so much that he is now sick with a nervous disorder. He is all I have. He has to be taken abroad immediately. I buried my husband not long ago, and who knows when they will start issuing us a pension....

What will a mother not do for her child. So I am asking you for my son's sake, do not refuse me. I am asking you for 225 rubles; if this should be difficult for you, please help as much as you can.

Not long ago, dear Batiushka, you helped my cousin, Princess Vera Shakhovskaia, and I beg you to respond to my request as favorably as you did to hers.... Your sentence will be the sentence of the Almighty.[80]

In other words, even where their material interests were involved, people did not treat Father John as their private resource, guarding any advantages they had received from him. Instead, they appear to have shared their good news and allowed their names to be used as a reference, suggesting that having received his beneficence was itself a kind of commodity that one could "loan" to others as a sign of favor.

The other group of people who felt that they had a *right* to ask were those who show a budding labor consciousness. They not only plead misery and ask for help but also identify the objective causes of their state. A worker writing in 1903 on behalf of other workers injured on the job shows the trust in the Tsar that Daniel Field and others have described as "naïve monarchism," and, in a phenomenon Reginald Zelnik has explored, links the Gospel with unionism and social justice. He is also one of many to link Father John with the Tsar for a host of reasons:

> Surely the Batiushka Tsar', and all the laws and their rulers, could not have forgotten these unfortunate people!... The insulted and the injured cripples sue for compensation for their injuries in court, but what happens then? The employers and the administration use all means possible—doctors, buying witnesses—to proved that the injured party was himself to blame. Or they drag on the case for two or three years and then find little cause....
>
> The worker is not able to support his family and the children given to him according to the Law of God, so his entire family degenerates ... they forget the Holy Scriptures of our Lord Jesus Christ, for whose labors people went to listen to Him and He rewarded them....
>
> I have already appealed to His Excellency the Procurator on January 28, 1903, and have turned to the Circuit Court which does not act lawfully, but no one has paid any attention. I have also addressed the Grand Duke Sergei Aleksandrovich, but all remains as before.... *What I have said shows that where the Batiushka Tsar is personally, there is truth and justice, and where he is not personally, then truth and justice are supplanted and overruled by finances.*
>
> *Please pass along this plea to the Batiushka Tsar, as you are his close counselor, and as there are no more other measures that can be taken.* If you do not pay attention to this, good Shepherd, I will have to try to address the Tsar personally.[81]

Such people depicted both Father John and the Tsar as courts of last resort "untainted" by the bureaucratic apparatus, standing above the usual hierarchies. Both, they believed, could restore both heavenly and earthly justice. To the people who sought out Father John, he resembled the Tsar in his capacity to override the conventional networks of power. The association with the Tsar emerged on other levels, including urban legends and politics. Monarchist contemporaries, for example, asserted that people placed Father John's portraits next to those of the Emperor because "as an all-Russian pastor and a shield of the Orthodox faith, in his activity he approached the feats of the all-Russian emperor, who is the anointed of God and a defender and preserver of the faith."[82] The similarity between the Emperor and the parish priest, then, reflected both charismatic blessings and real power.

Intercession and Intervention (*Zastupnichestvo* and *Khodataistvo*)

The unique perception people had of Father John emerges especially strongly in the area of intercession, a quality attributed to saints from the Virgin Mary downward. Such phrases as "Earnest intercessor" and "Having thee as an intercessor" recur throughout the prayers and hymns to saints of the Orthodox Church. Father John had an advantage over canonized saints, however, because he was alive, and hence could act—and be appealed to—in person. As befits his status as a priest in the world, he was asked to intercede before representatives both of the heavenly power and of the earthly one. In this respect, his association with the Tsar was practical: people not only believed Father John was *like* the Tsar; they believed he could intercede on their behalf *to* the Tsar. People consulted him when they believed that only the Tsar could overrule the clerical hierarchy. For example, he was asked to get through to Nicholas II to allow an otherwise unlawful joint Roman Catholic–Orthodox marriage ceremony, people whose local bishop had appropriated the family icon wanted his blessings to go to the Emperor if they were refused again, and so on.[83]

Most of the requests for intercession, however, dealt with financial matters. Help with jobs was the largest area. Because Kronstadt was close to St. Petersburg and because people believed Father John to be infinitely well-connected, many job-seekers from the provinces eager to come to the capital described how fruitlessly they had tramped from office to office and asked him to contact "some appropriately highly-placed person," repeating, "*Just one word from you* and [X] will give me a position."[84] In their eyes, Father John was a patron in every sense of the term. While members of the clergy seeking positions or augmented pensions formed one large group of seekers, most were workers, bureaucrats, and sailors from the Capital District.

Their insistence is understandable, for Father John's intervention could have the desired effect. On January 8, 1904, for example, he received a letter from Nikolai Speranskii, the Chief Military Medical Inspector, telling him that in response to his request, the former senior physician of the Second Kronstadt Infantry Regiment, Dr. Sobolevskii, had been re-assigned to the position of Senior Physician of HIM Maria

Fedorovna's Cavalry Regiment in St. Petersburg.[85] When Father John's intercession was unsuccessful, as when he was advised in 1905 that the assistant to the bookkeeper of the Kronstadt port could not get the position he wanted in the Admiralty because someone else had already been promised it, the authority (in this case, the Chief of the Main Navy Staff) sent a personal letter with an explanation.[86]

Patronage was not a one-sided path, with Father John knocking on the doors of the powers that be. It went in both directions, with both parties understanding that the other might be in a position to do them a good turn someday. Just as Father John regularly petitioned military, church, and government officials on others' behalf, so they approached him as well. Vladimir Sabler, then the assistant to the Ober-Procurator of the Holy Synod, for example, contacted him in 1904 to arrange employment in his convent for a woman who had studied in the Statistical Commission and was an excellent accountant.[87] Along with Father John's being the center of a constellation of prayer, then, he was also part of the St. Petersburg power network, both asking and asked for on others' behalf.

But not all the letters asking for Father John's intercession were after something tangible, or something that required any action other than prayer on his part. They are important because they show that the people who wrote to him were not only interested in the concrete help he could provide them, but valued his spiritual blessing as well. Their amalgam of practicality and religiosity shows that, to many, Father John was neither *only* a benevolent patron nor *only* a man of prayer (without diminishing the importance of either group); he was both. This separation of material and spiritual was neither fixed nor absolute in the worldview of most of those who wrote to him. In Soviet writing on religion, it became a cliché to say, along with Marx, that when people expressed spiritual sentiments or needs, they actually had material ones in mind. What one observes in the letters from businesspeople to Father John, however, is a clear appreciation of both the material and spiritual sides of their work. Pavel Barskov, who with his wife Elisaveta ran a mom-and-pop fruitsellers' on Mokhovaia Street in St. Petersburg, wrote: "Please pray before the altar of the Most High Creator for us wretched and foul sinners, as I have a shop and the right to trade, but my uncle is the one who buys me the goods, and, because I don't have any means with which to buy the goods myself, we end up paying more than we ought." The Barskovs did not pursue this line further, however; neither did they attempt to persuade Father John to approach the recalcitrant uncle. Instead, they professed the opposite:

> Dear Batiushka, pray for us sinful, wretched, foul, and unworthy Pavel and Elisaveta, may the Lord God help us and arrange matters for us with His all-knowing Holy Providence, *but not as we want, but as is pleasing to Him*, our Most High Creator and Lord Jesus Christ. And may He affirm us by His grace and help us sinful ones be firm and unshakable in all matters pleasing to Him, our only Savior and Lord Jesus Christ, that He may pour forth His grace on our business affairs.[88]

One cannot know for certain, of course, whether the Barskovs really meant that they wanted for things to turn out as God wanted and not as they hoped. They may have thought that Father John would be moved by their willingness to accept God's will, and thus be more inclined to pray for them than for someone who did not take God's will into consideration at all. But their final request for Divine grace to be poured forth on their business affairs, which is not one to be found in most letters, suggests at least some level of sincerity. They are emblematic of the pious businesspeople who turned to Father John for help.

The importance of Father John's purely spiritual blessing to people becomes clear in the cases when people called upon him even after they had taken all of the practical steps to assure something. In 1901, for example, Avgust Brilinskii, a forest inspector, explained that his wife Anna had begun an affair with the godfather of their youngest daughter. To help Brilinskii bring some distance between his wife and her lover, the Empress had interceded on his behalf for a job transfer to Kiev, and the director, Viktor Sergeevich Kochubei, had promised to see to it. What, then, was Father John's role to be? To pray for the transfer to go through as soon as possible, because Brilinskii felt it was imperative to get everyone, especially the children, out of the situation.[89] Thus, even though Father John was not expected to act upon any person directly, he was asked to affect the general spiritual constellation of the event.

Father John, in short, attracted people who saw their lives in religious terms, and there were clearly many of these in the Russian Empire. The combination of spiritual and material assistance they desired showed itself most strongly when he was called upon to intervene in legal cases. Most often, people claimed that they or their friends had been falsely accused. Given the traditional importance of the saint in working justice, righting wrongs and serving as "the counter-hero of the dispossessed," such appeals provide a testimony that Father John had taken on this attribute of sanctity in the eyes of those who called on him.⁹⁰ Thus the family of a Colonel Bezbryzhii from Warsaw explained how he had been lashed in the face by a drunken officer coming back from a picnic: he had fought back, and was now sentenced to eight years of penal servitude on Sakhalin. Bezbryzhii had had only one month of service left and had been loved by fellow soldiers and command alike; even many of the officers who knew of the incident were on his side. Although the court had followed the letter of the law, could not Father John persuade the Emperor to show mercy?⁹¹

Father John's status as holy defender of such "little people" extended beyond the Orthodox community. Roman Catholics, Jews, and Muslims within the Russian Empire also enlisted him in their service. In February 1898, for example, he received a plea from Magomet Rakhim Abdraimov and Akhmet Amirov, who mentioned that they heard from many people that his prayers could rescue one in minutes of unjust accusation:

> On June 10, 1897, some Kirghiz attacked our herd; they stole several horses and rams. Our comrade, Usendbai Kharanbaev, was attacked, and subsequently died. Evidence in the form of the animals' skins and heads was found after we reported the incident to the district leader. The two Kirghiz initially testified that the attack-theft had indeed occurred, but they were then bought off (along with two others) and accused *us* of killing him. We have been sentenced to eight years. We have filed complaints to the Senate, but to no avail.
>
> Please pray for us to the Almighty Judge who sees our innocence clearly. We are sure that your holy prayer will free us from undeserved punishment.⁹²

Part of this openness lies in the general Muslim acceptance of such Christian holy figures as Mary and Saint George the Dragon-Slayer. But the very fact that people approached Father John in this way shows that he had already become the kind of "transconfessional" holy figure who crossed denominational lines even as he defended Orthodoxy. In fact, given later representations of Father John as an obscurantist, it is instructive to note that during his lifetime he was not perceived as such by many people from other confessions; they considered him to be an impartial authority. In their letters, it is clear that his unique charisma was far more decisive than his being an Orthodox priest. Thus Nikolai Shanshiev explained that he had been born and baptized into the Armenian (Monophysite) faith, but knew no Armenian and had been going to a Russian (Orthodox) church from childhood. He now sought Father John's advice on whether he would be committing apostasy if he converted from the faith of his fathers: "I will tell you frankly, I would not approach anyone else so boldly with this kind of a request, but you are *first of all* a staunch, sincere follower of the Divine Christ, and *only then* an Orthodox priest. I believe deeply and sincerely that it means more to you to save and admonish a wavering soul than to fulfill any missionary obligation."[93]

Gottfried von Dorn, an eighteen-year-old Lutheran student in the Sea Cadet Corps, expressed similar sentiments in 1900. After learning that the Orthodox faith had seven sacraments to Lutheranism's two, he turned to Father John to learn just what the differences between the two faiths were. He cautioned that he saw no need to convert because he thought all religions were the same, and added that he was writing precisely because he wanted an objective opinion: "Here in the corps you cannot talk of such things, for everyone is partial to one or the other side."[94] The question of conversion seems to have been particularly charged for Father John's Jewish correspondents. Lazar Satz, for example, wrote Father John several times, outlining his desire to be a true Jew—and at the same time feeling uncertain as to whether he should convert, as had his brother. Especially striking is that, like Shanshiev, Satz clearly felt that he could trust Father John to provide an impartial opinion and asked for his prayers in any case.[95]

This high regard for Father John by the non-Orthodox extended outside the boundaries of the Russian Empire. Not only did people write to him from places ranging from Austria to the United States, they also came to see him in person. French admirals, Anglican divines, German tourists—all considered him a necessary part of their visit to Russia. One of Thomas Edison's students even recorded his voice on a phonograph, so that Father John's spoken greeting to Bishop Nikolai of Alaska may yet surface. This recognition by foreigners only reinforced his reputation in Russia as "a *universal* phenomenon."[96]

Prayers, Advice, Guidance, and Moral Support

While healing was the traditional prerogative of the holy man, and material help the patron's, Father John was just as important in the sphere associated with an elder (*starets*): advice and guidance. Letters asking for moral support make up almost as large a category as healing and material help. [97] It is these confiding letters that show how often the people who wrote to Father John craved not only a listener, but someone who could speak with Divine authority and advise them correctly, or otherwise take salvific charge of their fates. Women (twice as often as men) wrote him long letters asking for spiritual counsel, describing their lives in great detail. It is in these letters that one begins to understand how much he meant to the women who turned to him and how dependent they were on him, as was Olga:

> My darling Batiushka, please do not rebuke me in thine anger, neither turn me away from your generous and merciful protection and aright my fate because I cannot manage to direct myself.... I entrust myself to your hands like raw clay and ceaselessly entreat you, make this clay into God's vessel in order to accommodate the word of God and to preserve forever unto the ages. Please tell me directly where and how I ought to live.[98]

For some, he supplanted both traditional family ties and those of religious hierarchy:

> I have only one comfort in life, and that is when I write you all my sins—and when you accept them, dear one, I firmly believe that the Lord will forgive me.... Oh, how fortunate I would be if God were to bring me to have you hear my confession privately if I die ... remember me then, your prayers will rescue my soul from Gehenna. I have no more relatives or parents, and *their prayers are sinful anyway; you are the only one who is pleasing to God*.[99]

Most often, however, women described their own inner lives. In a pattern familiar in Medieval Europe, they told Father John that they wanted to live more piously, but felt constrained by their material realities, most often in the form of their families. Unmarried women who wanted to stop working for the family and to join a religious community reported opposition by their parents, especially by their mothers.[100] And, even more often than children against parents, spouses complained about one another. In a pattern familiar from women saints' lives, wives depicted husbands as being obstacles to their spirituality, particularly when it came to performing acts of charity.

Aleksandra Zelenova described the conflicts that could arise between spouses when one was significantly more pious than the other. Most notable is that, as an Orthodox Christian woman, she understood that she was supposed to obey her husband. But what was she to do when he did not act in a godly way? In a letter typically laden with Church Slavonicisms, she wrote:

> In the name of the Father and the Son and the Holy Spirit, Amen. Holy Father John, hear me from the depths of my heart. I cry unto you, help me with your word and your admonition. And I will accept it as the word of God. I am perishing in a life of sin and there is no understanding of God's will in me [*nest' vo mne razumeniia voli Bozhiei*]. I truly want to be saved and to enter into the knowledge of truth [*v razum istinnyi priiti*], but I do not know the true path on which I should go.
>
> I have been living as a married woman for five years now. My husband leads a sinful life, destroying both himself and me, and rages [*neistovstvuet*] against me, destroying my body and soul. I am suffering both physically and spiritually, and my spiritual torments sometimes surpass my strength, so that sometimes I all but despair of my salvation.

Occasionally, Zelenova would be driven to deciding that it would be better to pursue her own salvation and leave her husband, who both drank and insisted on sexual relations during the periods when the Church enjoined abstinence, and would go to stay with her relatives. When she did so, however, she felt anguish of another sort. While she could pray better in her parents' home and generally felt relieved, she wondered whether she was not going against God's will by leaving her husband. As she explained:

> When I am with my husband, I recall the words of the Gospel (that who loves father or mother or whomever more than Me is not worthy of me), and think that I am breaking God's commandment, in that I am fulfilling my husband's desire rather than God's will. But when I leave, then I suffer again, for I am sorry for my husband and think that without me, he will perish completely, and then recall the Gospel paralytic (whom He (the Savior) healed because of the faith of others).

Zeleneva sees the root of the problem in her ignorance, to which she frequently alludes. If she were sufficiently holy to be discerning, then her duty—that is, God's will—would be clear to her. But, for all that she has wracked her brain, it is not. She wants Father John to act as a spiritual father and to show her the way she ought to follow:

I beg you, Holy Father John, do not leave me without a word and do not disdain [*vozgnushaites'*] my sinfulness and my ignorance, that [*aki*] the fire of despair not consume me. My husband almost always goes drinking and wants there to be money for this and says I don't know how to live and that I spend everything and give it to my relatives and that he drinks because of me—while I suffer because I am living without doing anything good, and my works [income] do not go to God or to good deeds. Write me how I should live and *may I spend the money I earn myself as I wish without my husband's knowing, because he does not allow me to do anything good, and in what I should submit to him and what I should resist.* Help me as the one who was once [*nekogda*] wounded [*uiazvlennyi*] by brigands.... I know I am unworthy, but even the dogs eat the crumbs that fall from their masters' table.[101]

To women as pious as Zelenova, Father John offered one of the only legitimate venues at their disposal for escaping or subverting the authority of their husbands. Women who were not religious did not need his sanction in the same way, of course; they could find it in the protofeminist arguments that had come to the fore from the 1850s onward with the discussion of the "woman question." Women who wanted to live up to Orthodox notions of virtue, however, understood perfectly the potential contradiction involved in "Serve God above all" and "Wives, submit yourselves to your husbands in all things," or even "Honor thy father and thy mother." In their eyes, Father John was the only hope of reconciling the irreconcilable.

Men expressed also spiritual seeking and restlessness, but almost never mentioned parents. Unlike the prototypes depicted in the lives of the male saints, whose family conflicts focus on mothers—but exactly like their counterparts in the Pious Strugglers of Everyday series—their religiosity often seems to emerge as a rebellion against their married state, and focuses on their wives and children. A blind young man who had been married for three years wanted to know, for example, "Where is it better for me to be saved, should I leave my wife and children or not?"[102] Mothers, too, could perceive their children as being utterly incidental to the larger problem of their own spiritual lives—or even as posing the chief obstacle. For people hemmed in by family pressures, religion—and especially Father John's blessing—could provide a socially sanctioned escape. On July 23, 1899, the mostly literate Vasilii and Paraskeva Raspopov described the unhappy situation of one of their friends:

> One night after she had thoroughly scolded her child she went to sleep and in her dream saw the Lord Himself crucified on the cross and the Queen of Heaven suddenly she leapt up! very frightened and said a prayer, then went back to sleep ... and what do you think has happened to her since then? Although she goes to church, she rails and swears at the Lord Himself and the Mother of God and all the saints, and foul words never quit her mind. She used to be such a pious, God-fearing woman and what has happened to her now is very bad, she cries about it day and night and wants to abandon her children and leave to—she herself doesn't know where. She asks you, Batiushka, will you bless her to go on this path or not? She has four children, one smaller than the next, and she is very poor and sends you one ruble, please advise her in writing.[103]

In other words, since the children have caused the cursing, fleeing them may cure it. Whether or not it involved a step as dramatic as the leaving of one's family, however, many correspondents reported a desire to devote more of their lives to spiritual concerns, particularly as they grew older. While many historians have sketched the pattern of a cyclical religiosity in women's lives, suggesting that many women had to delay their religious impulses until they had fulfilled their childbearing and child-raising obligations, this phenomenon was not uniquely feminine.[104] Especially in peasant culture, becoming increasingly observant, fasting more strictly, celibacy, and reading only religious literature (if one were literate, of course) were respected, and sometimes expected hallmarks, of one's later years.[105] The pattern of later-life religiosity was not restricted to the peasantry, however. A 46-year-old man in government service could also express a desire to spend the remaining years of his life in repentance, and become psalm-reader in the Nativity church before the icon "Search for the Lost."[106]

A recurrent theme in the letters that people sent Father John is their spiritual isolation and their wishing they had someone to talk to about their inner lives. Their writing to him in such numbers, particularly from the provinces, suggests that other social and religious forums were not enough. People wrote to him because they wanted to both share their spiritual experiences and be guided by a reliable authority. When they felt that they had seen something extraordinary in the religious sphere, they approached Father John with none of the diffidence of those asking for money or prayers. It is as if being privy to an insight or vision gave them freedom or parity in approaching him. The barely literate Lukullian, for example, began his letter to Father John with the familiar *"Golubushka!"* and asks for his blessing: "I don't need earthly pleasures. My dearie, there would be no greater happiness on this earth if you would visit my humble cell, I need to tell you a great secret."[107]

Not only visions emboldened people in addressing him; the subject matter of those visions also led them to believe that they had been entrusted with a grave responsibility. The Tsar, and more broadly the notion of Russia's fate, figure prominently in virtually all of the visions that people reported to Father John. The eldress Evdokiia, for example, wanted to tell Their Imperial Majesties that they could find a great amount of gold and old weapons below the icon of the Kazan Mother of God, "but without your advice, Father John, I daren't do anything about this."[108] A mostly literate woman wrote him that "the great elder, Father Kornilii," had given her a prophecy to disseminate that had been revealed to him by the Lord Himself, "that great sorrows will befall our Sovereign and all Russia will weep everyone from the oldest to the youngest will suffer and there will never have been such a calamity as this." She wanted to carry out the command, but was not sure of how to proceed.[109]

It cannot be emphasized strongly enough that visions and prophecies were not the exclusive province of peasants, the uneducated, or the poor. Even someone as educated as Prince Vladimir Bariatinskii felt it "his sacred duty" to advise Father John by telegram from Tsarskoe Selo in April 1905 of a message from the beyond received by the American widow of Meissner, a former bureaucrat in the Ministry of the Interior. While praying at her son's grave in Tiflis (Tbilisi) for God to help Russia in the war with Japan, she heard a voice saying, "Until Russia turns to the Lord with prayer and fasts for a week, she will not be in a condition to overcome the foe!" Madame Meissner asked whether the requirements of fasting applied to the armed forces as well as to the rest of the country, and was told, "Of course not, as they have to preserve all their strength for the work which has been laid upon them!" When she asked the voice how she was supposed to tell the Russian people, she was told to tell Prince Bariatinskii and his wife, who must then tell Father John, who would in turn notify the people. The voice assured Madame Meissner not to doubt for an instant—this was the will of the Father of Heaven—and warned that if Russians did not turn to God for the requisite week of prayer and fasting, they would never recover from the consequences of the war.[110]

The apocalyptic quality of such visions was not new, but the predictions of doom for both the Tsar and the Russian Empire were. With the assassination of Alexander II in 1881, nationalities tensions, the explosion of terrorism, and the 1905 revolution, the visions' dread reflected real political and social anxieties, as did their counterparts in contemporary France.[111] Father John was the clergyman in Late Imperial Russia most consistently associated with dire predictions of Russia's impending fate. Did these visions, from so wide a range of sources, influence his own? Or did people simply wish him to confirm their prophecies with the help of his discernment? In either case, the similarity between the visions of Father John and those who wrote to him offers another reason for his popularity. His eschatological religiosity was perfectly attuned to that of the people who sought him out, and as far as could be from the contemporary "progressive trend" in academic theology.[112]

Here a clear difference between laity and clergy emerges. Unless their vision is sinister, laypeople delightedly shared their glimpses of the other world with Father John. Monks and nuns, by contrast, wanted to determine whether even apparently benevolent ones had not come from the Devil. Letters from clerics deserve special mention for other reasons. While Father John provided an example to many laypeople, he played an even more focused role in the lives of the clerical estate. Parish priests approached him for both professional and spiritual advice, reflecting the social orientation of the post-Emancipation parish clergy, and expressing a collegiality testifying to the social nearness they felt to him, rather than his distance. The solidarity of the parish clergy Manchester has identified transcended fame, fortune, and even holiness.[113]

More surprising, given the mutual suspicion that often existed between the "black" (monastic) and "white" (married) clergy, is the extent to which Father John attracted monks and nuns. After all, although nuns might maintain a lively contact with their relatives and intercede on behalf of other women, the monastic community was nonetheless a relatively closed environment, with discipline and obedience to one's superior enforced quite strictly. Most monks and nuns had few resources outside their monasteries to which they might turn.[114]

Father John's close relation with nuns and convents is more understandable than it initially appears, however. In more than a few ways, they shared a common lot. Priests in general (and Father John in particular) and nuns were more involved in works of charity and education, and more intimately involved in ministering to the lay communities around them than their monk counterparts. Both groups were far from the networks of episcopal power and prestige (although it was possible for a widowed priest to become a bishop, as was the case of Savva Tikhomirov, this was not common). In their service and lack of access to power, priests were the symbolic women in the all-male Orthodox hierarchy.[115] It is because of this perceived similarity of aims and lives that Father Georgii Shavel'skii, the Protopresbyter of the armed forces, wrote enthusiastically of the convents he had known and saved his bitterest criticisms for monks and monasteries.[116] It is also because of the greater activity of nuns in directly serving the poor, the needy, and the orphaned, that Father John threw far more of his support behind convents and nuns than behind men's monasteries, founding three convents and funding countless others.[117]

Nuns and Convents

Some of the nuns' letters to Father John dealt with practical problems —being transferred to another convent, writing on behalf of alcoholics, and so on. Many more, however, sought out Father John's advice on their spiritual lives, such as mastering the Jesus Prayer.[118] This is less surprising than it might seem. As a rule, the priest-confessor assigned to convents was not an ordained monk, but a married priest. This was done on pragmatic grounds: nuns, the hierarchy reasoned, would be less likely to fantasize about or approach a married priest; the priest himself, safely married, would be less likely to be drawn to his spiritual charges. While there is little evidence that romantic temptations were successfully minimized in this approach, it is clear that having a married priest for a confessor was not the most spiritually useful choice for nuns. The temptations, obligations, and potential for spiritual sophistication were quite different for a nun who was pursuing chastity, and a married priest who had family responsibilities. Moreover, some priests actually mistrusted the monastic life and sought to minimize the ascetic attempts of their charges.[119]

Abbesses, who were women with years of spiritual effort and discipline behind them, found it even more difficult to identify ordained clergy who could serve as companions and guides in the spiritual life. Some of them turned to such celebrated elders as those of Optina or Feofan the Recluse. Remarkably, however, in a testimony of how highly religious "professionals" perceived his progress in the spiritual life, others turned to Father John.[120]

Here, also, the relation between Father John and his correspondents was not one-sided. He valued the opportunity to have spiritual discussions with people whom he regarded as peers, especially Abbess Taisiia of Leushino. The publication and wide distribution of their correspondence, and Taisiia's later memoirs of her relationship with Father John, suggests that the edifying epistolary dialogue was a recognized genre with a large enough audience to warrant wide distribution. Taisiia's correspondence with a novice and the letters of Feofan the Recluse to an unnamed woman also fall into this category. Father John's presence in this company is unusual not in form or content but in his being a married priest advising nuns and monks rather the other way round.

Letters written by the monks resemble those of the nuns, indicating that both sexes shared the temptations of monastic life—disagreements within the community, physical attraction to a community member, whether or not to proceed to the next stage of the monastic life, and so on.[121] Because the monks could also be ordained priests, however, they had explicitly pastoral concerns, for which they turned to Father John—most of the concerns being those for which they could not readily find an answer, and thus comparable to the concern with classification Orthodox laity showed about the dead. One hieromonk, for example, wanted to know whether or not he should commemorate an apostate who had been ripped apart by wolves. Another hieromonk from Albania related in 1903 that local Muslims who were ill or suffering would come to his monastery and ask him to pray over them. He was afraid to bring holiness in the form of the Gospel, his stole, and so on, into contact with them, and asked Father John how best to proceed.[122] These were purely pastoral problems, virtually identical to similar questions posed by married priests.

But there were also questions specific to monks. The most spectacular example of monastic bewilderment before the ills and complexity of life in the world came from Hieromonk Kirill, an Athonite monk who had spent most of his life on the celebrated island of all-masculine monasticism. He had recently been reassigned to Odessa to the affiliate (*podvor'e*) of the Athos Monastery of St. Panteleimon and was stumped by the variety and gravity of the sins he now had to encounter.

> I have never had to encounter confessees like the ones in Odessa ... and because of this it is hard for me to absolve great sins at confession. At the same time, I don't see how I can apply the church strictures in all their force, and so I am utterly baffled as to what to do. Here are the most puzzling questions:
> 1. May one absolve a murderer who has committed this sin only

a few days before confessing it, and what sort of an *epitimia* (penance) should one give him?

2. May one absolve—and give the Holy Mysteries to: 1) a fornicator; 2) an adulterer; 3) men who commit bestiality (*skotolozhnik*); 4) a pederast (*muzhelozhnik*)—who committed the sin a few days ago? What sort of a penance should I give him?

3. What do I say to people who are living in sin, and do not want to stop?

4. What do I say to a married couple that practices withdrawal to avoid having children?

5. What do I say to men who lie with men, and women who lie with women?

6. Can lawful spouses who have had intercourse the previous night be allowed to communion?

7. May lawful spouses who have had relations "through the back way" be absolved? What about unlawful [unmarried] ones? And what sort of penance should they receive?[123]

One longs for Father John's response to letters like these. As well as providing a rare glimpse of sexual mores, including abstinence before communion, they also show that monks like Father Kirill, as well as laypeople and abbesses, sought out Father John for matters they did not feel they could entrust to anyone else. That they would approach a married priest attests to both his spiritual standing in the entire community of believers, without the usual division of laity, parish clergy, and monastics, and the extent to which those in every category could turn to him as a way of circumventing or supplementing their usual chain of command, without actually undermining it.

Gifts and Donations

The place that Father John held in people's minds and hearts can be gauged by the kinds of gifts, as well as the requests, he received. Poorer and less literate people, in particular, accompanied with a donation their request to pray for someone. Even when peasants had spent all their money on a trip to Kronstadt, they would still try to offer something to him, whether "two pounds of spruce oil and a little sugar (eat it in good health, our kind shepherd)"; a handkerchief, a towel, or a flower.[124] This pattern is strikingly absent among the nobility, who rarely referred to payment for services rendered. Either they considered the transfer (or the direct mention) of money somehow indelicate, or hoped to avoid it.

The gifts to Father John fall mostly into three categories: (1) posthumous gifts in people's last wills and testaments; (2) "Please pray for X and by the way have some Y," or (3) "Please accept N [rubles] and use them as you see fit." Whether or not the gifts are linked to gratitude, services hoped-for in advance, or as payment for services rendered, they convey the sentiment that Father John deserved something for his efforts. Their range is striking: he was offered everything from two hundred thousand rubles to six silver spoons and a bracelet.[125] He received carriages made in Novo-Petrovsk, cases of vodka from the Samsonov plant, fish conserves from Tomsk, and boxes of Orlov apples from Mtsensk. Both men and women often expressed their love in the form of handmade objects, such as a casket made by Georgii, the venerable recluse of Zadonsk, and countless embroidered belts, cuffs, down-filled gloves, and "a pair of warm socks I knitted myself."[126]

Gifts of this sort could make trouble for Father John. Echoing, "Why was this ointment not sold and the proceeds given to the poor?," hostile writers from both Protestant groups and the radical intelligentsia criticized Father John for appearing in costly clothing.[127] But the criticisms did not stick. Leaving aside the general acceptance of beauty and sumptuousness in liturgical art characteristic of both Orthodoxy and Roman Catholicism, most people understood the dynamics of gifts to a beloved person from the clergy. Hermione, the abbess of the Kliuchegorskii Kazansko-Bogoroditskii convent in Kuzushchagii uezd, for example, described how she and her sisters had sewn him satin vestments painted with gold. Father John would have had to have a heart of stone to resist the pleas of such women who had poured all of their energies into making something beautiful in the expressed hope that he would wear it "at least once." Moreover, liturgical vestments were something that could be easily passed on and given to others. Father John passed on many of his gifts to needy clerics, including a sick priest who wanted to die in one of John's old cassocks, and left detailed instructions in his will as to which priests would receive his cassocks, *riasa*s, and mitres.[128] In making a personal donation to Father John, people were making a donation to the Church.

The pragmatic approach of the givers and the nature of Father John's charity emerged in the kinds of gifts he received. It made sense for Voronezh merchants to send six sacks of buckwheat grain complete with a hulling mill, for liquor store owners to send bottles of wine, and for fishmongers to send marinated pressed caviar and smoked sterlet:

while Father John could not have eaten and drunk everything himself, he had several convents and the House of Industry to provide for. The old tradition of donating food, fruit, or wine to a monastery or convent on the anniversary of the death of a family member now assumed new forms: cafeterias from the House and other shelters, for example, provided opportunities for potential donors to sponsor commemorative meals for deceased loved ones.[129] If Father John's charity were still private and individual, it would have been difficult for him to use or dispose of all the in-kind donations; with all the poor who used the House of Industry daily, one could be assured that one's pickles, cabbage, and marinated mushrooms would find a good home and that the endeavor would be as "soul-saving" as the previous approach, which had focused on monastery donations. Similarly, knowing the extent to which Father John was besieged by poor clergy and churches, a man from Nizhnii Novgorod could send a set of liturgical vessels with instructions to give them to whoever needed them most.[130] Just as Father John was at the center of a network of prayer, then, so he was also the animator of a network of material support. Those who received something from him knew that they were not only getting it from him or from God, but from some concrete person as well, just as the givers knew that the eventual receivers would be linked with them and with Father John in love and God, in a new interpretation of traditional charity.[131]

While the emphasis on the personal may have been traditional, the form was not. The donations to Father John illustrate a gradual sea change in the patterns of Russian giving linked with the commemoration of the dead. While many people simply willed their money to him with the request to pray for the soul of "N," others asked his explicit guidance. He almost invariably suggested some cause that helped the poor rather than an ecclesiastical institution focused exclusively on prayer—a convent which was also a shelter and orphanage, or a parish church and school, for example.[132] In keeping with the old idea that the gifts most beneficial in a spiritual sense were anonymous ones, the givers invariably requested that "this holy deed remain between the two of us"—as, for example, when Aleksei Maitov wanted to commemorate his relatives by building a parish church in Siberia, "or anywhere in our Mother Russia, for that matter."[133] In many cases, the givers wrote that they did not feel competent to distribute their money in the most effective way; Father John knew which churches were neediest.[134]

As in other aspects of Russian religiosity, then, while Father John's emphasis on charity modified the traditional form of commemorating the dead, it also reinforced the general impulse to express charity in forms sanctified by the Church. And, as in other aspects of religiosity, the notion of Father John as patron extended to include the Tsar. Father John became not only the mediator between God and giver, but also between Tsar and giver. While his presumed closeness to the Tsar appeared more often in the context of helping people find jobs or commuting their prison sentences, in the context of gifts it was linked to popular affection for the monarchy. Just as Queen Victoria and Prince Albert received an eleven-hundred-pound round of cheese as a wedding gift from the farmers of the Cheddar district, so Father John was asked to pass along gifts to the Tsar. A barely literate letter from Evdokim Makarov Meshkov in Tver guberniia, who sent some honey, brings this out:

> I have the honor of presenting you with a little present from my bees and ask your blessing for this my production. I am also desirous of obtaining your portrait as a souvenir and as a blessing.
>
> Second, I would like to present my bee gift to our young Sovereign. This gift I would like to present for the year 1893, for the beekeeping exhibition. This exhibition enlightened me, it showed me all there was to know about raising bees and I wish to thank [him] for the way which was shown to me.
>
> But I am a peasant and barely literate, I learned at home I was never in any school anywhere, but I was in Moscow at the coronation of Alexander III. And also at Nicholas II.... The monarchs gave me an honorary certificate and the bee-keeping exhibition also awarded me with a certificate in bee-keeping. I would like to thank him for all of this but because I am a peasant and don't know who I can send it through please tell me how I might.[135]

The Attribution of Holiness and Its Impact on Father John

While Father John's responses to these letters were not collected, his response to the attention he received survives in his diaries. The key was that people responded to him *because* God had shown him favor. To someone who attached as much importance as did Father John to being a vessel and a priest of God, this recognition was a vindication, a sign that both *vox populi* and *vox Dei* had acknowledged his efforts. The efforts of decades had finally borne their fruit, creating the ideal union between people, priest, and God of which he had dreamed. He could barely contain the joy he felt at being the instrument of this unity. As he wrote in his notebook in 1894:

> What a great, untold wonder of God's mercy to me—that all the pious Orthodox Christians across the entire expanse of the Russian land are well-disposed to me and feel trust and love for me, and that for such a disposition and trust on their part the grace of God visits them and rescues them from ills and sicknesses, sorrows and attacks, when the Orthodox turn to me personally, by letter, and telegraph.[136]

Father John's perception of his own role is very revealing. He believed that people's devotion to him was an extension of their devotion to God. Moreover, he was God's representative, in the sense that devotion and respect to him found favor in God's sight. This identification of self with God came, of course, perilously close to the spiritual delusion technically described as *prelest'* (delusion).[137] Father John understood this. He sought to counter this risk by repeatedly reminding himself of the sources of his power: God, the liturgy, and especially the Eucharist. As he wrote on December 26, 1893:

> The grace of God which dwells in me *thanks to my sincere faith and prayer, because of my frequent, reverent partaking of the Holy Mysteries*, has made me dear, esteemed, glorified, and loved throughout all the ends of Russia and even outside it. And so I value the grace of God, truth, and holiness in myself with all my being and at all times and may I remain in truth and holiness for the glory of God and for the good of myself and others.[138]

On the face of it, this seems to be an unusually meritorious notion of grace. The more conventional interpretation is that grace is freely given by God and can vanish as quickly as it came, regardless of how hard the recipient thinks she or he is working for it.[139] Father John, however, had worked for grace more assiduously than most and did not minimize his own role in the process of its acquisition. His prayers now extended his boldness in addressing God for others to asking God for this grace to continue working through him.

By the 1890s, it seemed that he had all an aspiring saint could desire. God favored him, people all over the world acknowledged him, and a daily stream of healings testified to his unique access to grace. But precisely at the point when he appeared to be most securely a man of

God, the very things that had been the sources of his spiritual strength seemed to sap his time and energy. The Eucharist, of which he could still exclaim, "What wondrous, heavenly grace—partaking of the Holy Mysteries! What renewal! what heavenly peace! what lightness, sweetness!—what is earthly life after this? What is delight in food and drink?," was now also a stumbling-block to seeing as many people as possible.[140] He had to see people in order to pray for them and to perform the services they requested—and, by doing so, to raise money for the many social and religious projects and poor individuals he supported. In themselves these were laudable purposes. In becoming a public holy figure, however, Father John had to struggle to maintain that which had nourished him as a private one.

His notebooks reflect this struggle. During the 1880s, Father John first mentioned his irritation with people, particularly children, who went frequently to communion—the very thing he had once so ardently desired. He wrote in 1882: "I feel such ire at seeing them [children] brought up, and brought up so often, and I complain—I, who have communion every day, begrudge it to these beloved of the Lord."[141] Long lines at the chalice meant less time for *molebens*, to be sure. But why single out children? Perhaps because he did not have his own, Father John explained his antipathy to infants being brought to communion in terms of their lack of consciousness.

> They are also worthy of the Gifts, *although they do not recognize their importance and salvific quality*. I think, "They are brought up often—what for?"—and how much more often than they do I, a wretch, take communion—and remain a sinner? I should rejoice that, if there are no adults, at least children are sharing the immortal, spiritual meal with me. And remember what the Lord said to the disciples when they wanted to keep the children from going to Him.[142]

Less evident in Father John's objection to children's, and, later, certain adults', receiving communion was its frequency. Here the difference between Roman Catholic and Orthodox practice is instructive. The debate between infant versus adult baptism and communion in the early Church resulted in the adoption by the Orthodox of the position that the child, having a soul, ought to be baptized and given communion as soon as possible. In Roman Catholic practice, an infant was also baptized immediately, but communion was withheld until the age of seven. Orthodox children were first given confession at the "conscious" age of seven as well, but could receive Communion immediately after baptism; in fact, they could theoretically (like Father John) partake every day.[143] In response to his directions to partake more frequently, ever more Kronstadt mothers began to take advantage of this opportunity, thus occupying an ever-greater amount of Father John's time. More adults began to appear from the 1880s onward as well.

By the 1880s, Father John was so busy that his diary largely served as an appointment-book, and he often found his attention wandering to thoughts of the appointments he had to keep after the service rather than the liturgy itself. As early as 1883, he repented privately for his heart's not lying with his spiritual children when he confessed them, "but with the desire to finish as soon as possible so as to gather a more abundant [financial] harvest."[144] He had to plan his day minutely by that time, and knew that an early upset in his plans would create a domino effect, upsetting the hopes of many who had carefully arranged to see him later in the day. For all his care, this happened often. In the mid 1880s, letters to him begin to contain such reproaches as, "Please be so kind as to designate once again a time for our child's baptism.... We waited for you on Thursday from five to nine o'clock."[145]

The pressure to meet those who clamored to see him was constant. Father John had succeeded only too well. The sins for which he repented most frequently from the 1880s onward included "carelessness in prayer, extreme rushing, and occasionally lack of reverence to the holy work at hand."[146] All of these tendencies are, of course, occupational hazards, an inuring to the aspects of one's profession that were once so fresh and inspiring. His enchantment with serving the liturgy might have paled even without public attribution of holiness to him and the consequent demands for his extraliturgical services. Nevertheless, it is clear that the pressure to run to his appointments rather than a loss of reverence for the sacred as such, that now prompted Father John to race through his services. "Because I was hurrying to St. Petersburg," he confessed to his notebook in the late 1890s, "I rushed my *molebny*, especially the last one, and was punished with constriction and sorrow, and managed to regain [my] peace and boldness [before God] only with great effort."[147]

Father John was cornered. Every day, he received letters with piteous pleas for material help. In an extension of his principle of charity to everyone, he could leave no plea unanswered—hence, the endless pressure to bring in as much money as possible. On the other hand, he could hardly minimize the importance of communion only on the grounds that he was more busy. To make matters worse, as more people wished to have Father John come to their houses, so also many more wished to confess to and take communion from him. These mutually exclusive demands could strain him to the breaking point. As he wrote of a liturgy with many communicants in 1894:

> At the beginning I willingly and fervently give communion to people of every estate and income, but by the end I start to give way to impatience and disappointment, as if forgetting what great work I am doing ... and where do I hasten so from this work? To worldly distraction and vanity, to the satisfaction of my avarice, to gluttony, to love for this world, which is hostile to God! Then I repent.[148]

Ironically, then, the achievement of one his goals for Russian Orthodox Christians—more frequent communion and a more active sacramental life generally—meant as a consequence less time to devote to others outside the church building.

Father John's celebrity had other deleterious effects on the quality of his religious life. His sense of himself as a universal intercessor for the Russian land, which had begun to appear in the 1880s and was full-blown by the 1890s, came into conflict with his continuing responsibilities as a parish priest. Even as he traveled to the capital nearly every day, he still had to reckon with the requests of his Kronstadt parishioners—especially those of the poor, who had been his original constituency—for routine clerical services. He felt the tension keenly:

> Soon after the liturgy and after having partaken of the Holy Mysteries I was irritated and angry with my parishioners who had asked me to visit their sick with the Holy Gifts—because I had wanted, out of avarice, to make the rounds of the visitors by serving *molebens* and then to go to Petersburg for prayers and making money—even though the money is for charity and almsgiving.[149]

As the letters to him demonstrate, Father John had become a fulcrum for charitable donations: those who wished to help the poor sent their contributions to him, secure in the knowledge that it would help the "deserving" poor. As the scale of the giving increased, it created circumstances he had not foreseen: rather than being able to catch up with the needs of the poor, the poor themselves seemed to multiply like mushrooms. Petitioners began to haunt his every step, waiting outside his house and St. Andrew's for him to appear. He came to feel the persistence of the poor as a crushing burden and to dread going outside at all. For all of his recognizing the spiritual importance of giving charity, he began to feel the tension between his role as a prayerful intercessor for people and their priest—and as the giver who supported them materially. His diary entries reveal moments of crushing sadness at feeling unable to both pray and physically help. As he wrote on February 20, 1882:

> Today I became extremely upset because of the paupers, particularly because of the girls to whom I had given alms (2½ kopecks each) who continued to follow me even afterward, although I deliberately tried to go away from them, wishing to pray alone. Then about forty grown-up paupers came to me asking and I, already having been vexed by the persistent girls, flared up at the adults, sending them to the city's rich.—At the end of it all I was all morally shattered and came home.... I was forgiven by prayer in front of the Tikhvin icon of the Mother of God.[150]

It was both spiritually and materially vital to find some way of accommodating these conflicting pressures. Father John tried to accustom his seekers to certain patterns of giving, such as having them form lines of twenty and giving each "captain" a sum to distribute among his or her "regiment," but such efforts were in vain.[151] He became so hounded by the poor that he literally had to flee them. "Forgive me for running away from the pauper who was chasing me," he confessed to his diary in 1882. "I was saying to myself, 'I will give to everyone at their own time, at 3 o'clock, but I do not want to give at *every* place and *every* time, because there are so many, many of them.'"[152] Building the House of Industry had neither eased his burden nor lessened his sense that he must give to the poor directly, not through an institution, even one that he himself founded and financed. Indeed, the greater his fame for holiness and charity, the more supplicants appeared to feel that he was theirs rather than his own. Father John's early declarations that "the priest belongs to everyone, not to himself," had come true to an extent he had not anticipated.

The sense of the poor closing in inexorably about him, and of the holy man as public property, emerged palpably in Father John's notebooks from the 1880s onward. Seekers haunted his door and flocked around him to a degree that surpassed that of almost any other public figure. Although observers wrote admiringly of his serenity, his nerves were actually stretched to the breaking point. When he first became a sought-after celebrity, he swung from one extreme to another. He wrote in his diary in 1883:

> Today I did not go out on the street from six to eleven-thirty—so that I would not have to encounter the paupers who were awaiting my exit and my dole—but when I did finally go out, it was just my luck to encounter five of them (there had been a doling-out to the poor earlier, only not to this lot). I gave them two kopecks each, and one annoying boy began to beg persistently for more, and in vexation at him I thrashed him by the hair and went along the trading-quarter street for a walk (my head was pounding). The paupers came after me again, especially the deaf and one-eyed one; I grew angry at him because of his insistence and his persecuting me and firmly, with both hands, thrashed him by the hair; the others were frightened and went ahead quickly; I went ahead also; the one-eyed pauper at the end of the street came up to me again and I felt sorry for him—I gave him twenty kopecks, called over two more of them as well, and gave them ten kopecks each; then I got angry again and wanted to hit the big young fellow good and hard, but he ran away; then the boys began to pester me again and I ordered the policeman to take him away to the station for cadging. The boy started to cry, and I said to let him go. I have sinned, and I blame myself. I repent before the Lord, the Mother of God, all the saints, and all people.[153]

While Father John made no excuses for his behavior, it is a measure both of contemporary acceptance of corporal punishment—and their dependency on him—that his supplicants did not seem to find it unduly harsh. In fact, it attracted no mention whatsoever. Although father John blamed himself for "these crude manifestations of impatience and hard-hearted spite," there is no sense that his thrashing paupers or pulling them by the hair was anything more than "crude" or anything unusual; the relation between a holy man and his followers could clearly encompass an extraordinarily elastic range of behavior.[154]

Because of their growing clamor, Father John's assessment of the poor as a group began to change during the early 1880s. Their persistence was a far cry from the restraint he had noted in 1868, when he wrote, "One should always give poor boys alms with pleasure: they ask out of desperate need and, having received a sufficient amount, do not come asking again for a long time."[155] But here is a difference between a saint and a private citizen. When Father John had been regarded simply as an unusually kind-hearted priest rather than a holy man, the poor were more diffident about asking for help, and he was more inclined to be touched at their plight, vigorously defending them against accusations of vagrancy. Although he attempted even in the first years of his career to see to it that the money he gave away would not be misused, at that time he was less inclined to reproach those whom he suspected of abusing his confidence, and more intent on preserving his inner equilibrium. As he wrote in 1869: "If you know for certain that the paupers to whom you give money use it for bad purposes, do not become angry at them, but maintain your mildness and gentleness, laughing with them like Paul the Simple. Is it worth getting upset over money (which is ashes)?—remember your own life, sins, and circumstances before blaming them."[156]

By the mid-1880s, by contrast, his response was much more hard ("I condemn myself for my extreme fury at the paupers who follow me every day in a group—they are idle, with nothing to do, and ask me to give generously with insolent persistence").[157] Just as the poor had moved away from recognizing the individuality and mortal flesh of Father John and treated him as the repository of their demands, so he had become more inclined to treat them as a collective to whom he owed impersonal charity. This process of increasing impersonality on the part of both seekers and holy man, illustrated so well in Father John's changing relations with the poor of Kronstadt, may be an inevitable consequence of the shift in emphasis to the "holy" from the "man" in the holy man.

The change manifested itself not only with respect to the poor. Yes, Father John was glad that he was "loved by everyone, dear, celebrated, strong in faith, hope, and the love of Christ,"[158] but the tide of people wishing to see him physically exhausted him. He wrote on May 16, 1883: "Two women came to see me out of their spiritual love. They wanted to receive the Lord's blessing through me and express their spiritual inclination for me, *at seven a.m.* . . . and I was angry and indignant at the two of them and all of them, because at every time of the day, early and late, everywhere, they keep shoving me, keep trying to catch me."[159] It seems never to have occurred to Father John that he might be justified in resenting the loss of privacy, or that a certain amount of privacy might actually be necessary to preserve his spiritual life. Newspapers wrote dumbfounded accounts of the after-effects of his nationwide tours—during one such visit to Kharkov, all the gardens and orangeries on his host's estate were trampled into the ground by devotees who camped there in order to catch a glimpse of him; the local police were unable to stop them.[160] Father John himself was regularly knocked down, pulled in all directions, and even bitten by devotees who wished to have his "living" relics.[161]

It is a measure of how much this constant being in public demanded of Father John that his diary entries from this period read as laconically as "August 30, 1891. I have not written in my book for a long time—more than four months."[162] The notebooks that had once served as the repository of his aspirations, experiences, and struggles, had nearly lost their original function. The people who came to him were now the object of Father John's religious energies; *they*, rather than his diaries, were the arena of his religious life and his spiritual support.

The transference of his religious energies outward to his devotees also led to one of the most serious casualties of Father John's popularity: his relation with his wife. Earlier in their lives together, from the 1850s to the mid-1870s, she seems to have resigned herself to his single-minded pursuit of holiness and to have accepted her lot as marginal helpmeet. If Father John was not to be hers, at least he was no one else's either, and Elizaveta Konstantinovna could seek to create a hearth. She began to find most of her emotional solace in her sister Anna, and her nieces Ruth and Elizabeth, whom she raised herself. When Father John had been a private individual, he and his wife at least had their own spheres in which the other also operated—his at church, hers at home—and hence had to respect the authority of the other there. Moreover, in the beginning of his career Father John was regularly upbraided by his superiors and hounded by the Kronstadt authorities; Elizaveta Konstantinovna may well have pitied her beleaguered spouse. Going out was a duty rather than a pleasure, and Father John's domestic environment could provide a haven from the slings and arrows of his travails. Although hardly a marriage in which the two parties formed an integrated unit, it was a domestic arrangement that offered both parties a certain measure of autonomy and stability.

This *modus vivendi* changed for the worse with Father John's reputation for holiness. Once he began to acquire not only followers but devotees, relations with his wife deteriorated. Elizaveta Konstantinovna had accepted his spending his waking hours visiting the poor; she did not respond as calmly to the bevies of admiring women who gazed soulfully at Father John and gave him expensive presents. His suggesting to his wife that he shared intimate, rarefied spiritual bonds with these women that were beyond those of which she was capable infuriated Elizaveta Konstantinovna. Particularly galling to her was that Father John, who had resisted her own desires for closeness with

Fig. 4 Matushka Elizaveta Konstantinovna Sergieva. Photo courtesy of the Central State Archive of Cine- and Photo-Documents

him for so long, now seemed to be welcoming the advances of others. It was not only her imagination: after he became famous, his notebooks for the first time begin to record his being aroused by the women who flocked to see him, whether his own cleaning-woman or "a beautiful Countess in a white dress" (although he resisted).[163] Elizaveta Konstantinovna fought back with vigor. Whether because she had come to view religious observance with a jaundiced eye after living with Father John, she was busy, or out of a desire to provoke him, for a while she almost stopped going to church. Almost any incident became the pretext for a quarrel. Father John described one such instance in 1882:

> This evening I had a major unpleasant scene with my wife because I accused her of copying the key to my writing-desk and to its inner drawers and taking several things and some money. She flew me like an enraged lioness and was ready to tear me to pieces; she howled from fury like a crazy woman; she threatened to hit me on the cheek in front of the children; she upbraided me for my "broads"—that is, the pious women who have entered into spiritual communion with me in prayers, the sacraments, spiritual conversations, and readings—she abused me in the most dishonorable fashion possible, and exalted herself. Lord! Forgive her, she does not know what she is saying and doing. Enlighten her who is all overshadowed with earthly cares and sweets, grown fat and wide and having forgotten God.[164]

Father John began to suspect his wife of any number of deceits, from appropriating the rose-scented oil intended for the shroud of Christ used in the services on Holy Week to replacing the diamond buttons on the collar of his cassock "sewn on by persons who were devoted to me" with plain glass ones, thinking he would not notice.[165] His discontent with his domestic life finally erupted in 1883:

> Woe to me with my relatives, with their disrespect for church regulations, with their perpetual dainties—disgraceful in everyday life—their amusements, their laughter with the children Ruth and Elizabeth, with the cats and the dog,—with their laziness towards prayer, private and public. (They go to church [only] five or six times a year—God be their judge!) What kind of answer will they give for themselves and the children?—they want to rule and they rule indeed, fulfilling all of their wishes and whims.... And how they bring up the children! O horror! Without any respect for

the rules of the Church! They do not keep the fasts themselves and they are teaching the children to do the same: on the first week of Great Lent they eat cheese and eggs, not to speak of caviar and fish.—Who will make them listen to reason? They don't listen to me.[166]

There are descriptions that temper Father John's. One of the nieces paints a very different picture of pious, domestic idyll in her reminiscences, recalling how carefully Elizaveta Konstantinovna protected her husband's few hours of rest and how Father John refused to eat at home without the company of his wife, calling her his "angel."[167] Nevertheless, his account, however inclined to accentuate the negative, captures a fundamental accuracy. Having grown accustomed to reverence and devotion from his public, he was ever less inclined to accept being treated as an ordinary mortal at home. It is not surprising that, as he became more famous, the references to family and sociability in his notebooks gave way to the pleasures and pressures of life in public. His handwriting became larger and more untidy; his diary now served largely as an appointment book. With Father John's identification with society and development of a total view of the society in which he lived, the shift from parish priest and ascetic to public holy man was complete.

The surviving letters that people sent to Father John demonstrate the many levels of his appeal, from the material to the spiritual. They show that many different social groups in Russia shared the same symbols and a common experience of Orthodox Christianity, whether in the blessing of a cross for a child, a request for a prayer service, or a familiarity with liturgical language and Church Slavonic. Requests for healing from sickness and material help also cut across class boundaries, with a noble father as likely to ask for the cure of his sick daughter as a peasant mother, and an impoverished genteel spinster as desperate as a factory worker given the sack.

The letters asking for healing offer a unique perspective on the essentially religious mentality of their writers. This mentality emerges in a variety of ways: the associations they make between one's moral state and one's physical one, the notion that events are sent by God, the identification of sin and its consequences. People also show a familiarity with the notion of holiness, acquired in what was still an essentially religious culture. The key notion is that of *ugodnik Bozhii*, one who is *pleasing* to God, or God's favorite. Because an *ugodnik* has explicitly managed to find favor in God's eyes, his title conveys that his mission is to do the same for others who have yet to come so close. Moreover, both *ugodnik* and *zastupnik*—intercessor—have their roots in active verbs in common use at the turn of the century, and both describing actions *any* person could undertake: pleasing and defending or interceding on someone's behalf. The beloved holy person was identified, and described, for qualities that won favor in God's eyes and activities undertaken on behalf of other people.

Much the same thinking applied when people turned to Father John for religious advice. Because he was pleasing to God, he could discern God's ways and intent more clearly than the petitioner. Their phrase taken from the Orthodox liturgy, "You have been given the grace to pray for us," is emblematic. Father John was identified as a vessel of power, but this power was always understood to be the collective possession of the Church. Because of this, the correspondents felt no hesitation about asking for his prayers: both he and they belonged to the Church; his grace was *for* them.

The people who wrote to Father John expressed their religiosity in Orthodox terms. While they believed he had the power of prayer and intercession, it was still God who healed and decided. Their notion of holiness is best understood as a sense of a constellation, in which Father John stood closer to God than they, but was still in the same *place*. This sense of sharing the same cosmology and being in a shared endeavor is why people offered to pray for him, even as they asked his prayers.

Father John's apparently being able to achieve desired results through prayers changed the perceptions others had of him. Thanks to this, for the first time in Russian religious experience, a priest was called upon to perform the functions of uniquely endowed charismatic prayer previously associated exclusively with the monastic or non-worldly holy individual. Although he was still called to perform conventional priestly functions, the emphasis was less on the efficacy of the ritual as such than it was on the strength of his faith being able to infuse the standard rites with a power other priests seemed to lack. A *moleben* performed by Father John thus became less a random act of faith, form, or desperation and more of a certainty that one would get all the Divine help possible. Similarly, Father John himself began to be regarded not only as a virtuous priest, but as a uniquely empowered saint.

5

Contemporary Representations and Their Role in Spreading Saintly Celebrity

The letters to Father John from people of every social background represented a growing consensus that he was indeed a holy man. They were only one manifestation of his widespread veneration, however. While the letters represented the private, unmediated aspect of his homage, there was also a more public and a more deliberately constructed one. It was this public aspect that was stoked by a host of institutions and individuals, and it was this one that caused the Church hierarchy the most concern. The practical aspect of the homage included those individuals involved in the logistics of Kronstadt pilgrimages: the proprietors of lodging-houses, drivers of *droshky* and hansom cabs, and the Kronstadt-Oranienbaum-St. Petersburg transportation network. The promotional side included people who had experienced Father John's beneficence and wished to publicize it as an act of piety, journalists who were interested in him as a social phenomenon, and hawkers of souvenir scarves and postcards. Dedicated Orthodox writers who saw their task as compiling material for an eventual *vita* made up the next "layer" of image-makers. The last layer of the Father John homage was the Church hierarchy, who tried to keep an eye over all the actions and publications to make sure that they were acceptable. Together, these groups helped to make him the object of both a cult and an industry.[1] The interaction of their interests illustrates the dialectical character of Orthodoxy in Late Imperial Russia.

Here one must distinguish between the representations of Father John during his life, those after his death and before 1918, those of the emigration, those of the Soviet period, and those after 1988. While all representations played an important role in the furthering of his cult, this chapter will concentrate on the representations contemporary with Father John, for their makers faced a unique problem. No Orthodox Christian could be officially called a saint as long as he or she was still alive. Even those who believed Father John to be holy, therefore, had to watch scrupulously the expression of their homage to him to a far greater extent than those writing or painting after his death. Moreover, as long as he was alive, he could respond to the ways in which he was represented; after his death, it became far easier for others to express themselves without reservation. This chapter, then, will focus on the challenge that a *living* saint posed to his Orthodox milieu.

The act of spreading the word about Father John was simplest for those laypeople who had no official position within the Church, or who did not derive any portion of their steady income from Father John—and who wished, as an act of piety, to make more widely known their successful healing, sobriety, or whatever other good thing that had come to them through him. Most often, this took the form of writing brief accounts for local newspapers, such as the first unsolicited testimonials that appeared as a letter to the editor in the December 20, 1883, issue of *New Time*. Sixteen people who ascribed their healings to the prayers of Father John published an account of their previous ailments, a declaration of their thanks, and his "testament," which consisted of "Now live according to God's truth and go to Holy Communion as often as possible."[2]

Another form of testimony and expression of veneration consisted of setting Father John's prayerful musings from *My Life in Christ* to music. As long as the prayers had been previously published, and hence "vetted" by the clerical authorities, this was acceptable.[3] The problem came when people began to circulate prayer chain-letters. These chain-letters, a combination of magic, Orthodox formulae, and private enterprise, followed a similar format. Following the model of the widely distributed apocryphal "Dream of the Holy Mother of God,"[4] the writers claimed to have received one of Father John's "secret, effective" prayers, adding that, if the prayer were distributed and read a set number of times, one's wish would come true; if one failed to observe the conditions, misfortune would follow. Given that contemporary clergymen, including Father John himself, dismissed such prayers as superstition,[5] it is ironic that the contents of such "magic prayers" have come down to us thanks largely to his indignant repudiations, which he published in newspapers in a futile attempt to stop their distribution. One such prayer ran as follows:

> O Jesus Christ, we pray to Thee, Holy God, Holy Mighty, Holy Immortal One, have mercy on us and on all Thine world from all perishing. Thou hast redeemed our souls from sin by Thy blood. O, Pre-Eternal God, thine mercy is great, for the sake of Thy most pure Blood, always, now and ever, and unto the ages of ages.
>
> The condition of the prayer is this: whoever has this prayer has to pass it along to nine persons and to read it at least once a day with faith. Then you will be freed of every evil and misfortune, and if you don't do it, you will be subjected to evil and misfortune.[6]

In denouncing the prayer, Father John wrote the Kronstadt newspaper *Kotlin* in 1890:

> Once again there is a prayer supposedly composed by me going around.... This would-be prayer, which came out of some ignorant, and by no means a church, head, is not mine, and its afterword obviously belongs to some wheeler-dealer who is counting on the gullibility and superstition of the common people.... In the middle of March 1887 and in January 1889 I asked *The Kronstadt Herald* and other newspapers to make this fraud public; I am now repeating this humble request.[7]

It was a losing battle, however. Such "secret prayers" had been widely copied and circulated hand to hand for years, long before they came to be associated with Father John.[8] In a letter to Georgii Ramennikov, who had inquired about the Orthodoxy of one of the best-known prayers after seeing it in the possession of his mother and his wife, Father John himself admitted to having copied out "The Virgin's Dream" as a boy of ten ("But," he hastened to add, "When wise people enlightened me, I threw it into the fire.")[9] By 1908, the publication in both Russian newspapers and the *Frankfurter Zeitung* of at least one such "secret Father John prayer," which called for the deaths of both Lev Tolstoy and the minister of finance, Sergei Witte, would have serious political consequences.[10] In a similar association with politics, Father John also became the subject of such urban legends as his warning the Tsar not to venerate an icon presented to him by two students, and instead ordering a soldier to shoot at it—a Tatar holding two knives was hidden in the icon for an assassination attempt.[11]

The magical chain-prayers were only one aspect of earlier forms of aliturgical religiosity that became incorporated into the veneration of Father John. Identifying which such devotional forms survived and were deemed acceptable, and which were not, offers valuable information into the relatively unstructured practice of aliturgical Orthodoxy. Some forms were unlikely by definition. The practice of attaching rings, crosses, and other costly jewelry to efficacious images of Father John, as was done with such miracle-working icons in the St. Petersburg area as the Joy of All Who Sorrow and Kazan icons of the Mother of God,[12] for example, could not apply. The reason goes beyond the obvious one—that no icons of Father John could be placed in churches, or even painted, while he was alive. In the same way that exemplary nuns in Roman Catholic countries were described as "living rules," Father John was a living icon, himself receiving the veneration and gifts that would go to his image after his canonization. He was "decorated" with the jeweled crosses, costly satin, velvet, and brocade vestments embroidered with gold, and sable-lined *riasa*s in the way beloved icons were with seed pearls and precious stones.[13] (Such ex-votos as miniature random organs and limbs molded in wax or cast in tin from those healed were not used to honor Father John, although they were used with icons in Russia, as in Western Europe.[14])

The commercial side of the veneration was similarly independent, relatively straightforward, and paralleled the situation in such contemporary Roman Catholic pilgrimage sites as Ars and Lourdes.[15] By the 1880s, Father John was a celebrity. Thousands of people came on a weekly and, at peak times of the year, a daily basis to Kronstadt, hoping to see him and to take Holy Communion from him. All of them needed to eat, to drink, and a place to stay. As a result, hostels for pilgrims became a more lucrative source of income in Kronstadt than ordinary boarding-houses with a steadier clientele. Competition for the pilgrims was fierce: as visitors' accounts and letters describe, they would be met by hawkers just off the boat, urging them to use their services. Their hustling was noted both neutrally and sardonically by visitors, and satirized by Serebrov in *Times and People*.[16] Because all the hostels offered approximately the same services—a bed or mattress, a suitably pious atmosphere with religious literature (some sold by the Ioannites), votive lamps burning in front of icons, and regular readings of *akathists*—there was little that distinguished one from another save for the quality of the mattress and the proximity to St. Andrew's Cathedral.[17] There was, however, one service that all could provide in principle, but which none could guarantee, and that was the assurance that Father John would visit their residence on the very day when this or that pilgrim would be staying there.[18]

Simply put, the demand for Father John exceeded the supply. This disparity created a paradoxical situation. The crush of visitors, which was especially high at such traditional times as Great Lent, brought both a heightened atmosphere of piety and income to Kronstadt. But this popularity had its price. The greater the number of those wishing personally to see, touch, hear Father John, the more difficult such possibilities became—and the greater, by extension, became the possibilities for those who could somehow guarantee such contact. Father John was in an inescapable position. His main work was prayer and sacraments; he did not want to be his own impresario. While his diaries from the 1880s and 1890s mention his regret and remorse at wanting the occasional minute to himself, by the beginning of the twentieth century he had realized that it was impossible for him to see everyone, and that it was too taxing to try to sort out everyone personally. By the mid-1890s, as the press of seekers mounted, he began to use the services of people who occupied a place somewhere between a manager and a social secretary to sift through the crowds wishing to see him. To get through the screening of these "bouncers," visitors wishing to get through to him would prepare for weeks in advance, using what connections they could muster. On November 30, 1903, for example, one student persuaded the personal secretary of the Ober-Procurator of the Holy Synod to let him use one of his calling-cards as a means of entry, and did get in.[19]

It was rarely that simple, however. Although Father John paid these middlepeople respectable salaries, the temptation to accept "a little something" in exchange for promising some personal contact with him proved too much for them to refuse. As a result, such secretaries as Evgeniia and the notorious Vera Pertsova earned both small fortunes and the ire of those who tried to use them as go-betweens.[20] Even worse, in the eyes of the devotees, were the liberties the screeners allowed themselves. Frustrated seekers described, for example, how Evgeniia collected ten rubles personally for every visit to Father John she arranged (apart from the cost of the visit itself) and even insulted his wife;[21] or how, when accompanying him on a trip to Astrakhan, Pertsova stalked off with a *sac voyage* filled with donations and snapped, "Try sitting here without any money and see how far you get."[22] Other enterprising people quickly realized that, although they did not represent Father John in this way, they could claim they did, and could profit from making false guarantees. Even women who lived in the House of Industry confessed to this—not surprisingly, as by the early 1900s, half of the House had been converted into a pilgrims' hostel, with every room having three doors that were to be opened during Father John's visits, to make it easier for him to pass quickly from room to room without having to lose time by going out into the hallway.[23] The dealing reached such proportions that, by the beginning of the twentieth century, it was difficult to escape the conclusion that Father John's entourage was trading in his name and profiting from it.

By the 1890s, virtually the only people able to see Father John were those who could afford to pay for the privilege. Such women as Aleksandra Maksimovna Lebedeva, a wealthy manufacturer from Saratov, sold everything in order to be near Father John; she was given a flat in the rectory of St. Andrew's Cathedral as a reward. Once the screeners had taken everything from her, they stopped calling; only Father John continued to visit occasionally. The methods of his "secretaries" with regard to the less wealthy can be surmised from the letter a barely literate woman wrote to him in the late 1890s:

> You visited us on March 4—Petersburg side, Bol'shaia Grebetskaia, at the metalworker's. I had great sorrows because my husband drinks and asked Katerina Semenovna to bring you to see us and she designated the price of one hundred rubles for a *moleben* and so I pawned all my things, everything I had, but that came to only sixty rubles. And when Semen came, he grabbed the envelope and said, "Why isn't there a hundred rubles here? There's only sixty in this envelope," and I said I had nowhere to get the rest, then he said, "Well, then, we won't bring him," and I said, "May God's will be done," and then Semen said, "I'll add forty of mine." I said, "Go ahead, if you have them." Now both of them keep coming, he and Katerina, they keep grabbing me by the chest, asking for forty rubles and saying they are going to see the judge, and I say, "My arbitrator is dear Batiushka." Dear batiushka, if I had the money, I would give it to them, but I gave them everything I had and I have nowhere to get the rest, because my husband drinks it all away. Dear batiushka, please pray for his improving and forgive

me, the sinner Ografena, for writing to you—I am doing it because they won't give me any rest.[24]

The idealistic young pastor who would go from door to door in search of alcoholics' families to help had himself become one of the hard-to-reach elite. Father John did not deny the charge. When pressed by indignant acquaintances, he acknowledged that those who surrounded him were indeed selling access to him. But all he could say in justification, even as he admitted that "many among the believing Orthodox are displeased because of my people," was: "All right, let us say that I chase them away—do you think that it will improve matters any? Of course not. These have already made a fortune thanks to my name, while those who begin to traffic will be poorer than these and they will have to squeeze even more from the people."[25]

Father John's indifference, which seems here to border on cynicism, is a sign of how weary he had grown. Certainly the shadier of the secretaries took some of the luster off his image. Even those who admired Father John found themselves increasingly compelled to disconnect him from those who trafficked in him.[26] This corrupt atmosphere had several consequences: it helped create the atmosphere in which the Ioannite sect would flourish; it provided grist for such satirical representations as Protopopov's play *Black Ravens*; and it would make it easier for the radical press to attack Father John after the releasing of censorship restrictions from 1905 to 1907. Although getting through to him became increasingly difficult, however, it was not impossible, and enough people did continue to manage to see him that the hopeful crowds persisted. But whether or not they found a personal audience, almost all of the visitors bought souvenirs to bring home. The mementos that figure most regularly in visitors' descriptions are large portraits of Father John labeled "Dear Batiushka," souvenir scarves with reproductions of him and views of Kronstadt in the corners, enameled-tin mugs like the ones distributed at the disastrous coronation festivities at Khodynka field in 1896, icons of Saint John of Ryla (his patron saint), and little crosses, with objects blessed by him fetching the highest prices in their categories. The most widely bought items were postcards of Father John.[27]

References to these cards appear in virtually every visitor's memoir, and they seem to have been nearly omnipresent. It is not surprising: fixing for oneself as they did the features of Father John and of one's pilgrimage and costing one to five kopecks each, postcards were one of the cheapest mementos possible. Their omnipresence, however, conceals the difficulties that they occasionally posed. Because Father John's fame came at the end of the nineteenth century, he was one of the first cases for the Russian Orthodox Church's having to decide upon a policy for, to paraphrase Walter Benjamin, the liturgical act and the holy individual in an age of mechanical reproduction.[28] Because of Father John's rapidly growing reputation for sanctity, the reproductions made of him had to be both suitably dignified and highlight the qualities for which he was most famous—without, however, resembling icons, so as not to confuse the faithful. Decoding the cards of Father John thus shows how far the image-makers could go.

Before the mid-1880s, Father John was not famous enough to warrant special attention, and the photographs taken of him as a young priest are the poses typically chosen by contemporary photographers: resting his head thoughtfully on his hand, book in front of him on a small table with a crocheted doily, seated on a bench, holding the wide-brimmed black businessman's hat favored by Late Imperial Russian priests, and so on. Even though Father John was in his sixties and seventies at the height of his fame, photographs of him in his youth were still readily available in Kronstadt bookshops until the time of his death.

The photographs of Father John from the mid-1880s, when he became famous, are a different matter. Because most images on the cards came from posed photographs, taken by professionals in a studio, he appears in his best *riasas* and, as began to be awarded them, his state decorations (see Frontispiece).[29] Most often he appears sitting, only rarely standing. Both the choice of garb and the pose are telling. Appearing in full vestments outside a church was out of the question. Not only did Church canons limit the wearing of vestments to performing liturgical actions, vestments were iconic in the most literal sense of the term. Once canonized, a bishop or priest *had* to be depicted on his icon in vestments conveying his ordained state, as descriptively as the cross in the hand signaled the martyr.[30] For the same reason, it would have been inappropriate to show Father John in the act of giving a blessing (as was, though wildly inadmissibly, the nonordained Rasputin in a celebrated and widely reproduced photograph by Boule).[31] Not only was the gesture itself iconic; if reproduced, it would have meant that Father John would have had to pose in so reverent an action—he would, in effect, have been blessing the camera. The only exception to the prohibition were the photographs of his blessing the crowds from on board a ship, as these were taken live and the recipients were themselves visible.[32] Engravings or paintings of such images, on the other hand, were perfectly acceptable because they avoided this problem of recording a "live" liturgical action. Even being shown standing was problematic, as saints were depicted on icons full-face, either standing or cut off at the waist. To avoid any possible confusion with icons, Father John was usually shown with his face in three-quarters (as in contemporary passport requirements) and seated, to add a note of casualness (see Fig. 2).[33]

These guidelines were developed not systematically but ad hoc, with the religious authorities usually deciding that something encountered was undesirable rather than giving positive suggestions in advance. Paintings of Father John done in an iconographic style were explicitly forbidden in a Synodal ruling of July 1, 1895, after the military governor of Kronstadt and Vice-Admiral Kaznakov confiscated several such examples made in the enamel and painted-on-porcelain types characteristic of the late eighteenth and nineteenth centuries.[34] Similarly unacceptable as overtly iconographic were oleographs of Father John as Christ, surrounded by cherubim.[35]

Fashion, alas, was not on the side of the hierarchs. The turn of the century saw an infatuation with experimenting with traditional iconic forms. In the 1890s, it was in vogue to use famous people as subjects for icons: an icon of Saints Peter and Paul used the writers Alexander Pushkin and Vladimir Dal' as models for the apostles; Ilya Repin posed Vladimir Chertkov for one of his icons.[36] And these were relatively tasteful. In 1897, the *St. Petersburg Spiritual Herald* bemoaned the proliferation of such icon-novelties as crucifixion-in-a-bottle and strips of icons pasted on cardboard so that, if held one way, one saw Saint Nicholas, if in the other direction, Saint Barbara. As the *Herald* ruefully noted, Russians were still far from the point when icons might be treated as the holy objects they were and sold in such "decent" locations as churches and monasteries—and not regarded as simple necessities, like soap or twine, and hawked next to them on street.[37] Dubious Father John likenesses were part of this trend of mass-produced images "catering to the lowest desires." They proliferated to the point that the Synod stopped giving their earlier detailed rationales for their decisions: when one Theodore Friedman asked in 1893 for permission to issue a portrait of Father John on a *breloque* (watch-charm), for example, adding that Father John had already given his consent, the Synod wrote simply, "Inappropriate—denied" on his petition.[38]

Try as it might to forbid images of Father John that resembled icons, the Synod could do little about how any such images were used; and they could be used like icons whether or not they looked like icons. However realistic a photograph of Father John, if someone put it in her icon corner and said prayers in front of it, the damage was done as far as the Synod was concerned. When the Synod did begin to receive reports of people keeping Father John photographs in their icon corners, they reacted vigorously, stating categorically that this was wrong.[39] It is out of this gradual erosion of "appropriate" boundaries and the gradual popular attribution of sanctity to Father John that the Ioannite "sect" would arise.

Written Representations of Father John

Written accounts of Father John ranged more widely in both form and content than did his images. They included both articles by independent professional writers and journalists whose fancy was caught by Father John, and works by people who regarded themselves as his Orthodox biographers and who were writing with the aim of promoting his canonization. The groups differed sharply from one another both in the tone they used and the liberties they took in commenting on his purported sanctity.

In examining the professional journalists' Father John articles, one must bear in mind that, given the realities of censorship in the 1880s and early 1890s, the religious-edifying genre was relatively broad—and safe.[40] Father John was not only an interesting and marketable topic, he was also acceptable. But even without this practical consideration, such well-known journalists as Mikhail Menshikov of *Novoe Vremia* and Vasilii Rozanov covered him avidly. (Even the artist Nikolai Roerich published Father John's admonition to him of: "Don't get sick! You will need to work a good deal for the Motherland."[41]) These writers were not entirely disinterested. They concentrated on Father John's sanctity and popularity, but they often did so in order to draw unflattering comparisons between him and the Church hierarchs. Menshikov, for example, wrote regular articles on Father John, even suggesting, when the question of restructuring the Church administration arose in 1905, that he, "as a recognized living saint," inaugurate a new line of Patriarchs.[42] After Father John's death, Menshikov went further:

> A significant part of the clergy, chiefly the upper clergy, responded to him with a feeling of wounded jealousy. The mitre-wearers with the glittering diamonds on their *klobuk*s, their decorated *omophorion*s and *panagia*s, could not but notice that, with all their academic liberalism, with all the Tübingen-esque worldliness of their views, with all their artful mastery of court intrigues, they were infinitely lower than the Kronstadt priest—lower in the eyes

of both God and people. Without long arguments the people quickly reached the conclusion that he was the real thing, and *they* were somehow—not real.... They could never forgive the great priest of the Russian land this, and they blocked him as long as they could. It was only just before his death, when he was completely weak, that he was deemed worthy of being appointed to the Synod—he, some of whose devotees declared to be the living Christ come down from Heaven![43]

During Father John's lifetime, however, Menshikov generally restrained himself in speaking of his holiness, only letting down his guard in such unusually tense moments as the Kronstadt sailors' rebellion of 1905. Vasilii Rozanov, on the other hand, went as far as one could in publicly proclaiming Father John's sanctity. He wrote in 1905:

Is not all of the Russia of our day amazed and stunned at the appearance of this marvelous priest who has access to that which no mortal has—above all, the striking influence on the souls of those in his presence.... He does not dazzle with his intellect, as does Filaret; he is only of middling learning; but the murmur, "This is a saint," follows him everywhere. Perhaps, however, this is a recluse, a grim keeper of the fasts, a hermit? "I eat and drink with the publicans," he might apply to himself the words of Christ. He is constantly in public, among the people; yes, he is in constant motion, and in what motion! At his age people are weak and bent, but he seems for all the world like a young woman. Despite his seventy years, in all my life I have never heard anyone refer to him as an old man or an "elder." It is a little odd to even to try to imagine him sleeping, lying down, or resting....

Seeing him, the Russian people gives way to its wonder; they run after him in crowds; they kiss the hem of his clothing; they kiss the ground on which he walked; they rip apart any handkerchief, towel, or any object that he held in his hands and treasure these particles as "relics."...

"Heaven has come down to earth," "a wondrous person has appeared to us," "an angel in the flesh." The wave of movement around an ordinary priest who is a mere *protoierei* really is marvelous and miraculous. Through his meaning and significance and the people's attachment to him, "the living God" has eclipsed all the Metropolitans, all the official religious authorities, all the clerical "Sanhedrin."[44]

It was precisely such independent articles that, in stressing Father John's specificity and distance from the Church hierarchy, would fan his cult—and alienate the bishops who had to keep him in check. Like the laypeople who sent their "unsolicited testimonials" to newspapers as an act of piety, journalists and writers who were not affiliated with official Church publications had nearly free rein in singing Father John's praises and all but canonized him themselves. But neither Rozanov nor his epigones claimed to be speaking for the Orthodox Church. And there was the rub. It was, of course, only the Church hierarchy who could make such a decision; and even they could make it only once Father John were safely dead. The hierarchy, then, faced the challenge of dealing with and directing a truly popular phenomenon in an Orthodox direction.

It was not, however, simply a matter of hierarchs attempting to control their impetuous flock. Father John had champions among both the laity and lower-level clergy who wanted to impress upon their hierarchs that he was indeed saintly and ought to be canonized someday; many bishops felt the same way. They faced the task of presenting their enthusiasm and their case *in an Orthodox way*. Both groups—the "pleaders" and the "deciders"—saw themselves as being on the same side; each recognized the right of the other to its role. Once Father John was dead, the process could, in theory, proceed safely and neutrally. As long as he was alive, however, both sides recognized they had a spiritual obligation to keep him from getting into trouble, as it were. In singing his praises, they could not go so far as to risk his becoming proud and losing, in a reckless moment, all that he had so painstakingly acquired—a phenomenon they would have known all too well from the lives of the saints.[45] In other words, the pleaders, too, were responsible for both fostering and protecting Father John's sanctity—because the loss of it would be not only his but that of the entire Church. As a result, the pleaders voluntarily tried to restrain their descriptions and make them safely edifying; the deciders had to watch over all of the manifestations of religiosity connected to Father John to determine the same thing. This delicate process of balancing his various representations during his lifetime emerges most strongly with respect to the written accounts of the pleaders.

Some had as their aim simply promoting, or more widely disseminating, a personality "pleasing to God." These follow within the tradition and canons of the "edifying" genres generally; and indeed the reporting of Father John's life needs to be seen within the context of the genres of religious writing that existed in Russia during his time. Itinerant peddlers continued to hawk both prints and booklets on religious themes throughout Russia.[46] Besides the Scriptures and lives of the saints, which were being published by the Church in increasing numbers, there was also a wide range of "edifying" and deliberately popular material published by various institutions connected to the Church. These ranged from small leaflets such as the *Troitskie Listki* (Trinity sheets) intended "to provide the simple Russian people with edifying reading, and thus to promote their religious and moral education and enlightenment," to an entire series called "Strugglers of Piety."[47] Almost all of these narrative tales dealt with either individuals long dead or fictional men, women, and children who exemplified the virtues of self-sacrifice and abiding faith that the Church sought to inculcate. They offer a clue as to the reading public for the material published on Father John. Because he was so idiosyncratic, however, the edifying tales rarely provided literary models for the accounts written about him. Other contemporary parallels and literary models for Father John stories are saints' lives, the children's series "The Lives of Remarkable People," the tracts about pilgrimages to the Holy Land and Mount Athos, and, because Father John is described most often within the context of his own travels over Russia, travel writing in general.

It is here that the difference between contemporary accounts of Father John's life and those written decades after his death emerge most clearly. In a pattern typical for saints' lives, people writing years after the death of a saint would take pains to make their material fit within hagiographical canons.[48] Just twenty-five years after Father John's death, in a compilation of materials for his canonization, for example, Surskii anticipated queries of "How can you pray to Father John when he has not yet been canonized?" with the acerbic comment, "God Himself added him to the list of saints during his lifetime," using other people's visions of Father John on icons as supernatural proof of his sanctity.[49] Once Father John was canonized, his "iconization"—here used in the most literal sense of the term—became complete. The versions of his *vita* published in Russia in the 1990s, for example, assume a tone of epic distance and speak of Father John in much the language used in the earliest Russian saints of the eleventh centuries, with whom he is grouped as a national hero.[50] The émigré version of 1964, while putting more stress on Father John's politics, also followed the standard pattern of a *vita*.[51] (One of the only exceptions is S. L. Firsov, who sees a similar fin-de-siècle malaise in the Father John period and the turn of the twenty-first century: "Morality falling, crime rising, a growth of hatred and malice all around—all of this says that the social organism is grievously ill, just as it was in the beginning of the twentieth century."[52]) Father John's contemporaries, however, revealed a concern with their own time and an insistence on his relevance "to our days" that would of necessity pale with every passing decade. The details they chose to emphasize in their accounts yield important information on how he was perceived to be part of the hagiographical tradition and how that tradition itself was incorporating new elements.

First, and foremost, they emphasized his contemporaneity, his being a typical priest, someone who looked like everyone else. "He speaks in our language," "He knows us," "He is one of us"—these were all recurrent motifs. One can sense the almost palpable relief of people living in the world writing, "Despite his rigor, Father John is no stern ascetic—he drinks wine, he goes out in company."[53] After his death, by contrast, this one-of-us attitude vanished, with a hagiographic one taking its place. ("Although Father John said he was no ascetic, he said so only because of his extreme humility; in reality, he was the greatest of ascetics."[54])

At least one of the reasons Father John's contemporaries were enchanted by him was that, although he was extraordinary (which is, after all, why he had impressed the writers in the first place), he was extraordinary in an ordinary context. He was married. He lived in an ordinary-looking house near the center of a middle-sized town that was home to transient sailors. He read magazines. He taught in a high school. He thought that something really ought to be done about the poor. He had to deal with both the city and the Church bureaucracies. He believed that the wealthy ought to be more charitable, but this did not stop him from being delighted at getting invitations to their dinner parties. He was, in short, as worldly and as far from the image of a gaunt ascetic hermit or powerful bishop—the most familiar types of canonized holiness in nineteenth-century Russia—as one could be while still being considered close to sanctity.

It is not surprising, then, that contemporaries dwelled so affectionately on those qualities of Father John that they believed he shared with them. But of course Father John was not "just like" everyone else. It was his differences, after all, that made people pay attention to him. One of the enduring sources of his appeal was that, along with combining the religious types of priest and prophet, he also managed to combine extraordinary manifestations of Divine favor while seeming to remain "the priest next door," or "the boy from the country who comes to the city and makes good." The contrast would have been striking in any case, but it became all the more so because of how it was presented.

Fig. 5 Father John with his sisters.

Virtually every account of Father John published in his lifetime, especially before 1905, stresses his homely attributes alongside his supernatural ones. It is no accident that Father John is shown so often in photographs with his mother and sisters, who look like typical peasant women, or that his family hut and present house—solid but barracks-looking—were often depicted side by side, or that so many words and images alike would be devoted to scenes from his rural background.[55]

These are especially important because the traditional edifying genre now merged with the newer one of travel writing.[56] The interest in Father John merged with interest in local color and ethnography. A card showing several images of his trip to Ustiug, for example, had examples of Ustiug handicrafts next to a photograph of Father John being driven to church; an illustration of his trip to the Russian North had an inset of a young woman in local costume; the largest image on a card showing his trip to the Oneg lake district was that of an Olonets *izba*, and so on.[57] Similarly, Father John literature sought to broaden the appeal of the basic edifying story to attract a wider public; it did so by merging several existing successful literary forms. A specifically Romantic quality in describing Father John's life, for example, was the attention devoted to natural descriptions of the North and the importance attributed to nature as a formative influence and setting.[58] This was not specific to religious writing, of course. The lengthy descriptions of rivers, landscapes, and summer skies by Nikolai Gogol, Ivan Turgenev, Sergei Aksakov, and Lev Tolstoy were but the best-known manifestations of the nineteenth-century obsession with nature. For religious narratives, however, the accounts of Father John seem to be unusually laden with nature descriptions. Thus Aleksandr Semenoff-Tian-Shanskii wrote of Father John's native village of Sura in Arkhangelsk province: "The village is situated at the confluence of the rivers Sura and Pinega, a tributary on the right bank of the river Dvina, approximately 500 versts from the White Sea. Not far from the village loomed mountains and white alabaster rocks with caves and meadows; many birds and animals live in the forests."[59] S. V. Zhivotovskii, another biographer, went further in language that both anticipates that of a film treatment and recalls hagiographic descriptions of the saint's environment as wilderness:

> It is difficult to create good agriculture in a short time on this quicksand.... Everything has to be created in the most difficult conditions possible, as the northern summer is very short. Three months will go by in which the sun hardly ever goes down from

the horizon, and then the cold, foul autumn sets in. In the beginning of October everything here is almost covered with snow. The sun at first will appear for only a few hours, and then virtually disappears.

The long, harsh winter sets in.

The mail comes here only once a week.

Contact with far-off Russia is only by horse and reindeer.

For almost nine months all of nature is buried in deep sleep.

Deep silence reigns, disturbed only by the ringing of the bell calling the sisters to the convent church—and the wailing of the wind and the keening of the blizzard, which blend with the hungry howls of the wild animals.[60]

Finally, writers extended the connection with nature to Father John himself. Boris Zaitsev wrote, "The nature of the Russian people expressed itself very strongly in him—these light blue, utterly peasant eyes, full of wind and fields."[61]

The emphasis on nature was more than a stylistic device. Father John's own attachment to nature appears in virtually every work he published. In *My Life in Christ* alone, entries on nature, as when Father John compares the breaking up of frozen rivers and lakes in the spring to the separation of the soul from the body at death, for example, abound.[62] Reviewers of foreign editions similarly commented on his love for nature as a distinguishing feature of his work.[63] They emphasized how the young John experienced the power of nature during school holidays when he walked home from the Arkhangelsk boarding school for sons of the clergy, suggesting that it was on these journeys on foot of several hundred versts through forests and mountains with scarcely any human being to be seen that he developed his love of nature and the capacity for seeing God in it. They also attributed this experience of long walking, which paralleled that of pilgrims and holy wanderers, as forming his tendency toward extemporaneous prayer.[64]

The fondness for praying out of doors and addressing God through nature persisted in later life. For all of Father John's love for the Eucharist and the liturgy, he continued to prefer the out of doors for private prayer, beginning his day as a priest in Kronstadt with a half-hour walk and prayer alone in his garden at 4 A.M. This open-air quality and lyric celebration of nature recalls both Francis of Assisi and Sergii of Radonezh.[65] Such accounts of Father John's life, and his own references in sermons to nature, may explain their popularity among his listeners, most of whom were also from rural backgrounds and celebrated the feast of Pentecost by carrying in enough grass to cover the floor of their church, wrapping the icons with leaves, field flowers, and wreaths. The standing gonfalons and iconostasis would be so thickly covered with tree branches—in some cases, entire trees—that the parish church took on the appearance of a transplanted enchanted forest and the holiday itself was often referred to as "the earth's feast-day."[66] His references would have been more familiar to them than the learned sermons of the bishops.[67]

Biographers stressed other childhood influences besides nature. They felt that the effect of the stern landscape and climate were accentuated and reinforced by the poverty of Father John's native village. One observer wrote that "everything there created by the hands of men was poor and meager: modest wooden houses, two old ramshackle churches—the "Church of the Presentation" and the "St. Nicholas Church," in which the vessels were only of tin, the house in which Father John was born—not even a peasant's cottage, but rather a dilapidated hut."[68] Part of the emphasis on Father John's poverty was the suggestion that the works of human beings came off badly next to the works of God in the depressed context and helped to create a predisposition toward viewing all human endeavor as insignificant against the omnipotence of God. Other sources support this notion. While the Church provided many villagers with their primary source of stimulus and inspiration, this was especially true for the children of the clergy, as the philosopher Sergei Bulgakov wrote of his own childhood as the son of a provincial priest.[69]

Finally, late nineteenth- and early twentieth-century versions of Father John's life share a Horatio Alger–like emphasis on the material benefits that could accrue from following him. According to these narratives, after contact with Father John, people down on their luck could come into solvency. Even after his secretaries had made access to him difficult, he appears in stories as the ideal giver, kindly, discreet, and understanding, unlike the "usual" philanthropic agencies with whom he is contrasted. Typical is this 1900 eyewitness account of a poor student:

> [After Liturgy,] Batiushka begins to remove his vestments. A youth aged about sixteen in a school-boy's uniform comes up to him and timidly stretches out a paper to him.
> "Just tell me what you want," says Batiushka, continuing what he is doing with the haste that is typical for him.
> "It's for my education ... I don't have enough," come the broken words, uttered in a whisper.

Fig. 6 Tourist postcard of Father John visiting his homeland.

"How much do they want from you?"

"Fifty rubles."

Batiushka reaches his hand into his pocket and takes out some money. He takes out the amount and gets ready to give them to the asker, doing so "incidentally," without breaking off what he was doing before. For the first time, he looks at the youth standing in front of him, on whose cheeks tears are involuntarily streaming down. Who knows? Maybe he has already meekly submitted his request more than once, and for naught, and maybe he has come here as a last resort, which, if not filled, would shatter all his dreams for a bright future! If he were turned down here, then he would have left in complete despair. But here, *they listen to requests without any demeaning questions, without insulting his person,* they give him a saving anchor as easily as if he had asked for some trifle. Tears of gratitude poured from the eyes of the youth. Happy is he who can wrest such tears from people!

"Calm down, calm down, dear boy! I am very happy that I can help you." Batiushka patted the boy's inclined head. His eyes caught sight of the too-short sleeves of the school uniform, the splitting seams—and the hand that had been ready to give the amount requested quickly reaches into the pocket again and only then fulfills the request.

The youth went away happy, but soon returned. The fear of a mistake brought him back. Discomfited, he comes up to Batiushka again, the gift in his hand.

"Batiushka! You made a mistake: There's a lot more here!"

"No, there is no mistake," the Batiushka replies quietly. "That's for a coat ... for your books."[70]

There are countless variations on this theme of unquestioning generosity: the merchant who gave Father John an envelope with three thousand rubles and protested when he handed it immediately to a seeker without counting it; the woman whom he told to give her offering to the first person she saw, and who then hesitated when it was a well-dressed officer (who, as it turned out, desperately needed exactly that amount). In all these cases, Father John knew how much the seekers truly needed, and saw that they got it. With such stories in circulation, it is not surprising that so many people asked him for money.[71]

Even more formulaic were the success stories of men (they are always men) who had once been rich and lost everything through drink, reaching the "lowest depths" before being "resurrected" by Father John. The alcoholics' narratives follow the same pattern: a man who is wealthy (a variant: and has a flourishing business) begins to lead a dissipated life in the bars and clubs of St. Petersburg, supporting ballerinas, actresses, and other chic mistresses. In a few years, he has squandered everything, including his wife's money. He sinks so low that he begins to beat his wife and children, pawning their last pillow and blanket. Father John spots him in the House of Industry and tells him to come to church (or the reverse). He gets him to stop drinking, helps him with money, and arranges employment. Although the drinker claims he is unworthy, Father John maintains that he must go to communion. Our former alcoholic becomes a new man. He begins to treat his family well, he is at first poor but honest, and then he rapidly becomes a success. Everything he is he owes to Father John.[72]

Although the alcoholic's *vita* is as predictable as a saint's, it includes enough details to make people recognize every restaurant and brand name the repentant Bacchus gives. The appeal to contemporaries was that, while the alcoholic's *vita* obviously followed Gospel models, it was also both a Cinderella story and a Horatio Alger one. Because the story always includes a mistreated family who supports the alcoholic in his first tentative steps to Father John and whose domestic life becomes an idyll, moreover, we may assume that the audience for the alcoholic's *vita* were less the drunks themselves than their despairing wives or children. The high proportion of letters from alcoholics' wives and daughters to Father John bears out this guess. The alcoholic's *vita*, with its acute awareness of the misery the alcoholic's relatives endure, followed by a happy and supremely secure ending, must have read to them like a dream nearly impossible, but desperately hoped-for all the same. The repentant alcoholic's remorse for abusing his family must have seemed particularly haunting. If one bears the likely audience in mind, the details of the alcoholic's *vita* become all the more evocative. The very tone in which the alcoholic recounts his tale, in fact, sounds as if it were narrated by his reproachful wife.

Consider, for example, what B-v tells us:

> From my father, I received a house and one hundred and fifty thousand in capital. Besides that, I got three hundred thousand as my wife's dowry. [Subtext: she was wealthier than he, and he lost it all!] A sizable fortune, it would seem; with this I could have lived not only out my life painlessly and provided my family in every way, but also have brought some use to the fatherland as a citizen, businessman, industrialist, inventor, capitalist.... After all, I am

educated man, I had a government position.... [Subtext: he must have heard this every day!]

[The restaurants] Donon, Content, Pivato, and The Bear[73] are witnesses that I paid up to 3 rubles a cigar and up to 2 1/4 rubles for a glass of vintage wine. They are also witnesses that I would sometimes give 400–600 rubles for lunch or dinner "for two," sometimes several days in a row....

When my cash ran out and I had to pay everything by promissory notes, I mortgaged the house, but did not reduce my expenses one bit. After all, how could I deny Josephine her coach or Margarita her *collier*?... That would have been unthinkable, so I took out a second mortgage, started to pawn the securities, the diamonds ... then the creditors all turned up at once. *We had to sell the apartment and all our things* and *my wife and children and I moved into a furnished room.*... I switched to drinking raw vodka, became a hard drinker, and sank lower step by step to putting us in a doss-house. *My wife started to go out to do laundry....*

There is no word awful enough for my actions! From wealth and luxury I drove my wife and three small children to rags and poverty, I beat them, I tortured them, I dragged the last pillow out from underneath the baby to the tavern, leaving him to sleep on the bare floor. *My wife was a beauty. Look at her now.* Unfortunate woman, she goes unwashed and uncombed for weeks—she has just about sunk into idiocy. But *not too long ago she played an important role in society, she was the first at the balls, she organized receptions, she had a salon.*[74]

Once Father John enters the story, the tone changes to a less worldly and reproachful, more devout one. Father John's voice worked "like healing balsam" on B-v's wound. Suddenly images from childhood—Christ crucified, the Mother of God, angels—came flooding back and he fell to his knees. B-v could not bring himself to go up to the cross at the end of the service for fear of being chased away, however, having heard that Father John could "see right through you." Father John spotted him shrinking toward the wall and gestured for him to come nearer. The crowds parted for him. In their conversation, the emphasis on praying *together* and Father John's omniscience is characteristic of other such narratives:

"So you came to me, after all. You did well; let's pray together. You are very unhappy, but the ways of the Lord are unknowable...."

You are going towards Him, and this is your great fortune.... Has it been a long time since you stopped drinking?"

"Stopped drinking?" he asked. "But how did you know that I stopped drinking, Batiushka?"

"It's not hard to see an unfortunate drunkard in you, my son. You are not an evil person; the Christian in you has not died; but the enemy has vanquished you.... But it could be worse. The enemy could have destroyed your soul as well.... Thank the Lord for His mercy and ask for His help in your fight with the enemy!"

Father John led him to the side of the church to the holy icons and B-v went down on his knees. For the first time in twenty-three years B-v raised his eyes to heaven and his lips began to whisper words of prayer. O, what a state he was in! He trembled from some joyous agitation. His soul was lighter than it ever had been. Tears were pouring down his face. In this minute, he made peace with everyone in the whole world, with all his enemies and foes. He wanted to embrace all of them, so that they would all be as happy as he was this minute.

Also evident here are allusions to the Psalms ("I will lift up mine eyes to the hills" [121]) and ("and my mouth shall declare Thy praise" [103]). After Father John was canonized by the Moscow Patriarchate in 1990, the prayer he recited over B-v would become the standard "Father John prayer" recited at the end of every service in which his name was invoked, from the occasion of his canonization to *molebens* for wives on behalf of their alcoholic husbands.[75] It worked mightily on B-v: he fainted. By the time he recovered consciousness, Father John was gone; but he had left behind a member of the House's trustees with instructions to give B-v ten rubles and to tell him to come to confession and communion. The wife's voice returns:

These ten rubles were precious to B-v, because he and *his family had gone hungry* for several days. *His wife had managed to scrape up fifty kopecks* for his trip to Kronstadt, while *she and the children had certainly been left without a cent*. The happy, joyous B-v came home. His family had not seen him like that in a long time. They moved straight-away into a light-filled room, they bought some food, some boots for the children. Everyone prayed together at the housewarming. Before they had not read any prayers; lately they had not even had an icon; the children did not know the "Our Father." Now they decided to pray all together every morning and evening. How quietly, peacefully, and happily this day passed.[76]

Now enters the third voice of the alcoholic's *vita*: in its emphasis on the benefits of honest, physical work and the results of "culture" and dissipation described in prose as dismal as possible, it recalls the voice of Tolstoy in his last phase:

> He used to have a permanent *loge* in the theater, he knew many of the stars of the ballet and the operetta, he drank the best foreign wines as if they were water, and as a result—he kept yawning, had headaches, was depressed, and often regretted the time and energy he wasted.... Whereas the new happiness he found was not only constant, stable, and unchangeable, but it was *eternal*....
>
> B-v rolled logs for three days. He felt strong, healthy, brisk, and cheerful.... His family cheered up, too; it was now sated and happy too. Without drinking bouts, a ruble and ten kopecks were enough for all their humble needs....
>
> His wife and children were resurrected into a new life: they grew younger and healthier. There were already schools earmarked for the children; no one knew any more need of any kind.[77]

The last section, to the fairy-tale phrase "No one knew any more need of any kind," comes back to the dream of the despairing alcoholic's wife. Virtually all of Zhivotov's *Drunkards at Father John's* stories share this tone and structure, differing only in the extent of the drunkard's initial wealth and the depth of his degradation. Father John appears as the same kindly, Saint Nicholas–like helper (and the stories connected to Saint Nicholas seem to provide the closest prototype for Father John stories, for reasons that will be discussed below); the drunkard has already hit bottom and himself decided to seek out Father John. For all that they seem to have been cut from the same pattern, however, the compiler always takes pains to give such details as the source, the name and patronymic of the repentant drunkard, the age of the family members, the number of children, the length of time elapsed in each stage—all without any caveats about their having been changed to protect anyone's identity.

This lack of anonymity makes perfect sense. While the saint and the recipients are alive, the reporters tend to be so struck by the wonder of the events that they include as much information as possible to impress upon the listeners that "[t]his really happened, here is the people's address"; later, inquest commissions for canonizations sought out specific information as well.⁷⁸ The motivation here is different from those seeking to be healed of sickness who provided Father John with as many symptoms as possible in their letters, but it is identical to accounts of successful cures. In both the healing miracles and the alcoholics' *vitae*, the desired transformation has already occurred: the thing is to impress both its importance and its veracity on the reader. Similarly, the late nineteenth-century emphasis on accuracy emerges in contemporaries writing not that Father John was universally known, but that "his works are read everywhere on earth *between 30 and 70 degrees longitude.*"⁷⁹

It is this emphasis on veracity that yields the most valuable unwitting information about what was most likely to impress Father John's contemporaries:

> The transformation from a shy, lowered, humiliated rag-picker to a person with firm resolve, decisiveness, and almost exaltation occurred so quickly, that he needed only *a suit* to become completely unrecognizable....
>
> He stood straight, throwing his head slightly back, and each motion was accompanied by so much confidence that it was as if someone had just made him *a business consultant* or awarded him a *major decoration*....
>
> Within two years, Petr Ermolaevich opened up his own store; just recently he bought *a stone house*.⁸⁰

One last thing needs to be said about the alcoholics' *vitae*. Along with illustrating a progression from being rich as Croesus (they use precisely this expression) to the most bitter poverty to God-fearing bourgeois comfort, they also attempt to inculcate desirable standards of behavior. Even as the erstwhile alcoholic achieves respectability, the *vita* makes clear that this is not enough. He now practices what many Christian denominations refer to as good stewardship as well. Although the *vita* does not have Father John command the alcoholic to begin donating money—he limits himself to insisting upon confession and communion—in every case, the reformed drunkard and his family become paragons of solid burgher virtues:

> Every Sunday and holiday, the family went to church; every evening was dedicated to prayer and reading from the Holy Scriptures.... Not a single pauper was turned away. The parish church

became the object of his particular solicitude. He had the icon cases and the liturgical utensils gilded, he fixed the church chandelier, he bought icons—in a word, he did everything he could to ornament and beautify the church.[81]

Now I-v manages apartment houses and capital and makes large donations for good works. Drunkenness never tempts him, and he never takes anything alcoholic in his mouth.[82]

In short, as well as being the mouthpieces for the dreams of despairing family members, the alcoholics' *vitae* also served as *exempla*, providing both hopes and models for fallen men and their families. While Father John is central to the successful resolution of the plot, he is not the focus of the story; he is important mostly as a *deus ex machina* for the lay drinker.

The situation is different for the works that focus on Father John. The people who wrote narratives of his life in support of his eventual canonization draw directly on earlier hagiographic models: they describe his standing out even in childhood, his regular encounters with the Divine, and so on. Zhivotovskii, who visited Father John's native village at the height of his fame wrote, for example,

From long ago, Father John's relatives have grown accustomed to regard him as a special person, as someone not of this world. I learned here that even in childhood, the Psalm-reader Ilya Sergiev's son, the small, thoughtful Ivanushka, enjoyed the particular respect of his fellow-villagers. Let someone lose his horse—he or she will go to ask Ivanushka to pray; let some misfortune happen, or let someone fall sick—they go to Ivanushka once again.

But then the wondrous boy grew up, and his glory shone like the sun over Orthodox Rus'.[83]

In a similarly hagiographical account, another biographer quotes an old man as saying that "[h]e was prayer-like. When he was only a little boy, we saw him going to school: he would take off his boots so as not to wear out the goods obtained by his father's labors, and carry them in his hands. And first off he would go to church. He would stand on his little knees and pray—and go to school only after praying."[84]

Contemporary narratives of Father John included other hagiographical elements. The poverty of his birthplace inspired some of his admirers and biographers to think of the cave of the Nativity.[85] Others, more inclined to patriotism, drew comparisons with the serf background of the poet and scientist Mikhail Lomonosov.[86] Both attempts to seek historical parallels or precursors for events in the life of a holy person—not in a strict genealogical sense, or even in the sense of spiritual ancestry—recall the Byzantine *topoi* in the Orthodox liturgy. These allegories and similes sought to connect the saint to the pantheon that preceded him, and occasionally to the natural world as well. In this respect, the reference to Lomonosov is particularly telling. It suggests that, in their accounts of his life, Father John's contemporaries were seeking not only to associate him with the Russian classics but also to use him to link secular Russian heroes with events in religious history. To them, both religion and "canonized" culture were part of being truly Russian. This view was characteristic of a strain of Slavophile thought and illustrates how often people linked the religious and the secular, or even the Divine and the human, elements in Russian history. The blurring of the lines came through most in the figure of the Tsar, who was believed by the Orthodox Church as having been anointed by God and whose birthday, saints-day, and coronation anniversary were celebrated by state and church alike as holidays, with services, sermons, and military parades. Similarly, the inclusion of Lomonosov as a prototype in Father John's spiritual biography reinforced the notion that serving Tsar, art, and country were functionally equivalent to serving the Orthodox Church. (Other writers, by contrast, took pains to point out that Father John was not a typical "superfluous man" from literature, like Pushkin's Onegin, Lermontov's Pechorin, or Turgenev's Rudin.)[87] Later biographers drew even further-reaching parallels between religion and culture: in the 1990s, Nikolai Lisovoi noted that Father John was born on the very day that Pushkin composed his *Reminiscences about Tsarskoe Selo*—October 19, 1829—and suggested that such events in the spiritual life of a nation were more connected internally than was immediately evident.[88]

Even more telling was the stress that Father John's biographers—especially those who were themselves priests or monks—placed on his clerical background: a grandfather on one side a priest; family in clergy for at least 350 years. Father John's life is one of the first instances of the clerical background of a saint being emphasized in a *vita* (of course, partly because he was one of the very few married priests to be canonized). Russian hagiographies usually restrict themselves to citing the influence of the immediate family, particularly the parents of the future saint. When parents are cited in a *vita*, they fall into two categories: pious parents who set an example for the saint-to-be, or parents who object to the child's desire for an ascetic life and must either be won over to his side or overcome.[89] Because of the attempts throughout the nineteenth century to make the clergy open to men from all backgrounds, the manifestly positive effect of Father John's clerical genealogy was used as a defense against contemporary critics of the clergy's castelike nature.[90]

The emphasis on clerical lineage had another, earlier precedent. From the beginning of Christianity, the *vitae* of the holy sought to include what pertinent evidence existed as regards their origins; the lives of Augustine, Basil of Caesarea, and Gregory the Theologian show the spiritually influential role of their mothers or sisters.[91] In Father John's case, as with Gregory of Tours, several biographers used the clerical pedigree to suggest that over three centuries of service to the church had left their imprint to create an "aristocrat" of piety.[92] The abbot Konstantin exclaimed, for example, "How full of meaning is his career against the background of his genealogy! For he is the offshoot of an entire "dynasty" of priests and psalm-readers who served the same village church for over three hundred years! See how thick was the "levitical" blood that flowed in the veins of Father John!"[93]

Father John's hagiographers themselves faced the dilemma of the "priest's two bodies." As a saint, Father John's goal was his own salvation, with his primary responsibility to his own soul. As a priest, his goal was the salvation of his flock, with his primary responsibility to them. Both in his personal relationships and in the reporting of his life, it is important to know from which "body" he is acting. If Father John occasionally felt tension between the two—as regards his wife, for example—is it surprising that his biographers might, as well?

The personal-saintly aspect of the future *vita* had to establish Father John's "supernatural" religious pedigree, identifying his spiritual ancestors and prototypes as well as his biological ones. This would have been especially important for Father John, as he had no personal spiritual father, and his biological father died when he was relatively young. But the emphasis on spiritual ancestry comes from Christianity itself, with its emphasis on individual salvation. One's primary ties of both affection and responsibility go not to one's family, but to God ("He that loveth father or mother, ... son or daughter, more than me, is not worthy of Me" [Matthew 10:37]).

Father John's unusual family situation posed a challenge, and it is one that his contemporary biographers handled carefully. Although he felt the tension between family and religious obligations within himself, his biographers were invariably careful to stress both his life-long submission and devotion to his mother and his chaste, harmonious relation with his wife.[94] In fact, one of the many things that distinguishes representations of Father John from the pattern of a typical holy man is his apparent devotion to his family. His father died in 1851, the same year John entered the St. Petersburg Theological Academy. With John as the only son and the only family member with more than a rudimentary education, breadwinning responsibilities fell to him. Some accounts suggest that he felt the weight of family responsibility and offered to withdraw from the Academy to take on employment as a deacon, but his mother generously refused. All biographies mention that his fine handwriting and good behavior earned him employment in the Academy as a clerk and scrivener. Most also state that John earned nine (or ten) rubles a month and sent all of it home to his mother.[95]

These homely virtues of filial duty, particularly prized by the peasantry and the merchant classes, are usually absent from the *vitae* of monks and nuns. Of course, just as a clerical family tree was unusual in *vitae*, so part of the reason for the absence of family ties in the lives of men saints is the nature of the saintly genre. The lives of the earlier warrior princes emphasize military valor and service to the fatherland; those of ascetic monks or bishops usually stress family opposition and the tendency to run away to a monastery, with one's saintly life usually beginning in earnest only upon monastic tonsure.[96] For all of the emphasis on women's service to the family in didactic literature, the lives of the few Russian women saints also tend to follow this ascetic pattern, with such family-oriented saints as Ul'iana Lazarevskaia being the exception rather than the rule.[97] Father John introduced a variation into the pattern, first by his devotion to his parents as a child, and, second, in his saintly life beginning with his ordination. His being a married priest dovetailed neatly with a movement from the intelligentsia to force a more positive official recognition by the Church of family life.[98]

This implicit celebration of the family in Father John's life was more than paradoxical: he had virtually no independent family life to speak of, as his biographers knew. His chastity in marriage also played into the hands of such un-Orthodox thinkers as sectarians and Vladimir Solov'ev.[99] Father John's biographers all refer to the displeasure of his wife at his decision to remain chaste, which was evidently made without his consulting her and of which she learned only after their wedding (this is key, because if both had agreed, there would have been hagiographical precedent and no problem).[100] The more charitable hagiographers assume that Father John persuaded her to live with him as a sister with a brother with the words: "There are enough happy families without us, Liza. Let us dedicate ourselves to serving God and our neighbor."[101] (The parallel with the works and concerns of Lev Tolstoy is striking, whether in *Family Happiness*, *Kreuzer Sonata*, or in the opening lines of *Anna Karenina*.) In doing so, some claim that Father John is one of the "redeemed 144,000 virgins" referred to in the Apocalypse.[102] Those with a more sanguine view of human nature ascribe more forceful opposition to his wife. Some hold that in attempting to appeal to her husband's sense of obedience to church authority, she petitioned Metropolitan Isidor of St. Petersburg to remind him of his marital obligations; others that she pursued divorce; others still that her father—the dean whose position Father John had inherited by marrying his daughter—went to the authorities on her behalf.[103] One version of their encounter might as well have been taken from early Christian saints' lives. In this account, Metropolitan Isidor summoned Father John into his presence and threatened him with the loss of his position, divorce, and so on. Father John reportedly told him that "It is the will of God [that I live so], and you will come to know it," and walked out. The moment he left, the Metropolitan went blind, and his sight was not restored until he called Father John back, begged pardon, and asked him to pray for him.[104]

Leaving aside the inherently fantastic nature of this report, Father John never referred to it in his diary, even as he appears to have recorded every instance of his contact with the Metropolitan, over the course of thirty years.[105] Moreover, in the first years of his career, when this incident would have occurred, Father John doubted that the sort of miracles described in the apostolic period and in hagiography were possible in the current historical moment. The unlikeliness of such classical "revenge" incidents with the Divine punishing others on Father John's behalf, however, did not make them any less popular among many of his biographers.

One story described how three students decided to play a prank on Father John by having one of them pretend to be deathly ill and another pretend to be his distraught brother. After warning the three that they were joking with God, he prayed that they receive according to their faith—and the faker instantly became paralyzed. He recovered only after the two instigators had sought out Father John and repented.[106] Captain Stepan Burachek also claimed that he had witnessed someone making jokes about Father John be immediately burned in the face while lighting a cigarette, adding that the victim himself understood that he was punished for his "free-thinking."[107] A woman who asked for money, claiming falsely that her hut had been destroyed in a fire, received it (and thought privately, "So much for your clairvoyancy!")—only to return home and find her hut burned to the ground, alone of all those in the village.[108]

In making a case for this sort of "revenge" miracle, the writers cite such instances as the apostle Paul's blinding of Elymas the sorcerer as precedents. However, such contemporary religious journals as *The Wanderer* also regularly included similar accounts of Divine punishment, such as "God's Fearful Punishment of an Insubmissive Daughter," "A Manifest Execution by God for Not Venerating the Feast of the Prophet Elijah," and "How a Schismatic who Blasphemed Against Communion Was Brought to his Senses." Father John's contemporaries knew well the figure of God stepping on behalf of His own.[109]

The willingness of such proto-hagiographers as Bol'shakov and Surskii to include such dubious material—a willingness questioned by their more sober fellow hagiographers who were no less devoted to Father John—suggests both the proportions his image had achieved and the relative lack of control in the Russian Orthodox Church when it came to tempering the accounts of, let alone the activities of, holy men. In any case, his wife appears in contemporary biographies only long enough to establish his chastity and his ascetic overcoming of the bounds of nature, as well as—implicitly—his "right" to daily communion, after which she is not heard from again. She exists as an obstacle to overcome and the means by which Father John gets his parish; after this, most biographers either feel that she is irrelevant to Father John's future development or that she poses a nagging problem solved best by passing over silence. (It is no coincidence that photographs of her are so rare in the pantheon of family photographs, and perhaps also that, when she does appear, she looks either pinched or dour.)[110] Only in her own eulogies and in the Russian *vita* of 1990 is she praised as being the "ideal *matushka*."[111]

More important are the three spiritual ancestors whom Father John's biographers identify for him: Saint John of Ryla (Ioann Ryl'skii), for whom he was named; Saint Nicholas, in whose church he received his primary religious education; and Saint Serafim of Sarov, to whom a living link is established. Here the question arises of how much Father John cooperated with his public in fostering his own cult.[112] On the one hand, he had to guard against pride to avoid losing grace; on the other, he could not deny that he had been given unique grace and believed, using the same rationalization used to uphold the veneration of icons, that, in honoring him, people were honoring the Divine source.[113] The

Fig. 7 Father John and Elizaveta Konstantinovna with his godchild's family. Photo courtesy of the Central State Archive of Cine- and Photo-Documents.

line was very fine, and one can discern it first in the importance to Father John of Saint John of Ryla (d. 946), the Bulgarian hermit for whom he was named. After Father John became so famous that people flocked to celebrate his saint's day, he linked the attention showered on himself on the feast day he shared with the saint, both to deflect it from himself—and to indicate how people should perceive him. On one such October 19, for example, he thanked the crowds who had come to congratulate him with, "You have gathered here ... to honor *in my person* the servant of Christ and your fellow pray-er, the performer of Christ's Mysteries and one who strives to support you in your salvation and the leading of a God-pleasing Christian life, *and also* to venerate the great *Pleaser* of God, John."[114] Father John also named the convent he founded in St. Petersburg after his patron, so that it became known simply as "John's" (Ioannovskii)—allowing people to refer simultaneously to both the founder and the prototype. (This proved especially convenient, of course, when he himself was canonized.) His biographers were not so subtle. In one sermon Father John delivered on Saint Nicholas of Myra's feastday, the biographers were quick to "discern" that when he was praising Saint Nicholas and paraphrasing the troparion hymn to him, he was in fact speaking of himself, and condemning Tolstoy in the person of Arius:

> Today we are celebrating the memory of Nicholas the Luminary. He is mostly called a Wonderworker, however, because he performed and continues to perform so many miracles that it is impossible to describe them exhaustively. His very life was a miracle: he was the most right rule of faith and the strict denunciator of the then-contemporary heresy of Arius, who reduced the Son of God to the level of an ordinary creature. He was meek, humble of heart, accessible to everyone, compassionate, merciful, the sincere helper of widows and orphans, the defender of those unjustly persecuted and sentenced, chaste to the highest degree.[115]

The comparison ended with Father John's addressing the matter of miracles, particularly the contemporary assertion that all "so-called" miracles were explainable by natural causes. He said modestly that in his own service to many people, he had encountered "multitudes" of rapid and even instantaneous cures of the lame, the blind, and the deaf (without, of course, directly mentioning his own prayerful role in those cures). The reference to Arius is certainly not coincidental, either. Father John gave this sermon in 1898, when he had already crossed swords with Tolstoy more than once. By invoking Nicholas and Arius, he intended to summon up the specter of himself fighting Tolstoy and his followers, who denied the Divinity of Christ and saw the Gospels exclusively as a source of moral teaching.[116] To biographers, then, Saint Nicholas and Saint John of Ryla provided Father John's true ancestors, protectors, and prototypes—and, it seems, to Father John himself.

But to whom could he look as models if not the saints, after all? If Tolstoy could acknowledge Pushkin as a predecessor and influence, could a seeker of holiness refer in a similarly natural way to saintly predecessors without seeming vain or presumptuous? He could not, because of the obvious difference between artistic and spiritual mastery: Father John's creation was the salvation of his own soul, from which he could not separate himself as a writer could from his manuscript.

For fear of a fall, Father John had to avoid explicit parallels with other saints, while his biographers did not. (Only in letters to the Abbess Taisiia—herself a person of great spiritual rigor—could he write of a grace-filled service, "It seemed as if everything were aflame—I was inspired, too, and spoke like a prophet or an Apostle."[117]

Of all three spiritual "ancestors," the connection biographers made between Father John and Saint Serafim of Sarov is the most telling, especially after Serafim's canonization in 1903.[118] Nikanor, the archbishop of Kazan, stated point blank in the newsletter of his diocese that Father John was Serafim's successor in terms of holy glory, for all the difference in their ways of life. Nikanor was one of the first to declare that the change in religious styles between the ascetic monk and the married priest was a function of the change of the times. Father John used steamships and trains instead of standing in solitude on a rock, as did Serafim, because people needed him to be everywhere. "Because people are different now," Nikanor claimed, "they need to be acted upon in new ways peculiar to them."[119] Saint Serafim's spiritual authority also impelled some of Father John's contemporaries to establish a direct link between the two men through the person of the "eldress" Paraskeva Ivanovna Kovrigina. According to them, Serafim's favorite disciple, Ilarion, had specifically instructed Paraskeva to leave the Reshmin hermitage (*pustyn'*) and serve Father John, "the new luminary of the Church of Christ, who is shining in Kronstadt."[120]

This spiritual blessing and connection was intended to establish Father John's being "anointed" by Serafim to perform miracles, but such a connection is tenuous. Father John never made such a link himself, referring to Kovrigina publicly only as the pious woman who had encouraged him to pray for someone's healing (and disparaged her privately).[121] There were, to be sure, practical motivations for drawing the comparison. Identifying a connection to Serafim minimized Father John's idiosyncratic qualities, and made him appear less exceptional in the eyes of the Church hierarchy. Moreover, Saint Serafim had been canonized largely at Nicholas II's initiative. Perhaps Father John's biographers were hoping for the same, given that pupils of saints are better candidates for canonization.[122] Ironically, Soviet writers seeking to debunk religion followed the same path as the hagiographers—by establishing links between Father John and other saints. Rubakin, for example, compared Father John's exorcising of demons from "hysterical" women to the earlier practices of Saint Bernard.[123]

As well as establishing a spiritual genealogy for Father John, his contemporaries followed such other hagiographical conventions as attempting to foreshadow marvelous events to come in the life of the saint (a phenomenon that also occurred in *The Lives of Remarkable People* series, in which the "remarkable person's" accomplishments would be prefigured in the first twelve years of his or her life). The most recurrent instance of childhood promise, cited in Father John's own words, seems to draw from the classic life of Saint Sergii of Radonezh. As a student in the diocesan school for clerical sons, John Sergiev did very badly. As he describes it:

> My father received the smallest possible salary, so it was awfully difficult to get by. I already understood the burdensome position of my parents and therefore my inability to learn was a real disaster. I did not think much about the significance of learning with respect to my future, but I was especially sad that my father was spending his last resources for my upkeep, and all in vain.[124]

But then the first miracle of his life occurred:

> All were cleverer; I was the last in the class.... I began to get up at night to pray, which I preferred: everyone was asleep ... it was quiet.... I prayed most often for God to give me the light of wisdom for the consolation of my parents.[125] One night, as before, I could not understand anything we had gone over; as before, I read badly; I could not understand or remember anything the teacher had said. Such a depression fell upon me that I fell on my knees and began to pray fervently. I do not know whether I was in this state for long, but suddenly I was shaking all over. It was exactly as if a curtain had fallen from my eyes; it was as if my intellect had opened up in my head and I could clearly envision the teacher I had heard that day, his lesson; I even remembered what he had spoken of. And my soul began to feel light and joyous. I had never slept as calmly as I did that night. When it was barely light, I leapt from my bed, grabbed my books, and—oh, happiness—I was reading much more easily, I understood everything, and I did not only understand everything that I had read, but I could relay it. I sat differently in class than I had before: I understood everything, I remembered everything. The teacher assigned an arithmetic problem: I solved it and the teacher even praised me. In a word, in a short time I made so much progress that I was no longer the last student. The farther, the better I did in my studies, and by the end of the course I was one of the first in the class transferring to seminary.[126]

The similarity of this incident to one in the life of Saint Sergii of Radonezh and those of others saints who were unable to learn properly and gain the ability through divine intervention, shows to what extent Father John shared the mental universe of his biographers in reconstructing his childhood. Nevertheless, there are several differences. His account is autobiographical. In a culture that stressed and valued modesty even in its secular forms, Father John would have been inclined to minimize rather than to accentuate signs of special election: he mentions an event that stresses his own nullity and God's power.[127] Above all, Father John's account is realistic; no elder appears miraculously; he is bothered not so much by the fact of doing badly as by the consciousness that he is burdening his poor parents. Poor children felt keenly the crushing sense of being a liability rather than an asset, and sensed that they must justify their existence and repay their real material debt to one's parents, quite independently of whatever mutual affection both parties may have had.[128]

A more explicitly supernatural childhood incident, involving a vision, calls for more comment. The Abbess Taisiia of Leushino describes the event from a conversation with Father John: "Once, during the night, Vanya saw an extraordinary light in the room. He looked and saw in the light an angel in his heavenly glory. The little boy was troubled, but the angel calmed him by telling him that he was his guardian angel."[129] Given that Orthodox lives of the saints after the eighteenth century rarely contain cases of visions that do not pertain to icons (in striking contrast to the Roman Catholic nineteenth- and early twentieth-century visions of Mary), this event is unusual.[130] There may be less obvious parallels, however, which need to be noted.

One comes from the sphere of the visual arts. Even before the mid–nineteenth-century change proposed by Soviet art historians, who ascribed changes in iconographic style largely to the social and economic changes wrought by the Emancipation of the serfs in 1861,[131] German Romantic, French Catholic, and Victorian art had influenced Russian iconographic painting to the point of creating a new subgenre—religious pictures based on the biblical illustrations of Gustav Doré. One of the most popular images was that of two children walking hand in hand across a precipice against a waterfall, sometimes with a cross on the hillside (all stock Romantic images) with a tall, serene Guardian Angel hovering reassuringly behind them.[132] There was also a growing genre of edifying children's stories with a sentimental religious-supernatural element.[133] While this element, trickling down as it did from aristocratic circles, would hardly have reached the remote

John Sergiev, it would have affected Abbess Taisiia, the tale's recounter —she had come from a cultured family, was one of the granddaughters of the poet Aleksandr Pushkin, and had had several visions herself. In any case, both the visions of the angel and the immediate, almost supernatural response to prayer, reinforce the image of John Sergiev's childhood as unusually permeated with a sense of the closeness of the Divine and its responsiveness to entreaty.[134]

Another formative influence emphasized by biographers is his fondness for spiritual reading. Even more than the Psalter and the Desert Fathers, the texts used in the services he loved, Father John was drawn to the New Testament. As the Abbess Taisiia recounted him saying:

> Do you know what laid the foundations of my turning to God and what, already in my childhood, warmed my heart with love for Him? It was the Holy Gospels. My father had a New Testament and I loved to read this marvelous book when I came home for my school-holidays; the style and simplicity of narration made it accessible to my childish reasoning; I read the Gospels, enjoyed them and found them an irreplaceable consolation.... I may say that this New Testament was my childhood companion, my tutor, guide and comforter, and that from an early age I was familiar with it.[135]

It was this combination of scriptural, patristic, and liturgical reading that biographers claimed made Father John such a "harmonious, pure, and healthy being," and which made both his speech and his writings so immediate and vivid.[136]

Finally, most of his biographers refer to his initially wanting to become a missionary, whether to Alaska, Africa, or China.[137] At the time that John Sergiev was a student in the Theological Academy, this path was gaining in followers. The Orthodox Church had recently stepped up its missionary activity and seminarians could consider traveling to convert people who were now within Russia's territories.[138] Although it was more common for missionaries to be monks, by the nineteenth century, married priests such as Ioann Popov, who was later canonized under his monastic name of Saint Innocent, had also become active in Alaska.[139] The rationale usually given for John Sergiev's choosing to become a married priest is that after becoming acquainted with what struck him as the dissipated life of the capital, he decided that Russia "had enough of her own pagans."[140]

This seems to be retrospective cleverness, however. Father John himself never mentioned a tendency toward missionary work, emphasizing instead the long attraction of the priesthood.¹⁴¹ A more plausible and more original explanation for his not choosing missionary work has been offered by the abbot Konstantin. He suggests that John was so steeped in the patriarchal nature of his family and so dependent on it that he could hardly imagine anything beyond the priesthood and shied away from the path of monasticism and missionary work as something too extraordinary, sticking to the well-beaten track by marrying a priest's daughter who could provide a secure "position."¹⁴² In all, then, the Orthodox depictions of Father John written during his lifetime combine contemporary details along with typical hagiographical structure and motifs; these details would gradually vanish from ever-later versions.

Negative Representations

All the representations of Father John discussed so far have one thing in common: they are, at the very least, positive. But there were other, less favorable, depictions written during his lifetime. Most of the hostility he prompted came from his support of the autocracy during the 1905 Revolution, but he triggered negative representations for religious reasons as well as political ones. The strongest such attack came from the writer Nikolai Leskov.

Throughout the late 1870s and early 1880s, at the very time when Father John was catching the public eye, Leskov was moving gradually from familiar descriptions of Orthodoxy to a Tolstoyan anticlerical and antisacramental position. His accounts of Orthodox "types," which grew steadily more acerbic, reached their apogee with a work called "The Vigil-aunties" (*Polunoshchniki*). The novella, which was first published in the liberal *The Messenger of Europe* in late 1891, represented both an attack on establishment Orthodoxy and a retaliation for Father John's anti-Tolstoyan position.¹⁴³ Leskov hated Father John for exemplifying all that he had come to despise in Russian Orthodoxy, from sacraments, icons, and miracles to the cult of the saints. To Leskov, Tolstoy represented everything good in Russian religious life, and Father John everything evil. In a letter to Lidia Veselitskaia, he reduced the matter to its simplest terms: "You cannot love [both] Lev Tolstoy and John of Kronstadt."¹⁴⁴ "The Vigil-aunties" is a devastating satire not only of his entourage, but also of Father John himself, who is trounced in a religious debate by the Tolstoyan Klavdiia.¹⁴⁵

Leskov's animosity did not end there. He felt that Father John not only personified Russian Orthodoxy, he had individually repugnant qualities: praying over people individually and not in a group, choosing only curable people to heal, and so on. He expressed himself with full venom in private letters. In a letter to Prince Dimitrii A. Khilkov, another Tolstoyan, Leskov commented sardonically (in brilliantly used Church Slavonic) that a sure sign of Father John's perspicacity was his choosing to accept the invitations of Marks, the well-known publisher of atlases and the journal *Niva*, and Suvorin, the publisher of *New Time*, but not that of "the poor, righteous widow" Tifiaeva, a publisher who was seeking funding for her children's magazine, *Toy*.[146] Leskov even refused to call Father John by his proper name, referring to him instead as "Ivanov," "Ivan Il'ich," or "Perjean" (from Père Jean). Leskov also despised those who followed Father John and fanned his cult, especially those who he felt ought to know better. After Khilkov's children were forcibly baptized with Father John's assistance, even though their father had not wanted it, Leskov exploded to Tolstoy on December 14, 1893:

> The worst of all this is how people in contemporary society, who have lost all sense and conscience, respond to it. They say very little about it and when they do it is always wanly and dully and put the matter in this fashion: "Well, it all depends on how you look at it, it all depends on your point of view." ... The most important thing here is that Khilkov's mother began this "with PerJean's blessing," and whatever foulness Père Jean might do, it is all "holy." ... Even those from whom I would not expect it all toe the same line.[147]

Similarly despicable, in Leskov's opinion, were artists who painted pictures of Father John, and the periodicals that reproduced them. After *Art Survey* printed Vereshchagin's painting, *The Visit of a Sick Woman by Father John Sergiev*, in the first issue of 1891 along with a detailed account of his "wonder-working" activity, Leskov vilified the magazine's editor.[148] Earlier, he had written sneeringly of how a painter had just finished an oil called *The Temptation of Father John*. "One sees night, a study, the moon, a church through the window, he is dreaming over a book, a little devil holding a straw is tickling him behind his right ear; to the right is a young woman with a decollté 'down to there,' but he is tired and persists in dreaming."[149] He concluded:

> They have swallowed their Ivans the wrong way, but unfortunately have not choked on them. His "images" are being sold in

icon-shops next to saviors, Kazans, and "all saints." Publishing houses are falling over one another to get their hands on him and are now all spattered by him. While his glory and the stupidity of society continue to grow, like a particular kind of post over the place where you relieve yourself in a two-story pub in an *uezd* town.

Tolstoy himself, incidentally, shared Khilkov's and Leskov's sentiments, writing on August 3, 1890: "Your letter about John is marvelous; I guffawed the whole time I read it aloud. It is awful what they have done with the Russian people in nine hundred years of Christianity. They, particularly the women, are completely savage idol-worshippers."[150] While the most destructive criticism of Father John's milieu would come later, in connection with the Ioannite scandal, there was already a negative representation to provide a foil to the positive ones.

Responses of the Clerical Hierarchy

Leskov's and Tolstoy's dislike for Father John was fully in keeping with their neo-Protestant sensibilities. But men charged with maintaining Orthodoxy could be even more alarmed by both the presence of an unusual priest and the spontaneous, mass aspect of Father John's appeal. Individual charisma and elemental outbursts of devotion such as his seemed to undermine the institutional basis on which the grace of the priest had traditionally rested. He rekindled the same fear of charisma only barely bridled by church tradition and discipline and the sacraments that had historically characterized the uneasy relations between charismatic or mystical individuals and the church hierarchy, and that had expressed itself to a still greater extent most recently in episcopal animosity to the Optina elders.[151] Rozanov's sharp observation that Father John's charisma overshadowed that of conventional religious authorities was on the mark.

The nature of the official objections to Father John was both practical and principled. The practical objections were straightforward: Kronstadt was a bustling port town near the capital. Father John attracted more multitudes than had any monastic elder and was more in the public eye than they by virtue of geography alone; he was strategically well placed both to have crowds reach him conveniently and to attract attention. The nature of the principled objections to him was more complicated and changed over the course of his career.

In the first twenty-five years of his priesthood, Father John remained largely a local phenomenon and could be controlled relatively easily. Any infractions of discipline or custom on his part, such as his relations with his wife or his unusual involvement in the lives of his flock, were perceived as private rather than public phenomena and were handled accordingly. During this period of his career, the church authorities regarded him as a local curiosity—overzealous, perhaps, ultimately biddable. Although their written reactions to Father John at this time have not survived, they may be surmised from his diaries. In 1869, for example, he commented of his archpriest, "In private, he's fine, but in public, he puts a brake on me that is far too strong, even unreasonable."[152] Even if one allows for Father John's wounded feelings, the confirmation from contemporary secondary sources suggests that there was indeed tension. And although it is unlikely that Metropolitan Isidor of St. Petersburg was blinded for attempting to reprove him, his diaries do describe years of chilly treatment and rebuffs on Isidor's part. In 1867, he spoke of "my insult, my sadness, and my tears after the brusque, refractory reception I received at the Metropolitan's"; in 1890, at the height of his fame, he wrote, "Not once in thirty years has he greeted me in a fatherly way, with a kind word or look, but always in a demeaning way, with severity and harshness."[153]

The turning point in Father John's relation not only with the people who came to him but also the church hierarchy was the 1883 open letter to *New Time*. On the day after the letter ran, the Ober-Procurator brought it to the attention of the Synod. All the members were nonplussed; Isidor was displeased that "such a notice"—that is, one concerning a religious topic and proscribing a change in religious behavior—had been printed in a secular newspaper without being approved by the religious censor.[154]

The nature of the Metropolitan's objection goes to the heart of the suspicion Father John initially encountered on the part of the hierarchy. The bishops had been trying to exercise more control over religious observance and phenomena and to draw the lines more clearly over what was appropriate religious behavior and what was not. Monks and itinerant holy people had been the chief troublemakers in this regard; now individual charisma had sprung up from an entirely unexpected quarter. Father John and his admirers, it appeared, were seeking to extend and blur the very lines the church authorities were so earnestly seeking to draw.

Indeed, Father John's revision of the Synodal-era priesthood and support of the social forms of the early Church seemed to call into question the hierarchy's attempt to set boundaries. Why had he not entered a monastery rather than getting married if he had no intention of consummating the marriage? Why had the sixteen grateful people not expressed their sentiments in a religious newspaper so that the contents might have been approved by the necessary authorities? The issue was one of deliberately confusing the few areas of religiosity that were clearly defined: proper channels existed for pursuing chastity and the ascetic life; proper channels existed for expressing views pertaining to Orthodox beliefs and practices. Father John appeared to be taking on tasks for himself, including chastity and religious writing, that were seen as belonging to monks and bishops, and being outside the accepted boundaries of being a parish priest.

Another objection to his having stepped out of his proper sphere was the matter of maintaining control. From Peter I onward, the clergy had been treated as a separate branch of society, with its own courts, its own publications, and its own censorship. As well as providing the lower-ranked clergy with a certain measure of protection with regard to the other classes of the Russian population, this policy also maintained their isolation and their subjection to their superiors. Having laypeople praise a cleric in the lay press in the way they had Father John invited judgment by standards and individuals other than those of the Orthodox church, which could remove the priest from direct subordination to his religious authorities and allow him to appeal to independent public opinion.

In this sense, Father John was one of the first harbingers of a less easily manageable priesthood.[155] Because of his independent, charismatic appeal he triggered an official mistrust that persisted for decades. Despite the valiant attempts made by his official biographer, the Archimandrite Mikhail, to cite the honors he received as proof of his having risen to the heights of worldly as well as spiritual success, there is no record of Father John's being invited to serve in the major cathedrals of Russia. He never served, for instance, in the Dormition Cathedral or that of Christ the Savior, or in the most famous monastery in Russia, the Trinity-Sergiev Lavra.[156] Although he was among those invited to participate in the wedding and coronation of Nicholas II, he was not included in the festivities organized by the clergy proper, such as the canonizations of Feodosii of Chernigov and Serafim of Sarov.[157] Even after Father John had become famous and somewhat autonomous, bishops still insisted on their prerogatives where they could. In one instance in 1887, when (in an evocation of early Church practice) he backed a peasant candidate for the priesthood who enjoyed popular support but lacked formal seminary training, for example, the local bishop dismissed his petition in no uncertain terms.[158] Ministry of the Interior Censorship committees in both St. Petersburg and Moscow banned such publications as collections of spiritual verses dedicated to Father John, descriptions of him as a healer of drunkards, and accounts of his travels.[159]

Bishops were especially concerned with matters of church policy, such as the dispensations from the rules governing preparation for communion that Father John gave out so freely. Bishop Savva (Tikhomirov) once reprimanded him for an incident that had occurred during his visit to the Vyshnevolotskii Kazanskii convent. Father John had apparently allowed several nuns to take communion without previous confession from their spiritual father at the convent, and Savva investigated this infraction of monastic discipline, finally ruling that such allowances not be repeated.[160] The stumbling block here was very similar to that posed by the elders: the authority of the independently chosen spiritual father seemed to supersede and threaten that of hierarchical discipline. Many bishops were determined that dispensation was properly and exclusively theirs to give. On other occasions, Father John had to defend himself against accusations of theological slipperiness made by the celebrated recluse, Bishop Feofan.[161]

Not all of Father John's clerical peers were enthusiastic, either. While many admired him, others were aggrieved that he was running away with all the glory, making other priests look bad by comparison. They thought his distinctive mannerisms were "affected" and unnecessary; some even chased him out when he appeared in their churches.[162] Still other parish clergy were reluctant to have him participate in their churches because of the pandemonium his services aroused. "There is always a problem with the visits of Father John of Kronstadt. Any time he shows up, the church is always packed to the gills with people—they drag in the sick, they are all shouting and making noise, they fill the church full of dirt, and it takes a long time after his departure until you finally recover."[163]

The problem Father John posed went beyond being simply a matter of control. With his becoming a public figure, the irregularities posed a potential public, as well as a private or local, threat. The celebrated Bishop Feofan (the Recluse), who was in no way "responsible" for him, as was Metropolitan Isidor, wrote Father John a warning letter that was couched only in terms of the spiritual danger his efforts posed to himself and to others. Pursuing an ascetic way of life in the world was fraught with temptation for anyone who was not a monk, Feofan argued;

he was concerned both for the possibility that Father John might "fall fearfully" and be a cause for scandal and innuendo among both clergy and laypeople.[164]

The healing cited by the sixteen, and the many others who followed in their wake, posed another difficulty. The fact of miraculous occurrences was not necessarily problematic in itself: the nineteenth century had seen a gradual retreat from the rationalism of the ecclesiastical regulation and an embrace of the potentially supranatural. The obstacle lay in the source. When cures were attributed to Divine intervention, they were expected to occur through the veneration of icons, holy relics, or the intercession of reposed saints; instances of clairvoyance were common among elders and holy fools, but recovery from illness was most unusual. Father John caught the church unawares. The Orthodox Church in Russia had *vitae* of pre-modern healers, as well as those of Saints Nicholas or Cosmas and Damian, but it had nearly forgotten how to cope with a living thaumaturge. According to some accounts, Konstantin Pobedonostsev, the Ober-Procurator of the Synod, called in Father John for questioning precisely on the matter of reputed miracles. "Others have started out in the same way you have," Pobedonostsev is reported to have said to Father John, "How will you end up?"[165]

This account conveys the difficulty the Church authorities continued to encounter in seeking to check and channel unconventional forms of religious behavior. While there was a developed "negative" system of discipline to apply to various forms of misbehavior, including falsified reports of "miracles," there was as yet no corresponding positive mechanism of directing spontaneous religiosity. Unless one could point to actual infractions, the Church authorities could only watch and wait. In the similar case of Padre Pio, the stigmatic Capuchin monk who died in 1968 at the age of eighty-one, the Roman Catholic Church came down on the side of caution: Pio was silenced everywhere but in the confessional, forbidden to write letters or to preach. His biographer, a fellow priest, wrote approvingly, "Without these lines being drawn, there would have undoubtedly occurred a sort of mob canonization during his lifetime"[166]—which is precisely what occurred with Father John. (On the other hand, after Pio's death, he, too, is a full-fledged celebrity and industry, with Padre Pio snow shakers, air fresheners, and a shrine attracting more visitors than those of Lourdes or Saint Francis of Assisi.[167])

The Orthodox hierarchy, by contrast, allowed Father John's charismatic behavior to develop, checking it only in the cases of actual infraction. Their doing so was prompted by several motives. Because of perceived growing areligiosity in the second half of the nineteenth century, the Church might have been more willing to tolerate behavior that affirmed and encouraged piety.[168] But just as important was the Orthodox Church's belief that saintliness could develop "from below," and hence needed only watchfulness. In this context, Father John's being a priest—and one who was careful to couch every action in strictly Orthodox terms—was particularly important. As a priest from generations of clergy, Father John was seen by the hierarchy as being one of them, and hence more inherently trustworthy than a woman wanderer or even a monk.

Because of this attitude, Father John's reputation, initiated by an independent group of laypeople and a secular newspaper, remained in the public domain: it was a lay rather than a clerical initiative, although priests were quick to write accounts of their contact with Father John as well.[169] It is an indication both of the lack of a formal investigative mechanism on the part of the Orthodox Church and the extent to which lay beliefs continued to shape definitions of holiness that the accounts of Father John's "miracles" were collected and attested to by the laity and the parish clergy. Outside Russia, this tendency for the laity rather than the clergy to foster his cult persisted in posthumous accounts of his exploits as well.[170]

The hierarchy's objections to Father John come down to this: In his person, Father John combined two religious types that had hitherto been distinct, that of priest and that of the prophet or holy man, or institutionalized as opposed to personal charisma. The priest dispenses salvation by virtue of his office; even where personal charisma may be involved, it is the office that "confers legitimate authority upon the priest as a member of the corporate enterprise of salvation."[171] Given the importance Father John attached to the priest's being able to perform the sacraments, it is clear that he saw his own role in precisely these hieratic terms. He managed to combine these attributes, however, with the prophetic ones that had previously tended to exclude them—vital emotional preaching, a concern with social reform, clairvoyance, and healing. The root of his popular appeal was precisely his ability to provide both the immediacy of personal charisma and the sanction, and hence services, of legitimate authority.

In his combination of priestly office and personal charisma, Father John was the first example in Russia of a phenomenon that has become characteristic of the modern period. It has been increasingly the priest as often as the monk or pious layperson who both captures the religious imagination and speaks as one having authority. (Although this book concentrates on Father John and Russian Orthodoxy, one may note a similar phenomenon in Roman Catholicism, beginning with Jean-Marie Vianney in nineteenth-century France. More recently, liberation theology may be taken as the most extreme example of a politically and socially committed priesthood.)[172]

After the publicizing of his healings, Father John became a celebrity, his image both spread and created by those who clustered around him. To a certain extent, he cooperated in the process. His cult grew as well. Kronstadt became a pilgrimage site, and the spreading of his fame became an industry. Bishops watched the process to make sure it remained within the bounds of Orthodoxy. Their fears as to spontaneous lay canonization were proved justified when the Ioannite sect emerged at the turn of the century.

6

The "Ioannites" and the Limits of Veneration

As bishops feared, Father John's charisma and its representations contained dangerous ambiguities as well as blessings. The esteem in which some people held him led them beyond the boundaries of acceptable Orthodox behavior, of which the "Ioannites" were the most extreme manifestation. It was difficult to pin them down: were they pious but misguided Orthodox Christians whose awe before Father John pushed them too far—or were they sectarians cloaking their beliefs and practices under the guise of a revered Church figure? Were they cult members and kidnappers—or one of several nativist, anti-intellectual strains of radical right activism?

The Ioannites, like the eschatological Old Believers of the seventeenth century, were a phenomenon more complicated than any of these categorizations would suggest. Initially, they were laypeople with little formal education drawn to Father John for his burning faith and his warnings that Russia must recover its Orthodoxy and stick to the narrow path before it was too late. Unlike so many clergy who seemed to be permeated with the spirit of liberalism, rationalism, and progress—all anathema to the Ioannites—Father John spoke in a voice the Ioannites understood. To them, he *was* Orthodoxy. But they took their appreciation in an unexpected direction: they claimed his charismatic gifts for themselves. Despite Father John's repudiations, the Ioannites clustered around him, gathered in communes, and began to travel over the Russian Empire seeking both funds for and recruits to their own brand of emotional piety. Their vision extended to politics: the Ioannites defended autocracy, and attacked the forces of modernism they perceived in the religious hierarchy, the secular bureaucracy, and the so-called Jewish press.[1] Their challenge to mainstream Orthodoxy and liberal politics alike has made them one of the most misunderstood and misrepresented religious phenomena in twentieth-century Russia.

It is the uncertainty over the Ioannites' relation to Father John that puzzled many people. Heretical groups such as the Arians, Novatians, and Manicheans, after all, had usually themselves taken the names of their leaders, but the Ioannites, like the Strigolniki and the Judaizers in medieval Russian history who were named by their opponents, were so dubbed by a hostile press. Moreover, the Ioannites faced foes both within the establishment Church and in the radical press—two normally opposed groups. The cleavage lines that split Russian opinion on the Ioannites thus did not correspond to the classical lines of early twentieth-century political conflicts. What made matters even more confusing is the extent to which the Ioannites were represented, and misrepresented, by all sides. Contemporary Church writers, for example, devoted their energies to demonstrating where the doctrinal errors of the Ioannites lay, grouping the Ioannites within the spectrum of existing sects in Russia. This involved stressing Father John's disavowal of the Ioannites and their "sectarian" profile.[2] Likewise, moderate journals, who felt compelled to defend the Orthodox Church, were careful to distinguish between Father John and the Ioannites.[3] To the radical press, the Ioannites were a convenient front for attacking Father John, his mainstream devotees, and his politics. The "excesses" of the Ioannites were useful insofar as they could reflect unfavorably upon their supposed source.[4]

While the positions of outside representers are clear, it is far more difficult to determine how the Ioannites described themselves. Until the relaxing of the censorship in 1905 and 1906,[5] the Ioannites had no forum for their publications; their words come down to us largely through the prism of such authorities as the Holy Synod and the police, using the Ioannites' voices for their own purposes;[6] inquiring letters to Father John are the closest eyewitness source.[7] Even once leading Ioannite figures began to publish individual pamphlets and a weekly journal called *The Kronstadt Beacon* (*Kronshtadtskii Maiak*), it is not clear to what extent "followers" subscribed to their opinions: both Church authorities and reporters were careful to distinguish between the motives and actions of the Ioannite "leaders" and the "dark, simple flock;" and the individual Ioannite beliefs show a great variety.[8] The most obvious example of how problematic it is to classify the so-called Ioannites is that they themselves never used or accepted the term, insisting to the end that they were only Orthodox Christians. They remain an invaluable case study of a sect from its origins as unconnected individuals to the gradual perception of common strands among these individuals' behavior—both by outsiders and by themselves.

In this discussion, the usage of the term "Ioannite" will follow that of Russian publications during the Ioannites' heyday from 1890 to Father John's death in 1908, and not the many ways it was constructed after 1917. After exploring the ways in which the Ioannite profile differed from conventional Orthodoxy (although the Orthodoxy of the Ioannites as such will be less central than the question of why it was so important to Church contemporaries to establish whether the Ioannites were "truly Orthodox," and why that mattered so little to the radical press), the discussion will trace the group's development. It will examine the ways in which the Ioannites were used and depicted by outside agencies, contributing to the formation of an Ioannite "type." The dynamics of this manipulation shed new light on the interrelation of clergy, government agencies, and the press in shaping religious policies, particularly during the shelter scandal of 1907–9. The discussion will then examine how the Ioannites reacted to this onslaught, at first defending themselves and then taking the offensive. Most important is the extent to which the Ioannites embodied the peril to the Orthodox Church that Father John's reputation for living sanctity posed. While the Church decided in 1908 that the Ioannites were a kind of right-wing deviation within Orthodoxy, their "excesses" are important precisely because they provided an "other;" they established how far one could safely go in showing reverence for Father John. In the Soviet era, their "otherness" would be redefined and used for very different purposes.

Definitions

Just who were the Ioannites? Initially, it was very difficult to perceive that they were in any way different from Orthodox Christians. Part of the confusion was that, thanks to the broad understanding of holiness in Russia, the behavior and beliefs of the Ioannites seemed to be quite close to the typical behavior of those who honored Father John. Like many of the Orthodox faithful, the Ioannites held that he was a specially chosen vessel of God. They stood in awe of his miracles and admired his unstinting generosity to the poor and needy. And their behavior reflected this veneration. Like many of the Orthodox faithful, the Ioannites kept images of Father John—whether portraits, photographs, or the lithographs that an indefatigable chain of peddlers spread over Russia—in places of honor in their homes. They, too, treasured tangible signs of his blessing: candles, *prosphora* (blessed bread), icons, holy water, and other objects that had been in contact with him were treated with reverence. Similarly, many Orthodox and Ioannites believed that Father John prayed to God using different prayers than did other priests, and sought to obtain the texts for their efficacy. Finally, unlike such groups as the Baptists or Pashkovites, the Ioannites insisted on their devotion to the Orthodox sacraments of confession and communion. Much of the religious behavior of the Ioannites, in short, so resembled the conventional manifestations of Orthodox piety that it was very difficult to distinguish them from typical, if extraordinarily fervent, Orthodox Christians. It was this similarity that would so plague the attempts of religious and political authorities to identify the Ioannites and to determine how properly to deal with them.

Nevertheless, there were differences, and it was these differences that gradually came to the authorities' attention. The Ioannites believed that the world as they knew it was about to end—probably after a revolution—and that they could find salvation only by going to God in the person of Father John. Some taught that Father John was the Prophet Elijah, others Jesus Christ, others God of Sabaoth.[9] Even "The Truth About the Ioannite Sect" (*Pravda o sekte ioannitov*), an Ioannite apologetic, read: "God has appeared in the flesh within the Kronstadt *batiushka*. He has justified himself in the spirit. He has revealed himself to the angels and is preached among the peoples."[10]

Such characteristically ambiguous phrasing raised eyebrows. In what sense did the Ioannites mean that God had appeared in Father John? Other texts were problematic as well: "We are fortunate, brethren, that in our days *we can see the Lord on earth walking among us, abiding in* the great, righteous man, dear Father John of Kronstadt"; "Anyone who blasphemes the Holy Trinity *dwelling in* the true pastor, Father John of Kronstadt, will be destroyed"; and "Go to Kronstadt and obtain the Bridegroom, Christ," and so on.[11]

The next step was to join a community of like-minded devotees—but not an established convent or Father John's own House of Industry. Both Orthodox forms of community would have put too many limits on the Ioannites' behavior: convents ran according to rules and discipline that had little to do with the Ioannites' emphasis on eschatology and charisma—if anything, a convent would have sought to uproot these individualistic tendencies; it would certainly have discouraged the Ioannites' rituals that far too closely resembled Holy Eucharist.[12] Moreover, the convents had strict admission standards including entrance fees, which the Ioannites were usually too poor to provide.[13] Similarly, the House taught trades and encouraged Orthodox observance, but its emphasis on the practical put off the ardent Ioannites.

This brings us to the next distinguishing feature of the Ioannites: their unwillingness to be directed by Church and state authorities, including Father John himself. According to Orthodox teaching, submission to the Church hierarchy, and, by extension, to a spiritual elder, was indispensable to salvation.[14] The Ioannites, by contrast, believed that they alone possessed the truth and that it was their prerogative to label hierarchs and clerics as being "false" pastors.[15]

The Ioannites subverted traditional Orthodox notions of hierarchy in other ways. While they revered Father John, a clergyman, they did not maintain the strict gender roles characteristic of Orthodoxy. The presence of female leaders and the similarity of men's and women's roles distinguishes the Ioannites (and many other sectarian groups) from the far more clearly defined gender(ed) functions in the Orthodox community. While the Ioannite publicists were all men, almost all the recruiters, book-peddlers, and heads of communes were women. Moreover, next to Father John, the Ioannites' leading spiritual figure was Porfiriia Kiseleva, a woman to whom many referred as the "Mother of God." The overwhelmingly female proportion of the Ioannites would be used against them both by the Synod and the radical press, who wrote with dismay of the women's "speaking with power."[16]

In a final distinction from Orthodox behavior and beliefs, the Ioannites traveled, preached, recruited, and sought to reproduce church rituals. In Orthodox practice, teaching and preaching was the exclusive province of a male clergy; leadership roles for laypeople, and women in particular, were limited. Individuals of holy life could excite admiration and emulation, but women wishing to form communities—particularly women from the lower classes—often ran into official resistance.[17] The Ioannites, by contrast, preached their own interpretations of Scripture and, in a spectacular example of uncanonicity, sold what they claimed was "Father John's communion" in bottles for a ruble each.[18]

Initial Clerical Responses and Representations

These elements took time to crystallize. Initially, Ioannitism was not a movement, but a cluster of common traits observed in individuals acting independently. The peasant Vasilii Kondratov in Gdov district in 1892, the peasant woman Klipikova in Samara in 1895, a wanderer named Maxim in 1896—all were reported as preaching that the end of the world was at hand and that Father John was Christ Himself, Who would soon come in glory.[19] It was not yet clear that the incidents were connected in any way, and they were treated on a local basis, often with the diocesan bishop sending Father John directly to the offender's home parish for admonishment.[20] It is because of the ad hoc nature of the complaints that their common traits took several years to identify. In the meantime, confused priests who encountered such suspect visitors to their parishes began to contact Father John directly.

In 1900, for example, Father Aleksei Zlatoustov from Pokrovskii uezd told Father John that three women had arrived from Kronstadt preaching that he was the only true, lawful pastor in Russia (and immortal besides), that one should therefore pray to him and to his portraits, that money was the seal of the Antichrist, and that people ought therefore to leave their jobs, turn over their money, and travel to him for confession. Father Aleksei, who was young and inexperienced, asked Father John to respond to the most vexing questions in writing so that he could "calm [his] upset people in time."[21] Other priests reported parishioners who regarded Father John as the Lord come in glory, citing John 1:6 ("There was a man sent by God, his name was John") and who, like many sectarians, taught that marriage was fornication.[22]

Zlatoustov's request gives one pause. It is not surprising that peasants, soldiers, and laypeople generally wrote Father John to report that "people who call themselves your disciples are teaching the Gospel in an unhealthy way, calling you God and saying that we have to leave married life and give away all we have: who are they?"[23] But that priests seriously posed such questions suggests the extent to which Father John had recast traditional categories. He had transformed the performance of the sacraments; he had kept his virginity within marriage (which many Ioannites used to argue for a life of radical chastity). He had become increasingly apocalyptic in his sermons; such a man might have sent out disciples as well. The key for Orthodox priests, then, was determining whether or not the wanderers had Father John's blessing. Had the itinerant orators limited themselves to preaching that the end of the world was at hand, or had they identified a layperson as the

Fig. 8 Father John in the company of colleagues and friends, including, in the first row, priests Grigorii Petrov (far left) and Filosof Ornatskii (left of Father John) and art critic Vladimir Stasov (third from left). Father John's wife, Elizaveta Konstantinovna is second from right. Photo courtesy of the Central State Archive of Cine- and Photo-Documents.

source of salvation, they would have been pegged immediately as sectarians. Because they linked themselves with Father John, however, many priests hesitated.[24]

The priests' position was complicated by an additional factor. They were the local guardians of Orthodoxy, charged with maintaining *proper* worship and belief among their flocks. They had to answer not only to God and their parishioners but also to their bishops. Before reporting to the hierarchy, the priests would have wanted to exhaust all their other resources and be sure of the ground on which they stood. In the case of the Ioannites, the court of appeal next to Father John himself were the local diocesan journals, which served as clearinghouses for knotty pastoral problems.[25] It is because of such articles as "Father John's new admirers in the Don *oblast'* [region]" that priests all over Russia quickly became aware of the existence of the "new admirers"—and helped to create a taxonomy of the new phenomenon, for it is in these articles that the Ioannites' characteristics were first tabulated and an attempt was made to place them within known types.[26]

Equally decisive was Father John's own unequivocal response to the so-called admirers. This must be emphasized, for critics later suggested that Father John did little to discourage the adulation he received. These charges are not borne out by the evidence.[27] He not only traveled to denounce, he also wrote invectives on the as yet unclassified abusers. He did so in response both to the religious authorities and to laity. One of the first such instances came in 1895, when Vladimir Sabler, then the assistant to the Ober-Procurator, forwarded to him a report from Vissarion, Bishop of Kostroma and Galich. In his diocese, a peasant woman named Pelagia Vasilievna Kabanova had portraits of Father John standing in front of her icons and blocking them from view; he prayed to him as if he were Jesus. When threatened with arrest, she said of him, "I am ready to endure all for my Savior." Sabler asked him to "bring Kabanova to her senses." Father John tried to do so in a detailed letter of March 12, 1895. Despite his many women followers, he emphasized women's ignorance and susceptibility.

> The fanatical, ignorant, and senseless false teaching of Pel. Kabanova occurs among ignoramuses and senseless people, *especially* women, and *sometimes* illiterate and ignorant men....
>
> I never gave Kabanova, nor anyone else, any ground for regarding me as Christ—me, someone sinful and weak! God's grace, and my having served for many years in clerical orders, have so enlightened my spiritual eyes and strengthened my faith in the Lord and the Holy Church, as well as making me realize my own weakness and sinfulness, and my constant need of God's grace,—that I never thought of myself so highly, and in fact realize that I am weaker and more sinful than anyone else. I can only wonder at Kabanova's absurdity and the delusion, and so now denounce her:
>
> Leave your raving and your absurd, senseless innovation; bring your repentant head to your pastors and judges whom you have discomfited with your pernicious innovation, and believe the way all Orthodox Christians believe and confess ... there is no name

under the heavens before which to bow down save that of Jesus Christ.... Who sits at the right hand of the Father, who abides with his faithful and who will abide invisibly in His Church to the end of the age.—And if we spread any news other than the Good News of God's Word, may we be anathema, as the Apostle says.[28]

Similarly, when a soldier named Semen Tarabrin implored Father John to tell him whether it was true that he was God, Porfiriia Kiseleva the Mother of God, and Kronstadt the Heavenly Jerusalem, for example, Father John scrawled on the letter, "O nonsense! O absurdity!" and answered immediately.[29] These statements began to be published after several people begged Father John to do so in an attempt to cut off the spread of the dubious teaching.[30] Of these, his comments on an *akathist* composed in his name by the peasant Ivan Artamonov Ponomarev are particularly expressive.

An *akathist* was an Orthodox liturgical verse form to Jesus Christ, the Mother of God, established saints, or miraculous icons. While composing an akathist was occasionally undertaken as a form of personal devotion, it could not be used during gatherings without Synodal approval; composing an akathist to someone living and hence uncanonized was out of the question.[31] Ponomarev, however, was deterred by neither convention nor reticence. As well as referring to Father John as "great and holy," his akathist also referred to him as "God made visible," "Judge of all the world," and addressed him as "Trinity."[32]

Even if Ponomarev had limited himself to calling Father John a saint, it would have been inappropriate. The apparent identification of him with God Himself was too much. Archbishop Vissarion of Kostroma sent Father John a copy of the akathist with instructions to deal with it. Father John did. He fired off a letter to Ponomarev that was reprinted in *Kostroma Diocesan News* in 1902. The letter shows him at his most outraged:

> Who gave you, blockhead, the idea of writing this akathist? Satan, I suppose. How dared you, dolt, use my name for evil purposes and compose an akathist—something which is only appropriate for saints—to me, a sinful person (even though I am a priest)? Are there any blasphemies you did not pile up in it? No person in his right mind can read your trash. And you read these raving words of yours to simple, uneducated, open-hearted people—and they believed you, lunatic and pretender? Pathetic! What was your intent in composing this balderdash? Setting up your own schismatic society, setting up your own meetings and separating kind, simple

people from God's Church? Does the holy Church not have its own, divinely inspired akathists? Who do you think you are? You have forgotten the most important thing, which is that you are an ignoramus, a raving idiot who doesn't make any sense. I *curse* your akathist. Tell *that* to everybody who listens to you and follows you.[33]

This spirited response, however, did not prove enough to dissuade Ponomarev. He continued to disseminate his akathist, his beliefs in Father John's unique holiness, and turned the water Father John blessed for him into a source of income. Why was not Father John's condemnation enough to stop Ponomarev? In the usual Orthodox practice of spiritual discipline, an elder's upbraiding should have quashed a follower's misguided initiative. Perhaps Ponomarev explained away the condemnation as proof of Father John's humility. Perhaps he saw the rebuff as a concession Father John was forced to make by the Church authorities.[34] In any case, Ponomarev's ignoring of the energetic rebuttal was typical of other Ioannites, "leaders" and "followers" alike, which suggests that Father John was for them a convenient focus for religious energies that did not always prove to have a great deal in common with him; a peg to hang their hat on, as it were.

Both in his letters and his visit to Ponomarev, Father John was speaking in his two bodies—as a seeker of holiness and an Orthodox priest. While he thanked God daily for how much people loved him and for the grace he had received, he was genuinely horrified that someone could tempt fate by calling him divine. Even stronger than his dismay, however, was his wrath at what he saw as the trespassing of Ponomarev and those like him. There was no question for Father John, or for most of the other Orthodox clergy or hierarchy, as to whether laypeople were entitled to their "voice," in the sense of preaching, composing akathists, or setting up their own meetings with no clergymen present to keep them in check. They were not. Father John, for example, told Ponomarev's fellow villagers to listen in all cases to their pastors and not to any troublemakers—that is, to laypeople taking their own initiative. As soon as it emerged that the so-called admirers had little desire to follow their supposed leader, most of the clergy turned against them.[35]

Early Press Representations and Police Reports

The press perceived and represented the Ioannites in a way very different from the clergy. It is extremely telling that what the clergy labeled teachings, the press called ignorance. Their descriptions, however, were similar. According to the newspaper *Russia*, which reported the news on September 9, 1901, fifteen young women visitors to the village of Sus'tie told the villagers that the end of the world was at hand, that Father John was a messenger sent by God, and that everyone who wished to be saved must go to Kronstadt to serve him. The women added that no occupation was more pleasing to God than weaving decorative wreaths (in Kronstadt, under the guidance of more experienced elders) and that they themselves and their leader, Pet'ka, were saving themselves by leading this godly way of life in Kronstadt near Father John. The reason the paper was reporting this piece of news was that by the time the villagers summoned a priest to investigate these curious visitors, they had vanished, taking three girls from the village with them.[36]

The way in which the story was presented by the newspaper was very different from Church representations. *Russia* paid no particular attention to the young women's references to Father John or to Kronstadt, which were key for the clergy. Instead, its reporter was struck by the appallingly low level of "enlightenment" that the reception of the visitors seemed to suggest. "There are educational institutions constantly operating in the village," he wrote,

> There are spiritual and secular pastors to be had, "Big Brother" is right there (there are six estates by the village), and *still* ... girls show up out of nowhere blathering all kinds of nonsense, and this nonsense is immediately and greedily welcomed and accepted by everyone.... It is just as if these people had never known anything educational, it is just as if they were some kind of savages.[37]

The journalist went on to ask the reader if he or she did not think that there was something here to think about. His question was rhetorical, and set the tone for many journalistic accounts that would follow. The kind of eschatological, "be-prepared-for-the-end-of-the-world-and-watch-out-for-the-Antichrist," mentality that the women in Sus'tie showed was something that most educated Russians shrugged off impatiently, even viscerally, as being the worst of "village darkness." *Russia* left the article as a piece of local backwardness exemplifying rural Russia; its reporter showed no interest in the future fate of the three girls who had left with the visitors. But the Department of Police did. They also wanted to know more about the "Pet'ka" the young women had referred to, and contacted the Ministry of Internal Affairs of Novgorod Province—within which the village of Sus'tie was located—for more information.[38]

Fig. 9 Father John surrounded by seekers. Photo courtesy of the Central State Archive of Cine- and Photo-Documents.

The information the Ministry provided bore a striking resemblance to that of the clerical press. According to their report, Petr Trofimov had worked in a factory in St. Petersburg until a machine had torn off his left hand. He had then made his living as a peddler, and for the last two years had wandered from monastery to monastery in prayer (which, incidentally, the Ministry regarded as being behavior so typical it required no comment). Trofimov often went to see Father John in Kronstadt and read his books. He had persuaded several girls to travel around Russia with him singing psalms.

The trio sang well, which attracted villagers. But they also tried to persuade people to go with them to Kronstadt for a collective confession before Father John. In this case, Trofimov had managed to persuade the peasant Ivan Petrov, his wife, and a girl (not three girls, as *Rossiia* had claimed, suggesting a greater degree of coercion and vulnerability). The young woman had stayed in Kronstadt and was now engaged in weaving wreaths there; her father had visited her; both claimed to be satisfied with her situation.[39]

The Ministry provided additional testimony from peasants who were present when Petr Timofeev and his companions performed at the house of Timofei Ivanov. According to them, the trio sang spiritual verses and prayers about Father John and others, "but it was difficult to understand their meaning."[40] It is not clear whether the peasants really found the verses hard to understand or whether they were protecting themselves until the authorities made it clear what their opinion was supposed to be. But the authorities did quote the peasants as saying that one had to regard Father John as God and that he was "better than our *popes*." It is not clear whether the phrases were the peasants', Trofimov's, or the Ministry's. The two ideas being presented in the same breath, however, suggests either that the trio had an extremely elastic notion of the divine, or that they were being misinterpreted. The three also called themselves "Father John's servants" and "apostles." Finally, the visit reported by *Rossiia* was not something new—according to the villagers' testimony, every time Trofimov came, he took someone with him to Kronstadt.

The Mobilization of the Government: Police Department and Holy Synod

The police mulled over the implications. The unauthorized movement of people, especially minors, from place to place was no longer their chief concern: the element of religion now meant that the matter had to be forwarded to the powers that be. And so they forwarded the Trofimov file to the Ober-Procurator, Konstantin Pobedonostsev.[41]

The actions of the police, the Ministry of the Interior, the Ober-Procurator, the local bishop, and the Holy Synod in the early stages of the affair illustrate the ways in which the authorities in Late Imperial Russia worked together on cases of suspected religious deviation. From the point of view of the Orthodox hierarchy, the culprits were the "ringleaders" of Father John's misguided admirers. They were charlatans, whether their aim was profit or sectarianism. Non-Orthodox religiosity that involved taking money from peasants was synonymous with exploitation. Equally important, however, was the Church hierarchy's emphatic disassociation of Father John from his supposed followers. Their insistence shows to what extent he had overcome suspicion and established himself in the eyes of the bishops as being solid and one of their own.

For in formulating his response on December 29, 1901, Pobedonostsev had consulted with Gurii, the archbishop of the Novgorod diocese. Archbishop Gurii had said that in his opinion Trofimov, like "the other leaders of Father John's devotees" (of whom he was clearly well aware) was using Father John's name as a cover. In fact, according to Gurii, the rabble-rousers were pursuing some mercenary aim—either simple lucre, or the formation of a "pernicious" sectarian group. Pobedonostsev commented only that he had felt it his duty to advise the Minister of the Interior of Gurii's assessment—and to add that for his part, he would deem it appropriate to deport Trofimov from the *guberniia* (province) of Novgorod and to keep him under strict police surveillance.

The element that most preoccupied the Synod in the Trofimov affair, then, was the possible formation of a new sect. The elements that most attracted the attention of the police were that of the unauthorized movement of people from place to place and financial exploitation.[42] Despite the different emphases of Church and police, however, *all* the charges were criminal offenses before the freedom of belief and freedom of press laws passed in February 1903 and October 1905.[43] The appropriate agency—in this case the Synod—outlined policy as concerned religion, the Ministry of the Interior approved it, and the police carried it out. If the police suspected a sect before being advised that one existed, they first contact the Ministry of the Interior—especially the Department of Foreign Confessions' Spiritual Affairs—who then contacted the Synod for policy guidelines. The police forwarded the Trofimov file to the religious authorities because they needed an explicit directive.[44]

Both in the Trofimov case and the ones that followed, the Synod sought to make the strongest possible case against the suspected sectarians. In a 1904 "Ioannite" (they still had no label) case, the extent of the Synod's involvement in shaping the Ioannite profile and stacking the official deck against them is particularly evident.

Case (*delo*) number 3069, initiated on December 9, 1904 (thus after the first "freedom of belief" law) was an attempt made by the Chancellery of the Synod to attract the attention of such "civil" agencies as the police, the Minister of the Interior, and the Moscow Procurator. Their presentation of the case is especially important for the terms in which it is expressed, and for those details that the Chancellery felt would most impel the police and the procurators to take action.

In their report, the *meshchanka* Maria Alexandrova and the peasant Nataliia Ivanovna Sukhanova first stood accused of peddling religious books. Because literature "of spiritual content" was subject to its own laws and standards, questioning the women's authorization to sell it was a logical course for Spiritual Consistory to follow. And it emerged that while the books were those approved by the censorship (in other words, the women were not selling any nonimprimatur, possibly sectarian, texts), the women did not have the legal right to sell them: this was the first strike against them.[45]

The Chancellery went on to claim that Alexandrova and Sukhanova declared that Father John of Kronstadt was the true Lord God, "for Jesus Christ had become incarnate in him." One of the proofs was that the two wore photographs around their necks of Father John decorated with cherubim, which they would remove, "insisting" to an audience that consisted largely of women that they also pray before them and venerate them. They then did the same with a photograph of a woman whom they called the "Queen of Heaven" and the "Immortal Mother of God."[46]

By repeatedly emphasizing the largely feminine composition of the gathering, the Chancellery was perhaps hinting at the notion of irrational, easily swayed women and implying that the presence of men might have acted as a restraining influence. They also stressed that during the prayers, the women placed the photographs before those praying in place of icons, which the audience apparently acknowledged.

This raises a host of interesting questions. How readily did people accept visual substitutes for icons, as long as there was something in front of which to pray (a contention made by foreign observers earlier in the nineteenth century)? Father John was a known quantity, but what of the mysterious Queen of Heaven? In accepting photographs of the "Immortal Mother of God," were the peasant women responding chiefly to the spiritual authority of Father John and the holy wanderer generally? How familiar were they with photography? Could they have assumed that this was only the latest of more than a hundred known icon types of the Mother of God? Would they have seen any reason to distinguish between the photographs and the mass-produced realistic lithograph-icons that had become so widely spread? It remains an open question as to how readily Russian Orthodox believers accepted new figures in their domestic shrines.

Once the prayers were finished, Alexandra and Sukhanova gave those present water to drink and *prosphora* supposedly blessed by Father John to eat. While the Chancellery described this action (and, by implication, sought to condemn it) as "they gave them communion" (*prichashchali*), it is not clear whether the women saw their actions in these terms, or described them in that way. In itself there was nothing uncanonical or un-Orthodox in laypeople's drinking holy water and eating holy bread without clerical supervision. Every Orthodox Christian was supposed to keep a supply of the water blessed at the feasts of Theophany (January 6) and Mid-Pentecost for domestic or emergency use; the pious often began their day with partaking of this holy food and drink.⁴⁷ The practice of giving or sending *prosphora* blessed at pilgrimage sites or on the day of one's feast day was also widely spread. It would thus have been expected for those who had been to Kronstadt to share their bounty of grace with their neighbors. By labeling this behavior "communion," and the anointing of the women with oil supposedly blessed by Father John "chrismation," the Chancellery was seeking to cast Alexandrova and Sukhanova in the most suspicious light possible. In any case, whether it concerned water, bread, or oil, Alexandrova and Sukhanova were careful to emphasize the connection of the elements with Father John. Whatever grace the two women had, they claimed to have it only insofar as they had access to him.

These were the religious misdemeanors. The Chancellery added material accusations as well. Alexandrova and Sukhanova sold as holy objects scraps of fabric, which they claimed came from Father John's *riasa*s and the dresses of the "Immortal Mother." They sold sand that they claimed Father John and the woman had walked on (which supposedly could cure all ailments); copper crosses that they passed off as being silver ones; books and pictures of him at inflated prices. They told a woman wearing a silver chain and gold earrings that such luxurious objects were sinful, and urged her to turn the jewelry over to them (so that they could give it to Father John, who would in turn give it to a poor sister in Christ), and had even persuaded people to sell all they owned "for pennies" and accompany them to Kronstadt. All in all, according to the report, the women were extorting money under the guise of donations to Father John. At the end of its report, the Synod Chancellery declared vigorously that Alexandrova and Sukhanova were members of a gang of swindlers (still nameless) organized by Porfiriia Iv. Kiseleva, the so-called "Oranienbaum Mother of God," and a man named Mikhail Petrov (the "Archangel Michael"). They claimed that Porfiriia also had convinced people that she was Father John's chief assistant and had already extorted hundreds of rubles from the unwary. And so the Chancellery concluded its case.[48]

The Ministry of Justice of the Moscow Palace of Justice's Procurator was not completely convinced. They contacted the police on January 7, 1905, to see whether the Chancellery's evidence was sufficient to posit the existence of a "gang of swindlers," and asked for more information. The police replied that Porfiriia, of whom they were aware, had been behaving much more carefully after being searched in 1902. They acknowledged that a for-profit group did exist with her as their focus. They conveyed the somewhat surprising news that Father John visited Kiseleva every time he passed through Oranienbaum (it emerged afterward that he was her confessor) and that, to ensure access to him, she regularly and generously heaped money and gifts upon his entourage.[49] And, because of the mention that Father John had some contact with Porfiriia and her group, the matter ended without any official course of action being decided upon.

In St. Petersburg, because the opportunities for observing the Ioannites firsthand were greater, both police and religious authorities had a much more nuanced perception of the Ioannites' activity. By April 9, 1905, the St. Petersburg Provincial branch of the Ministry of the Interior had determined that a well-organized group did exist for the purposes of soliciting money. The group was headed by Porfiriia Ivanovna Kiseleva ("the Mother of God"), Mikhail Petrov (the "Archangel Michael"), Elizaveta Korchacheva ("Solomoniia the Myrrh-bearer"), and Nazarii Dmitriev ("John the Theologian"). The Ministry ruefully concluded, however, that it was very difficult to prosecute them because, first, the blasphemous labels appeared to come from the "ignorant and fanatical mass of worshippers," and not from the leaders themselves; second, even when people had been tricked out of all their money, they preferred to remain silent. Nevertheless, they warned the Governor General, given that newspapers had already begun running articles depicting Porfiriia in a most unflattering light, one ought not to leave her activity unpunished; it was high time to resolve the complaints raised against her as quickly as possible through the legal system. The best way to do this was to appoint about one or two undercover agents per guberniia to amass evidence.[50]

The Most (Mis)Represented Ioannite

Porfiriia I. Kiseleva, the "Immortal Mother of God" who attracted so much attention, was the most notorious of the Ioannites. She organized one of the largest Ioannite communities, based first in Oranienbaum and then in Kronstadt, playing a central role in Ioannite prayer meetings. In Ioannite literature, she was celebrated as "a pure, inviolate virgin ... mistress not of this world, but whose dominion comes from the Church of Christ," who "labored more than [saints] Mary Magdalene, Nina [of Georgia], and Thecla," and whom "the Lord visited in the person of Father John of Kronstadt."[51] Several Ioannite canticles to her choose as their prototypes Orthodox hymns to female martyrs, as in:

> Dieva mudraia Porfira
> Ty stradala za Khrista,
> Khrista kamen' mnogotsennyi
> Ty imiela u sebia.

(Wise virgin Porphyra, thou hast suffered for Christ and had his precious stone with thee.)[52]

One could take the verses and the photographs as being curious examples of popular piety—if it were not for the strict Orthodox prohibitions against composing any such texts to living people. Porfiriia's giving blessings and accepting religious honors were accepted by the Ioannites but were emphatically not Orthodox behavior. For these reasons alone, it is not surprising that she became the focus of Orthodox criticism. People wrote Father John to warn him that Porfiriia's claims to be the Mother of God were encouraging imitators.[53] Others commented darkly that this "virgin" had been visited by a midwife in an Oranienbaum maternity ward and that she had a generally shady past.[54] The radical writer Aleksandr Serebrov, who visited Porfiriia's flat, described her as "a buxom woman with a disgustingly hanging lower lip," adding by way of explanation that "in her youth, Porfiriia had been a prostitute."[55]

Kiseleva's financial activity was even more suspect. One woman wrote

Father John a pleading letter, saying that her husband wanted to sell everything they owned and leave her. Vasilii Pustoshkin, who said that he had God's grace, had ordered him to do so in order to be "saved" by Porfiriia.[56] Several men described how their wives had fallen under Porfiriia's influence and run away with all of the funds in the joint bank account, adding plaintively that they cared less about the lost money than getting their wives back.[57] Others described Porfiriia's minions as claiming to be Father John's representatives and to be collecting for him, which was an invariably successful undertaking.[58] As Porfiriia's exploits began to be reported by the press, Father John began to receive letters from people ranging from peasants to students, asking him indignantly to put an end to "this mockery of the Church."[59]

Porfiriia's most sensational representation, however, would be in *Black Ravens*, a play written by an erstwhile Orthodox missionary, V. V. Protopov. She was depicted as Mariia Guseva, a woman who posed as the Mother of God incarnate to cynically exploit her gullible followers. Guseva's gestures, turns of phrase, and appearance were modeled on Porfiriia's, and did much to bury her reputation (hence the "suffering for Christ" referred to in the Ioannite canticle).[60]

Father John and the Ioannites Connected in Print

Black Ravens was one of the first literary works that deliberately linked Porfiriia and her associates with Father John. In one scene, for example, an actor made up to look like Father John appears to give Guseva his blessing. Guseva also speaks of Father John as having taught her all she knows when it comes to robbing the Russian people blind. This linkage between him and the enterprising group upset even the liberal members of the Orthodox Church.[61] The Ioannites themselves, however, did all they could to foster the sense of connection to Father John. One of the chief ways of doing so was through their press organ, a weekly journal called *The Kronstadt Beacon*.

The initial aim of the *Beacon* seemed simple: the collecting of "Ioanniana" for the purposes of Father John's eventual canonization. A typical issue, for example, would begin with an excerpt from one of Father John's sermons. (The sermons had all been published previously in authorized editions.) The back cover of every issue read:

> We remind everyone of the opinion of the renowned luminary and recluse, Bishop Feofan [the Recluse], on the dear batiushka's

homilies: "As far as concerns Father John of Kronstadt," writes the wise and holy recluse, "know that he is truly a man of God. And his books are good. Here are the bright thoughts of a soul which lives in God. Read them [while] making the sign of the cross."[62]

A closer examination reveals, however, that the publications and aims of the *Beacon* went far beyond the purportedly modest agenda. First, the recruitment strategy was evident. The *Beacon*'s editorial staff "heartily encouraged" its subscribers to purchase both the journal and its inexpensive editions with sermons by Father John *"for distribution and sale among the populace"* (emphasis mine). Moreover, although the editors of the *Beacon* claimed that their book warehouse "offered all the works of Father John of Kronstadt *and other spiritual writers* to meet the spiritual demands of the Russian people," there were far more collections of dubious spiritual verses dedicated *to* Father John than there were works *by* him. While the journal boasted of a largely clerical (and mythical) body of contributors, the books offered were actually written or compiled by the decidedly lay Vasilii Pustoshkin or Nikolai Bol'shakov and had such titles as *"The Twentieth Century and the End of the Age," The Red Summer Has Passed, but there is Nothing in the Garden*, and *How One Should Live In Order To Be Rich*. But while a close reading of the publications revealed ambiguity bordering on heresy—which was the point of view of the clergy—to a less expert audience, such as many policemen, the illustrations of Father John on the *Beacon* covers and the use of such existing popular religious genres as the spiritual verse created the impression that the Ioannites were only a particularly ardent, if slightly "tetched," group of Father John's admirers. Despite the growing swell of letters expressing dismay at the Ioannites' use of his name and the people abandoned by spouses and parents, so far the Ioannites were of interest mostly to Church and state authorities. What thrust them into the public eye was the shelter affair.

Shelters and Scandal

It began innocently enough. A recurrent motif in the Ioannite encounters with villagers was the call to "sell all you have and follow me." While all were called to live in Ioannite communities in Kronstadt, young women and children were the ones most prone to go. Given that minors—and, often, women—needed parental consent to live outside the family home, it may seem strange that so many parents would consent to release their daughters and sons in the hands of relative strangers. But the piety of the parents, the Ioannites' guarantee that the children would be looked after in an Orthodox way and would learn a trade, and Father John's own reputation for finding work and shelter for the poor at the House of Industry, were a potent combination. To many peasant parents, it seemed that by going to Kronstadt with Father John's pious representatives, their extra mouths might get a better break in life, a chance to see the world, and the spiritual advantages of being near a living holy man, all at once. In a climate where children were regularly farmed out to relatives (not to mention simply left on the doorsteps of orphanages), the offer of the Ioannites appeared a sensible, and perhaps even heaven-sent, opportunity.

That was how it seemed. And then in the autumn of 1907 one newspaper after another began to publish sensational exposés about the conditions in the shelters. The children were undernourished, exploited, overworked, and made to follow regimes of prayer that would make monks faint. The girls might even have been, they hinted darkly, sexually abused. The adults were either brainwashed or duped. After a furious press campaign, the shelters were raided and closed down in 1909.

But it then emerged that matters were not so simple. Some voices began to claim that the children had been well-fed, clean, and happy with the Ioannites; that they were in the shelters with their parents' consent, that they had been traumatized by being snatched away by brute force, and that their religious beliefs were being mocked in the "Jewish-owned" children's homes in which they had now been forcibly placed. In a rage of attack and counterattack, papers ranging from *The Bourse Gazette* to *Penny* delighted in printing what they called "the gory details" and "the naked truth." Other newspapers countered by calling the descriptions lies, even libel. In the resultant confusion, Orthodox practices and dietary rules, freedom of belief, freedom of assembly, and the rights of parents and state to children's bodies were furiously debated. The debate carried a particular edge because it was 1907. The old censorship laws had been lifted and the attempts to neutralize the revolutionary movement had failed. The Ioannite shelter case provided a forum for both expressing the social turmoil and allowing an attack on religiosity of whatever sort.

The initial impetus for the shelters was this: Father John's piety was well-known; so was the success of the House of Industry in teaching its clients trades enabling them to earn a living. It is not surprising that enterprising people chose to emulate, or capitalize upon, both. While the Orthodox Church might have preferred them to support the House itself, initiatives similar to Father John's were also hailed as positive examples of an "active" Orthodoxy.[63]

The Ioannites drew on Father John's reputation, but followed a different path. They had two distinct recruitment strategies. One, as we have seen, urged adult villagers to come with the Ioannite representatives to Kronstadt to lead a God-fearing life because the end of the world was near. The members of the Ioannite communities lived communally, did not marry (or, if married, lived apart from their spouses), and worked to recruit others. The younger and more attractive were trained as salesmen-preachers, who traveled around Russia with bags of religious books, photographs of Father John, and wreaths for decorating icons and gravesites, calling others to join them in Kronstadt.

Another approach targeted parents concerned for both the economic and spiritual future of their children. They were encouraged to send their children to Kronstadt to learn a trade that would allow them to support themselves in an environment that would protect them from the baneful influences of the modern city and foster their spirituality. Although there is no evidence that the less able-bodied were singled out by the organizers, many of those children that left with the Ioannites appear to have been unsuited for heavy agricultural work, whether because of age or infirmity. Occasionally the two approaches were combined, as in the cases of recently widowed women with children to support. Once arrived, the younger children were put to work making the wreaths and decorated photographs that their elders would peddle. The communities were thus meant to be fully self-sustaining economic units, engaged in "soul-saving" work and way of life. Regular visits to St. Andrew's Cathedral in Kronstadt where Father John served formed part of their weekly or monthly routine.[64]

This, at least, was the strategy. The children were usually sent off with a certain amount of clothing and funds, depending on their parents' means. Within weeks, however, many parents received letters asking for large sums of money—signed with their children's names, but not in their handwriting. When parents grew suspicious and checked, it emerged that the letters were frauds and that their children had been picked clean of their possessions.[65] When they expressed their outrage to the authorities, the pressure on the police became fierce and had an immediate effect.

Some children were sent home to their mothers.[66] Father John himself published an open letter in *The Russian Pilgrim* denying any connection between the recruiters and his beloved convent in St. Petersburg, which they were defaming; he denied that he had allowed anyone to sell his works; he called the police to investigate these "dens." This repudiation was reproduced by the thousands for distribution by parish priests, and the St. Petersburg Urban Prefect's Office launched a full-scale investigation.[67]

The press had a field day. The tenor of newspaper articles rapidly grew ever more sensational, describing children kidnapped by members of a religious cult who then abused their charges, beating them, feeding them inadequately, dressing them in rags, having them sleep on the floor, and forcing them both to work inhumanly long hours and to engage in suspect rituals.[68] Articles with such headlines as "CHILDREN HORRIBLY TORTURED—CHILDREN IN THE IOANNITES' CLAWS—CHILD MARTYRS" emphasized the children's pallor, their open sores, and their general air of dullness.[69] Doctors from the Society for the Protection of Children testified that they found children "in horrible physical condition, incapable of enduring their forced marches to services on the Karpovka [at Father John's convent] from their shelter beyond the Warsaw station."[70] The Ioannites' apocalyptic pronouncements were described as "false rumors about the imminent end of the world."[71] To heighten the sense of outrage at abused children, an Ioannite woman was quoted as saying that the health of the children's bodies did not matter; the health of the souls did.[72] Some journalists called for an immediate closing of the shelters. Others allowed that, however unattractive a spectacle the Ioannites presented, they had a right to exist—until, that is, it concerned children and both their physical and mental health. At that point, society had a right to intervene.[73]

The article that most worried the Prefect, however, was one that appeared to challenge the police directly. It appeared in *The Petersburg Gazette* on September 29, 1907. The headline read, in capitals and boldface, "THE SHELTERS.—CORNER DWELLERS.—BLESSED WREATHS.—TWO JEWISH GIRLS MISSING." The article began by reporting that "the kidnapping of two Jewish girls which has disturbed all Oranienbaum has been connected to these shelters." Despite the sensationalistic opening, there turned out to be no link between the Ioannites and the two missing girls. More pertinent to the police was a series of pointed questions posed by the reporter to an employee of the Prefect's office. The reporter hammered away at the police's not being aware that the shelters were "these kind of" institutions. Instead of asking the reporter just what he meant, the hapless policeman tried to explain that because the managers of the shelters had complied with all official requirements and behaved correctly, they had assumed that the children were only part of so many corner dwellers in Petersburg.

But the *Gazette* reporter's target was less the police than it was Father John himself, and the connection it sought to make between him and the shelters. As far as the police knew, Father John never visited the communal flats, but the parents of the children often combined a visit to their children with a trip to Kronstadt. The reporter seized on this: "You mean to say that only the children of the Ioannites, or of Father John's devotees, end up in these shelters?"

The equation of "Ioannites" with "Father John's devotees" came so quickly that it was nearly imperceptible. The gap between honoring Father John and being an "Ioannite" shrank to nothingness. The article pushed the supposed connection further. In describing the high prices the wreaths fetched as supposedly being blessed by Father John, for example, the *Gazette* wrote, "In the eyes of the fanatics, this religious sanction made the wreaths especially valuable; they ascribed miracle-working powers to them. One need only put such a wreath on one's head—and the person becomes party to Father John's heavenly grace." Thus, under the guise of exposing the "fanatic sectarians," the reporter was able to denigrate the general principle of venerating tangible objects associated with a saint—whether clothing, relics, or any object blessed by him. To those looking for an opportunity to poke fun at pious Orthodox practices, the Ioannites were a gold mine: by sneering at "sectarian abuses," the anti-Orthodox could ridicule Orthodox forms as well.

It was this aspect of the Ioannite scandal that proved so difficult for many Russians. One could be upset, as an Orthodox Christian, at the trafficking of charlatans; it was easier yet to express righteous outrage at potential child abuse. But if one felt uneasily that the criticism came a little too close to home, one began to feel some sympathy precisely for the "sectarians" one would have liked to condemn. If, moreover, the reporters' Orthodoxy was dubious or nonexistent, it became all too easy to wonder whether the press campaign against the Ioannites was not an excuse to undermine Orthodox customs and beliefs themselves. Protopov's *Black Ravens* had been the first such foray. But in some cases, the equation of the Ioannites with Father John and mainstream Orthodoxy was offensive to the point of blasphemy. Aleksandr Amfiteatrov, for example, wrote a parody of an Orthodox vesperal verse to be performed "at the Ioannite zeals and other festivities of Russian holy foolishness like unto them, chiefly at the meetings[74] of the righteous Father John Il'ich Sergiev, the wonderworker of dry Madeira, who is of one essence with the black hundreds, the old wives' prophet, the blessed bribe-taker, and who prays for all rogues and thieves:"

Plutie tikhii
Khmel'nyia slavy!
Bliz tebia, sviashchennago,
Bliz tebia, blazhennago,
Zhulik na mazurikie
I vor na plutie!
Vyvedshe tebe iz t'my na solntse,
Videvshe sviet gazetnyi,
Zhdem do kontsa
Eshche nemnogo,
Chtoby tvoi plutni prokuror nakryl!

[O gladsome cheat of the drunken glory! Near you, sacred and blessed one, there is a crook for every thief! Now that we have led you from the darkness to the sun, having beheld the newspapers' light, we wait until the end—for the procurator to expose your tricks!]⁷⁵

Amfiteatrov's verse, as a parody of one of the most revered hymns of the Church, was particularly offensive to Orthodox sensibilities, but other linkages between Father John, the Ioannites, and Orthodoxy were almost as blatant.⁷⁶

It would have been difficult to find a single periodical in St. Petersburg that did not mention the "Ioannite scandals" from the end of 1907 to 1909. It is all the more striking, then, that the police appear to have pursued virtually every reference. No sooner did an article promising "new sordid revelations" appear than a memorandum left the Prefect's desk the next day with the clipping attached, the address of the presumed shelter circled, and a terse "Get back to me on this ASAP" appended. The second series of reports are notable for their detail. The second Petersburg precinct, for example, wrote of the shelters at 13–14 Teriaevskaia and 8 Ordinarnaia that there were

> thirteen girls aged 6–9 and forty-five women aged 18–30 at the former; fourteen boys aged 4–8 and ten women of the same age as the foregoing in the latter. The children are dressed in ordinary clothing, while the adults are entirely in black. The children are accommodated on mattresses and plank beds; the adults sleep on the floor. The apartments are kept immaculately clean and neat, which was also verified by Special Inspector Lanskii. They are fed with Lenten [vegan], but good and healthy, products. Both the

children and the adults spend their time in weaving wreaths and making [artificial] flowers for sale in the provinces with the claim of having been blessed by Father John of Kronstadt; they also sing religious hymns, have edifying discussions and readings, and attend church services at the convent located in the same area—no. 45 at the Karpovka quay.[77]

Other police reports were more negative, describing the exhausted appearance of the children, which they attributed to improper food and a lack of fresh air, given that the children spent virtually all of their time inside the apartment.[78] But there was clearly a divergence between the uniformly horrific descriptions of the newspapers and the wide range of conditions reported by the police. Even allowing for the different aims and perspectives, the discrepancy is striking. Most surprising is that while some children clearly showed signs of exhaustion, others had a "cheerful and healthy appearance," told the investigators that they had not had to work, that no one forced them to pray, that they had gone to bed at midnight and got up at 5 A.M. with a rest in the afternoon. They thought that they had received good food, and enough of it.[79]

Their testimony suggests that a great deal of the conditions in the Ioannite shelters lay in the expectations and the previous experiences of the beholder. A poor peasant orphan might find shelter life quite different than did the children of an educated widow, urban reporters, or the Chairman of the Society for the Care of Poor and Sick Children.[80] Even if the situation was lacking by reigning urban standards, those standards were still often higher than those previously encountered by peasant children. When questioned by her priest from home, for example, one girl from the Urals said that at first she had missed her parents, but then found life at the shelter a good time: they were driven around in a car (actually, a tram, the priest noted) and she thought that Kronstadt and Petersburg were better cities than Perm.[81] It is hard to disagree with her assessment. It is this discrepancy that needs to be kept in mind as the contradictions in the various reports become more glaring and harder to reconcile.

Closing the Shelters

After a campaign that lasted nearly two years, the St. Petersburg authorities finally closed the shelters in July 1909, transferring the children either to their guardians or to shelters run by such established wards as the Chairman of the Society for the Care of Poor and Sick Children.[82] In the end, the Prefect acted on organizational grounds. Because the Ioannite shelters taught the children work skills, they could be regarded as trade workshops or vocational schools, for which the Ioannites had no permission.[83]

This was not the end of the story, however. Many children begged not to be taken. After being forcibly moved, they protested at having their Gospels taken away and being given novels instead. Their parents filed claims that the administration, in removing their children from the shelters without their consent, had denied the children their freedom. One father, referring to the sexual examination to which his daughter had been submitted, was particularly insistent that she had been "violated." The parents were better organized than the administration had expected: as well as petitioning the Ministry of Justice, they contacted almost every agency and well-placed official they could think of, including Petr Stolypin.[84] Indignantly claiming that their children were moved without their consent from Orthodox supervision to that of people who mocked their beliefs and religious dietary constraints, they charged that the religious freedom of Orthodox Christians was at stake.[85] They claimed that the alleged bad conditions of the Ioannite shelters were libel and defamation by the "Jewish" press, thus seeking to create the impression that the Ioannites were a Russian phenomenon, while its critics were either foreign (in the case of Russian Germans) or non-Orthodox (in the case of Lutherans, Roman Catholics, and Jews). In short, the Ioannites sought to turn the closing of the shelters, and all of the "persecution" they had encountered, into a conflict between the Russian and the alien, the traditional and the new.[86]

Particularly effective in the campaign was the leadership of Nikolai Nikolaevich Zhedenov, a nobleman and member of the Union of the Russian People. His letter-writing campaign in defense of the Ioannites spread to almost every governor and minister in Russia.[87] Zhedenov claimed to defend parents' rights to assign their children wherever they pleased, and the rights of Orthodox Christians to live according to their convictions, and not to arbitrary standards imposed by a foreign bureaucracy and a hostile press. He then distinguished between three groups of so-called Ioannites: those "hooligans" who threatened Father John with outbursts during services, those recipients of miracles who exalted him (whom he compared to fans of ballerinas and opera divas), and hardworking, honest Russians who chose to live in groups for economic reasons; all needed different approaches. The Ioannites were not a sect, but Orthodox Christians, and were not being persecuted by the Church, but by secular authorities who were themselves far from Orthodoxy.[88] Finally, he noted, the Ioannite production of wreaths was described as a "worthless, parasitical" activity. By these standards, many examples of Russian folk creation could be dismissed, including the Suzdal school of iconography.[89]

The campaign, which utterly ignored the role the dogmatically focused Synod had played in the tracking of the Ioannites, had some success. A nativist backlash began. Such radical right publications as *Zemshchina* played on people's fears of the bureaucracy by stressing that the children in the shelters had been seized and moved because their papers were not in order; the implication, none too thinly veiled, was, "It could happen to you!"[90] The moderate *St. Petersburg Gazette* commented, "Let's say that the Ioannites are fanatics, let's admit that they are heretics, but let's face it: the children do not want to leave them—they cry and fight off anyone who tries to make them. Recall Dostoyevsky: are all the good intentions in the world worth a single child's tear?" The *Gazette* also acidly pointed out that there were plenty of hungry children the Society for the Prevention for Cruelty ought to help before seizing the Ioannite children, who probably did not want to leave because they were well-fed and well-treated. They noted that the accounts of corrupted girls and sores were fabrication: after a thorough medical inspection, it emerged that all the children were healthy; all the girls were virgins. After comparing the persecution to that of the revolutionaries, they concluded that perhaps one ought to fight the Ioannites, but not using such "medieval" means.[91] Even the left-leaning *New Voice*, which referred to earlier accounts of Father John's "miracles" as fantasies woven by a shackled press, spoke out against any official persecution of the Ioannites: it was time, they felt, for Russian society to get out of its diapers and not count on any state agency to speak for it; all the Ioannites deserved were contempt.[92]

Ioannite Reaction

The shelter scandal, the attacks in the press, an increasingly unified and hostile front on the part of the Orthodox clergy, who were now pressing for an official Synodal condemnation of the Ioannites as heretics—all of this created a situation in which the Ioannites felt that the forces of the world were truly arrayed against them, thus increasing their eschatological tendencies even as they fulfilled them. It also meant that they could now discern who their enemies were. Moreover, it gave them a far stronger sense of themselves and their differences from "mainstream" Orthodox Christians.

Because of this growing sense of group solidarity, the Ioannites' strategy changed during 1908. They had acquired experience in dealing with outside agencies and the Imperial system, which they now began to turn to their advantage. Their tone in both publications and encounters with officials moved from one of defensive articulation to one of aggression. It is precisely in their successful attempt to publicize their position, however, that the Ioannites overplayed their hand: they showed how far they had moved from what most people understood as Orthodoxy.

A series of "rebukes" issued by the Ioannite leaders to Orthodox bishops, for example, attacked Orthodox clerics hostile to the Ioannites as "wolves among sheep," articulating an image of the Ioannites as new apostles and true Christians who could and should distinguish between true and false pastors. Once a layperson assumed the right to judge everything for herself, as the Ioannites did after 1907, she cut the Orthodox hierarchical principle at its root. "The Church of Christ is in Danger," an Ioannite publication from 1908, for example, was one long diatribe against the Orthodox clergy in the form of scriptural quotations with connecting sentences explaining their application to the contemporary situation: it told true believers to resist the "notables" warned against by Jeremiah, who, although they know God's law, have destroyed "the yoke and the bonds" (Jeremiah 5:5). Also typical was the exclusive reliance on Scripture and the absence of any quotations from Church Fathers (which is hardly surprising, as the Fathers usually emphasized subordination to the legitimate hierarchy).

The play *Black Ravens* gave the Ioannites another opportunity to attack the establishment Church. While they were as upset as the Synod about the mockery of Orthodoxy, they used the fact that the play was written by an Orthodox missionary, and the very principle of the church's using the stage to promote a message, to criticize modernizing tendencies within the Church. The worst examples were Protopov, the former missionary who had written the play, and the church journals *The Bell* and the *Missionary Overview*.[93]

Most interesting are the claims the Ioannites made for being a beacon of true Orthodoxy in the turbulent revolutionary climate. The laws passed as a consequence of the 1905 Revolution and the political institutions that emerged were anathema to the Ioannites: "Not a single true Christian who loves the Faith, the Tsar, and the Fatherland has entered the State, Tsarist Duma;" priests in left parties were "Judas-betrayers, conscious murderers who have given themselves to Satan."[94]

They interpreted the Book of Ezekiel in light of post-1905 Russian politics: in Chapter 39, which begins with the words, "Therefore, thou son of man, prophesy against Gog," "son of man" was taken to refer to Father John and "Gog" to the Duma.[95] The introduction of freedom of conscience and the equality of religion it implied was key for the Ioannites, who saw themselves as the faithful remnant: while (they believed) the official Church was constrained by its connection with the government from speaking out, they could. They claimed that because of the new law, flocks were freely departing from Orthodoxy to Roman Catholicism, with many "false" pastors are actually expressing their sympathy for this mass conversion. Finally, the Ioannites claimed that the liberal press was deliberately preparing the ground for an armed uprising against Jesus Christ, the Church, and the Autocratic Tsar, God's anointed.[96]

Of course, many of the people to whom Pustoshkin refers were Uniates who had been forcibly converted to Orthodoxy earlier. Moreover, many Christians, including Orthodox clergy and Father John himself, at least thought it possible that the Duma might be an opportunity to provide a Christian witness.[97] But to Pustoshkin, Bol'shakov, and other Ioannites, any departure from "truth" was tainted with the spirit of the world; a recognition of the subtleties or the complexities of the Church are altogether missing. This distinction between the insistence on unique possession of truth and a broader sense of inclusivity on the part of those who feel responsible for the catholicity of the whole Church is, of course, one of the classic distinctions between sect- and Church-consciousness. So are the apocalyptic, chiliastic beliefs that the Ioannites share with such groups as the Old Believers. Pustoshkin and Bol'shakov—and those for whom they claim to speak—possess this quality in abundance.[98]

Official Condemnation

The Ioannites succeeded in throwing sand in the eyes of the authorities. On August 23, 1909, even the Department of Spiritual Matters of Foreign Confessions in the Ministry of Internal Affairs had to ask the Chancellery of the Ober-Procurator of the Synod whether the Ioannites were considered faithful members of the Holy Church, or regarded as a religious group that had definitively broken with Orthodoxy.[99] The Orthodox Church decided to resolve the ambiguity surrounding the Ioannites once and for all at the All-Russian Kiev Missionary Convention.

There, a majority of 112 to 14 voted to define the Ioannites as a sect (the milder option would have been "a religious-mystical tendency").[100]

The discussion surrounding the vote, however, reveals that the attitude of the clergy was more ambiguous and nuanced than the final result suggests. The Petersburg missionary preacher Dmitrii I. Bogoliubov, for example, felt that it was still not clear that "Ioannitstvo" was indeed a sect. He thought it was a distinctive expression of Orthodox religiosity, analogous to right-wing patriotic political organizations, and that, rather than condemning "Ioannitstvo," the Orthodox Church ought to nurse it and direct it. Bogoliubov warned that if the Convention declared the Ioannites to be a sect, they ran the risk of pushing people who so far were only suspect into actually forming a dangerous sect. He urged his colleagues to introduce discussions with the Ioannites instead, in the hopes that through dialogue, the excesses would fall away and that these "mostly good and naïve" people would have something useful to offer the Church; Andrei, Bishop of Mamadysh, expressed similar sentiments.[101]

The voices of others carried the day, however. The motion passed, and the Ioannites were officially labeled a sect similar to the *khlysty*.[102] This ruling was key in establishing all further policies that affected the Ioannites, particularly once the Synod approved it soon after.[103]

All Orthodox Christians, for example, were now warned against participation in *The Kronstadt Beacon*. The clergy was instructed to exercise great caution toward anyone who appeared sympathetic toward the Ioannites, requiring their recantation from the Ioannites' chief delusions before performing any sacraments for them. The clergy was also to warn their parishioners against going to Kronstadt for fear of possible Ioannite abuses. Those laypeople who persisted in Ioannitism after admonishment were to be excommunicated.[104] Similarly, the Council of Ministers headed by Petr Stolypin, felt that the so-called Ioannite sect was actually a criminal organization and hence should be persecuted like all such others; they contacted the Synod for guidance in formulating future policy.[105]

The Ioannites and the Union of the Russian People

The growing condemnation made it imperative for the Ioannites to find allies within established organizations, so that they could either merge or pursue their own activities under the umbrella of an organization that was under no risk of being closed down. This was easier than it seemed. Because of their spirited defense of autocracy and Orthodoxy, their hatred of modernity, and their anti-Semitism, the Ioannites seemed natural companions-in-arms for the Union of the Russian People (URP). The apparent similarity of both groups' aims (every issue of *The Kronstadt Beacon* stated that "the direction of the journal is religious-moral, in the spirit of the Orthodox Church and of Russian nationality"), the similar personality profiles of members (Nikolai Zhedenov, for example, was active in both organizations), and the recognition Father John had given the URP, led members of both groups to seek a rapprochement.

But plans for a merger quickly foundered. The stumbling blocks were Father John's repeated condemnations of the Ioannites and their being labeled a sect by the Orthodox Church. For all that the URP felt sympathy for fellow monarchists and anti-Semites, they had their own reputation to worry about. If they were going to maintain their own status as a respectable, Orthodox body, they had to keep their noses clean, as it were. Hence the Orthodoxy of the Ioannites was key in the URP's decision.

On July 23, 1908, the Iaroslav chapter of the URP took the first step in clarifying the relation of the Ioannites to Father John. Their representatives met with him in the Vaulov Dormition skete, which he had founded in Iaroslav province. According to them, as soon as they brought up the Ioannites, Father John spat to one side in disgust and said, "I have anathematized them repeatedly before, and now, before witnesses, I anathematize them again." He denied any connection to *The Kronstadt Beacon* and gave the URP his blessing in fighting against the Ioannites—but, perhaps aware of the accusations of violence brought against the URP, he urged them to fight using legal means only.[106]

Despite the report of the Iaroslav chapter of the URP and the Kiev condemnation, the Ioannite question caused a temporary split within the Union. The Union's leadership refused to support the Ioannite cause and expelled the Ioannite leaders from the Union's ranks. While they regretfully acknowledged that some individual members harbored pro-Ioannite sympathies, the URP "officially and categorically" declared that it had nothing in common with "Ioannite fanatics" and that ascribing holiness to anyone was the sole prerogative of the Orthodox Church.[107] The newspaper *The Bell*, which had most consistently criticized the Ioannites from a conservative, Orthodox position, reported indignantly that when the URP newspaper *The Russian Banner* folded, the Ioannite *Storm* took over its mailing list: the closest comparison, they said, would be themselves closing and their subscribers receiving the "Jewish *Bourse*" instead; the act would sow confusion among 'the best Russian people' as to who was who.[108] But the Union's Alexander Nevsky section in St. Petersburg welcomed the Ioannites, and became the chief "outside" spokesmen in their defense. The latter included B. A. Vasil'ev, Nikolai Zhedenov, and the Abbott Arsenii (Minin), a former missionary and Athonite monk.

The Ioannov Brotherhood

Together, the three decided to create a new organization called the Ioannov Brotherhood, which opened on September 8, 1909. Its stated aims were the glorification of Father John's memory through the compilation and writing of a *vita* and establishing philanthropic institutions in his name. As had been typical for the early Ioannites, the Brotherhood did not support any of the institutions Father John had himself founded, whether the House of Industry or any of the convents. Their affiliation with the radical right cause is evident. Article 4 of the Bratstvo charter, for example, reads: "Eligible candidates for the Brotherhood must be Orthodox Russian people who hold sacred their oath of loyalty to the Anointed of God, the Emperor and All-Russian Autocrat, and who reject the false teachings of the materialists, socialists, revolutionaries, and Freemasons."[109] It was precisely because the Ministry of Internal Affairs chose to interpret the Brotherhood as an essentially political and conservative organization (like that of the Brotherhood of the Archangel Michael) and Father John as a philanthropist, rather than as a religious figure, that they approved its existence on these secular grounds.[110] Once Nikolai Bol'shakov and the better-known Ioannites joined the Brotherhood, however, both Synod and police began to follow its activities more closely.

It emerged that the Brotherhood was not founding any educational or philanthropic institutions, as its charter had stated, but was pursuing largely religious aims. According to a police investigation, sample weekly lectures from September 20 to October 1 listed their topics as "On God's Dread Judgment," "On Seduction and Conversion from Orthodoxy," and the like. At Brotherhood meetings, moreover, Arsenii regularly preached antisectarian sermons in which he "exposed" Baptists, Pashkovites, and Frederic William Farrar, the contemporary English religious writer, but defended the Ioannites. Once the St. Petersburg Special Office on Societies, which had initially approved the registration of the Brotherhood as a legal society, was informed of this "deviation from the organization's initial nature," they ordered it closed.[111]

The Twilight of the Ioannites

Besides the Kiev designation of Ioannitism as a sect in 1908 and the closing of the Brotherhood in 1909, there were other setbacks for the Ioannites. Nikolai Bolshakov died unexpectedly on January 2, 1910. The Society in the Memory of Father John was formed with the express purpose of salvaging his "bright name and works" from the Ioannites' misdeeds. The police continued to watch like hawks for any signs of Ioannite activity, including claims that it was spreading among the St. Petersburg garrison. It seemed as if the steam would go out of the movement.[112]

But this was not the case. From 1909 to 1913, some people continued to sell all their property and live in Ioannite communities headed by local "prophets."[113] Ioannite preachers were reported as far afield as Vologda, Vladimir, Piatigorsk, Kislovodsk, the Caucausus, Samara, Saratov, and Minsk.[114] Now that Father John was dead, their teachings were more disparate than ever. Some predicted that Nicholas II's rule would soon end with his murder, and that the Antichrist would reign in the person of Lev Tolstoy (or Sergei Witte).[115] Some sought a public debate with Tolstoy; others preached against marriage and eating meat, but for free love.[116] In a combination of folk medicine and exorcism, a peasant named Fedor Lobodin used a book entitled *A Gospel Interpretation*, which he claimed had been blessed by Father John, to heal and exorcise peasants in Voronezh.[117] New "Christs" appeared to take Father John's place—Chursikov in Petrograd, Koloskov in Moscow, Stefan Podgorny in Ukraine.[118] A group of teetotalers appeared whose members called themselves the "Ivanov Brothers" (*Ivanovskie bratsy*).[119] The activity was so varied that some newspapers began to suggest that the Ivanovskie Bratsy, the Ioannites, the Baptists, and the Adventists were seeking to form a united anti-Orthodox, and especially anti-Orthodox missionary, front.[120]

Official confusion persisted as well. When queried by local authorities as to how to proceed with reported Ioannites, the central authorities operated with an astonishing amount of crossed signals. In a memorandum of March 28, 1910, for example, the Department of Spiritual Matters of Foreign Confessions, responding to a query from the

Governor of Tomsk Guberniia as to how to proceed with regard to recently spotted Ioannites, advised him that

> [g]iven that *so far as we know* the Ioannites *have not formed a sect* with dogmatic or canonical teachings distinct from those of the Orthodox Church—instead, they appear to be a sort of pietistic organization pursuing moral self-perfection—they should be treated not from a religious, but exclusively from a general, civic point of view.[121]

The Court Hoffmeister responded in a similarly disingenuous vein to the Tobolsk governor in 1911 that the Ioannites were not a sect but a pious group of people whose only aim was the eventual glorification of Father John, adding that after 1906 legislation, preliminary censorship laws had been abolished and Ioannite publications could not be persecuted on these grounds.[122]

How is it possible that representatives of the Ministry and the Court could be at such variance with the Synod and the ruling of 1908? Clearly, the Synod's approval of the 1908 All-Russian Missionary Convention in Kiev had not been strong enough. On April 13, 1912, a special session of the Synod was held devoted exclusively to the Ioannite issue. Ioannitism was now officially declared a khlyst-type sect; Kiseleva, Pustoshkin, Nazarii, and Zhedenev were held responsible; special pronouncements were prepared for the Orthodox flock clarifying the issue.[123] It is a sign of how much the Ioannites had succeeded in permeating official discourse, however, that even their Orthodox enemies absorbed some of their language. Such pamphlets as *The Ioannites Have Been Damned by Father John of Kronstadt*, published in 1912, read, "These heretic Ioannites have been damned by Father John, and, *through him*, by God Himself."[124]

The Ioannites belong to a long series of popular religious movements seeking to recapture "true" religion and to waken others to the dangers of imminent apocalypse.[125] In the Late Imperial Russian context, they are also part of a larger nativist, right-wing response to modernization and secularism. The Ioannites attracted much more attention than millenarian religious groups usually warranted, however, because of their claim to be Father John's "true" followers. Because he was such a widely known, widely revered symbol of Orthodoxy—and one who had himself transformed so many categories of Orthodox behavior—the actions of the Ioannites inevitably reflected not only upon Father John himself, but upon Orthodoxy as well. The Ioannites thus not only caused an identity crisis in the Orthodox Church, but also provided an easy target for the radical press: by attacking the "illiterate, anti-Semitic Ioannites," one could smear Father John as well. Post-1990 representations would tacitly rehabilitate the Ioannites by incorporating their literature, but, in Late Imperial Russia, the Ioannites were perceived as a threat to both Father John and to Orthodoxy.

7

The Politics of Orthodoxy, Autocracy, and the Revolutionary Movement

The attributions of "intercessor" and "witness" affected Father John politically as well as spiritually, for his fame coincided with the rise of the revolutionary movement. As a result of this challenge to the status quo, both he and many of his followers were shaken out of their acceptance of the monarchical order as a given. Once it dawned on them that tsars could be murdered, as was Alexander II in 1881, and that the Orthodox establishment could come crashing down around them, as it almost did from 1905 to 1907, they responded viscerally. Father John took upon himself the mantle of defender of the ideal of "Orthodox Russia" as, from the 1880s onward, the prophetic aspect of his priesthood came to the fore. The growth of his parish to encompass all of the Russian Empire meant that his pastoral responsibilities became political. Along with spending more of his life in public, Father John also began devoting more of his energy to defending the political and religious order and attacking the dangers he saw emanating from Lev Tolstoy and the radical intelligentsia. When it seemed as if Russia might actually crumble in the 1905 Revolution, he was so appalled that he threw in his support behind the revolution's most vociferous opponents. This symbolic backing of the radical right branded him for decades, eclipsing the other aspects of his life until the end of the twentieth century. Moreover, because he was regarded as holy, his politics forced many Russians to question whether allegiance to Orthodoxy and its holy people meant allegiance to the autocracy as well—even though Peter the Great had removed the office of Patriarch and instituted the Synodal Church. The conflict was between those who supported the separation of Church and State, and those who still defended the Byzantine ideal of Church-State symphony; between secular and religious society, between human and divine right. In a decision that would have far-reaching consequences for the image of Orthodoxy, Father John chose the latter in each instance.

Father John had a total Christian vision of the world, which governed his notions of what contemporary Russia ought to be like. This vision had several characteristics: the true life of the Christian was not on earth but in heaven, all people were equal before God, and the world (or at least Russia, as the leader of Orthodox Christian nations) ought to be governed by Orthodox Christian principles. This conception of a Christian order defined his social and political opinions.

The most important characteristic of Father John's total conception was his notion that the true life of the Christian was not on earth but in heaven; earthly life was at best a shadow of the eternal life to come. Before the assassination of Alexander II, Father John was essentially practical and apolitical; when he thought of society, it was in terms of realizing biblical and Christian ideals of charity and spiritual equality. At the beginning of his priesthood, contrary to the Slavophile conception of Russia as a uniquely Orthodox homeland, "natural, simple, and harmonious," he rejected the notion of any "chosen" country; he did not idealize any political order, whether contemporary Russia or early Byzantium.[1] Typical of the few even remotely political comments he made in the 1850s and the 1860s was the diary entry, "Saying 'Our father which art in heaven,' and so on, means that our fatherland is Heaven."[2] Where Father John did expressly use the image of the king, it was largely reflexive; the image of the king in Orthodox clerical writing (and in Russian life) was so omnipresent that it seemed a natural example of certain principles: "Just as the name of His Royal Highness is constantly written and pronounced in decrees in the king's chambers and offices, so in church, where God's grace is particularly present, God's name in the Trinity is constantly invoked."[3]

As with many Russians, Father John's attitude to authority in general and that of the king specifically, and the terms in which one might express one's objection to them, changed with the assassination of Alexander II on March 1, 1881. The event marked a watershed in Father John's notions of the role of the ruler and of stability in Russian society. He first mentions the assassination in a brief entry of March 2, where he refers to having received the "frightful news of the murder of the Sovereign Emperor by a bomb while he was exiting his sledge." Initially he thought of the event in religious terms broadly conceived: he was moved to think of the power of repentance and wrote of the terrorists that "even the killers of the Lord, if they had repented, would have been saved"—a position very similar, incidentally, to that of Tolstoy and others who petitioned Alexander III for the killers' pardon.[4] Almost immediately after the assasination, however, Father John took a more epic and vengeful interpretation: "Evil and predatory vultures have swooped down upon our gentle Sovereign and ripped him to bits, and with him other innocent people, and streams of martyrs' blood have begun to flow. May the Lord render unto these vultures in human skin according to their actions, and may he give those murdered incorruptible wreaths."[5]

In the days that followed, Father John gave himself up entirely to speculate on the implications of the assassination for Russia and the fate of the Emperor in the next life. He abandoned his lesson plans and spent classes reading aloud newspaper accounts of the Emperor's death to his class. He saw the murder in religious terms as a cross to bear and perhaps as a way of redeeming Alexander's previous errors. When he tried to make sense of the assassination, Alexander II became a kind of Christ-figure, dying for the sins and the ultimate salvation of his people:

> We have an awful act of villainy; our beloved Sovereign is killed by a certain hand. But where is the Lord, then? Why did He did not deliver him? Has he forgotten us? No, he did not forget us, and He did not avert this. He struck us like lightning, allowing such a misfortune to strike us—in order to wake us from our sinful slumber, for us to come to our senses, look about ourselves, recognize the abyss of our sins, repent, and improve.[6]

Despite this conclusion, it was difficult for Father John, with his abiding belief in the power of liturgical prayer, to accept that God would allow the murder of "the Patron of the Church, for whose power, victory, peace, health, overcoming the enemy and the adversary She [the Church] daily brought earnest prayers," especially given that all of Russia had recently "prayed especially for his deliverance from death from villains" (this referring to the previous attempts on the life of Alexander II). He wrote in bewilderment and anguish, leaving his sentences unfinished, "Can it be that the Lord has not heard the prayers of the Church ... he heard them, and accepted them."[7]

The labeling of Alexander II a martyr was not specific to Father John, of course. Most other conservative individuals and institutions responded in a similar vein. Such newspapers as *The Moscow News*, for example, referred to the Tsar with such religious terms as "Tsar-Martyr" and "Tsar-Sufferer." The historian Vasilii Tatishchev compared Alexander to "that good shepherd who lays down his life for his sheep."[8] The construction of a special church on the site of the killing was a project emphasizing such religious and mythological references.[9] Father John's was thus but one voice in the general conservative and monarchist sentiment. To him, as to the readers of *Moscow News*, it was only one step from calling the king a martyr for his people to declaring his death a moral tragedy for Russia and equating his killers with the enemies of Russia in a moral sense—equating them, indeed, with all the forces of evil threatening Christian Russia. Although Father John had not regarded Russia as being a particularly Christian country before the death of the Tsar, the murder of Alexander II appeared to him to be a sign of Russia's moral crisis.

> What is this? An open, insolent war of our own against our own, against the king and all of his subjects? For now everyone is stricken, if not physically, then morally, emotionally.... But, insolent and blind, they [the killers] are warring against themselves ... they are destroying their criminal, evil seed—the seed of the antichrist. Yes, the antichrist: for they are [of] his spirit. They are warring against everything that is sacred for all Christian peoples and kings; by overthrowing the kings they want to establish anarchy and crude tyranny, faithlessness, immorality, illegality, fear, and horror. But they will not be able to pull it off. God is with us, u[nderstand] a[ll] y[e] n[ations] a[nd] s[ubmit] y[ourselves], f[or] G[od] i[s] w[ith] u[s], O ye powerful, submit yourselves, for if ye again strengthen yourselves, ye shall again be vanquished.[10]

Even this surge of religious-patriotic fervor, however, did not suddenly eclipse the faults of the Russian Empire in Father John's eyes. The Tsar's death was not a redemption of people's sins, as was that of Christ, but a warning, a punishment, and a sign that people needed to improve.

The murder of the king was sent to us by God to wake us up.—And everyone has come to their senses! Everyone is crying, oh-ing and ach-ing!—But is that all we need? We need moral cleansing, profound national repentance, a change of morals,—Christian ones for pagan ones. Let us wash ourselves, let us cleanse ourselves, let us make peace with God—and he will make peace with us and will eat away and destroy all enemies of the king and the people as if they were pulp.[11]

He did not understand repentance in an exclusively sacramental sense. Despite the threatening tone of the last phrase, Father John reminded Russians of the social ways in which they needed to improve their lives, calling for the rich and the strong to care for the poor and the weak.[12]

The assassination of Alexander II was the turning point in Father John's relation to autocracy in the person of the ruler. The Tsar's dying a "martyr's death" symbolically changed the status of the ruler in his eyes. Before the killing, the Tsar was largely an abstraction to Father John. Afterward, the ruler gradually came to incarnate for him the religious aspects of the old order and the positive qualities of tradition and stability versus the negative ones of revolutionary change. When, in 1883, he found something to criticize in the next monarch's policies, for example, he quickly reproved himself ("Lord! It is not for me, it is for you to judge the King—and you set your judgment over him in all the earth.... How then can we, with our near-sighted, sinful judgments, *dare* to interfere in your judgments?").[13]

Father John's new appreciation of the monarch was informed by other political events. The most significant, changing both his standing in society and the importance he attached to the ruler, was his role in the last days of Alexander III. Although his fame was near its height by the early 1890s, Father John still encountered suspicion and hostility on the part of the clerical hierarchy.[14] His being invited to minister to the dying Alexander III had the effect of, if not removing these suspicions altogether, at least making it difficult to express them publicly.

The nature of this visit is still shrouded in misunderstanding. It is undeniably true that Father John was summoned to the Emperor's bedside and asked to give him last rites. But he was not, as was asserted afterward, particularly close to the Imperial family or the court, nor was he their confessor.[15] The invitation came about as the result of a suggestion by the Grand Duchess Aleksandra Iosifovna, who was the wife of Alexander III's cousin. The Emperor's own knowledge of Father John was at best cursory—but he did acknowledge Father John's all-Russian fame, as the following conversation he had with Countess Aleksandra Andreevna Tolstaia (the writer's cousin) suggests:

ALEXANDER III: Tell me who you think are the most remarkable and popular people in Russia. I know how honest you are and I am certain that you will tell me the truth. Of course you mustn't think of including me in the list.
COUNTESS TOLSTAIA (smiling): Very well, I won't include you.
ALEXANDER III: But who will you have, then? That's what I'm interested in.
TOLSTAIA: First of all, Lev Tolstoi.
ALEXANDER III: I expected as much. Who else?
TOLSTAIA (thinking): There is one more person I can name you.
ALEXANDER III (impatiently): Who is it, then? Who is it?
TOLSTAIA: Father John of Kronstadt.
ALEXANDER III (laughing): I had forgotten about him. But I agree with you.[16]

Countess Tolstaia, incidentally, was not the only person to link Father John and Tolstoy. The journal *New Path* described both men as being "religious phenomena of similar force"; the Iuriev (Dorpat) University chose both simultaneously as honorary members (which honor Father John consequently rejected).[17] In any case, although Alexander III had heard of Father John, it is clear that his acquaintance was limited to the public knowledge virtually any Russian newspaper reader of the 1890s would have had. Nikolai Vel'iaminov, Alexander's personal physician, even claims that the Emperor shared Pobedonostsev's distaste for Father John's "originality."[18] By the time it became evident that Alexander was gravely ill, however, Father John was so widely known for working extraordinary acts of recovery from illness that a member of the Romanov family might have reasonably suggested that he be asked to pray at Alexander's bedside. While he was invited to attend to the dying Emperor in Livadia in 1894, it was as a court of last resort, not as someone who had enjoyed a previous trust.

Nevertheless, his reaction to this invitation was powerful. People had already identified his role as that of Russia's intercessor before God. What better manifestation of this role, and to what better purpose might it be turned, than to praying for the dying Tsar? Despite his lack of success—Alexander III died several days after his arrival—he tried to turn the occurence to his favor in an account of the visit that was widely printed in newspapers and cited throughout Europe and the

United States.[19] The section that most emphasized his connection to both the crown and to the Russian people described Alexander's last words:

> The Sovereign wished me to lay my hands upon His head, and I held them there for a long time. The Sovereign was fully conscious and asked me to rest a bit, but I said that I did not feel any fatigue and asked him, "Is it not difficult for Your Majesty to have me hold my hands on Your head for so long?" He said, "On the contrary, I feel better when you hold them there." Then he deigned to say, "Do the Russian people love you?" "Yes," I replied, "Your people love me." "They love you," answered the Sovereign, "because they know who you are and what you are."[20]

Alexander's affirmation of Father John's importance, witnessed by the assembled Imperial family, was the best-publicized testimony Father John had ever received. He did not blame his own prayers for his failure to heal the Tsar; instead, he reproached all of Russia and concluded with an admonition to the Russian people:

> Do not weep and do not lament, Russia! Although you were not able to win healing for your King through prayer, your prayers did win Him a quiet, Christian end—and a good end crowned His glorious life,—and that is the most precious thing of all. Now also love His Heir, the Emperor Nikolai Aleksandrovich, who received a sacred behest from His Sovereign Father—to follow in his steps.[21]

Father John saw nothing incongruous about applying his role of intercessor and spiritual father of Russia to draw a moral imperative from the Tsar's death. Similarly, his readiness to ascribe psychological motives to actions of the Imperial Family—the reasons for Maria Feodorovna's wishing to have communion, for example—was in keeping with his identification as "the pastor of all Russia." But what was self-evident to Father John, and what his correspondents echoed in associating the two "Batiushkas," was not welcomed by the Palace. The forwardness of someone who was, after all, only a parish priest, ran against the grain of the conventional phrases used to describe any members of acts of the Royal House. In his eagerness to turn the Tsar's demise into an edifying lesson, Father John appeared to be oblivious to Imperial protocol.

It is not surprising that because of this "familiarity," Father John disconcerted those who were charged with preserving and maintaining the Romanovs' public image, particularly the conservative press. Their assessment of his account reflects the mixed opinion of what behavior was deemed appropriate for a religious figure. Although Father John submitted his text for publication in *New Time* almost immediately, there was some dispute on the editorial board as to whether it was appropriate for publication. Aleksei Zhemchuzhnikov commented to the paper's publisher, Aleksei Suvorin:

> The profound interest of this article lies in the esteemed Father John's describing everything he saw and heard, everything to which he was a witness.... The concluding appeal of the author to "grieving Russia," however—"Now love also his Heir, who received from His Sovereign Father His sacred behest: to follow in His steps"—are full of emotion and impressive—but we think that when the subject concerns such an emotional family matter as the behest received from One's dead Sovereign Father, *no one*—not even when governed, as here, by the most reverent and best intentions—save for the Monarch himself may announce it publicly, in whatever expressions and in whatever circumstances He himself deems appropriate.... Moreover, persons of all social conditions and estates, without exception, ought to restrict themselves to citing only those words which His Imperial Majesty has made public up to this point.[22]

Zhemchuzhnikov was operating largely under the principle of Imperial privacy and prerogative to control the Imperial image. The implicit rebuke to Father John in the last paragraph—that everyone without exception must operate within a certain framework of discretion in discussing the Imperial family—is tempered by his acknowledgment of Father John's repute and his stress that this principle applies to everyone. Suvorin, however, questioned Father John's motivation more directly, and flatly accused him of taking too active an interest in his own promotion:

> Your remarks are absolutely justified. When I received Father John's article, my first inclination was to send it back to him and to suggest that perhaps he ought not write about himself, and so on. But the Sovereign himself, for whom I have always cherished the warmest feelings, emerges in this account as such a dear and

such a Russian person—so much more genuine and more simple than Father John himself, who is now the most popular person in all of Russia—that I ordered it to be typeset and sent to the Imperial Court, without whose permission we cannot print such things in any case....

Father John has inquired why the article is taking such a long time to appear. He has evidently become a bit seduced by his own popularity, but I do not think he will gain much with this piece—[23]

And *New Time* was a conservative publication. Suvorin's impatience with Father John suggests the extent to which even moderate laypeople, not only bishops, had begun to question his celebrity, which his visit to the Tsar only increased. In fact, the immediate result of the visit was the association of Father John with the Palace by Church hierarchy, laity, and foreign press alike. Although Father John had been renowned before the visit to Alexander III, his position in terms of the church hierarchy was only completely secure after the encounter. After the visit, his diaries stop mentioning attempts by clerical superiors to restrain him. The process that had begun with the assassination of Alexander II now had reached its apogee: Father John's sermons began to equate Orthodoxy with the temporal success of Russia.[24] The visit to Livadia had crystallized his attitude toward the monarchy as a political ideal.

This is not to say that the encounter with Alexander III signaled an abrupt change. Instead, Father John's first direct contact with the Imperial family was one of the stepping stones on his path from being relatively unpolitical to becoming convinced that even the flawed Orthodox order he knew was preferable to what the revolutionary movement augured. The assassination of Alexander II, the popularity of Lev Tolstoy, the unexpected death of Alexander III, and above all the revolutionary movement—all of these mark the points of evolution of Father John's consciousness toward active defense of the existing order.

Father John was not alone in this progression. Many of his correspondents followed a similar path and expressed similar sentiments. Several elders of the Optina monastery ascribed the fires, storms, and cholera that swept Russia in 1848 as a natural reflection of the revolution in Europe. The celebrated bishop-scholar Ignatii Brianchianinov bewailed the preoccupation of Russian society with things French: "What will happen to us, what will happen to Russia, which continues to see France as the Promised Land and Paris as the New Jerusalem?" Serafim of Sarov went even further in his apocalyptic predictions. In the eyes of the early and mid-nineteenth-century religious eschatologists, Russia and Orthodoxy were under attack as never before. In their alarm before a changing world, they began to lump together indiscriminately the forces of evil (materialism, secularism, the West) and adopt Uvarov's formula of "Orthodoxy, Autocracy, Nationality" as emblematic of the essence and the stability of the old order.[25] The lesson was clear: Russians must resist Europe's supposed materialism and stick to their own ways. If Russia did not heed the call to piety and Orthodoxy, a catastrophe of apocalyptic proportions would follow. Laypeople were as prone to this eschatological frame of mind as monastics. Count A. P. Tolstoy (the former Ober-Procurator of the Holy Synod), for example, turned to the Optina elder Amvrosii in 1871 with a request to interpret a dream in which Filaret, the Metropolitan of Moscow, read a large book with the words "Rome. Troy. Egypt. Russia. The Bible" on one of its pages. The elder interpreted it in the following manner:

> Although Russia is currently regarded as an Orthodox and independent state, nevertheless elements of foreign unbelief and impiety have penetrated and taken hold in us, and threaten us with the same fate that met the forgoing countries.... This could mean that if in Russia, too, because of disdain for God's commandments and because of the weakening of the rules and regulations of the Orthodox Church and because of other reasons piety will fall into decline, then surely must follow the final execution of that which is uttered at the end of the Bible, that is, in the Apocalypse of John the Theologian: "The Antichrist will come in the times of anarchy."[26]

Eschatological sentiments only grew with the revolutionary movement. While letters on politics to Father John remained a minority, from the 1890s onward, politics began to exist as a separate category in his correspondence. It is in this area, more than any other, that the specific profile of his writers emerges, especially after 1904. In the religious sphere, he attracted people of virtually every age, religion, nationality, and social background; in the political one, he received letters only from dedicated monarchists or those who were wavering between political parties. He was ignored by almost every committed liberal from the Constitutional Democrats leftward. In most cases, it is nearly impossible to establish which came first: Did Father John's opinions determine who his audience would be, or did the limited nature of the opinions he encountered form his own, or both? It is enough to say that his conservative tendencies were at least reinforced, and in some cases actually spurred on, by the letters he received.

In one case, ironically, it was Father John's "liberal" position that prompted a flurry of angry right-wing response. Immediately after the Kishinev pogrom in 1903, both Father John and Bishop Antonii (Khrapovitskii) denounced the ghastly events in no uncertain terms in sermons and in the journal *Missionary Overview*. The impact of their condemnation was so great, in fact, that an editor from Odessa requested permission to publish them as a separate brochure—which was distributed so assiduously by the Jewish community that the Archbishop of Kishinev warned the Oberprocurator it might be counterproductive.[27] Even Tolstoy declined a friend's request to make a public statement of outrage about the pogroms, because he felt that "Father John has already said, and admirably, what every person who has not turned into an animal thinks and feels. Any further comment seems hardly necessary."[28] But Father John's condemnation of the pogroms also earned him the hatred of anti-Semites. A typical post-Kishinev letter to him read: "Father John, *Judas*, you were esteemed by the Russian people until now! Now you are a guardian of the yids and their slave and minion. You only know to drink the blood of Christians."[29]

Father John promptly turned this hate mail over to the police. Such threats, however, along with letters from Kishinev claiming that the pogrom had been a set-up and that the first shot had come from a Jewish doctor who killed an innocent peasant, led him to temper his initial unequivocal indignation with an apology to the Christians of Kishinev for his previous "one-sidedness."[30] This about-face shows that, although Father John did not share the visceral anti-Semitism that often characterized the extreme right, it was all too easy for him to be influenced by the one-sided information he received (there were no letters from the Jewish community about the pogrom). It also recalls his initial mild pastoral and evangelical response to the assassination of Alexander II in 1881, giving way to a more political one. It is not surprising that the priest Georgii Gapon, who would later become famous for leading the demonstration to the Winter Palace on "Bloody Sunday," criticized Father John for vacillating.[31]

Other events influenced Father John's opinions as well. After the laws on religious tolerance passed in 1903 and 1905, for example, Orthodox peasants from the Western provinces, and especially the heavily Polish areas, began to complain to Father John that the local Poles were pressuring them to convert to Roman Catholicism. Orthodox priests in those regions also wrote of Catholic propaganda, saying one of the most successful ploys was the claim that Father John himself had converted to Catholicism and taken the Pope's blessing.[32] There were no letters, however, from formerly closet Uniates who were glad to have the opportunity to practice their faith openly. Given the imbalance and his own predisposition, it is not surprising that Father John gave generously to the Orthodox population of the area.

The most distraught letters with politics as their subject, however, are those written during the revolutionary turmoil that reached its peak during the revolution of 1905–7. Most people simply asked for Father John's prayers after peasants set fire to (or robbed) their estates, or after their children became involved in the revolutionary movement.[33] Letters from the most educated are a litany of shock and dismay, filled with such phrases as "It is fearful to think of what awaits our dear fatherland, all of these strikes threaten something terrible, the Church and the Orthodox faith are in danger, as is our dear Tsar-Batiushka and his Heir."[34] To the people who were shocked by the events of 1905, Father John was a symbol of security and stability, someone who could be counted on to direct the country to its proper path.

Conservative political organizations also began to contact Father John after 1900, asking him whether he might agree to become an honorary member. Just as such organizations as the Society for the Prevention of Cruelty to Animals and the Vilna Students' Mutual Aid Society had petitioned him to serve as a stamp of approval that would attract other donors, so, in a time of political upheaval, organizations that wished to support Orthodox and national ideals sought out Father John to serve as their symbol. The Kazan branch of the Russian Gathering, for example, invited him to become an honorary member "as the one who prays for the Russian land, as a true servant of our Lord Jesus Christ, and as a person who firmly defends the basic Russian foundations (*ustoi*)."[35] When these organizations contacted him, they did so in measured and general language, asking for his prayers that the organization might "worthily serve for the good of the Fatherland."

He did not disappoint them. From 1905 on, many right-wing political organizations, including the Russian Gathering (in both the St. Petersburg and the Kazan chapters), the Kharkov chapter of the Union of Russian Men, the Russian People's Union in the name of Michael the Archangel, and the Russian Patriotic Society, enlisted him as an honorary member. The extent to which Father John had become adopted by the "institutional" far right is evident from the publication of his sermons and essays by radical right and conservative factions in the government. His reputation was used to bolster their own.[36]

Other people, especially the less literate, described their confusion. A shop assistant from Moscow asked him which political party one ought to sign up for, and which not, explaining that he had just joined the trade-and-industry party, "But maybe one ought not to join any party at all."[37] Some attempted to reconcile their Christianity with their radical sentiments, asking him to intercede for the "unfortunate sailors and soldiers who had gone crazy" during the recent Kronstadt uprising, "that they might not perish at the hands of executioners—who are their own brothers."[38] Letters expressing the most confusion came from peasants. One such group from Saratov wrote him of the newspapers in their area that had "tempted all their villages." "Please tell us how to respond to these fairy tales and how to defeat the enemies," they asked, adding earnestly, "Dear Batiushka, they are writing very bad things about you."[39]

Other mostly literate people asked for his prayers "that during the present time of troubles and disturbance the Lord might enlighten our minds ... that we might not be thrown off from the true path."[40] Most interesting here is that even as Father John's less literate correspondents trusted him to guide them, they showed far less confidence in their own ability to stick to the "true path." Their letters would form the basis of his belief that the peasants were good at heart and well-intentioned, but fully capable of going astray politically without clear guidance. The most explicit statement of an essentially religious mentality confronted with new political choices and responsibilities came from a peasant named Aleksandr. He wrote:

> I dare to ask for your blessing, your prayers to the Lord, and your instruction setting me on the right path, as I have gone astray because of my pride, my high-mindedness, and self-will, and have fallen into a powerful temptation, which allow me to describe:
>
> I always feared and avoided books which were not of spiritual content and read only spiritual ones. But then on November 30, 1905, the *volost'* chose me as their plenipotentiary for the elections to the State Duma. Right away I got the idea that I was better than everyone else. The other plenipotentiary understood that according to the October 17 manifesto, the one on freedom of the word, that the word was something spiritual and that the Sovereign was God's instrument who would return to God. We discussed it together privately and determined that we must ask the Sovereign to pardon everyone guilty, that he did not give them life and did not have the right to take it away. So we went to Vologda to three churches to pray.[41]

Aleksandr then went on to recount how, seized with a sense of his political and religious responsibilities, he began to pray loudly for everyone living and dead "with unnatural cries," feeling cold inside and feverish outside. He then walked along the streets calling all to church and repentance, and, finally, during Liturgy on December 17, 1905, first thrashed around before an icon of the Savior crying out that he was unworthy—and then, just as the Gospel was to be read, had a vision of the Savior coming toward him with the angels. The vision must have made him faint, because he reports that the church's deacon later told him that he was taken to the police station. Aleksandr had since gone to confession and communion two or three times, but could not rid himself of a bewildering welter of thoughts on truth and mystery. He implored Father John to pray for him for God to forgive him and to set him on the true path (he added that he wanted to visit him, but after all that had happened, his wife would not let him out of her sight). On the other hand, no letters survive from peasant deputies who went to the Duma without suffering spiritual crises. If their voices were not represented in his correspondence, the letters from people like Aleksandr would form the dominant impression, confirming Father John in thinking that political representation was beyond the "simple people" and only confused them.

Most decisive in forming Father John's views, however, were the letters that directly challenged his apoliticism and called him to action. Some of the demands came from the radical right:

> The residents of the Northwestern region cannot understand the calm silence—or the voicelessness—of Father John, who is so respected by everyone. His silence is especially mysterious at a time like now, when his fatherland, which needs both moral and material help, so needs to hear his voice.... This is a pogrom which is attacking all of Holy Russia. There was a time when Father responded to every need; now, just when his fatherland needs him most, Father John's voice is not heard—strange, even more than strange! In earlier times like these, we had unforgettable pastors like Avraam Palitsyn and others—is Russia barren of them now? It cannot be.... Respond to Russia's sorrow, embolden her![42]

But not all of the letters summoning Father John to political activity came from people who perceived the 1905 Revolution as a pogrom targeting Russia and Russians. He received letters from supporters of the political changes as well. Whether the calls to action came from the right or the left, however, he was charged with a moral responsibility to speak out:

> There is nothing left to do except to seek help from our clergy. The current situation is almost hopeless for all of the lower classes who do not belong to the "bureaucracy." ... Father John, pay some attention to the needs of the people in Russia, who need not Cossack whips (which the damned "bureaucracy" uses), but those rights which the Sovereign Emperor promised and which the students and everyone who understands stands for.... Maybe when you read my letter, you will say, "That's not my business." No, Father John, no one has more business than you to speak out, because Russia and the people trust you more than anyone else, and you have access to the Sovereign. And who better to come to [our] defense than you, spiritual pastors—after all, you will have to answer for this, the pastor has to answer for his sheep.[43]

Father John responded quickly. The letters he received not only echoed his own repugnance at revolutionary terrorism, they explicitly called him to action. The sermons he preached from 1900 onward must be understood in this light. His correspondents would have thrust upon him the role of "Russia's conscience" even if he had not wanted it himself; as it was, his followers made it clear to him that they believed he had both the duty and the responsibility to speak out. But Father John's own decades-long conviction that it was the obligation of the priest to "denounce" would have prompted him to do so; the letters to him simply provided added incentive and confirmation. When he did speak out, it was not in measured tones. His last sermons expressed his dismay at the upheavals and his fear that an imperfectly Orthodox order might fall to something far worse. They raised piety and patriotism to nearly an equal status, changing his image from being an essentially religious figure to that of being the exponent of typical equations of Orthodoxy with Russian might and identity. Father John grew particularly strident during the 1905 Revolution.

> Look what is happening in this kingdom at the present time: everywhere students and workers are on strike; everywhere there is the noise of parties who have as their goal the overthrowing of the true monarchical order established by God, everywhere the dissemination of insolent, senseless proclamations, disrespect for the authority of the ruling powers established by God, for

"there is no power but of God: the powers that be are ordained of God": children and young people imagine that they are the masters and commanders of their own fates; marriage has lost all meaning for many and divorces at will have multiplied to endlessness; many children are left to the whims of fate by unfaithful spouses; some kind of senselessness and arbitrariness rule.... Finally, an unpunished conversion from Orthodoxy into any other faith whatever is allowed; even though the same Lord we confess designated death in the Old Testament for those denying the law of Moses.[44]

If matters continue like this in Russia and the atheists and the anarchist-crazies are not subjected to the righteous retribution of the law, and if Russia is not cleansed of its many tares, then it will become desolate like the ancient kingdoms and cities wiped out by God's righteous judgment from the face of the earth for their godlessness and their wickedness: Babylon, Assyria, Egypt, Greece-Macedonia.

Hold fast, then, Russia, to your faith, and your Church, and to the Orthodox Tsar if you do not wish to be shaken by people of unbelief and lawlessness and if you do not wish to be deprived of your Kingdom and the Orthodox Tsar. But if you fall away from your faith, as many intelligents have fallen away, then you will no longer be Russia or Holy Rus', but a rabble of all kinds of other faiths who wish to destroy one another.[45]

The tidal wave of 1905's political murders and antigovernment terrorism also stunned Father John.[46] He began to use allegories to support the regime. In his reading, Moses became the "Autocratic Leader," "as if their King," of the Israelites by Mount Sinai who began an "impious revolution." When Moses said, "Put every man his sword by his side, and go in and out from gate to gate throughout the camp, and slay every man his brother, and every man his companion, and every man his neighbor," Father John clarified to his listeners that this meant the slaying of each revolutionary. He concluded,

> This is how holy people suppressed a revolution among their people and by doing so saved their people from moral rotting decay, and this was pleasing to God. After forty days everything returned to its usual order.
> What is this if not an instructive example for our wicked time and the unbridled Russian revolution?[47]

Finally, the war with Japan became an occasion for him to restate his political credo and express apocalyptic dread:

> This bloody war of ours against the pagans is also God's righteous judgment for our sins. The final, universal, dread judgment of God is drawing ever closer as a consequence of the fearful overflowing of evil on this earth. Now all sorts of untruths are spreading over the earth like an ocean; there is no end to human wilfulness, the doors are open to all sorts of delusions and vices. The laws of God are flouted; creatures have forgotten their Creator; sinful people in their pride have imagined themselves to be innocent; those defiled with all sorts of impurities have forgotten their impurities. The ox knoweth his owner, and the ass his master's crib, but Christians have repudiated their Christ, their Savior [Cf. Isaiah 1:3]....
>
> Our intelligentsia youths have subverted the social and educational order, they have taken politics and the law-courts upon themselves without having been called to do so by anyone; they have taken to judging their masters, their teachers, the government and all but kings themselves; together with their head, Lev Tolstoy, they have judged and condemned the universal and fearful Judge Himself.... Verily, the day of the dread Judgment is near, for the deviation from God which was foretold has already occurred and the forerunner of the antichrist has already revealed himself [Tolstoy], the son of perdition, who opposeth and exalteth himself above all that is called God, or that is worshipped.[48]

The references to Tolstoy are not coincidental. From the 1890s onward, Father John had been moving to an ever greater condemnation of the celebrated writer. Ironically, as the Iuriev (Dorpat) University noted, the two had much in common: complicated relations with their dutiful wives, a desire for asceticism, and a reputation for being spiritual giants. The similarities ended there, however. From a social point of view, as many observers noted, they represented the old conflict between the elite aristocracy and the educated intelligentsia (*obshchestvo*), on the one hand, and the common people (*narod*), on the other.[49] From a political point of view, the two stood on opposite sides as well. Tolstoy's dislike for all forms of authority, his pacifisim, his overt desire to bring down the Russian Tsar, army, and Church all coincided with the period when Father John was becoming increasingly aware of the threats to the old order. But the biggest difference, of course, was religious. After all, the Tolstoy denied the main dogmas of Orthodoxy: he taught that Christ was not divine, but simply a virtuous human being; Mary was not a virgin, but an unwed mother; that none of the sacraments were necessary. His irreverent depiction of the Eucharist in *Resurrection* was especially offensive to an Orthodox believer. Finally, he attacked the Orthodox Church directly, calling it pagan, coercive, and idolatrous.[50]

The battle lines were drawn. Just as Father John had drawn social implications from his reading of the Gospels, so he now predicted the implications for society of Tolstoy's teachings. Dostoyevsky had written in *The Brothers Karamazov*, "If there is no God, then all is permitted"; Tolstoy's "perverted" conception of the Divine, Father John felt, would lead to similar nihilism.[51] A collection of his anti-Tolstoyan diatribes was published in 1902. After repeatedly excoriating the writer, Father John concluded that Tolstoy "according to scripture, ought to have a stone hung round your neck and be lowered with it into the depths of the sea; you ought not to have any place on earth."[52]

Such statements outraged such radicals as Bonch-Bruevich, who wrote a response so scathing that one could practically see the froth on his mouth.[53] In 1908, the Secretary of the State Council, Ioann Iakunchikov, sent as a curiosity to the Minister of the Interior a clipping from the *Frankfurter Zeitung*, which claimed to be a prayer written by Father John, calling on God for the deaths of both Tolstoy and Sergei Witte, who were "destroying Russia." The Minister wrote back, saying that the matter needed to be investigated and that, if proven false, it might be necessary to sue the German newspaper. "I would think," he added tartly, "that the people who represent Russia abroad might be a bit less cavalier as to how the public opinion of Western Europe is being systematically turned against her."[54] Although Father John initially denied the text, it emerged that he had previously approved the publication of a book that had contained it.[55] These prayers raised the eyebrows of the intellectual community, to put it mildly, and—along with the sermons—established Father John as one of the leading voices of the religious far right.[56] The claim that the autocracy had Divine right, the repeated call to submit to authority of whatever sort as also divinely instituted, and the repeated use of "senseless" in referring to contemporary political phenomena were characteristic of the language he used.

It is thus not surprising that the intelligentsia came to regard Father John as personifying the most obdurate elements in the Orthodox Church. When he had limited himself to working among the poor and criticizing corrupt and inefficient government institutions, he was cited approvingly as an example of the "healthy, life-giving forces that may still be found in our Orthodox Church." When he attacked the foundations and the very existence of those whose vision of Russia rested on different premises, they responded with a declaration of ideological war. Upon the lifting in 1905 of the censorship restrictions that had forbidden the negative depiction of clergy in the press,[57] Father John became the focus of anticlerical sentiments in the radical press and singled out among all the clergy and the hierarchy as the emblem of clerical reaction.

Some of the comments were purely gratuitous, as when a priest was arrested for seducing a minor and *New Thought* asked, "What does Father John, the wonder-worker of Kronstadt, have to say about this?"[58] Much of the other commentary was as trivial. The connection with the lower classes that posthumous accounts would depict favorably was now emphasized in an unflattering fashion: "The scum of Kronstadt, who have grown accustomed to receiving nickels and blessings from Father John, are alarmed at "Batiushka's" departure. They think that the intelligentsia has driven him out and are planning to revenge themselves against it."[59] Similarly insubstantial was the suggestion that Father John was out of date, that such a new type of fashionable clergyman as the monk Iliodor was *le dernier cri*. A conversation of two society ladies was reported:

COUNTESS LOLO: Oh, this [referring to Iliodor] is a phenomenon and a frightening phenomenon. Just think: twenty-three years old, a beauty and a monk....
PRINCE ANATOLE: *Le père Jean en beau et en jeune.*
PRINCESS TATA: Oh, what *père Jean*—he [Iliodor] is something really extraordinary, a bit frightening, they say, and bewitching.[60]

Most was made, however, of the apparent contradiction between Father John's reputed holiness and his association with the Union of the Russian People. That other clerics would associate themselves with the right-wing organization was only to be expected, the leftist newspapers and scandal sheets implied, but it was compromising and surprising for someone who was a popular saint. The newspaper *Russian Word* was quoted as reporting that the Arkhangelsk student mutual aid society had voted to exclude Father John of Kronstadt from its membership because of his politics and returned his contribution of one hundred rubles.[61] An editorial in *New Thought* stated simply:

> I am not at all surprised that foreigners residing in Russia refuse to understand contemporary Russian newspapers ... their healthy minds simply cannot reconcile those unnatural combinations that so characterise contemporary Russian life. For example: The God-loving pastor John of Kronstadt blessed the banners of the "truly Russian" people and read them "truly Russian lectures." How can the godly John of Kronstadt compromise himself by ties with the Union of the Russian People?[62]

Most serious was the accusation that, through his association with the Union of the Russian People, Father John had implicitly condoned political assassinations and pogroms. (His earlier calls for Tolstoy's death and the references to Moses putting down rebellion through violence did not help.) As *The Break* charged on December 7, 1906: "Why are you silent and do not subject to Church censure the "celebrated" Kronstadt Right Reverend John Sergiev who in the last few days has blessed the pogrom banners and killings, and has [thus] openly confessed before all his rejection of Christ?"[63]

Father John had not blessed any assassinations, of course, but the association with the Union would stick. It is worth asking why. The phenomenon of clerics espousing extreme right politics is neither unusual nor specific to him.[64] But the radical labeling of Father John as a "Black Hundredist"—repeated so consistently in the Soviet historiography that one might assume the terms were synonyms—is remarkable given how relatively insignificant Father John's political activity actually was.[65] He never became involved in the Duma; he took no part in the strategic planning and demonstrations of the Union of the Russian People, as did Father Ioann Vostorgov and the monk Iliodor.[66] Moreover, in 1905 Father John was seventy-seven years old. He complained repeatedly of his physical infirmities and, although he was officially appointed to the Holy Synod, never actually attended a single session—on grounds of illness—something that would have been his dream earlier. He was too frail to take part in meetings and marches.[67]

The limits of Father John's willingness to take an active part of whatever sort in the turbulent political life of the "first revolution" became painfully evident during the sailors' rebellion in Kronstadt in October 1905. The event made it clear that he was damned if he took part in politics, and damned if he did not. Rather than seeking to exercise any influence over the crowds, Father John left Kronstadt for a safe haven until the rebellion had been brought under control. The radical press pilloried him mercilessly for this dénouement; several of the leading

Fig. 10   Cover of *Pulemet*, 1905. Satirical depiction of Father John's leaving Kronstadt during the sailors' rebellion. Courtesy of The New York Public Library, Slavonic Collection.

satirical journals printed devastating cartoon depictions of his "slinking away." On November 5, 1905, for example, *The Arrows* had as its cover a line drawing of Father John fleeing mutinous Kronstadt with the caption "He has departed from evil and done ... good" (an ironic reference to Psalm 33[34]:14); *Machine-Gun* ran a derisive article captioned "Exodus from Kronstadt."[68] Political verse also lampooned Father John, as did A. A. Weinberg in "The Minister's Complaint":

> Matrosy obratilis' v bandu,
> Kto byl saper—stal khuligan,
> Miatezhnyi Shchmidt beret komandu,
> Bezhit blazhennyi Ioann.

(All the sailors have formed a gang; the sapper's become a hooligan, The riotous Schmidt is taking command, while blessed John is fleeing town.)[69]

Fig. 11 Postcard of Father John returning to Kronstadt from St. Petersburg across the ice at night. Such treks were part of Father John's daily routine.

The poet Sasha Chernyi used the Kronstadt riots to link Father John with representatives of the the police, the government, and any representative of authority in Tsarist Russia in a 1906 version of "Who Lives Well in Russia?":

> Popu medotochivomu—
> Razvratnomu i lzhivomu,
> S idieei monarkhicheskoi,
> S raspravoiu fizicheskoi ...
>
> Nachal'niku gumannomu,
> Bankiru inostrannomu,
> Liubimtsu gubernatoru,
> Manezhnomu oratoru ...

Sysknomu otdieleniiu
I Menshikovu-geniiu;
Otshel'niku Kronshtadtskomu,
Fel'dfebeliu soldatskomu ...

Vsiem im zhivetsia vieselo,
Vol'gotno na Rusi ...

(The false, dissolute honey-streaming priest, who favors the monarchical idea and physical reprisal, the humane superior, the foreign banker, the governor's favorite, the Manège orator ... the criminal investigation department, and Menshikov, the genius, *the recluse of Kronstadt*, the sergeant-major ... all of them live joyously and freely here in Rus'.)[70]

Even the *St. Petersburg Gazette* noted that the clergy of St. Andrew's Cathedral—with the exception of Father John, who had left in the morning—had organized a solemn church procession in an attempt to dissuade the rioters, but to no avail.[71] Despite this near-universal criticism for his disappearance from the public eye in Kronstadt's most acute moment, other radical journalists actually accused "Father John and his hooligans"— of *organizing* the disorders that "the politically conscious among the soldiers" had tried to restrain.[72] Even Trotsky repeated the charge, saying of the Kronstadt rebellion, "The major role in this was played by the gangs of the well-known miracle worker John of Kronstadt, who carried with them the most ignorant of the sailors."[73] But the charge of fomenting rebellion was, of course, absurd. It was Father John's refusal to act that darkened his image, as most radical newspapers asserted: "They are no longer sending Father John Sergiev large donations from the depths of the provinces. After his flight from Kronstadt his fame has faded. The tramps ... are gloomy. The handouts of money to them have stopped."[74]

Even Father John's supporters were disturbed by what appeared to be his faint-heartedness. The journalist Mikhail Menshikov, who had written glowingly of his sanctity, for example, attached even more importance to Father John's leaving Kronstadt during the sailors' rebellion than did his radical colleagues. He wrote in *New Time* on October 30, 1906:

The first thing I think of in these tortuous days is Father John of Kronstadt. There is someone who must be suffering bitter minutes!

> To serve for half a century in Kronstadt, to be glorified as the wonder-worker of all Russia for a quarter of a century, to acquire worldwide fame ... to create an enormous pilgrimage with himself as the object ... and [then] to be forced to realize that his immediate flock—15,000 mutinous sailors—lack any religion whatever, any spiritual discipline, or any respect for him, who is pleasing to God—say what you will, this is difficult. They say that Father John tried to address the churning crowd but was so unsuccessful that he left Kronstadt along with the masses of other residents. I do not know the details and dare not assert this—but if it is true that the pastor of souls abandoned his flock in these fearful, Satanic days, how can he, whose faith is profound, stand before the altar of God and lift his eyes to Him?
>
> They will say, "But Father John is a parish priest, while the sailors have their own priest, their Protopresbyter." Yes,—but Father John knows perfectly well, and cannot *not* know, that compared to him, all of these protopresbyters and metropolitans are nothing. They do not possess this highest degree of apostolic grace—the gift of healing; they do not work miracles.... Alone of everyone alive now, only he can be certain that after his death votive lamps will burn before his image and fervent prayers will be said to him. To know all this and to see how far he stands—in essence—from the souls who are closest to him—it is hard![75]

In a roundabout way, Menshikov had identified the reason for Father John's being singled out for press vilification. Although other clergymen were far more politically active than Father John, only he was considered holy. Memoirs of communist agitators regularly mention their dismay at being told by workers, "You may be right about other priests, but there are righteous people among them—there is Father John of Kronstadt."[76] Thus, although other clerics got the title of "Black Hundredist," their authority may not have been all that high to begin with; Father John's was, so he became the focus of radical attacks.

Interestingly, despite his earlier sensitivity to criticism, he bore up remarkably well under overt humiliation. He wrote to Abbess Taisiia after she expressed her commiseration that he took lightly all the mocking of "evil people" and that he remained the same "slave of God" as ever. "The Lord will retaliate for me," he told her confidently, "for whoever touches me maliciously is touching the apple of God's eye." While he acknowledged the falling-off of upper-class followers, he noted that the common people and children still flocked to him.[77]

Father John's views on how political, intellectual, and cultural life in Russia ought to be conducted affected his reputation and standing not only among the liberals, the intelligentsia, and the radical press, but among more conservative people as well. When he began to insist that his position was the only admissible one, he disconcerted those Orthodox Russians who felt that their faith did not imply a blanket rejection of forces for change, and might actually support change.[78] His reputation for holiness made their response to him even more problematic: What was one to do if a man of God expressed political views one found disturbing or even repugnant?

Although Father John's devotees showed a range of reactions, they fall into several broad categories. There were those who sought to overcome their misgivings and to accept his views as Divinely inspired, and those whose opinion of him altered negatively—whether by accepting that he, and indeed any saintly figure, might have flaws that left unaltered his essential sanctity, or by questioning his holiness, or by questioning the meaning of holiness itself. Such opinions survive in the letters Father John received in response to his sermons against Tolstoy and his defenses of autocracy. By the end of the nineteenth century, and particularly after 1903, Father John's sermons appeared regularly in such newspapers as *The St. Petersburg Police Gazette* and *The Moscow Gazette* as well as from St. Andrew's pulpit, thus reinforcing his public association with the most conservative Russian organs and institutions. The responses reflect as much consternation with his association with the official political right as with his opinions.

Most striking is the consistent amazement expressed at Father John's stance. His charitable work and his criticism of social inequity had given him the reputation of a positive force within religion, one that was automatically associated with reform in the broadest sense. It came as a bitter surprise to some to realize that his calls for social reform and a sincere desire to improve the lot of the poor did not imply a wish for political change as well. A tone of confusion and disappointment characterizes many of the letters. One man wrote:

> When I read the words of your sermon against count L. Tolstoy in the police newspaper (a fine place for such sermons), I was completely discomfited. Can it be possible: John of Kronstadt—and a sermon like that. The readers do not see an enlightened and humane pastor, but a fanatic with the most narrow worldview imaginable, not only in a religious sense but simply in a logical one.

The man went on to oppose the forces of progress and culture supposedly exemplified by Tolstoy to those he believed were the worst aspects of Orthodoxy exemplified by Father John: "Around [Tolstoy] and around other worldly writers nestles everything living, wise, ideological, and cultured, while around Father John huddles hypocrisy, sanctimony, and a hive of hysterical and psychopathic women glorifying fantastic miracles and miraculous phenomena."[79]

This is one of many instances of the association of Father John with female devotees, and one of the first implications that the devotion of women rather than men is a sign of the inferiority on the part of the object of devotion. Other writers were troubled by the stridency of his tone:

> I happened to become acquainted with your words of denunciation directed against Count Lev Tolstoy uttered in God's temple and often recounted on the pages of the *St. Petersburg Police Gazette*. Besides that, I happened to read a copy of your letter to the Dean of the University at Iuriev in which you came down like a thunder-cloud on the former, insulted at the simultaneous selection of you and the Count as honorary members of the University.
>
> And now I cannot find inner calm: how to reconcile your diatribes, so alien to the spirit of Christian gentleness, tolerance, and forgiveness for all, and your [earlier] letter [on spirituality] with its marvelous words, which I enclose?.[80]

A fellow priest named Aleksandr Liubimov questioned Father John's writing: "God continues to endure Tolstoy, as He does any unrepentant sinner, in order that He may punish them all the more strictly and increase in accordance with their guilt their eternal torment."[81] Nowhere among any of the "famous or holy" writers the priest had read had he encountered Father John's sentiment that God would keep people alive *in order* to punish them all the more harshly afterwards. Such a notion, he thought, mocked the endless goodness of God. On the contrary, Liubimov timidly wrote, God punished people *reluctantly*, and prolonged the lives of great sinners, even giving them great temporal boons, in order that they might come to repent and improve. Father John's categorical condemnation of Tolstoy deeply bothered the conscientious priest:

> Can it really be, esteemed Father John, that you clearly forsee the perdition of Count Tolstoy when you say that "God suffers him for

long in order to punish him the more strongly in the next life?" If so, then is it not useless, and perhaps even contrary to God's will, to pray for him?—I will not conceal from you that I, upon reading the above, was confused to no small degree, for I had earnestly prayed and continue to pray to God for the conversion of the perishing Lev N. Tolstoy, for his coming to recognize his grievous delusions, and his repentance, that the great and marvellous works of God may be manifest in him (as was the case with Tolstoy's brother, who had communion before his death).[82]

These were the "conscientious objectors." But Father John found enthusiastic supporters as well. Even their style echoed his own. It was clear that even as his opinions disturbed some, they heartened and emboldened others, who evidently saw him as their spokesman. While other clerics may have expressed similar points of view, Father John's supporters felt that he was one of the few who fought radical publicists on their own ground: in the pamphlet, the newspaper, and the published book, not only the sermon or the complaint uttered behind closed doors. People drew on the opposition that Nikolai Leskov had first articulated, identifying Tolstoy and Father John as the opposing forces struggling for Russia's future. Their sense of besiegement is accompanied by a resentment that their voices are not the dominant ones in public discourse, and that the language in which public discussion is being conducted is something alien and opposed to their own. To such correspondents, Father John appeared to be the only person who dared voice their own opinions. Like Father Charles Coughlin in the 1930s, Father John became a "surrogate spokesman for the dissaffected."[83] They adored him for bringing their own dimly felt impulses into the public arena and helped make those impulses a force to be reckoned with. In effect, he gave them back their voice and their presence in the public realm. As several women from Kiev wrote,

> You, dear Batiushka, have raised your authoritative voice loudly and fearlessly against the Russian antichrist. O, continue, we pray you, for the sake of our dear Russia, continue the great work you have begun—work which is fully worthy of you—of struggle with the dangerous false prophet! You are the only one who has the strength to measure swords with the monstrous titan who has filled the minds and hearts of the perishing youth; you alone can boldly reckon with the newspaper lackey-liberals as well.... We believe that you, holy Father, can preserve Russia from the fearful

calamity threatening her; you, and you alone, with all the potency of your spiritual power and your capability of worthily battling with the Russian adversary.[84]

As Father John grew so famous that his pastoral responsibilities symbolically extended to all of the Russian Empire, his views on how society ought to function touched a social nerve. This is not surprising. His defense of Divine right and attacks on secularization were consistent with a tradition that insisted upon the dominance of religion in social and intellectual life and one that identified revolutionary change with apocalyptic evil. It was a familiar point of view; no one commented on its novelty. Indeed, both Father John's admirers and detractors recognized that in this respect he was representative rather than original. The reason that he became associated with these radically conservative views more than any other clergyman who voiced them was because of his status as a holy figure. For an ordinary cleric to express the sentiments that Russia needed the Tsar in order to exist, that the intelligentsia was on the road to perdition, that constitutions were delusion and revolutions were disaster was predictable, certainly not inconsistent; for one thought to be godly, it raised the question of whether Orthodoxy was inherently fated to perpetuate its association with the Tsarist government. Precisely because Father John had been regarded as one of the brightest lights of the Orthodox Church, both because of his sacramental pastoral theology and his work among the poor, his final political credo was all the more devastating to those who wanted to explore political alternatives for Russia at the beginning of the twentieth century. Despite his initial criticism of the old order, once the very existence of that order was threatened in the revolution of 1905, Father John cast in his lot unreservedly with the most extreme of conservative forces. That his doing so was seized upon so fiercely by his contemporaries suggests how much Russians at the turn of the century had invested in Orthodoxy and their holy people, and how violently they responded when these expectations were either dashed or fulfilled.

8

Posthumous Legacy

As is characteristic for saints' lives, Father John's death in December 1908 was a momentous occasion. It provided the occasion for his devotees to mourn their loss, to celebrate his passing into the next life, and to begin openly speaking of him as holy. It also signaled the beginning of the interim stage in the saga of the saintly struggler: the period after his death, but before his canonization. As in other saints' lives, Father John's tomb in St. Petersburg became a new locus for God's presence, with reports of new miracles assiduously collected by those seeking his official glorification by the Orthodox Church. Nicholas II, who had already initiated several canonizations during his reign, set the wheels in motion for Father John's permanent nationwide commemoration in an Imperial Rescript that was broadly interpreted by the Holy Synod. Political events since his death affected this otherwise characteristic path, however. Because of the Revolution of 1917 and the Civil War, which resulted in a large-scale emigration from Russia and the replacement of Orthodox autocracy with communism and official atheism, Father John became as much a political symbol as a religious one. His unusual double canonizations, in 1964 by the Russian Orthodox Church Abroad, and in 1990 in Russia by the post-perestroika Moscow Patriarchate, show how differently the strains of Russian Orthodox Church practice interpreted their most politically invested recent saint. The hostility Father John provoked in those unsympathetic to his vision of Orthodox Russia has also acquired new nuances.

Father John's Death and Funeral

Father John died at the age of seventy-nine at 7:40 A.M., December 20, 1908. His funeral was one of the biggest and longest Russia had ever known. Train tickets from St. Petersburg to Kronstadt were sold out; virtually every available cart, sledge, and *kibitka* from Oranienbaum was rented. Father John's body was taken first to St. Andrew's Cathedral, where liturgy and *panikhida* were served in the morning and a *parastas* (funereal all-night vigil) in the evening. The cathedral remained open through the night to the next morning. People came to bid their farewells in an unbroken stream.[1]

The ceremony did not end there, however, for Father John was to be interred not in Kronstadt, where he had served for fifty-three years, but in the convent he had founded in St. Petersburg. His coffin was transferred over the ice to Oranienbaum behind the 94th Enisei Regiment and several military bands playing the standard nineteenth-century piece of "enlightened" civic religion, "How Great is Our Lord in Zion."[2] A crowd of twenty thousand singing Orthodox funeral hymns followed on foot. Brief *litya* services were served at such important sites along the way as the Naval Cathedral, the Theophany church, and the chapel dedicated to the late Admiral Makarov in Kronstadt, the train station in Oranienbaum, and St. Isaac's Cathedral, the Warsaw station, and the Holy Synod in St. Petersburg. People hung out of windows and climbed on roofs and fences to catch a glimpse of the cortège. These frequent stops for brief services were necessary because admission to the funeral at the Karpovka convent cathedral was by ticket only. By attending a *litya*, a resident of St. Petersburg could bid farewell to Father John in much the same way that she could light a candle in a chapel in lieu of a church. Those who accompanied Father John from Kronstadt to his final resting place walked twenty-five *verst*s in one day.[3]

The choice of the Karpovka convent for Father John's interment proved decisive in establishing which location would serve as his chief pilgrimage site. As was characteristic for Christian saints, the location of the saint's relics was key; if this differed from where he had spent his life (as happened when the relics of Saint Nicholas were moved from Myra to Bari), it did not matter. For just as people clamored to see and touch the saint while he was alive, so now they sought the same immediate, physical contact with the repository of grace.[4] St. Petersburg was a more convenient location than Kronstadt in many respects: it was on the mainland, all roads went there and, once one arrived, one could easily make one's way to the Karpovka. Certainly to the convent itself, Father John's presence became a constant source of both grace and income.[5] It was for this reason that the Kronstadt authorities sued over the suspicious circumstances of Father John's last will, drawn up by the Karpovka abbess Angelina when he was deaf and barely conscious, and leaving everything to her convent. They, like Angelina, wanted to profit from Father John after his death as they had during his lifetime.[6] His

Fig. 12   Father John's funeral procession. St. Petersburg, December 1908. Photo courtesy of the Central State Archive of Cine- and Photo-Documents.

Fig. 13   The St. John Convent on the Karpovka river. St. Petersburg.

apartment was to be turned into a combination of chapel and house museum, but this would be far more difficult if his more important belongings were transferred to the Karpovka convent, as they eventually were. Although a domestic shrine was ultimately set up in Father John's former living quarters, it did not draw visitors as a pilgrimage site. Attempts to set up supplementary shrines in the form of the crypt of Father John's mother and the chapel over his wife's grave did not take hold, either.[7]

This is not surprising, for their importance was now purely historical. True, Father John had had relatives and had lived in his flat for over fifty years—but what difference did it make, when one could still have access to him in the form of his relics? The difference between saints and other popular heroes emerges clearly here. It is interesting to visit, say, Monet's house and gardens at Giverny. It is the business of an Orthodox saint, however, to provide his devotees with continued access to Divine grace through his prayers and through his mortal body. Father John may have died, but to his devotees he was still present in both person and spirit; his saintly career had only begun. New post-mortem healing miracles began to be collected by the nuns at the funeral, and then in the burial chapel.[8]

Steps Toward Canonization, 1909–1917

Nicholas II began the process of enshrining Father John's memory in an Imperial Rescript dated January 12, 1909. Describing Father John as "a great beacon of Christ's Church and the pray-er for the Russian Land, a holy righteous man [*pravednik*]," the Tsar called for an annual nationwide commemoration of the date of Father John's death, and for a similar commemoration to occur in the year to come for the forty-days' anniversary.[9] He also expressed the hope that the Holy Synod would head larger initiatives.[10]

The Synod was quick to respond. On January 15, 1909, it issued a statement calling for the publication of Nicholas's Rescript, and memorial services in civil and military churches alike. It also called for seminary scholarships to be established in Father John's name, for Father John's portraits to be displayed in religious schools, seminaries, and academies; to have his works be made part of the homiletics curriculum; to establish religious schools bearing Father John's name in Arkhangelsk, to name a newly completed school in Zhitomir after him, and to promote the Karpovka convent to "first-class" status. This process of enshrining Father John began in his lifetime, but then it was local and from the bottom up, with—for example—parish schools petitioning the Synod to be named after Father John because he was their primary or sole donor.[11] After Father John's death, the highest religious authority in Russia and Nicholas II added an extra impetus.[12]

These steps to enshrine Father John's memory and hold him up as an example took other forms. In a collection of eulogies spoken at his memorial services and published soon afterward, church leaders opposed him to liberal tendencies within the Church. Bishop Aleksii of Taurida contrasted him positively to liberals and freedom fighters, asking forgiveness for even uttering these "epithets" in church.[13] Above all, bishops and priests noted that Father John had shown that there was but one way to serve society and the people: not through external changes but through every person's individual spiritual rebirth.[14] They used Father John's death to condemn such initiatives as parish reforms because those reforms "began from the wrong direction"—that is, through drawing up external regulations and charters, and not beginning with the spiritual regeneration of the parish.[15] After his death, then, Father John became a symbol used expressly against structural church reforms.

Representations of Father John written after his death in 1908, but before 1918, also added several new elements, with his eventual canonization in mind. The most valuable source for such accounts is the Society for the Memory of Father John of Kronstadt that, from 1908 onward, began to collect and publish reminiscences. The journal *Kronstadt Pastor*, which was published from 1912 to 1917, also published both memoirs and miracle testimonies. The work of amassing material continued even after 1917, but ground to a halt by the early 1920s.[16] In these last official accounts, several new elements emerge. The first is a shift from the earlier stress on Father John's "supra-classness" to his being labeled a man of the common people. Lieutenant-general David A. Ozerov wrote in 1912 of a visit Father John had made to Terioki during the 1904–5 war with Japan, for example:

> I am standing next to the Batiushka, our own Father John, I am looking at the crowd near the porch—and it seems to me that all of our Rus' is here, our holy, exhausted, simple, own Rus': *ignorant little peasants, worn-out little soldiers, nuns who are none too swift*, and above all them Father John, whose fervent and unwavering faith consoles and heartens everyone—*simply, artlessly, without discourses and intellectualizing*—in the old, Russian, ancient, biblical way.[17]

This emphasis on the lower classes vanished after the Revolution of 1917. Once the old social and political order had disappeared, the class differences that seemed so palpable after Father John's death seemed less important to writers; both émigré and post-1988 Russian publications return to emphasizing Father John's "universal" appeal.[18] Nevertheless, between Father John's death in 1908 and the Revolution of 1917, the impact of radical criticism and the Ioannite scandal was so strong that intelligentsia writers found it hard to imagine that they, too, had once championed Father John, finding it more convenient to pigeonhole him with the "common people." This also may be connected with the Church's staking its hopes on the common people, as opposed to educated society.[19]

The second shifting of representations after Father John's death is a greater emphasis on his women followers, which was—as were similar emphases on the feminine in France and the United States—mostly negative.[20] Aleksei Makushinskii, a boy soprano at St. Andrew's Cathedral from 1891 to 1904, recalled later that "it was mostly women who completely lost their reason [when they learned that Father John's carriage would pass], flinging themselves under the hooves of his horse with the words, "Praise the Lord, I have suffered for Christ!""[21] Similarly, a priest spoke of Father John's "tearing himself out of the grip of his overly excited admirers and—especially—admiresses [*pochitatel'nits*]."[22] Given that these writers wished to record their *favorable* impressions of Father John, it is striking that they emphasized the lower-class background, "ignorance," and femininity of his audience—particularly when, while he was alive, visitors to Kronstadt took pains to record the variety of ages, social backgrounds, and gender mix. Other eulogists turned this emphasis on women expressly to Father John's advantage. The deaths of Dostoyevsky, Tchaikovsky, and Mendeleev only resonated in the cultured part of the population, "not penetrating to the popular depths at all," they wrote; the deaths of such military leaders as Suvorov or Skobelev were felt more broadly, "but their names are almost alien to the feminine half of the population." It was only "holy" Father John who managed to capture the entire popular imagination, "and all the love of the more loving half of the nation—women." By capturing women, Father John had symbolically captured the nation's heart.[23] This generally negative focus on "exalted" and "abnormal" relations between women and celebrated religious figures may also have been a subtle way of undermining the relations of the Empress (and, by extension, the Imperial regime) with Rasputin.[24] Of all his different aspects, Father John's political pronouncements were the most muted between 1908 and 1917. With the decisive vanquishing of the 1905 Revolution and the old order he defended so hotly still in place after his death, his politics seemed less important than his saintly virtues.

Father John's Cult After 1917: Politics, Reality, and Representations

All of this posthumous apoliticism changed after the Revolution of 1917 and the Civil War. Father John's cult went largely underground in the USSR, and traveled abroad, thanks to an emigration that numbered in the millions. Virtually all of the émigrés lived in difficult circumstances, constantly worrying about finding documents, work, and shelter. In many of their minds, Father John rose again as the practical and spiritual helper he had been in Russia. Such laymen as Petr Matveevich Chizhov in Helsinki began to compile information about

Father John to inspire others. In Belgrade, I. K. Surskii served as a clearing-house for both biographical information and miracle accounts, which were published as a two-volume study in 1938. The émigré clergy, too, described him as a model pastor, occasionally comparing him to Saints John Chrysostom and Gregory the Theologian.[25] Just as he had been linked to Saint Serafim of Sarov during his life to establish his spiritual genealogy, so after his death people noted connections between him and the Optina elders, especially elder Varsonofii.[26] After World War II, when a significant part of the European emigration came to the United States, the main keepers of the cult became the Memorial Fund of Father John of Kronstadt, founded in 1954 and located in Utica, New York. With Father John as their exemplar, the Fund provided material help to needy Russian émigrés and re-issued such key sources of Ioanniana as *My Life in Christ*, and Archbishop Evdokim's *Two Days in Kronstadt*. They also kept up-to-date miracle accounts and, after Father John's canonization by the Russian Orthodox Church Abroad in 1964, became the first church in the world dedicated to *Saint John of Kronstadt*. The modest charitable activity of the Memorial Fund now extends all over the world, including Russia itself.[27] Without minimizing the charitable work of the Fund, however, its chief function has been the preservation of historical memory. With little contact between religious Russians within Russia and the émigrés of the period from the 1930s to the 1970s, the Fund was one of the only sources of information about Father John.

The St. John of Kronstadt Press in Liberty, Tennessee, by contrast, deliberately de-emphasizes Father John's Russian context. Although it was founded by American converts to Orthodox Christianity who are associated with the Russian Orthodox Church Abroad, it stresses Father John's universal qualities of piety and charity. The missionary and English-language emphases of the Press most influence this shift away from the specifics of Late Imperial Russia. He has even become a new, specifically American, cultural marker. Because Father John's birthday coincides with Halloween, holding religious services to honor him on that day reminds Orthodox Christians in the United States not to take part in celebrations of witches or demons.

Political Representations

The Utica-based Memorial Fund and the St. John of Kronstadt Press in Tennessee chose to reflect the wide nature of Father John's service. Liberal Orthodox thinkers emphasized his spirituality, such as his continuity with Saint Serafim of Sarov in the tradition of hesychasm, and the links of his *My Life in Christ* to the fourteenth-century theologian, Nicholas Cabasilas.[28] His specifically political legacy, however, found other adherents. The assessment of Father John as a prophet warning of the evils of revolution would be propagated most assiduously by the hierarchy of the Russian Orthodox Church Abroad. To these émigrés, who represented the most conservative elements of pre-Revolutionary Russian society, Father John was the prophetic voice that should have been listened to in order to avert the catastrophe that had scattered them over the ends of the earth. They were the heirs of those who had collected and published his "New Stern Words" and "Denunciatory Sermons" while he was still alive. In such publications as *Father John as a Prophet Sent by God to Bring Russia to Its Senses*, they repeated his last message to the Orthodox flock, now "sadly proven": Russia was on the brink of destruction, revolution would mean disaster, Russians must hold fast to their faith and to their Tsar or the very name of the country would vanish.[29] Father John's last sermons became the cornerstone of their own politics. They embraced his sentiments so fervently because they—and Russia—had paid the price. They bemoaned so many of their fellow émigrés' continuing to hold "the very beliefs that brought Russia to perdition," claiming that as long as those working for a new Russia continued to think only in this-worldly terms and did not heal their spiritual decay, they would be doomed to failure: "This is why neither the White movement [in the Civil War] nor the so-called Russian Liberation Army [of General Andrei Vlasov, in World War II] succeeded."[30] To the Russian Orthodox Church Abroad, the canonization of Father John in 1964 explicitly cast a vote before God for the ideals of church-state symphony, Holy Rus', and even the Third Rome.[31]

It is not surprising that the liturgical texts written about Father John composed in emigration dwell on this aspect, calling him "a mighty rampart of the Orthodox dominion of Russia ... true intercessor and ally of pious sovereigns."[32] Although the troparion and kontakion used by the Russian Church Abroad are supranational and suprapolitical, emphasizing the wide range of his sanctity, the akathist composed in the early 1930s by Hiero-Schemamonk Pachomius on Mount Athos and adopted for liturgical use after Father John's 1964 canonization includes such phrases as

> Do thou now grant enlightenment to *the children of Russia that are in the grasp of the darkness of error and in the power of impious traitors*, that they may come to know their wretchedness and, turning to the Lord, may cry out to him in repentance: Alleluia!

> New signs of the wrath of God befell us because we did not wish to heed thy divinely-inspired words, for *the Russian realm hath fallen and hath been given over into the power of cruel atheists* who have destroyed the honored monastic habitations, have defiled the holy temples, have grievously afflicted all pious people, and have given over a multitude of the clergy and laity to martyrdom.[33]

Father John's canonization in the emigration, then, was as much a condemnation of the Revolution of 1917 and an approbation of the principle of church-state symphony as of his personal holiness. His politics provided one of the cornerstones of the determinedly anti-Soviet and anti-Moscow Patriarchate position of the Russian Church Abroad. As successive generations born in Australia, Europe, and the Americas grow ever further away from the Russian political context, one wonders whether this emphasis will continue to serve Father John's cult outside of Russia.

Within Russia, however, the émigré emphasis on Father John's politics has played an important role. It is one of the many twentieth-century instances of a diaspora keeping alive a rightist tradition that is forced to go underground in the homeland. Even despite the relative lack of contact between the USSR and the outside world, the two sides managed to inform one another. The apparitions of Father John in the Soviet period, for example, were publicized in the émigré press—*and* in Soviet antireligious texts of the 1970s, which, ironically, served the purpose of acquainting Russian readers with otherwise obscure pieces of knowledge. We can thus observe an odd progression: Father John's far right politics were maintained overtly by part of the Russian emigration and clandestinely by people in the Soviet Union, both of whom managed to contact and to reinforce one another over the years. On the other hand, those politics were derided by the officially atheistic Soviet press and liberal writers outside of Russia. After perestroika, and Father John's canonization by the Moscow Patriarchate in 1990, these rightist tendencies could again go public. At the close of the twentieth century, we see that Father John has traveled the full circuit: texts about him originated in Russia from about 1900 to 1935, they were reprinted abroad from 1938 to 1988, reprinted *again* within Russia from 1990 onward, and distributed thereafter both in Russia and in the emigration.[34]

Within the Soviet Union, depictions of Father John's politics split in two opposite directions. If the émigrés felt nostalgia for their pre-Revolutionary way of life while struggling in Paris and Berlin, the sensations of despoilment and siege were all the more acute in the Soviet Union of collectivization, destroyed churches, and the purges. Not surprisingly, Father John's politics were depicted in an even stronger—and more polarized—form within Soviet Russia than they were in the emigration. Such documents as "Father John's Dream," for example, used the form of a vision Father John supposedly had in 1908 to attack such Soviet phenomena as the "Living Church," the killers of Nicholas II, and anyone wearing a five-pointed red star. The images of the "Dream" were schematic and graphic: in it, aborted fetuses join the ranks of everyone martyred for the Orthodox faith, and stinking worms crawl among the "godless, heretical books spreading the stench of their false teachings throughout the world."[35] The dream's depictions of the Antichrist, stamped foreheads, and animals come directly out of the prophecies of Daniel and the Apocalypse. With the first Five-Year Plan, forced collectivization, and the all-out persecution of the Orthodox clergy, all of which did more to upset lived religion than the October Revolution itself, the always-latent eschatological motifs in Orthodoxy became key. To those who felt that they were indeed living in the last days, Father John, Tikhon of Zadonsk, and Serafim of Sarov became important symbolic figures not because of their personal kindness or their emphasis on the prayer of the heart, but for their eschatological pronouncements. They remembered, for example, that Saint Tikhon had prophesied that the last Patriarch would bear his name, that Saint Serafim had had the fates of the last Tsars revealed to him, and that Father John had turned away some infants brought him for a blessing, saying that they would grow into "live devils."[36]

Father John's remains were desecrated and sealed off for decades. The Karpovka convent was turned into a warren of warehouses and offices in the late 1920s; St. Andrew's was blown up in the 1930s and a park with a statue of Lenin installed in its place.[37] Because of this, he was no longer accessible in his mortal flesh, although people "accidentally" dropped objects in front of the now-sealed basement window of his crypt to drop to their knees, or gathered on his feast day to pray across the street.[38] Instead, he began to appear in visions. In a 1919 account, Father John miraculously appeared to inspire Silaev, a Bolshevik sailor from the Almaz cruiser and Cheka commmissar, to repent and become a leading counter-revolutionary.[39] He also appeared with Sergii of Radonezh and Serafim of Sarov to serve requiems for all those who died without burial.[40]

People linked the visions of these intercessors to wonder-working wells and fountains, as in a 1930s apparition of a well on a collective farm, with Father John's image reflected in its water.[41] Because wells and springs have been key sources for local piety in antiquity and Europe, but slightly less so in Russia, the iconoclasm of the Soviet period had the effect of shifting lived religion away from icons and toward "natural" phenomena—a phenomenon that deserves further study.[42] The villagers who provided these reports found it logical that saints now roamed the earth. Their traditional sources of religion—icons, religious processions, church services, chapels, priests—had been taken away or destroyed; it thus made perfect sense (although they acknowledged that it was "incredible") that the reposed saints would appear in person as sources of inspiration and consolation.[43]

Not all of Father John's epiphanies in the Soviet period were beneficent; the revenge motif familiar from earlier accounts also figures. One account describes Father John's appearing at a Komsomol antireligious meeting. One of the infuriated communist youth throws a bottle at him, but it passes through the figure of the mysterious priest, who disappears; only the words "Father John of Kronstadt" suddenly appear on the wall. Although this vision disconcerts the communist agitators, they explain it as "popes' tricks," and continue their program. Suddenly, on a cloudless winter day, there is a flash of lightning that blows out the door of the Komsomol club. The audience is hurled out but unharmed; the atheist agitators burn to death. Local newspapers describe the event as vicious arson by anti-Soviet elements, but of course the village knows better. To avoid arrest, the three youths vanish and become wanderers, spreading the faith and the story of what happened to them.[44]

In another Father John apparition described in a 1934 letter, a collective farm worker reported seeing a priest walking in the field with a handsome young soldier who "looked just like George on the icons, or maybe it was the Archangel Michael." After recovering from the shock of seeing a priest at all—they had vanished from the public eye after persecutions by the mid-1930s—the older people said the priest looked like Father John. He blessed the believers' plot on all four sides, then went to the *sovkhoz* (state farm) section. When communists tried to chase him away, he told them that because the field was under Satan's dominion, and not God's, they would be punished for their atheism. The two apparitions vanished after attempts to seize them. Ten minutes later, the field burst into flame and was burned out; the believers' private plot was untouched. As in the other incident, *Izvestiia* attributed the event to religious "wreckers," citing the priest and the young soldier as suspects.[45]

In these Soviet-era visions that appear in clandestine documents, then, Father John is placed within a long tradition of apocalyptic visions; he acts as a defender of the faithful and enemy of the atheistic Soviet regime.[46] Now that people's icons had been confiscated, Father John's portraits became their replacements, "only we hide them, so as not to provoke the Communists." People also began to carve icons from wood, including images of Father John, which they claimed worked healing miracles.[47] He even appeared in literary works, thinly disguised by Mikhail Bulgakov in the fantastic novel describing Satan's visit to Stalin's Moscow, *The Master and Margarita*, as "the writer Johann from Kronstadt."[48]

Official Soviet publications simply reversed the image, repeating earlier radical formulae: Father John was "a monarchist, Black-Hundredist, and reactionary, who passed himself off as being a miracle-worker."[49] Paradoxically, at the height of the struggle with the "vestiges" (*perezhitki*) of religiosity in the 1970s, the Soviet press performed the function of publicizing and disseminating the very views it was fighting. In keeping with their schema of international forces of reaction conspiring together to fight communism, they ascribed great importance to both the émigré rightists and their comrades within the Soviet Union. Through this attention, Soviet publicists allowed both these groups to persist in attaching great significance to their struggle, for "international communism" and "international liberalism" were fighting them. By deliberately blurring the lines between the émigré and homegrown oppositionists, moreover, Soviet writers continued the tradition of pre-Revolutionary radical writers describing the Ioannites.

Post-Revolutionary Ioannite History

The Ioannites, too, continued to exist after Father John's death. Initially, they met the fate of other popular religious movements seeking to operate within the framework of a Church: by and large, if the hierarchy withholds its approval, or explicitly condemns the movement, it tends to die out. And the Ioannites did begin to dwindle away over the decade after Father John's death. Only right-wing newspapers bothered to report their activity; there was no coverage at all after 1913; they would probably have been forgotten even without the Great War. They survived, however, through a freakish quirk of circumstance, thanks to the Soviet power that was hostile to them.

The people persecuted as Ioannites in the Soviet period included people who displayed the earlier "prototypical" Ioannite patterns of behavior—*and* typical Orthodox Christians who honored Father John's memory. The reasons for conflating them were both religious and political. In the first decades of Soviet power, honoring Father John tended to mean adopting and repeating his apocalyptic, eschatological, antirevolutionary statements in the light of what was perceived as bitter reality. To those burned by the Revolution, his dire prescriptions of the apocalypse that would come to Russia seemed to be all too true after 1918, but this was especially so for the Ioannites. The 1920s' pronouncements of Father John apparitions strikingly resembled earlier Ioannite eschatology.[50] Moreover, Soviet authorities inherited the radical penchant for equating Ioannites with Father John's followers generally; others simply did not know there might be any difference. Finally, and most important from the point of view of the new regime, the devotees of Father John shared a decidedly antirevolutionary, and often monarchist, orientation, whatever their exact religious beliefs. They could thus be equated in terms of political and eschatological views, if not in their Orthodoxy, the niceties of which mattered little to the new regime. In a 1938 raid in Tver, for example, the secret police discovered a group of "Ioannite" conspirators disguised as a cooperative of Red Toilers, with pictures of both Father John and the late Imperial family in their possession—an echo of the *sovkhoz* worker's comment that these portraits had come to replace icons. Although these were not explicitly religious symbols, their owners' attachment to the iconic figures of the old regime was condemnation enough. As *The Atheist* reported, they received their "well-deserved and just punishment."[51]

During the 1950s, the shades of the Ioannites were summoned again.[52] Just as the Ioannites had served as synonyms for monarchist or antirevolutionary Orthodox Christians in the twenties and the thirties, so now they began to serve as a code word for their émigré heirs. In 1958, the fiftieth anniversary of Father John's repose, the Russian Orthodox Church Abroad began to publish articles and books devoted to preparing the ground for his coming canonization. This gave Soviet authorities a new opportunity to attack that "insubordinate jurisdiction." The Ioannites were now re-resurrected in the guise of the Russian Orthodox Church Abroad, who were also described as "black-hundredist, counter-revolutionary monarchist ideologues." The official Soviet conflation ran as follows:

> After the victory of the Great October socialist revolution, the ideological continuers of the monarchist-Black Hundredist party

were the so-called followers of the "old church" (the followers of Patriarch Tikhon). In our day, the ideological heirs and successors of this line are various Orthodox sects: the *molchalniki* (the Silent Ones), the Ioannites, the true Orthodox (the Iosifites, the IPTs [Istinnaia Pravoslavnaia Tser'kov] and IPKh [Istinno-Pravoslavnye Khristiane]) and others. One should note that, even before the revolution, the ideologues of Orthodoxy, *especially John of Kronstadt,* succeeded in strengthening the influence of the Church among the backward parts of the population. After the revolution, the Ioannites, *the followers of the Kronstadt sanctimonious,* made up the most reactionary stratum within Orthodox sects ... their White-guard emigrant leaders, like Bishop John of San Francisco, are lackeys of imperialism who still hope for a restoration of monarchy in Russia.[53]

As late as 1988, *Orthodoxy: An Atheist's Dictionary* continued this line, describing the Ioannites as "obscurantist, reactionary, fanatic followers of John of Kronstadt," and singling out the Russian Orthodox Church Abroad as the prime "example" of the sect.[54] Thus, in the eyes of the Soviet regime, opposition to communism and honoring Father John defined Ioannitism; the 1908 Synodal condemnation of the Ioannites on purely religious grounds was utterly lost sight of. Western treatments have discussed the Ioannites largely within the Soviet period, placing them within the context of such other oppositional eschatological sects as the Fedoristy, Innokentevtsy, and the *imiaslavtsy* (name-glorifiers), although Eugene Clay argues paradoxically for their Orthodoxy. Because the Ioannite patterns of behavior disappeared in the émigré context, émigré historians of religion have minimized the Ioannites' importance.[55]

The Canonization of Father John by the Moscow Patriarchate and Its Effects

The canonization of Father John by the Moscow Patriarchate posed a challenge to those in the hierarchy who wanted desperately to have some version of him that was "politically correct." Given the wildly politicized Soviet publications of the previous decades, this was not easy. When Father John was canonized by the Moscow Patriarchate in the summer of 1990, both the anti-Soviet émigré position and the Soviet-era condemnations of Father John struck the liturgical writers as equally awkward—after all, their bishops and predecessors had colluded with the Soviet government. Their ingenious solution was to avoid any explicit mention of politics or prophetic clairvoyance—and, in doing so, to make Father John fit their own image. By emphasizing his Russian-ness, the Patriarchate writers sought to make clear their geographical—and, by extension, spiritual—continuity with Father John. Their troparion hymn to him brings this out:

> Defender of the Orthodox faith, intercessor for the *Russian* land, a rule for pastors and an image for the faithful, preacher of repentance and the life in Christ, reverent servant of the Divine Mysteries, and bold pray-er for people, righteous father John, healer and most marvelous wonderworker, *glory of the town of Kronstadt* and adornment of *our* Church, pray to the All-benevolent God to give peace to the world and save our souls.

Compare this to the supranational sentiments of the troparion of the Church Abroad, which emphasizes Father John's universal importance:

> With the apostles thy sound has gone forth unto the ends of the world; with the confessors thou didst endure sufferings for Christ; thou didst liken thyself unto the holy hierarchs in thy preaching of the Word; and with the venerable hast thou shone forth in the grace of God. Therefore, the Lord hath exalted the depths of thy humility higher than the heavens, and hath given us thy name as a source of most wondrous miracles. Wherefore, O wonderworker who livest in Christ forever, take pity in thy love upon people in misfortunes; hearken unto thy children who with faith call upon thee, O righteous John, our beloved pastor.[56]

In a more subtle justification of collusion with the Soviet government, the Patriarchate's kontakion suggests that the Moscow Patriarchate may have temporarily entered hell, but it survived, and both Christ and Father John approve their choice: "Today the Kronstadt pastor stands before the Tabernacle of God and earnestly prays for the faithful to Christ, the Leader of Pastors, who gave the promise: 'I will establish My Church, and the gates of hell shall not overcome it.'"[57] This liturgical downplaying of Father John's "inappropriate" politics, however, runs counter to the attempt of a faction within Russia seeking to revive his political message. Books about contemporary heresies and sects in Russia conclude with chapters headed "Without Orthodoxy There is No Russia," including quotations from Father John forseeing the re-establishment of "an even stronger and more powerful Russia" if Russia, on the bones of its martyrs, builds anew on its traditional foundation.[58] Such statements as "Father John forecast a stern punishment for Russia if the Russians broke with Vladimir's great work and carelessly destroyed the Covenant with God, if they do not repent and return to the historic path of Holy Rus' and restore this Union," ensure the survival of his symphonic political views within Russia, if not within the Patriarchate's hierarchy.[59] The radical critique is not dead, either. After Father John's canonization in Russia in 1990, the indefatigable professional atheist, Nikolai Gordienko, fired off a brochure entitled "Who is John of Kronstadt?" intended to "expose" his autocratic, antiparliamentary sentiments.[60]

Nevertheless, the Moscow Patriarchate has an ace in the hole—Father John's burial site, although not necessarily his remains. In 1923, Father John's relatives petitioned to have his body removed from the Karpovka location and reburied first in the Smolenskoe cemetery, and then it appears, in Bogoslovskoe; it is unclear if and where he was actually reburied. Despite the ambiguity over what lies beneath the marble headstone, however, the old sense of holy man as *genius loci* is palpable in the restored Karpovka convent.[61] Along with St. Peter, Alexander Nevsky, and Blessed Xenia, Father John has been identified as one of the holy patrons of St. Petersburg. His association with material help and curing alcoholics has obvious ties to contemporary Russian reality, and the popularity of his cult within Russia seems assured for some time to come.[62]

Representations

Nonpolitical representations of Father John in Russia also changed after his 1990 canonization. The emphasis on his popularity shifted once again to a broad perspective, exceeding claims made him about him in the past or abroad. Here hagiographers were helped by existing practice. There is no such thing as a generic Orthodox saint: one must fit into such existing categories as apostle, martyr (or passion-bearer), monk or nun (*prepodobnyi/aia*), bishop (*sviatitel'*), prophet, warrior, or virgin.[63] *Otets*, a film about Father John made in St. Petersburg in 1991, followed the émigré troparion by claiming that he was one of the rare individuals to encompass all these categories within himself. According to *Otets*, while Father John has been labeled as "holy righteous" (*sviatoi pravednyi*, the accepted term for married saints), he was also an apostle because he was a missionary to all of the Russian Empire; a holy monk (*prepodobnyi*) because of his chastity and his efforts in instituting monasticism (he founded four convents and supported many others); a holy hierarch (*sviatitel'*) because, while not being formally a bishop, his pastoral growth was such that he did exercise this "eagle" role over Russia and was one of the proposed candidates for the office of Patriarch; prophet because he predicted the fall of the Tsar and perdition for Russia; and a martyr because he fell victim to the lies and slander of the press, as well as being physically assaulted with knives.[64] While there is clearly some hyperbole here, it is more than rhetoric. Father John did overlap more categories of holiness than many saints, and it is this polyvalent nature of his holiness that most emerges in the eyes of the Russians at the end of the twentieth century who recognized, and represented, him as holy.

The 1990 *vita* also raises the status of Father John's *matushka*, making her a full partner in her husband's pursuit of holiness. It declares that "Matushka Elizaveta shared in her husband's prayers and good works.... He loved her very tenderly, and how could he otherwise.... Matushka was her spouse's first adviser and shared his joys and sorrows."[65] This new emphasis on sharing and mutual devotion diverges from the 1964 *vita* and contemporary accounts, which mentioned Elizaveta Konstantinovna's protests about her husband to the Church hierarchy. All the versions are based on the same scanty, inconclusive evidence, but the image they present of Father John and Matushka Elizaveta's married life is strikingly different. Because the second *vita* is not based on any supporting evidence, new or otherwise, it reflects not so much reality as a change in sensibility on the part of the hagiographer: at the turn of the twenty-first century, it appears more pleasing to present the life of spouses as a joint project, rather than to describe marital discord as part of an ascetic effort. Earlier generations, however, found the image of Father John as a solitary ascetic struggler, overcoming the objections of both his wife and his hierarchy, either more convincing or more attractive.

Most ironically, the canonization of Father John by the Moscow Patriarchate in 1990 signaled not only an acknowledgment of his holiness, but the rehabilitation of the Ioannites. Either from ignorance, or working from the premise that those claiming devotion to Father John and persecuted by Soviet rule must be paragons, even the Ioannite leaders condemned by the pre-Revolutionary Synod have been incorporated into the mainstream of Orthodoxy in Russia. Nikolai Bol'shakov's posthumous work on Father John, *The Source of Living Water*, was

Fig. 14 Icon of Saint John of Kronstadt made by the nuns of the St. John Convent. St. Petersburg, 1992.

republished in 1995 with the blessing of the late Ioann, Metropolitan of St. Petersburg and Ladoga. The book includes citations from letters to *The Kronstadt Beacon* referring to it as "your esteemed journal," claims that the Ioannite peddlers healed a sick boy with their medals, and a spliced photograph purporting to depict Father John with Porfiriia Kiseleva and "the ascetic struggler, elder Nazarii." It also makes the novel case that one of Father John's early followers, Paraskeva Kovrigina, was the true power behind his throne and an Ioannite *avant la lèttre*—assertions not supported by any other evidence.[66] Father John's being safely dead, buried, and canonized means at least to some bishops within the Moscow Patriarchate that the theological threat the Ioannites posed during his lifetime has been declawed.

Conclusion

Father John of Kronstadt marks a turning point in modern Russian religious history. Even as he was the outgrowth of traditional notions of sanctity, he also proved to be the harbinger of new ones. His combination of social radicalism, personal charisma, political conservatism, and celebrity continues to inform Russian Orthodoxy and parallels religious phenomena in Europe responding to the challenge of modernization.

In many respects, Father John's background was typical of the Late Imperial churchman. He came from rural clerical origins, attended church school, then seminary, and inherited the parish of his wife's father (who was also, characteristically, from the clerical "caste"). His work to improve the lot of the poor, ardent preaching, and Eucharistic fervor exemplified the ideal "modern" Russian priest. In his public, priestly body, he personified the outward, service-oriented focus begun by women's religious communities. This turning outward, however, for all that it recalled early Christianity, ran against the reigning notion that holiness was the prerogative of icons, relics, or ascetic nuns and monks far from the world. In his combining the traditional asceticism that had characterized holiness—lifelong virginity and food discipline—with an emphasis on sacramental fervor and serving in the world, Father John forced his contemporaries to redefine their notions of sanctity. In a pattern similar to those of Jean-Marie Vianney and Padre Pio in Roman Catholic Europe, he created the type of the "holy priest" in modern Orthodox Christianity.

People became convinced that Father John was holy when they became healed as a result of his prayers. In the Christian tradition, healing had long been a manifestation of divine power, from Jesus' miraculous healings in the Gospels and those performed by the apostles to those of saints, especially after their deaths. In recent memory, however, living thaumaturges had become nearly extinct, partly because of the post-Petrine eighteenth- and early nineteenth-century Church hierarchy's suspicion of the people's reaction. Father John himself encountered this hostility when sixteen of the grateful healed described their cures in a major newspaper, but overcame it. Almost single-handedly, he moved the phenomenon of religious healing from the sphere of folk prayers back into the "acceptable" arena of the Church clergy.

Father John proved to be the intersection between lay and institutional notions of Orthodoxy in other ways. From the point of view of the laity, healing was a sign of God's clear favor, and the holy man was public property; they themselves were as much a part of the Church as their hierarchy; they wanted to publicize their experiences as a sign of piety. Father John's fervent liturgical celebration, his charity, and his healing abilities embodied the qualities Orthodox laypeople valued most, which is why they responded to him so enthusiastically. He combined the qualities of priest and prophet, of both personal and institutional charisma. This was precisely the sort of independent behavior that the hierarchy mistrusted, however, and they kept a sharp eye on his "originality." Father John's appeal to women and their role in spreading his celebrity prompted initial suspicion as well, for the classification of women's religious sentiments as ignorant, senseless "old wives' tales" was well-established in the Russian Orthodox Church. Ironically, the radical press would go even further in equating women's piety with backwardness, suggesting that this disdain ran across theological and even ideological lines.

The introduction of the media, whether conservative or radical, helped to form the character of the Father John phenomenon and itself raised the suspicions of the hierarchy: thanks to newspapers, magazines, and postcards, Father John became a celebrity in the modern sense. A broad section of the population came to know him through massively reproduced images and words (his own, those attributed to him, and those said about him); people sought him out just to be able to say that they had met him; they cast him as an expert on virtually every subject. His being invited to minister to the dying Emperor Alexander III made him internationally famous as well as known to those in the Russian Empire. In its broad publicity and large scale—mass pilgrimages made possible by an ever-expanding transportation network, mass reproductions of postcards, scarves, and souvenir mugs, mass public confessions to accommodate the numbers of crowds, special newspapers for devotees, and empire-wide confraternities—Father John's image differed sharply from those of pre-modern Russian saints, and set a new prototype irrevocably linked to the modern age.

Why, then, did the Church hierarchy accept Father John? If they had wanted to, they could have gone after both him and his admirers, as did the Ober-Procurator of the Holy Synod at the first signs of his celebrity. But Father John was obedient enough to his hierarchy to win its acceptance (as was his contemporary, the curé of Ars, to his bishops). Moreover, he encouraged people to those Orthodox forms of piety—a more active sacramental life, charity—that the hierarchy itself wished to foster. Finally, he was an ordained clergyman, and hence inherently more reassuring to the hierarchy than a layperson would have been. To the more thoughtful bishops, he was a sign of Orthodox Christianity's continued vitality in the face of modernity and a successful Orthodox response to the changes wrought in traditional society by political reforms, social changes, and industrialization.

But the doubters had a point. The potentially subversive aspects of living holiness became evident when Father John's most extreme followers called him God—or Jesus, or the Archangel Michael, or John the Baptist—come to earth. While Father John was quick to condemn them, the appellations suggest the extremes of fervor he inspired. Together with Lev Tolstoy, he came to symbolize the polarity of the choices facing Orthodox Russians: to move toward a private, unmystical, antisacramental neo-Protestantism and reject the association with the autocracy—this was Tolstoy's position—or to revivify Orthodoxy from within, seeking a more lively sacramental and more charitable Christianity than the version they had known. Tolstoy and Father John identified the same social and moral ills—depravity, material excess, and social inequality; they attacked them in nearly identical terms. Parts of Father Ioann's diaries read as if they had been lifted out of the pages of *What is Art?* or *The Kreuzer Sonata*; Tolstoy's later puritanism is nearly identical to Father Ioann's. Despite the similarity of their language and their critiques, however, they came to represent the extremes of "progressive" and "reactionary" opinion in Late Imperial Russia.

The reason for this split does not lie only in the nature of the religiosity of the two men, but in their different attitudes to the revolutionary movement. After the assassination of Alexander II in 1881, and particularly during the revolution of 1905, Father John preached unambiguously in support of the old ideal of political and religious "symphony." He gave his blessing to such radical-right organizations as the Union of the Archangel Michael and the Union of the Russian People. For all of his initial criticism of the existing order, as soon as the autocracy was seriously threatened, Father John came down unequivocally on the side of those who championed the most extreme adherence to Tsarism. It is difficult to imagine a more vociferous or consistent exponent of the notions that Russia's strength and meaning lie only in its Orthodoxy, that the autocracy is the most congenial form of government for Russia, and that political reform would open the flood-gates to revolution, which would be an unmitigated disaster. Although his apocalyptic view of Russian history and the threat of revolutionary change as heralding the age of Satan were no novelty, and his actual political involvement was far surpassed by others, the radical press targeted Father John as a symbol of religious reaction. In a backhanded way, the vehemence of the attack actually underlined the power of his international fame and reputation for holiness.

Nevertheless, it is largely because of his politics that Father John became a challenge and a stumbling-block, both for contemporaries and those who inherited the problem of determining the proper role of the Orthodox Church in Russian politics and society. Was the monarchy indeed the only appropriate form of government for an Orthodox country? Was it possible to be both Orthodox and liberal, or even Orthodox and revolutionary? Given the tumult Russia went through in the decades after Father John's death in 1908, it is not surprising that his politics would long overshadow his other aspects. After the Revolution of 1917 and the Civil War (1918–21), the Bolsheviks' opponents began to hail him as the prophetic voice that could have saved Russia from doom. His image became even sharper than it had been while he was alive. During the upheavals of the First Five-Year Plan (1928–32) in particular, peasants reported apocalyptic visions of Father John together with avenging angels; both devotees and persecutors linked him with Nicholas II and "counterrevolutionary elements."

The Russian Orthodox Church Abroad continued the politicization of Father John, using him to disavow the Revolution and support monarchy for Russia in its canonization of him in 1964. By contrast, the Moscow Patriarchate chose to ignore Father John's politics. When canonizing him in their own turn in 1990, they emphasized instead the social aspects that had the most resonance in contemporary Russia: his unstinting help to the poor and to alcoholics' families, his ability to heal, and, finally, his Russianness itself. For all these attempts, his politics still find followers in Russia. In this sense, Father John is but the first of so many modern candidates for sanctity—such as Patriarch Tikhon, Nicholas II, and virtually all of the new martyrs and confessors of Russia—whose canonization implicitly carries with it a rejection of the Revolution and its after-effects. For better or worse, holiness in modern Russia after Father John has become political, and it is likely to remain so for years to come.

In the largest sense, however, the Father John phenomenon is neither strictly Russian nor strictly Orthodox, but a general manifestation of traditional religiosity facing modernity and mass culture. In fact, in some respects, Father John has much in common with miracles and prophecies contemporary to him in Roman Catholic Europe. As with the Marian apparitions in Germany, France, and Portugal, and the fame of the curé of Ars, Father John's success is a sign of the Church hierarchy's ultimate willingness to embrace the accoutrements of modernity in advancing its own cause. Partly because of the challenges posed by modernization in all its forms—industrialization, revolutionary political movements, more widespread literacy—both the Russian Orthodox and the Roman Catholic Church decided to accept emotional, personal, and frankly supernatural forms of piety they had discouraged in the eighteenth century. As a result of Father John and his European religious counterparts, lived religiosity in the modern world has assumed a national scale in addition to the traditional small-scale forms—local shrines, parishes, saints, feasts—that had previously characterized it. In Late Imperial Russia, as in contemporary France, Germany, and Spain, holiness itself became associated with national virtues in the face of an "impersonal" modernity.

Like other modern religious phenomena, Father John of Kronstadt continues to engage the society with which he has had a dialectical relationship. He tried to transform it, and it regularly recasts him in its own image, continuing to call on him when he has corresponded to its needs. For all of the specifics of modernity, then, at least one aspect of the challenge to holiness remains. While saints strive for eternity, their enduring appeal on earth rests on how much sympathy and identification they continue to inspire in their mortal heirs.

Notes

Introduction

1. For different perspectives on the controversial canonization of Cardinal Alojzije Stepinac, accused of collaborating with the Fascist Ustasha regime's massacres, see Marco Aurelio Rivelli, *Le génocide occulté, état indépendant de Croatie 1941–1945* (Paris: L'Age d'Homme, 1998); Robin Harris, "On Trial Again," *The Catholic World Report*, August–September 1998, 41–43.

2. See especially Gregory L. Freeze, *The Parish Clergy in Nineteenth-Century Russia: Crisis, Reform, Counter-Reform* (Princeton: Princeton University Press, 1983); Simon Dixon, "The Church's Social Role in St. Petersburg, 1880–1914," in Geoffrey A. Hosking, ed., *Church, Nation and State in Russia and Ukraine* (New York: St. Martin's Press, 1991); Jennifer Elaine Hedda, "Pastoral Care and Social Activism in the Russian Orthodox Church, 1880–1905" (Ph.D. diss., Harvard University, 1998); Laurie Manchester, "Secular Ascetics: The Mentality of Orthodox Clergymen's Sons in Late Imperial Russia" (Ph.D. diss., Columbia University, 1995); Brenda Meehan, "From Contemplative Practice to Charitable Activity: Russian Women's Religious Communities and the Development of Charitable Work," in Kathleen McCarthy, ed., *Lady Bountiful Revisited: Women, Philanthropy, and Power* (New Brunswick, N.J.: Rutgers University Press, 1990), 142–56; Adele Lindenmeyr, *Poverty Is Not a Vice: Charity, Society, and the State in Imperial Russia* (Princeton: Princeton University Press, 1996).

3. See, in particular, the work of Natalie Zemon Davis, "Some Tasks and Themes in the Study of Popular Religion," in Charles Trinkhaus, ed., *The Pursuit of Holiness in Late Medieval and Renaissance Religion*, Papers from the University of Michigan Conference on Late medieval and Renaissance Religion (Leiden: Brill, 1974), 307–36; Michael Carroll, *Veiled Threats: The Logic of Popular Catholicism in Italy* (Baltimore: Johns Hopkins University Press, 1996), 5–6; and Craig Harline, "Official Religion–Popular Religion in Recent Historiography of the Catholic Reformation," *Archive for Reformation History* 81 (1990): 239–62.

4. See, for example, the identification of "rural" with "popular" in Vera Shevzov, "Popular Orthodoxy in Late Imperial Rural Russia" (Ph.D. diss., Yale University, 1994), 13–17. For peasants, see Marina M. Gromyko, *Mir russkoi derevni* (Moscow: Molodaia Gvardiia, 1991). For workers, see Reginald E. Zelnik, "'To the Unaccustomed Eye': Religion and Irreligion in the Experience of St. Petersburg Workers in the 1870s," in Robert P. Hughes and Irina Paperno, eds., *Christianity and the Eastern Slavs*, vol. 2: *Russian Culture in Modern Times* (Berkeley and Los Angeles: University of California Press, 1994), 49–82; Dave Pretty, "The Saints of the Revolution: Political Activists in 1890s Ivanovo-Voznesensk and the Path of Most Resistance," *Slavic Review* 54, no. 2 (summer 1995): 276–304.

5. William A. Christian Jr., *Local Religion in Sixteenth-Century Spain* (Princeton: Princeton University Press, 1981), 178; Eamon Duffy, *Stripping the Altars: Traditional Religion in England circa 1400 to circa 1580* (New Haven: Yale University Press, 1992); Leonard Boyle, "Popular Piety in the Middle Ages: What Is Popular?" *Florilegium* 4 (1982): 188.

6. See the discussion in David Hall, ed., *Lived Religion in America: Towards a History of Practice* (Princeton: Princeton University Press, 1997), vii–21.

7. Ernst Kantorowicz, *The King's Two Bodies: A Study in Medieval Political Theology* (Princeton: Princeton University Press, 1957).

8. For the connection between saint and cult, see Aviad M. Kleinberg, *Prophets in Their Own Country: Living Saints and the Making of Sainthood in the Later Middle Ages* (Chicago: University of Chicago Press, 1992), 7.

9. For studies outside Russia see, in particular, Barbara Corrado Pope, "Immaculate and Powerful: The Marian Revival in the Nineteenth Century," in Clarissa W. Atkinson et al., eds., *Immaculate & Powerful: The Female Sacred Image and Social Reality* (Boston: Beacon Press, 1985), 55–79; Ann Douglas, *The Feminization of American Culture* (New York: Knopf, 1977).

10. The standard examples include Nikolai M. Nikol'skii, *Istoriia russkoi tserkvi* (Moscow and Leningrad: Central Commitee of the Union of the Militant Godless of the USSR, 1931; 3d ed., Moscow: Politizdat, 1983); N. A. Smirnov, ed., *Tserkov' v istorii Rossii (IXv.–1917 g.): Kriticheskie ocherki* (Moscow: Nauka, 1967); A. I. Klibanov, ed., *Russkoe Pravoslavie: Vekhi Istorii* (Moscow: Politizdat, 1989). For Western portrayals in the same line, see Richard Pipes, "The Church as Servant of the State," chap. 9, in his *Russia under the Old Regime*, 2d ed. (New York: Macmillan, 1992), 221–48.

11. See, most notably, Gregory L. Freeze, "Handmaiden of the State? The Church in Imperial Russia Reconsidered," *Journal of Ecclesiastical History* 30, no. 1 (January 1985): 82–102; Robert L. Nichols and Theofanis Stavrou, eds., *Russian Orthodoxy Under the Old Regime* (Minneapolis: University of Minnesota Press, 1978); Charles E. Timberlake, ed., *Religious and Secular Forces in Late Tsarist Russia: Essays in Honor of Donald W. Treadgold* (Seattle and London: University of Washington Press, 1992).

12. This notion was developed before the revolution by Prot. G. S. Debol'skii, *O liubvi k otechestvu i trudie po slovu Bozhiiu*, 4th ed. (repr. Moscow: Izd. "Pravilo Very," 1996).

13. The most important pre-revolutionary studies are Nikolai I. Bol'shakov, *Istochnik zhivoi vody. Opisanie zhizni i deiatel'nosti otsa Ioanna Kronshtadtskago* (St. Petersburg: Tip. "Graficheskii Institut" Br. Lukshevits, 1910; repr. Izd. 'Tsarskoe Delo,' 1995); V. M. [Arkhiepiskop Evdokim (Meshcherskii)], *Dva dnia v Kronshtadte, iz dnevnika studenta* ([Sergiev Posad:] Sviato-Troitskaia Sergieva Lavra, 1902); Mikhail (Semenov), ierom., *Otets Ioann Kronshtadtskii, Polnaia biografiia s illustratsiiami* (St. Petersburg: Sinodal'-naia tip., 1903). Even in those instances where writers are clearly bothered by Father Ioann's politics, as in Sergii Chetverikov, *Dukhovnyi oblik o. Ioanna Kronshtadtskago i ego pastyrskie zavety* (Jordanville, N.Y.: Holy Trinity Monastery, 1958), and G. P. Fedotov, *A Treasury of Russian Spirituality* (Belmont, Mass.: Nordland Publishing Co., 1975), 346–49, they choose to emphasize the more positive religious aspects of his career.

14. See, for example, the inaccuracies in Father John's obituary in *The New York Times*, January 3, 1909: JOHN OF CRONSTADT DIES IN POVERTY (www.nytimes.org).

15. Walter Laqueur, *Black Hundred: The Rise of the Extreme Right in Russia* (New York: HarperCollins, 1993), 50; Bernice Glatzer Rosenthal, ed., *The Occult in Russian and Soviet Culture* (Ithaca: Cornell University Press, 1997), 396.

16. I. K. Surskii, *Otets Ioann Kronshtadtskii*, 2 vols. (Belgrade, 1938–41, repr. Forestville, Calif.: St. Elias Publications, 1979–80). For a critique, see Protopresbyter Georgii Shavel'skii, letter of June 12, 1939, Bakhmeteff Archive, Rare Book and Manuscript Library, Columbia University, New York.

17. Aleksandr Semenoff-Tian-Shanskii, *Otets Ioann Kronshtadtskii* (New York: Izd. A. Chekhova, 1955); idem, *Father John of Kronstadt: A Life* (Crestwood, N.Y.: St. Vladimir's Seminary Press, 1979); Alla Selawry, *Johannes von Kronstadt, Starez Rußlands* (Basel: Verlag die Pforte, 1981).

18. Karl Christian Felmy, *Predigt im orthodoxen Rußland, Untersuchungen zu Inhalt und Eigenart der russischen Predigt in der zweiten Hälfte des 19. Jahrhunderts* (Göttingen: Vandenhoek & Ruprecht 1972); Georgii Florovsky, *Puti russkago bogosloviia* (Paris: YMCA Press, 1937); Wolfgang Heller, "Johannes von Kronstadt," in *Biographisch-Bibliographisches Kirchenlexikon*, Bd. III (Herzberg: T.Bautz, 1992), 448–51; Louis-Albert Lassus, "Jean de Cronstadt, prêtre de Dieu—ami des hommes," *Contacts*, no. 94 (1976): 143–54; Nicolas Zernov, *The Russian Religious Renaissance of the Twentieth Century* (New York: Harper & Row, 1963).

19. See, for example, *Iz zapisnoi knizhki sviashchennika* (Moscow: Blagovest, 1996).

20. Letters to Father John are in the Central State Historical Archive of St. Petersburg (TsGIA SPb, f. 2219, op. 1 [Ioann Sergiev {Kronshtadtskii}, 1856–1908]).

21. The personal collection of Catherine Bortoli Doucet contains a letter from Father Ioann dated July 27, 1905, numbered #8994 by Father John's office. If they had mailed out nine thousand letters by the end of July in 1905, this corresponds to a rate of 1,285 outgoing letters a month, or about 15,500 a year.

Chapter 1

1. Although Russian historians of the Soviet period emphasized instances of nonobservance—people not going to confession, for example—in any given year, statistics actually show a consistently high level of observance. See B. G. Litvak, "Russkoe pravoslavie v XIX veke," in *Russkoe pravoslavie: vekhi istorii* (Moscow: Politizdat 1989), esp. 372–73, and L. I. Emeliakh, *Istoricheskie predposylki preodoleniia religii v sovetskoi derevne* (Leningrad: Gos. muzei istorii religii i ateizma, 1975), 122–25; also Gregory L. Freeze, *The*

Parish Clergy in Nineteenth-Century Russia: Crisis, Reform, Counter-Reform (Princeton: Princeton University Press, 1983), xxix.

2. See James Cracraft, *The Church Reform of Peter the Great* (Stanford: Stanford University Press, 1971), 242–51.

3. See the predominance of holy fools and wanderers in Pavel Novgorodskii, comp., *Raiskie tsvety s russkoi zemli* (Sergiev Posad, 1912).

4. See Golubinskii, Evgenii, *Istoriia kanonizatsii sviatykh v russkoi tserkvi* (Moscow, 1903), 109–98. Some priests of "holy life" did enjoy local esteem, however. See Prot. Luka Vasil'evich Efremov, *Dobryi pastyr': Kratkoe opisanie zhizni otsa Ioanna Borisovicha, sviashchennika Preobrazhenskoi tserkvi goroda El'tsa (1750–1824)* (Voronezh, 1893).

5. Cyril referred to the consecrated sacrament as "most dread," or *phrikodestatos*, which literally means "that which makes one's hair stand on end" (translated in Dom Gregory Dix, *The Shape of the Liturgy*, 2d ed. [London: Adam & Charles Black, 1975], 200).

6. See N. Kostomarov, ed., *Pamiatniki starinnoi russkoi literatury* (Moscow, 1862), 4: 186.

7. Even in the early twentieth century, *Novaia Zhizn'* described the St. Petersburg director of the city telegraph as circulating a memorandum among his subordinates "suggesting to them that they confess and partake of the Holy Mysteries during Great Lent" (*Novaia Zhizn'*, no. 383 [March 2–15, 1906]: 3). Similarly, Bishop Alexander (Semenoff-Tian-Shanskii) quotes civil servants as referring to their preparation for communion with "I am going to render God his due." Bishop Alexander, *Father John of Kronstadt: A Life* (Crestwood, N.Y.: St. Vladimir's Seminary Press, 1979), 32.

8. See Hans Belting, *Likeness and Presence: A History of the Image Before the Era of Art* (Chicago: University Of Chicago Press, 1994), 46, and esp. chap. 12, "The Iconostasis and the Role of the Icon in Liturgy and Private Devotion," 225–60.

9. For a contemporary call to pastoral charity referring explicitly to the Great Reforms spirit, see Iakov (Arkhimandrit), *Pastyr' v otnoshenii k sebe i pastve* (St. Petersburg, 1880). For aims to form popular taste, see Jeffrey Brooks, *When Russia Learned to Read: Literacy and Popular Literature, 1861–1917* (Princeton: Princeton University Press, 1985), 300, 302, and 306–11. Cf. also the discussion in Gregory L. Freeze, "'Going to the Intelligentsia': The Church and Its Urban Mission in Post-Reform Russia," in Edith W. Clowes, Samuel D. Kassow, and James L. West, eds., *Between Tsar and People: Educated Society and the Quest for Public Identity in Late Imperial Russia* (Princeton: Princeton University Press, 1991); and Simon Dixon, "The Church's Social Role in St. Petersburg, 1880–1914," in Geoffrey A. Hosking, ed., *Church, Nation and State in Russia and Ukraine* (London: Macmillan, 1991), 178–92.

10. *Ukazatel' statei, Pomieshchennykh v Dushepoleznom chtenii v techenie desiati liet, ot nachala izdaniia v 1860 do 1869 goda* (Moscow, 1870). Dostoyevsky relates a similar experience in *The Brothers Karamazov* when the elder Zosima describes having his life changed at hearing the Gospel read during a liturgy of presanctified gifts. The spiritual classic *The Way of a Pilgrim* also begins with the pilgrim-to-be being struck by the words "Pray unceasingly" in the epistle from Saint Paul (1 Thess. 5:17) read at liturgy.

11. See, for example, prot. Aleksandr Preobrazhenskii, *O Bogosluzhenii Pravoslavnoi Tserkvi s Podrobnym Ob'iasneniem Vsenoshchnago Bdeniia i Liturgii* (St. Petersburg, 1884).

12. Nikolai Bystrov, "Religiozno-nravstvennye sobesedovaniia v Il'inskoi tserkvi pogosta Muraveina, Ostrovskago uezda," *Pskovskie Eparkhial'nye Vedomosti*, no. 22 (November 15, 1896): 388.

13. Fedor L'vov, *O penii v Rossii* (St. Petersburg, 1834), 42. For a discussion of the

evolution of church music in the nineteenth century, see Vladimir Morosan, *Choral Performance in Pre-Revolutionary Russia* (Ann Arbor: UMI Research Press, 1986), chap. 3 ("The Emergence of a National Choral Style").

14. For a contemporary overview of missionary activity, see Evgenii K. Smirnov, *A Short Account of the Historical Development and Present of Russian Orthodox Missions* (London: Rivingtons, 1903; repr. Liberty, Tenn.: St. John of Kronstadt Press, 1998).

15. See the review of P. Znamenskii, *Istoriia Kazanskoi Dukhovnoi Akademii za Pervyi (Do-Reformennyi) Period Eia Sushchestvovaniia (1842–1870)* (Kazan, 1891–92), by A. Pypin in an offprint from *Vestnik Evropy* [n.d.], 710–11, 732. See also Robert Geraci, "Window on the East: Ethnography, Orthodoxy, and Russian Nationality in Kazan, 1870–1914" (Ph.D. diss., University of California at Berkeley, 1995).

16. See Thomas A. Kselman, *Miracles and Prophecies in Nineteenth-Century France* (New Brunswick, N.J.: Rutgers University Press, 1983), 113–40.

17. "Old Belief" refers to the seventeenth-century schism in which many Russians resisted Patriarch Nikon's reforms in Church language and ritual. See Roy Robson, "Liturgy and Community Among Old Believers, 1905–1917," *Slavic Review* 52, no. 4 (winter 1993): 713–24. For Protestantism, see Andrew Blane, "Protestant Sects in Late Imperial Russia," in Andrew Blane, ed., *The Religious World of Russian Culture, Russia and Orthodoxy*, vol. 2: *Essays in Honor of Georges Florovsky* (The Hague and Paris: Mouton, 1975), 267–78.

18. "Avtobiografiia," in Aleksandr Nikolaevich Strizhev, *Sviatoi Pravednyi Ioann Kronshtadtskii v Vospominaniiakh Samovidtsev* (Moscow: Izd. Otchii dom, 1997), 14.

19. Aleksandr Semenov-Tian-Shanskii, *Otets Ioann Il'ich Sergiev* (New York: Izd. A. Chekhova, 1955), 22.

20. Mikhail (Semenov), Hieromonk, *Otets Ioann Kronshtadtskii: Polnaia biografiia s illiustratsiami* (St. Petersburg: Sinodal'naia tip., 1903), 8, 25.

21. He and his admirers saw it as being a clear sign from God; Communist critics dismissed it as cynical calculation. See Vasilii E. Rozhnov, *Proroki i chudotvortsy: etiudy o mistitsizme* (Moscow: Politizdat, 1977), 78–79.

22. "Zhitiie sviatogo pravednogo Ioanna, Kronshtadtskogo chudotvortsa," *Zhurnal Moskovskoi Patriarkhii*, no. 10 (1990): 59–60.

23. *Dobrotoliubiie, tom pervyi* (unspecified prerevolutionary edition, repr. by Sergiev Posad: Sviato-Troitskaia Sergieva Lavra, 1993), 23–24; P. R., "Vazhnoe znachenie dnevnika dlia prikhodskogo sviashchennika," *Rukovodstvo dlia sel'skikh pastyrei*, no. 16 (1876): 475–88. For diaries' value as a surveillance tool, see "Prakticheskoe i nravstvennoe znachenie bogoluzhebnykh zhurnalov, zapisei o vnebogosluzhebnykh chteniiakh, pastyrsko-missionerskikh dnevnikov v dele vysshago nabliudeniia za tserkovno-prikhodskoi zhizn'iu," *Sankt-Peterburgskii Dukhovnyi Vestnik*, no. 42 (October 17, 1897): 840–41.

24. Ernst Kantorowicz, *The King's Two Bodies: A Study in Medieval Political Theology* (Princeton: Princeton University Press, 1957); "K chemu zovet nas sviatost' o. Ioanna Kronshtadtskogo," in Arkhimandrit Konstantin, *Chudo russkoi istorii. Sbornik statei, raskryvaiushchikh promyslitel'noe znachenie Istoricheskoi Rossii*. Jordanville, N.Y.: Holy Trinity Monastery, 1970), 224–25.

25. The classic Orthodox point of view is that theologians must also be ascetics or at least people of personal holiness—see, for example, St. Gregory of Nyssa, Maximus the Confessor, Symeon the New Theologian, et al. For recent arguments to this effect, see Prot. Mikhail Pomazanskii, "Ocherk pravoslavnago mirosozertsaniia o. Ioanna Kronshtadtskago," in *Piatidesiatilietie prestavleniia prisnopamiatnago otsa Ioanna Kronshtadtskago,*

iubeleinyi sbornik (New York: All-Slavic Publishers, 1958), 66–82; Bishop Auxentios, in *Orthodox Tradition* 11, no. 3 (1994): 69.

26. For another contemporary example, see Feofan [Govorov], *Primery zapisyvaniia dobrykh myslei, prikhodiashchikh vo vremia bogomyslia i molitvy...* (Moscow, 1903; repr. Saratov: Blagovest, 1997).

27. For studies of spiritual elders in Orthodoxy, see S. I. Smirnov, *Dukhovnyi Otets v Drevnei Vostochnoi Tserkvi (Istoriia Dukhovnichestva na Vostoke)* (Sergiev Posad, 1906); I. M. Kontsevich, *Optina Pustyn' i eia vremia* (Jordanville, N.Y.: Holy Trinity Monastery, 1970).

28. The State Archive of the Russian Federation (Gosudarstvennyi Arkhiv Rossiiskoi Federatsii; hereafter GARF), f. 1067, op. 1, d. 1, l. 1ob. (1856). The use of the feminine gender is used to suggest Father Ioann's use of the feminine *tvar'* rather than the neuter *sozdanie*.

29. Mikhail (Semenov), *O. Ioann Kronshtadtskii*, 8–10, 15–16.

30. GARF, f. 1067, op. 1, d. 1, l. 28ob; d. 3, l. 2ob.

31. Ibid, d. l. 1.

32. Mikhail (Semenov), *Otets Ioann Kronshtadtskii*, 38, 66–69; V. M. [Archbishop Evdokim (Meshcherskii)], *Dva dnia v Kronshtadte; iz dnevnika studenta*, 2d ed. (Sergiev Posad, 1902), 437–42; P. M. Chizhov, *Otets Ioann Kronshtadtskii, Zhizn', deiatel'nost', izbrannye chudesa* (Jordanville, N.Y.: Holy Trinity Monastery, 1958), 8.

33. GARF, f. 1067, op. 1, d. 3, l. 9; d. 4, l. 10.

34. Ibid., d. 1, l. 53.

35. Ibid.

36. A rare example of identification is found in the Paschal canon, particularly irmos 3, troparion 2 ("Yesterday I was buried with Thee, O Christ; today I arise with Thee. Yesterday I was crucified with Thee; now glorify me also in Thy kingdom..."); *Velikii Sbornik. Chast' Tretiia iz Triodi Tsvetnoi* (Jordanville, N.Y.: Holy Trinity Monastery, 1956), 8.

37. GARF, f. 1067, op. 1, d. 1, l. 16 (1856).

38. Ibid., d. 1, l. 4ob.

39. Ibid., d. 1, l. 65ob. For Western parallels, see Caroline Bynum, *Jesus as Mother: Studies in the Spirituality of the High Middle Ages* (Berkeley and Los Angeles: University of California Press, 1982), 23–48.

40. GARF, f. 1067, op. 1, d. 12, l. 1.

41. Ibid., d. 4, l. 63.

42. Ibid., d. 13, l. 22ob (1875). See the description in Saint John Climacus, *Prepodobnago otsa nashego Ioanna, igumena Sinaiiskoi gory, Lestvitsa*, 7th ed. (Sergiev Posad, 1908), iii–iv.

43. For the essential premise of the development of the elder—withdrawing in order to later serve society—see E. N. Sumarokov, "Starchestvo i pervye Optinskie startsy," in *Starets Makarii Optinskii* (Kharbin: Bratstvo im. s. Ioanna Bogoslova, 1940), 10–11. For a critique of social service without personal asceticism, comparing the "humanistic, philanthropic" G. Petrov and Father John, see *Tverskiie Eparkhial'nye Vedomosti*, no. 20 (May 25, 1909): 404–7.

44. GARF, f. 1067, op. 1, d. 12, l. 39ob (1874).

45. A. S. Kravchenko and A. P. Utkin, comps., *Ikona. Sekrety remesla* series. Moscow: Vek Rossii/Style A Ltd., 1993), 78.

46. GARF, f. 1067, op. 1, d. 12, l. 22 (1874).

47. Ibid., d. 4, l. 132. "Collectors" were a common type, particularly among the peasantry. Either a monastery would send out monks to canvass for donations or a layperson

would independently wander around Russia collecting money for a monastery or shrine. (Bishops criticized the practice: see the comments of Bishop Ioannikii of Arkhangelsk in *Pskovskie Eparkhial'nye Vedomosti*, no. 24 [December 15, 1896], 445.) Nekrasov's *Vlas* is the most famous literary example.

48. GARF, f. 1067, op. 1, d. 10, l. 69ob (1867). Compare to the more balanced assessment of Macarius of Egypt: "Within the heart are unfathomable depths.... It is but a small vessel; and yet dragons and lions are there, and there poisonous creatures and all the treasures of wickedness; rough, difficult paths are there, and gaping chasms. There likewise is God, there are the angels, there Life and the Kingdom, there Light and the Apostles, the heavenly cities and the treasures of grace: all things are there." *The Limonarion* (London: Faber and Faber, 1976), 131.

49. GARF, f. 1067, op. 1, d. 3, l. 67. Compare to Bishop Ignatii Brianchianinov, *The Arena: An Offering to Contemporary Monasticism* (Jordanville, N.Y.: St. Job of Pochaev Press, 1983), 209ff.

50. GARF, f. 1067, op. 1, d. 8, l. 46 (1864).

51. Ibid., d. 12, l. 11 (1869).

52. Ibid., d. 23, l. 169ob.

53. Ibid., d. 8, l. 46. See the discussion of priests' accountability for erotic dreams in S. V. Bulgakov, *Nastol'naia Kniga dlia sviashchenno–tserkovno sluzhitelei. Sbornik svedenii, kasaiushchikhsia preimushchestvenno prakticheskoi deiatel'nosti otechestvennago dukhovenstva*, 2d ed. (Kharkov, 1900), 1:778.

54. GARF, f. 1067, op. 1, d. 23, l. 36.

55. Ibid., d. 24, l. 38ob.

56. Ibid., d. 4, l. 89. The reference is probably to Abba Arsenius, who only changed the water for his palm-leaves once a year. See Benedicta Ward, trans., *The Sayings of the Desert Fathers: The Alphabetical Collection* (Kalamazoo, Mich.: Cistercian Publications, Inc., 1984), 11.

57. GARF, f. 1067, op. 1, d. 12, l. 9ob.

58. Ibid., d. 13, l. 9ob.

59. Ibid., d. 12, l. 1. The latter reflects an emotional, Roman Catholic, strain that made its way into Russian Orthodoxy through the Kievan Theological Academy in the eighteenth century. It expressed itself in such previously unknown genres as meditations on the Passion and the akathist "To the Most Sweet Jesus," of which Father Ioann was very fond. See d. 4, l. 2, when Father Ioann notes buying this akathist in the Synodal bookshop. For a discussion of the general trend toward "sweetness," see Georgii V. Florovsky, *Puti russkago bogosloviia* (Paris: YMCA Press, 1937), 107–22.

60. Abba Poemen, in Ward, *Sayings of the Desert Fathers*, 184; Symeon the New Theologian, *The Discourses* (New York: Paulist Press, 1980), 314.

61. GARF, f. 1067, op. 1, d. 12, l. 44; emphasis mine.

62. Ibid., d. 9, l. 26ob.

63. See the discussion of food discipline patterns in Caroline Bynum, *Holy Feast, Holy Fast: The Religious Significance of Food for Medieval Women* (Berkeley and Los Angeles: University of California Press, 1987), 73–149.

64. GARF, f. 1067, op. 1, d. 1, l. 20 (1856).

65. See the scale of the meals suggested in Molokhovets, Elena, *Classic Russian Cooking: Elena Molokhovets' "A Gift to Young Housewives,"* Joyce Toomre, trans. (Bloomington: Indiana University Press, 1993).

66. GARF, f. 1067, op. 1, d. 12, l. 74.

67. Ibid., d. 12, l. 89ob.

68. Ibid., d. 13, ll. 58, 60ob, 68ob, 69; d. 14, ll. 3, 38ob, 84.
69. Ibid., d. 23, l. 1; d. 14, l. 93; d. 8, l. 69; d. 14, l. 2ob.
70. Ibid., d. 4, l. 130.
71. Ibid., d. 9, l. 71ob (emphasis mine). Clergymen who had experienced nocturnal emissions had to examine their conscience and serve Liturgy only if they were sure they had not "brought it upon themselves" by excessive food, drink, or sleep. Bulgakov, *Nastol'naia Kniga*, 1: 779.
72. GARF, f. 1067, op. 1, d. 8, l. 46; d. 3, l. 109.
73. See also Abba John the Dwarf, "He who gorges himself and talks with a boy has already in his thought committed fornication with him" (Ward, *Sayings of the Desert Fathers*, 86.)
74. GARF, f. 1067, op. 1, d. 8, l. 53ob.
75. V. M., *Dva dnia v Kronshtadte*, 382.
76. John Chrysostom, for example, believed that virginity was a return to the authentic nature of the human being (*De virginitas*, xiv [PG 48.544]). Gregory of Nyssa similarly believed that sexuality was absolutely antithetical to the original state of human nature (*De virginitate*, ii [PG 46.324]; xii [PG 46.369]). This attitude was closely tied to early gnosticism (see Hans Jonas, *The Gnostic Religion: The Message of the Alien God and the Beginnings of Christianity* [Boston: Beacon, 1963], xvii, 31). For the survival of the idea of a sexual fall in Rabbinic literature, see J. M. Evans, *Paradise Lost and the Genesis Tradition* (Oxford: Oxford University Press, 1968), esp. 32–33, 46–55, and 60.
77. Although Gregory of Nyssa, like Philo and Origen, saw Adam as representing the spiritual element in the human being, and Eve the fleshly one (see *De hominis opificio*, xvii–xviii [PG 44.189–96]).
78. See Eve Levin, *Sex and Society in the World of the Orthodox Slavs, 900–1700*. Ithaca: Cornell University Press, 1989, chaps. 1 and 6.
79. See Metropolitan Evlogii, *Vospominaniia* (Paris: YMCA Press, 1957), 143–44; and Laurie Manchester, "Secular Ascetics: The Mentality of Orthodox Clergymen's Sons in Late Imperial Russia" (Ph.D. diss., Columbia University, 1995), 550–60; The Central State Historical Archive of St. Petersburg (hereafter TsGIA SPb), f. 2219, op. 1, d. 31, l. 159.
80. For early Christian examples of this phenomenon, see the lives of Galaction and Episteme, Chrysanthus and Daria, Julian and Basilissa, Marcian and Pulcheria, and Melania and Valerian, in Monk Moses, *Married Saints of the Church* (Wildwood, Calif.: St. Xenia Skete, 1991), 4, 25, 43, 138–39). For the medieval period, see Dyan Elliott, *Spiritual Marriage: Sexual Abstinence in Medieval Wedlock* (Princeton: Princeton University Press, 1993).
81. See Paul's epistle to the Ephesians 5:20–33, read at Orthodox ceremonies of matrimony.
82. Bulgakov, *Nastol'naia Kniga*, 1051.
83. The subtle denigration of marriage has a long history, but the Sixth Ecumenical Council, in which bishops were forbidden to have wives, was key. See *Pravila sviatykh apostol, sviatykh soborov vselenskikh i pomiestnykh i sviatykh otets s tolkovaniiami* (Moscow: Izd. Moskovskago Obshchestva Liubitelei Dukhovnago Prosvieshcheniia, 1912), 6–8; Ioann (Sokolov), bishop of Smolensk, *O Monashestvie Episkopov* (Pochaev, 1904), 5–25.
84. Bulgakov, *Nastol'naia Kniga*, 771.
85. Cited in Peter Brown, *The Body and Society: Men, Women and Sexual Renunciation in Early Christianity* (New York: Columbia University Press, 1988), 203.

86. See the exchange between a city priest and his country cousin to this effect in Nikita P. Giliarov-Platonov, *Iz perezhitago: avtobiograficheskie vospominaniia*, 2 vols. (Moscow, 1886–87), 1:45–46.

87. See André Vauchez, "The Virginal Marriage of Elzéar and Delphine" and "Conjugal Chastity: A New Ideal in the Thirteenth Century," in his *The Laity in the Middle Ages: Religious Beliefs and Devotional Practices* (Notre Dame and London: University of Notre Dame Press, 1993), 185–90, 191–203) for medieval Western examples. For a Russian example, see the life of Ul'iana Lazarevskaia in Serge Zenkovsky, *Medieval Russia's Epics, Chronicles, and Tales* (New York: E. P. Dutton, 1974) 391–98.

88. The third canon of Dionysius states that marital abstinence must be by mutual consent (*Pravila sviatykh otets s tolkovaniiami* [Moscow, 1884], 17–19).

89. See Nadejda Gorodetzky, *Saint Tikhon of Zadonsk: Inspirer of Dostoyevsky* (Crestwood, N.Y.: St. Vladimir's Seminary Press, 1976), 61–62.

90. "Aleksei the man of God as an image of self-denial for a legion of Russian ascetic strugglers," in Novgorodskii, *Raiskie tsvety s russkoi zemli*, 209–10.

91. GARF, f. 1067, op. 1, d. 3, l. 8ob.

92. Ibid., d. 8, l. 19.

93. See the warnings of M. Tsialovskii in the introduction to Sof'ia Tolstaia, *Dnevniki Sof'i Andreevny Tolstoi, 1860–1891* (Leningrad: Izd. M. i S. Sabashnikovykh, 1928), viii.

94. GARF, f. 1067, op. 1, d. 9, l. 8ob.

95. Ibid., d. 8, l. 60ob.

96. Ibid., d. 9, l. 14; d. 13, l. 56ob; d. 9, l. 59; emphases mine. The reference to the image of the Church usually refers to the marriage union itself rather than either party in it (cf. the epistle read at the rite of matrimony, Ephesians 5:20–33, concluding with the words, "This is a great mystery: but I speak concerning Christ and the Church"); Isabel Hapgood, comp., *Service Book of the Holy Orthodox-Catholic Apostolic Church* (Englewood, N.J.: Antiochian Orthodox Christian Archdiocese, 1975), 298.

97. GARF, f. 1067, op. 1, d. 9, l. 12.

98. See such edifying exhortations as Grigorii Diachenko, *V podarok detiam. Iskra Bozhiia. Sbornik razskazov i stikhotvorenii, prisposoblennykh k chteniiu v khristianskoi shkole dlia devochek sredniago vozrasta* (Moscow: Izd. Pazadelova, 1903).

99. GARF, f. 1067, op. 1, d. 9, l. 62.

100. Ibid., d. 9, l. 66ob. The metaphor is unconsciously apposite: by refusing his wife physical relations, Father Ioann has in effect deprived her of her own cubs.

101. Ibid., d. 4, l. 64.

102. Ibid., d. 4, l. 65.

103. Ibid., d. 4, l. 10.

104. Ibid., d. 3, l. 4.

105. See James A. Brundage, "Carnal Delight: Canonistic Theories of Sexuality," *Proceedings of the Fifth International Congress of Medieval Canon Law, Salamanca, 21–25 September 1965*, pp. 375–78.

106. GARF, f. 1067, op. 1, d. 8, l. 8.

107. Ibid., d. 9, l. 10ob.

108. Ibid., d. 23, l. 39.

109. Ibid., d. 23, l. 101. For food as control, see Darra Goldstein, "Domestic Porkbarreling in Nineteenth-Century Russia, or Who Holds the Keys to the Larder?" in Helena Goscilo and Beth Holmgren, eds. *Russia, Women, Culture* (Bloomington: Indiana University Press, 1996), 125–51.

110. GARF, f. 1067, op. 1, d. 4, l. 65. For sons' perceptions of *matushki*, see Manchester, "Secular Ascetics," 222–29.
111. GARF, f. 1067, op. 1, d. 9, l. 33ob. See the accounts of I. K., Surskii, *Otets Ioann Kronshtadtskii*, 2 vols. (Belgrade, 1938–41; reprt. Forestville: St. Elias Publications, 1979–80), 1: 9–11; and Mikhail (Semenov), *Otets Ioann Kronshtadtskii*, 30.
112. GARF, f. 1067, op. 1, d. 12, l. 35.
113. Ibid., d. 3, l. 28 (1857).
114. Ibid., d. 3, l. 59.
115. Ibid., d. 3, l. 46ob.
116. Ibid., d. 11, l. 31ob.
117. Ibid., d. 11, ll. 29ob–31ob (1871). Twelve years earlier, by contrast, he had reminded himself, "Initially I spoke this same village language" (ibid., d. 3, l. 1a).

Chapter 2

1. Hieromonk Mikhail (Semenov), *Otets Ioann Kronshtadtskii: Polnaia biografiia s illustratsiiami* (St. Petersburg: Sinodal'naia tip., 1903), 37–38. For the Synodal condemnation of *iurodstvo*, see The Russian State Historical Archive (hereafter RGIA), f. 834, op. 2, no. 1701, fol. 2. I thank Eve Levin for bringing this reference to my attention.
2. Mikhail, *Otets Ioann Kronshtadtskii*, 52.
3. See Admiral D. V. Nikitin (Fokagitov), *Na beregu i v more* (San Francisco, 1937), 7–13.
4. See Khomiakov's letters to Palmer in W. J. Birkbeck, ed., *Russia and the English Church During the Last Fifty Years* (London, 1895).
5. The State Archive of the Russian Federation (hereafter GARF), f. 1067, op. 1, d. 4, l. 19ob.
6. Arkhimandrit Serafim (Chichagov), *Letopis' Serafimo-Diveevskago Monastyria*, 2d ed. (St. Petersburg, 1903), 360.
7. Basile, "Grandes Règles," in Dom David Amand, *L'Ascèse Monastique de Saint Basile, Essai Historique* (Maredsous: Editions de Maredsous, 1948), 118–28.
8. See Feofan (Govorov), *Pis'ma k raznym litsam o raznykh predmetakh very i zhizni*, 2d ed. (Moscow, 1892), 271.
9. GARF, f. 1067, op. 1, d. 12, l. 13.
10. See the reminiscences of P. P. Levitskii, *Prot. Ioann Il'ich Sergiev Kronshtadtskii: Nekotorye cherty iz ego zhizni* (Petrograd, 1916), 4–7.
11. GARF, f. 1067, op. 1, d. 12, l. 43ob.
12. Ibid., d. 8, l. 63ob.
13. Ibid., d. 12, l. 6ob.
14. Ibid., d. 14, l. 5.
15. Ibid., d. 1, l. 16.
16. Ibid, d. 1, l. 16ob–17. Here Father John anticipates some of the miracles with which he would later be credited.
17. So many people wondered why miracles no longer happened as they did in early Christianity that Bishop Innokentii preached a sermon specifically on that subject. See his "Slovo o tom, pochemu Dukh Sv. ne tvorit nynie chudes?" in Priest M. A. Potorzhinskii, comp., *Obraztsy russkoi tserkovnoi propoviedi XIX vieka* (Kiev: tip. K. N. Milevskago, 1882), 185–98.

18. GARF, f. 1067, op. 1, d. 1, l. 28ob.

19. Dom Gregory Dix, *The Shape of the Liturgy*, 2d ed. (London: Adam & Charles Black, 1975), 33.

20. Ignatius, "Epistle to the Magnesians," in James A Kleist, ed., *The Epistles of St. Clement of Rome and St. Ignatius of Antioch* (London: Longmans, Green, and Co., 1962), esp. 70–71, 128.

21. See the discussion in Protopresbyter Michael Pomazansky, *Orthodox Dogmatic Theology: A Concise Exposition* (Platina, Calif.: St. Herman of Alaska Brotherhood, 1984), 246–54.

22. As he told bishops in his diary, "We can be not only your servants, but your counselors too, as the Holy Apostles regarded the presbyters, honoring them by having them participate at the apostolic councils. Bishops now fight for the most part with ink, pens, and paper, and not with living words or by example." GARF, f. 1067, op. 1, d. 12, l. 74.

23. V. M., *Dva dnia v Kronshtadte*, 385.

24. Alexandr Semenoff-Tian-Shianskii, *Otets Ioann Kronshtadtskii* (New York: Izd. A. Chekhova, 1955), 53.

25. Ibid, 52.

26. Prot. Ioann Il'ich Sergiev, *Moia zhizn' vo Khriste, ili minuty dukhovnago trezveniia i sozertsaniia, blagogoveinago chustva, dushevnago ispravleniia i pokoia v Boge. Izvlecheniia iz dnevnika*, 2 vols. Moscow, 1894; repr. Utica, N.Y., 1957), 1:33.

27. GARF, f. 1067, op. 1, d. 1, l. 53.

28. Ibid., d. 3, ll. 132, 86ob.

29. Ibid, d. 3, ll. 97ob, 102; later in Sergiev, *Moia Zhizn' vo Khriste*, 2:25–26.

30. Sergiev, *Moia zhizn' vo Khriste,*. 2: 25.

31. Ibid., 2:311–12. This is another instance of Father Ioann's having internalized scripture: the last phrase is from John 6:63. Compare to the images of Christ's wound as a breast giving milk in Caroline Walker Bynum, *Holy Feast and Holy Fast: The Religious Significance of Food to Medieval Women* (Berkeley and Los Angeles: University of California Press, 1987), plates 25–27.

32. For eucharistic miracles, see Bynum, *Holy Feast and Holy Fast*, 50–51, 63–64.

33. GARF, f. 1067, op. 1, d. 4, ll. 65ob, 58, 84. Interestingly, to rid himself of the eucharistic doubts, Father John prayed not to Jesus Christ but to Mary, whom he then fervently thanked.

34. Sergiev, *Moia zhizn' vo Khriste*, 2: 275. The selection is commenting on John 6:56 (also used in the Orthodox Church as the Communion verse for Mid-Pentecost).

35. Ibid., 2: 314.

36. Ibid., 1: 175. Icons of Christ have the Greek abbreviation for this phrase in Christ's halo, with the intent of linking Christ to the One who appeared to Moses in the burning bush. For a fuller discussion of imagery associated with Jesus Christ, see Leonid Ouspensky and Vladimir Lossky, *The Meaning of Icons* (Crestwood, N.Y.,: St. Vladimir's Seminary Press, 1983), 69–72.

37. See the enthusiastic comments on this phrase in Alexander Whyte, *Father John of the Greek Church: An Appreciation* (New York: Fleming H. Revell Company, 1898), 38–40.

38. Sergiev, *Moia zhizn' vo Khriste*, 1:168–69. Father Ioann is paraphrasing I Corinthians 15:45.

39. Sergiev, *Moia zhizn' vo Khriste*, 2:283.

40. GARF, f. 1067, op. 1, d. 14, l. 26.

41. Metropolitan Antonii (Khrapovitskii), *Uchenie o Pastyre, Pastyrstve i ob Ispovedi*

(New York: Izd. Severo-Amerikanskoi i Kanadskoi eparkhii, 1966), 289. See also Johann von Gardner, *Bogosluzhebnoe penie Russkoi Pravoslavnoi Tserkvi: Sistema, sushchnost', istoriia*, 2 vols. (Jordanville, N.Y.: Holy Trinity Monastery, 1980–82), esp. 1:58–72.

42. K. Glizhinskii, *Iz ob"iatii umiraiushchei bursy v gornilo zhizni. Ocherki poslednikh dnei bursy i sovremennago razvala tserkovno-prikhodskoi zhizni* (Ekaterinburg, 1912), 68.

43. Prot. I. Popov, *Nezabvennoi pamiati dorogogo batiushki o. Ioanna Kronshtadtskago* (St. Petersburg, 1909), 29.

44. The Russian State Archive of Literature and Art (hereafter RGALI), f. 525, op. 1, d. 414, l. 10 (the reminiscences of Konstantin M. Fofanov).

45. E. Makharoblidze, "O. Ioann Kronshtadtskii, kak sovershitel' Bozhestvennoi Liturgii," in *Piatidesiatilietie prestavleniia prisnopamiatnago otsa Ioanna Kronshtadtskago* (New York: All-Slavic Publishers, 1958), 89.

46. The Central State Historical Archive of St. Petersburg (hereafter TsGIA SPb), f. 2219, op. 1, d. 72, l. 2. Other unfavorable voices described Father John as the "Imperial church actor." See T. G. Morozova et al., *V. G. Korolenko v vospominaniiakh sovremennikov* (Moscow: Goslitizdat, 1962), 136.

47. Sviashchennik M. Paozerskii, "Vpechatleniia pervago sosluzheniia o. Ioanna Sergieva (Kronshtadtskago) na bozhestvennoi liturgii," *Sankt-Peterburgskii Dukhovnyi Vestnik*, no. 32 (August 8, 1897): 620.

48. See *Tipikon, siest' izobrazhenie china tserkovnago, iazhe zovetsia Ustav* (Moscow, 1885).

49. V. M., *Dva dnia v Kronshtadte*, 48.

50. Ibid., 48–49.

51. Ibid., 56; emphasis mine.

52. GARF, f. 1067, op. 1, d. 13, l. 4ob. For a contemporary discussion of the Protestant movement and its influence in Russia, see Nikolai Leskov, *Velikosvetskii raskol: Lord Redstok, ego uchenie i propoved': ocherk sovremennogo religioznogo dvizheniia v Petersburgskom obshchestvie* (Moscow, 1877). For the non-Orthodox churches in St. Petersburg, see V. V. Antonov and A. V. Kobak, *Sviatyni Sankt-Peterburga, Istoriko—tserkovnaia entsiklopediia v trekh tomakh* (St. Petersburg: Izd. Chernysheva, 1996), 3:215–76. For Father John's critiques of Protestants, see GARF, f. 1067, op. 1, d. 4, l. 12; d. 14, l. 19ob.

53. For a typical compilation, see A. I. Almazov, *Apokrificheskiia molitvy, zaklinaniia, i zagovory* (Odessa, 1901).

54. GARF, f. 1067, op. 1, d. 4, l. 132.

55. See priest M. Paozerskii's criticism of Father John's throwing aside his belt as "originality"—only to repent when, at the end of the service, he saw someone wrapping up Father John's shirt and undershirt for cleaning: they were as dripping as if just out of the water. Paozerskii, "Vpechatleniia," 621.

56. For example, abstain from meat, dairy products, sexual activity, and alcohol. See Leonid Heretz, "The Practice and Significance of Fasting in Russian Peasant Culture at the Turn of the Century," in Musya Glants and Joyce Toomre, eds., *Food in Russian History and Culture* (Bloomington: Indiana University Press, 1997), 67–80.

57. See the canonical commentaries, especially that of Dionysus, in *Pravila sviatykh otets s tolkovaniiami* (Moscow, 1884), 14–17; and Eve Levin, *Sex and Society in the World of the Orthodox Slavs, 900–1700* (Ithaca: Cornell University Press, 1989), 101–22, for female impurity in the context of the Slavs; Marina Warner, *Alone of All Her Sex: The Myth and the Cult of the Virgin Mary* (New York: Vintage Books, 1983), chap. 3, for the evolution of the taboo in the Roman Catholic West.

58. See the confessions to Father Ioann confirming this notion in Nadieszda Kizenko, "The Making of a Modern Saint: Ioann of Kronstadt and the Russian People, 1855–1917" (Ph.D. diss., Columbia University, 1995), 189–254.

59. Glizhinskii, *Iz ob'iatii umiraiushchei bursy v gornilo zhizni*, 69.

60. GARF, f. 1067, op. 1, d. 4, l. 1a ob; Aleksii Makushinskii, "Vospominaniie byvshago pevchago Kronshtadtskago Andreevskago Sobora," in *Piatidesiatilietie prestavleniia prisnopamiatnago otsa Ioanna Kronshtadtskago*, 43.

61. See the reminiscences of Maria Makeeva in RGIA, f. 834, op. 4, e. khr. 1668, l. 7–7ob; and O. V. Shustin, *Zapis' ob o. Ioanne Kronshtadtskom i ob Optinskikh startsakh, iz lichnykh vospominanii* (Bielaia Tserkov: Pravoslavno-missionerskoe Kn-vo, 1929).

62. GARF, f. 1067, op. 1, d. 14, l. 72.

63. Sergiev, *Moia zhizn' vo Khriste*, 1: 230–31.

64. Vs. S. Soloviev, "Otets Ioann," *Sever*, no. 49 (1888): 14–15.

65. Ioann Il'ich Sergiev [Ioann Kronshtadtskii], *Neizdannyi dnevnik; vospominaniia Episkopa Arseniia ob otse Ioanne Kronshtadtskom* (Moscow: Pravoslavnoe Blagotvoritel'-noe bratstvo vo imia vsemilostivogo Spasa, 1992), 52.

66. See the communion healing miracle reported in Vladimir E. Lebedev, "Moe vospominaniie o poiezdkie k o. Ioannu v Kronshtadt," *Pskovskie Eparkhial'nye Vedomosti*, no. 21 (November 1, 1896): 370–71.

67. Letter from a nun in TsGIA SPb, f. 2219, op. 1, d. 12b, part II, l. 146.

68. V. M., *Dva dnia v Kronshtadte*, 45.

69. Nikita P. Giliarov-Platonov discusses the importance of the confessional technique in parish assessment of a priest in *Iz Perezhitago: avtobiograficheskie vospominaniia*, 2 vols. (Moscow, 1886–87), 168–69. See also *Dobryi pastyr': biografiia o. Ioanna Kronshtadtskogo, pis'ma k batiushke i vospominaniia o nem* (St. Petersburg: Izd. Aleksandro-Nevskoi Lavry, 1994), 12–13.

70. GARF, f. 1067, op. 1, d. 4, l. 4.

71. Ibid, d. 4, l. 1a ob. For churches incorporating this feature, see Nikolai V. Sultanov's Cathedral of the Holy Apostles Peter and Paul in Peterhof. N. Sultanov, *Opisanie novoi pridvornoi tserkvi Svv. Pervoverkhovnykh Apostolov Petra i Pavla, chto v Novom Peter-gofie* (St. Petersburg: tip. "Obshchestvennaia Pol'za," 1905), 12–13.

72. Ibid., d. 4, l. 42ob.

73. Bishop Alexander [Aleksandr Semenoff-Tian-Shanskii], *Father John of Kronstadt: A Life* (Crestwood, N.Y.: St. Vladimir's Seminary Press, 1979), 39.

74. Vianney was made the patron of all French priests in 1905 and of "all priests in the universe" in 1929. Phillipe Boutry and Michel Cinquin, *Deux Pèlerinages aux XIXe Siècle, Ars et Paray-le-Monial* (Paris: Editions Beauchesne, 1980), 146–50.

75. TsGIA SPb, f. 2219, op. 1, d. 40, l. 42.

76. Makharoblidze, "O. Ioann Kronshtadtskii," 87.

77. TsGIA SPb, f. 2219, op. 1, d. 40, l. 30; emphasis mine. See also the reminiscences of Maria Makeeva, RGIA, f. 834, op. 4, ed. khr. 1668, l. 4–5ob, on the linking of devotion to the Eucharist and to Father Ioann.

78. See Protopresbyter A. Shmeman, *Evkharistiia: Tainstvo Tsarstva* (Paris: YMCA Press, 1984), esp. 15–19.

79. GARF, f. 1067, op. 1, d. 4, l. 41.

80. Ibid., d. 23, l. 30ob.

81. Ibid., d. 26, l. 17.

82. See Priest M. A. Potorzhinskii, comp., *Obraztsy Russkoi Tserkovnoi Propovedi XIX vieka*, 3d ed. (Kiev, 1912), 727.

83. For the new attention paid to preaching and consequent changes in both ritual and architecture, see Simon Dixon, "The Church's Social Role in St. Petersburg, 1880–1914," in Geoffrey A. Hosking, ed., *Church, Nation and State in Russia and Ukraine* (London: Macmillan; New York: St. Martin's Press, 1991), 180ff.; for early Christian practice, see Dix, *Shape of the Liturgy,* 437.

84. See, among others, the descriptions in The State Museum of Ethnography (Gosudarstvennyi Muzei Etnografii; hereafter GME), Rukopisnyi otdel, f. 7 (Tenishev), op. 1, d. 1439, l. 11; d. 1436, l. 40. See also the discussion in Marina Gromyko, *Mir russkoi derevni* (Moscow: Molodaia Gvardiia, 1991), 126–29.

85. See S. I. Smirnov, *Drevne-russkii dukhovnik: Izsledovanie po istorii tserkovnago byta* (Moscow, 1913), 255–83 ("Ispoved' zemlie"). See also the prayers read on Trinity Sunday Vespers, which include the words "and against thee, Mother Earth, I have sinned with my soul and body" (Evgenii Golubinskii, *Istoriia russkoi tserkvi,* 4 vols. [Moscow, 1880–1907], 2:399–400).

86. GME, f. 7, op. 1, d. 1739, l. 9; d. 1101, l. 1.

87. Gromyko, *Mir russkoi derevni,* 126.

88. V. M., *Dva dnia v Kronshtadte,* 69. The familiarity of Orthodox formulae such as this one and the extent to which people unconsciously identified with them, however, is also evident here from the use of the word "our."

89. Cf. Edmund Heier, *Religious Schism in the Russian Aristocracy, 1860–1900* (The Hague: Nijhoff, 1970), 12–14.

90. V. M., *Dva dnia v Kronshtadte,* 70.

91. Vasilii Rozhnov, *Proroki i chudotvortsy: etiudy o mistitsizme* (Moscow: Politizdat, 1977), 88.

92. V. M., *Dva dnia v Kronshtadte,* 60.

93. Aleksandr Serebrov, *Vremia i liudi: vospominaniia, 1898–1905* (Moscow: Moskovskii rabochii, 1960), 33.

94. V. M., *Dva dnia v Kronshtadte,* 69–70.

95. Levitskii, *Prot. Ioann Il'ich Sergiev Kronshtadtskii,* 23.

96. Arkhiv Ustnoi Istorii Rossiiskogo Gosudarstvennogo Gumanitarnogo Universiteta, fond Pskovskoi ekspeditsii, l. 6. Max Weber made a similar argument in discussing the high emotions characterizing the hearing of a mass or the witnessing of a mystical play which did not however translate into any increased personal moral responsibility (*The Sociology of Religion* [Boston: Beacon Press, 1964], 152).

97. Archpriest Valentin Sventitsky, *Six Lectures on the History of the Mystery of Repentance: Against General Confession* (Jordanville, N.Y.: Printshop of St. Job of Pochaev/Holy Trinity Monastery, 1996), 46.

98. Popov, *Nezabvennoi pamiati,* 31.

99. Bishop A. Semenov-Tian-Shanskii, in V. A. Desiatnikov, comp., *Ioann Kronshtadtskii* (Moscow: "Patriot," 1992), 292.

100. Boutry and Cinquin, *Deux Pèlerinages,* 147.

Chapter 3

1. The State Archive of the Russian Federation (hereafter GARF), f. 1067, op. 1, d. 4, l. 1a ob. The quote is from 2 Corinthians 8:14–15.

2. Ibid., d. 4, l. 98.

3. For Varvara A. Shkliarevich's work among these suburban poor, see "Mirskaia

chernitsa," *Khristianin*, December 1907, in Pavel Novgorodskii, comp., *Raiskie tsvety s russkoi zemli* (Sergiev Posad, 1912), 283–90.

4. GARF, f. 1067, op. 1, d. 23, l. 144ob. For a description of the social tensions in Kronstadt, see the account of Hieromonk Mikhail (Semenov), *Otets Ioann Kronshtadtskii: Polnaia biografiia s illustratsiiami* (St. Petersburg, 1903), 38.

5. GARF, f. 1067, op. 1, d. 3, l. 29ob.

6. Ibid., d. 3, l. 91.

7. Ibid., d. 4, l. 38.

8. Ibid., d. 14, l. 14 (1874); d. 3, l. 8.

9. Ibid., d. 4, l. 75. The words Father Ioann uses here—*milovat'*, *milostynia*, *pomiluite*—share a common etymology. See Vladimir I. Dal', *Poslovitsy russkago naroda: sbornik poslovits, pogovorok, rechenii, prislovii, chistogovorok, pribautok, zagadok, poverii, i proch* (Moscow, 1862), 2: 231.

10. Tikhon (Zadonskii), "On the Duties of the Rich and Poor," in *Sochineniia*, 15 vols. (St. Petersburg: tip. Ivana Glazunova, 1825–26), 1:173.

11. Mikhail Bakunin, *God and the State* (New York: Dover Publications, 1970), 75. This would change by the turn of the century. See Jennifer Hedda, "Pastoral Care and Social Activism in the Russian Orthodox Church, 1880–1905" (Ph.D. diss., Harvard University, 1998).

12. GARF, f. 1067, op. 1, d. 14, l. 77.

13. Ibid., d. 12, l. 1a.

14. Ibid., d. 14, l. 47.

15. Ibid, d. 9, l. 57ob.

16. See I. N. Ukhanova, ed., *Khudozhestvennoe Ubranstvo Russkogo Inter'era XIX Veka: Ocherk-Putevoditel'* (Leningrad: Iskusstvo, 1986), esp. chap. 2, "Istorizm. 1830–1880-e gg."

17. See especially "Khram i Dvorets," in Aleksandr Shamaro, *Delo Igumenii Mitrofanii* (Leningrad: Lenizdat, 1990), 135–89; and Helena Goscilo, "Keeping A-Breast of the Waist-land: Women's Fashion in Early-Nineteenth-Century Russia," in Helena Goscilo and Beth Holmgren, eds., *Russia, Women, Culture* (Bloomington: Indiana University Press, 1996), 47–52.

18. GARF, f. 1067, op. 1, d. 12, l. 50. For the scope of construction and architectural trends in mid–nineteenth-century Petersburg, see Andrei L'vovich Punin, *Arkhitektura Peterburga serediny XIX veka* (Leningrad: Lenizdat, 1990), esp. chap. 1, "Ot klassitsizma k eklektike." Father John supported *church* construction, of course; government incentives did as well. See A. V. Krasko, "Kupecheskaia Blagotvoritel'nost' v Peterburge XIX-nach. XX v. (na primere sem'i kuptsov Eliseevykh)," in "Sikh zhe pamiat' prebyvaet vo veki (Memorial'nyi aspekt v kul'ture russkogo pravoslaviia)," Materialy nauchnoi konferentsii, 29–30 noiabria 1997 g. (St. Petersburg: Rossiiskaia Natsional'naia Biblioteka/Fond po izuchenii istorii pravoslavnoi tserkvi vo imia Svt. Dmitriia Rostovskogo, 1997), 114.

19. GARF, f. 1067, op. 1, d. 3, l. 78; emphasis mine.

20. Compare to the ideas of Sergei Bulgakov described in Bernice Glatzer Rosenthal, "The Search for a Russian Orthodox Work Ethic," in Edith W. Clowes et al., eds., *Between Tsar and People: Educated Society and the Quest for Public Identity in Late Imperial Russia* (Princeton: Princeton University Press, 1991), 57–74.

21. Dal', *Poslovitsy*, 601.

22. Vasilii O. Kliuchevskii, "Dobrye Liudi Drevnei Rusi," public lecture given at a benefit for victims of a bad harvest; reprinted in his *Tserkov' i Rossiia: Tri Lektsii* (Paris: YMCA Press, 1969), 64.

23. *Pribableniia k Tserkovnym Vedomostiam*, no. 1 (1909), quoted in T. A. Sokolova,

comp. and ed., *Sviatoi Pravednyi Ioann Kronshtadtskii—Sbornik* (Moscow: Novator, 1998), 35–36.

24. See Nikolai Dobroliubov, "The Organic Development of Man in Connection with His Mental and Spiritual Activities," in his *Selected Philosophical Essays* (Moscow: Foreign Languages Publishing House, 1948), 72–103.

25. Compare to a similar progression in the case of Fedor Rtishchev, who moved from almsgiving to founding two hospitals. Kliuchevskii, "Dobrye Liudi," 81.

26. GARF, f. 1067, op. 1, d. 14, l. 91.

27. Ibid.

28. A. Nikolaevskii, *Velikii pastyr' zemli russkoi* (Munich: Izd. V. Prostetovskii, 1948) p. 27.

29. GARF, f. 1067, op. 1, d. 14, l. 1.

30. The Russian State Historical Archive (herafter RGIA), f. 796, op. 174, d. 743, l. 1; Georgii Apollonovich Gapon, *Zapiski Georgiia Gapona Ocherk rabochago dvizheniia v Rossii 1900-kh godov* (Moscow, 1918), 45–46.

31. The Central State Historical Archive of St. Petersburg (hereafter TsGIA SPb), f. 2219, op. 1, d. 1, l. 79.

32. See Prot. Theodor van der Voort, "Praktika i Bogoslovie Blagotvoritel'nosti v Russkoi Pravoslavnoi Tserkvi," in N. A. Pecherskaia, comp., *Pravoslavnoe Bogoslovie i Blagotvoritel'nost' (diakoniia), Sbornik statei* (St. Petersburg: Vysshaia religiozno-filosofskaia shkola, 1996), 123.

33. An average of 22,600 people per year worked in the House. The workshop offered a four-year training program in sewing and dress-making, with students keeping whatever money they earned. For a description of the House's services, see V. M. [Arkhiepiskop Evdokim (Meshcherskii)], *Dva dnia v Kronshtadte, iz dnevnika studenta* (Sergiev Posad, 1902), 172–94; and Adele Lindenmeyr, *Poverty Is Not a Vice: Charity, Society, and the State in Imperial Russia* (Princeton: Princeton University Press, 1996), 170–74.

34. Mme. Rimsky-Korsakov was presented with an icon on October 19, 1892, with thanks from Father Ioann for her ten years of service in the House; see TsGIA SPb, f. 2219, op. 1, d. 26, l. 141. For a discussion of women's involvement in charity in late imperial Russia, see Lindenmeyr, *Poverty Is Not a Vice*, 13–16, 125–29; and Brenda Meehan-Waters, "From Contemplative Practice to Charitable Activity: Russian Women's Religious Communities and the Development of Charitable Work," in Kathleen McCarthy, ed., *Lady Bountiful Revisited: Women, Philanthropy, and Power* (New Brunswick, N.J.: Rutgers University Press, 1990), 142–56.

35. GARF, f. 1067, op. 1, d. 23, l. 2ob.

36. See, for example, TsGIA SPb, f. 2219, op. 1, d. 13, l. 57–58.

37. GARF, f. 1067, op. 1, d. 23, l. 71.

38. See such notebook entries as "From November 25 to December 4, I was in Moscow on a leave of absence to raise money for the DT." Ibid, d. 23, l. 122.

39. RGIA, f. 1574, op. 2, ed. khr. 708, ll. 81–82.

40. GARF, f. 1067, op. 1, d. 23, l. 38ob.

41. For receipts from 1889–1908, see TsGIA SPb, f. 2219, op. 1, d. 22.

42. For fundraising letters from 1874 to 1908, see ibid, d. 47.

43. Cf. I. V. Preobrazhenskii, *Novyi i traditsionnyi: dukhovnye oratory oo. Grigorii Petrov i Ioann Sergiev (Kronshtadtskii). Kriticheskii etiud* (St. Petersburg, 1902).

44. Letter of January 30, 1907, in TsGIA SPb, f. 2219, op. 1, d. 47, l. 118.

45. The Duma reference is to the policy of resettling have-nots and vagrants in Kronstadt that began in the 1850s. Zaccheus was the tax-collector for the Roman authorities

who repented and told Jesus Christ he would recompense the people from whom he had unfairly extorted money (see Luke 19:8). GARF, f. 1067, op. 1, d. 23, l. 16.

46. Ibid., d. 13, l. 37ob.
47. Ibid., d. 12, l. 61.
48. Ibid., d. 13, l. 65ob; emphasis in original.
49. Ibid., d. 11, l. 26.
50. Ibid., d. 13, l. 71.
51. Father John also blamed his primary school education: "My being intimidated and bullied, and because of the cruel way some of the older students and teachers treated me"; for his "losing faith in himself and thinking too highly of others." GARF, f. 1067, op. 1, d. 24, l. 40 (1896). For clerical education in Russia, see Nikita P. Giliarov-Platonov, *Iz perezhitago: avtobiograficheskie vospominaniia*, 2 vols. (Moscow, 1886–87), 1:39–46, 97–106; Laurie Manchester, "Secular Ascetics: Russian Orthodox Clergymen's Sons in Secular Society, 1861–1917" (Ph.D. diss., Columbia University, 1995), 241–385. For religious education in general, see Ben Eklof, *Russian Peasant Schools: Officialdom, Village Culture, and Popular Pedagogy, 1861–1914* (Berkeley and Los Angeles: University of California Press, 1986), esp. 40–42, 155–76 ("The Church Parish School").
52. See the students' reminiscences in Nikolai I. Bol'shakov, *Istochnik zhivoi vody. Opisanie zhizni i deiatel'nosti otsa Ioanna Kronshtadtskago* (St. Petersburg, 1910; repr. Izd. "Tsarskoe Delo," 1995), 76–102.
53. GARF, f. 1067, op. 1, d. 23, l. 3.
54. Max Weber develops this idea in *The Sociology of Religion* (Boston: Beacon Press, 1964), 44–46.
55. Simon Dixon, "The Church's Social Role in St. Petersburg, 1880–1914," in Geoffrey A. Hosking, ed., *Church, Nation and State in Russia and Ukraine* (New York: St. Martin's Press, 1991), 180ff; Hegumen Chariton of Valamo, comp., *The Art of Prayer, An Orthodox Anthology* (London: Faber and Faber, 1973), 264–70.
56. GARF, f. 1067, op. 1, d. 1, l. 66. Note Father John's use of the word *cathedra* for himself, normally used to apply exclusively to bishops.
57. Ibid., d. 3, l. 102ob.
58. Ibid., d. 4, l. 30.
59. Ibid., d. 10, l. 58. Father John thought that such translation projects ought to begin with the octoechos, or book of eight tones, that was the cornerstone of daily vespers and matins Orthodox services.
60. Ibid., d. 10, l. 65ob.
61. Ibid., d. 9, l. 58ob.
62. Ibid., d. 11, l. 16ob. The reference is to Psalm 50.
63. Ibid., d. 10, l. 74ob.
64. One woman, for example, confessed that she went to weddings and listened to music. TsGIA SPb, f. 2219, op. 1, d. 31, l. 121.
65. GARF, f. 1067, op. 1, d. 9, l. 74ob. Iurii Lotman and Boris Ouspensky have argued that the absence of purgatory in Orthodox doctrine contributed to the dual, or binary, worldview of eighteenth-century Russians (Iurii M. Lotman and Boris A. Ouspensky, "Binary Models in the Dynamics of Russian Culture to the end of the Eighteenth Century," in Alexander D. Nakhimovsky and Alice Stone Nakhimovsky, eds., The *Semiotics of Russian Cultural History* [Ithaca: Cornell University Press, 1985], 30–66). As Eve Levin pointed out to me, however, the lack of Purgatory does not necessarily lead to dualism, and suggests seventeenth-century sermons as a better antecedent (personal communication, 1998).

66. GARF, f. 1067, op. 1, d. 8, l. 15.

67. See the descriptions of contemporaries in Dmitrii A. Zasosov and Vladimir I. Pyzin, *Iz zhizni Peterburga 1890-1910kh godov* (Leningrad: Lenizdat, 1991), esp. 116–28.

68. GARF, f. 1067, op. 1, d. 11, l. 3ob. The reference (*prilozhi im zla, Gospodi; prilozhi zla slavnym zemli*) is to Psalm 54:5 and the verses read by the priest at the Bridegroom services of Holy Week.

69. GARF, f. 1067, op. 1, d. 14, l. 80; emphasis mine. This accusation—that the white clergy knew its flock intimately while the black clergy was removed from its concerns and realities—was central to the tensions between the parish clergy and the monks who made up the episcopate. See Gregory L. Freeze, *The Parish Clergy in Nineteenth Century Russia: Crisis, Reform, Counter-Reform* (Princeton: Princeton University Press, 1983), 123–25.

70. GARF, f. 1067, op. 1, d. 11, l. 16ob.

71. Ibid., d. 15, l. 81; emphasis in original.

72. Hugh Seton-Watson, *The Russian Empire 1801-1917* (Oxford: Clarendon Press, 1967), 184.

73. GARF, f. 1067, op. 1, d. 3, l. 3.

74. Nikolai Iv. Novikov, *Istoziia o nevinnom zatochenii boiarina A. S. Matvieeva* (Moscow, 1776); Nadejda Gorodetzky, *Saint Tikhon of Zadonsk: Inspirer of Dostoyevsky* (Crestwood, N.Y.: St. Vladimir's Seminary Press, 1976).

75. GARF, f. 1067, op. 1, d. 10, l. 37ob. Although not as extremely as under Paul I, in the late 1860s the way men dressed still reflected accurately their employment and station in life. See T. T. Korshunova, *Kostium v Rossii XVIII-nachala XX veka: iz sobraniia Gosudarstvennogo Ermitazha* (Leningrad: Khudozhnik RSFSR, 1979).

76. The phrase "our common holy life" again suggests that Father John is linking himself and the Orthodox Church to the people, setting all apart from the intelligentsia. GARF, f. 1067, op. 1, d. 9, l. 36ob.

77. Aleksandr Semenoff-Tian-Shanskii explains Father John's indifference to secular art by his background—nature and direct contemplation of the divine would serve the function music and painting did for others (*Otets Ioann Kronshtadtskii* [New York: Izd. A. Chekhova, 1955], 188). Compare to L. N. Tolstoy's *What Is Art?*, ed. Gareth Jones (Bristol: Bristol Classical Press, 1994).

78. GARF, f. 1067, op. 1, d. 26, l. 54ob.

79. By the end of the 1860s, he was mapping out how he might emulate the prophets. See Ibid., d. 14, l. 42.

80. Ibid., d. 14, l. 42ob.

81. Ibid., d. 10, l. 43ob.

82. The Russian equivalent to the carnival period of Mardi Gras is the week (known as *Maslenitsa*, or Butter-Week) before Great Lent. It was the custom in some areas to wear masks and cross-dress in the period between Christmas and Theophany (*sviatki*, December 25–January 6). This incident from the 1870s is quoted in the reminiscences of Levitskii, *Protoierei Ioann*, 6–7.

83. See the account in E. N. Sumarokov, "Starchestvo i pervye Optinskie startsy," in *Starets Makarii Optinskii* (Kharbin: Bratstvo im. s. Ioanna Bogoslova, 1940), 52–78.

84. See, for example, TsGIA SPb, f. 2219, op. 1, d. 8, l. 52; d. 12, ll. 22 and 55; d. 14, l. 29ob, 40ob; d. 23, ll. 31–31ob.

85. Ibid., d. 23, l. 63ob.

86. Ibid., d. 23, l. 156.

87. Ibid., d. 9, l. 73.

88. Ibid., d. 13, l. 50ob.
89. Ibid., d. 14, l. 70ob.
90. Entry of March 16, 1881, in ibid., d. 23, l. 2.
91. Ibid., d. 23, l. 12ob.
92. Leskov depicted the sensitivity of the social implications in receiving a priest's blessing in *Soboriane*, when the priggishly anticlerical Termosesov suddenly reached for the astounded Father Savelii's hand—and then betrayed his ignorance by approaching the deacon Akhilla for another blessing—when only those with the rank of priest or higher were supposed to give them (Nikolai S. Leskov, *Soboriane* [New York: Izd. Im. Chekhova, 1952], 231–32. Similarly, Father Savelii had no intention of greeting the local noblewoman Plodomasova with anything other than a bow; she had to request his blessing and herself moved to kiss his hand "which he had in every wise sought to avoid" (57–58).
93. GARF, f. 1067, op. 1, d. 12, l. 1.
94. Ibid., d. 13, l. 51ob.
95. Ibid., d. 8, l. 67ob.
96. Ibid., d. 13, l. 67ob.
97. Ibid., d. 12, l. 61ob.
98. For a discussion of the implications of the status differences between "tserkovnosluzhiteli" and "sviashchennosluzhiteli," see Freeze, *Parish Clergy in Nineteenth-Century Russia*, 155–64.
99. GARF, f. 1067, op. 1, d. 13, l. 51ob; d. 14, l. 84. Most interesting here is Father John's sense that the "audience" had its own perception of his lines that ran counter to his own.
100. Ibid., d. 23, l. 162.
101. Ibid., d. 13, l. 51ob; d. 14, l. 84.
102. Ibid., d. 12, l. 39ob.
103. Ibid., d. 3, l. 85 (1857).
104. Ibid., d. 10, l. 28a.
105. Ibid., d. 23, l. 56.
106. Ibid., d. 10, l. 1a ob.
107. Ibid., d. 9, l. 20ob.

Chapter 4

1. Evgenii Golubinskii, *Istoriia kanonizatsii sviatykh v russkoi tserkvi* (Moscow, 1903), 11–15.
2. "Beseda s Sarapul'skimi pastyriami," *Tserkovnye Vedomosti*, no. 39, 1904; reprinted in Aleksandr Nikolaevich Strizhev, comp. and ed., *Sviatoi Pravednyi Ioann Kronshtadtskii v Vospominaniiakh Samovidtsev* (Moscow: Izd. Otchii dom, 1997), 16.
3. V. M. [Arkhiepiskop Evdokim (Meshcherskii)], *Dva dnia v Kronshtadte, iz dnevnika studenta* (Sergiev Posad, 1902), 301.
4. The Central State Historical Archive of St. Petersburg (hereafter TsGIA SPb), f. 2219, op. 1, d. 12, l. 9.
5. Ibid, d. 13, l. 48.
6. Ibid, d. 14, l. 65ob.
7. See Peter Brown, *The Cult of the Saints: Its Rise and Function in Latin Christianity* (Chicago: University of Chicago Press, 1982), 113–20.
8. Cf. Claude Lopez-Ginisty, *A Dictionary of Orthodox Intercessions* (Liberty, Tenn.:

St. John of Kronstadt Press, 1997), 3–5. For analogous Muslim traditions, see Fatima Mernissi, "Women, Saints, and Sanctuaries," *Signs* 3 (1977): 101–12.

9. Vasilii O. Kliuchevskii, *Drevnerusskie zhitiia sviatykh, kak istoricheskii istochnik* (Moscow, 1871), 361, 417–23, 438.

10. TsGIA SPb, f. 2219, op. 1, d. 9v, l. 335; d. 9g, ll. 4, 12, 21.

11. See John Hutchinson, *Politics and Public Health in Revolutionary Russia, 1890–1918* (Baltimore: Johns Hopkins University Press, 1990).

12. Stephen Wilson, ed., *Saints and Their Cults: Studies in Religious Sociology, Folklore, and History* (Cambridge: Cambridge University Press, 1987), 18–21.

13. This figure includes not only TsGIA SPb, f. 2219, op. 1, dd. 9a–e, labeled explicitly as "Letters for healing," but all those in which a request for healing is made (for example, a letter classified as "letters from nuns" may ask for healing; a letter asking for money may also ask as an afterthought for respite from chronic asthma).

14. Letter of April 3, 1901, in TsGIA SPb, f. 2219, op. 1, d. 19a, l. 127ob. For attitudes to "women's diseases," see Vladimir Zhuk, *Mat' i Ditia. Gigiena v obshchedostupnom izlozhenii*, 9th ed. (St. Petersburg, 1911), 16–18, 63–68.

15. Compare to the teachings of the Manichaeans and other dualistic sects in Dimitri Obolensky, *The Bogomils: A Study in Balkan Neo-Manichaeism* (Cambridge: Cambridge University Press, 1948), 1–27.

16. TsGIA SPb, f. 2219, op. 1, d. 9g, l. 210.

17. Ibid., d. 9e, l. 228.

18. Ibid., d. 9g, l. 227.

19. Ibid., d. 9g, l. 304.

20. Ibid., d. 9a, l. 130; emphasis mine.

21. Ibid., d. 9a, ll. 149ob.

22. Ibid., d. 9g, ll. 23, 244, 178. For clerical recognition of cursing's power, see "Materinskoe prokliatie" (Pavlograd, 1866), in *Rasskazy sel'skikh sviashchennikov o divnykh iavleniiakh milosti Bozhiei i groznykh sud'bakh Ego* (Moscow and Riga: Blagovest, 1996), 74–75.

23. TsGIA SPb, f. 2219, op. 1, d. 15, ll. 87, 231.

24. Ibid., d. 11, l. 188.

25. Cf. Charles Stewart, *Demons and the Devil: Moral Imagination in Modern Greek Culture* (Princeton: Princeton University Press, 1991), 38–39; Sergei Maksimov, *Nechistaia, nevedomaia, i krestnaia sila* (St. Petersburg, 1903).

26. TsGIA SPb, f. 2219, op. 1, d. 9d, l. 38.

27. Letter of April 20, 1901, in ibid., d. 9b, ll. 70–70ob. The only woman to do so wrote a confession rather than a letter.

28. Simon Dixon, "The Church's Social Role in St. Petersburg, 1880–1914," in Geoffrey A. Hosking, ed., *Church, Nation and State in Russia and Ukraine* (New York: St. Martin's Press, 1991), 178–84.

29. Father John's pamphlets against drinking include *"Imeiushchie ushi, slushaite!" Slovo protiv p'ianstva* (St. Petersburg, 1902; repr. 1996); *Probudites' pianitsy! i plach'te, vse p'iushchie vino!* (St. Petersburg, 1910); *O dushepagubnom p'ianstve, maternom slove, i tabakokurenii* (St. Petersburg, 1915; repr. 1995).

30. TsGIA SPb, f. 2219, op. 1, d. 15, l. 48; emphases mine.

31. Yannick Ripa, *Women and Madness: The Incarceration of Women in Nineteenth-Century France* (Minneapolis: University of Minnesota Press, 1990), 73.

32. TsGIA SPb, f. 2219, op. 1, d. 15, ll. 271, 273.

33. Ibid., d. 15, l. 259; d. 11, l. 229.

34. For a discussion of the phenomenon, see Ripa, *Women and Madness*, esp. 31–79. However, in 1840s Germany, Griesinger argued that women were incarcerated in greater numbers not because of their departing from culturally conditioned norms, but because everyone socially inferior, uneducated, and poor was more likely to go insane and hence more likely to be committed (Klaus Dörner, ed., *Madmen and the Bourgeoisie: A Social History of Insanity and Psychiatry* (Oxford: Blackwell, 1981), 26, 284. Compare this to Laura Engelstein's argument for the Russian specificity of other sorts of female "deviance" (*Keys to Happiness: Sex and the Search for Modernity in Fin-de-Siècle Russia* [Ithaca: Cornell University Press, 1994], 96–127).

35. V. E. Rozhnov, *Proroki i chudotvortsy: etiudy o mistitsizme* (Moscow: Politizdat, 1977), 83–85; P. B. Gannushkin, "Sladostrastie, zhestokost' i religiia," in *Izbrannye trudy* (Moscow: Politizdat, 1964), 80–94.

36. Priests were instructed to identify those not going to confession and communion for possible sectarian membership. See I. S. Belliustin, *Description of the Clergy in Rural Russia The Memoir of a Nineteenth-Century Parish Priest* (Ithaca: Cornell University Press, 1985), 176; Gregory L. Freeze, *Parish Clergy in Nineteenth-Century Russia: Crisis, Reform, Counter-Reform* (Princeton: Princeton University Press, 1983), 7.

37. TsGIA SPb, f. 2219, op. 1, d. 12b, part II, l. 123.

38. Ibid., d. 9d, l. 223.

39. Letter of January 29, 1902, in ibid., d. 9b, l. 135.

40. Ibid., d. 9b, l. 237. Barbara Alpern Engel explores some of the reasons the father-in-law was favored in *Between the Fields and the City: Women, Work, and Family in Russia, 1861–1914* (Cambridge: Cambridge University Press, 1994), 20–21.

41. For an Orthodox perspective on the place of doctors in the healing process, and on holy doctors, see Heinz Skrobucha, *The Patrons of the Doctors* (Recklinghausen: Aurel Bongers, 1967), 5–18.

42. Letter from Dr. Sheveleva on behalf of Maria Baranova, in TsGIA SPb, f. 2219, op. 1, d. 9b, l. 63.

43. See, for example, ibid., d. 9g, ll. 44, 46, 48, 87, 146, 192, 212, 219, 227, 246, 333–34.

44. Ibid., d. 26, ll. 130–31.

45. Ibid., d. 9g, l. 367.

46. Letter of January 14, 1897, in ibid., 9a, ll. 107ob.

47. Ibid., d. 19a, l. 246; emphasis mine.

48. Ibid., d. 60, ll. 1–3. See I. K. Surskii, *Otets Ioann Kronshtadtskii*, 2 vols. (Belgrade, 1938–41; reprt. Forestville: St. Elias Publications, 1979–80), 1: 245–46. The claim that Father Ioann had raised the dead was recalled in the context of Alexander III's illness (Surskii, *Otets Ioann Kronshtadtskii*, 1: 107). For the "resurrection" of people taken for dead, see Mitrofan (Monk), *Kak zhivut nashi umershie i kak budem zhit' i my po smerti*, 6th ed. (St. Petersburg, 1897), 97–99.

49. K. M. Saltykov, *Intimnyi Shchedrin* (Moscow-Petrograd: Gosudarstvennoe Izdatel'stvo, 1923), 20–23.

50. Rozhnov, *Proroki i chudotvortsy*, 105–6.

51. Brown, *Cult of the Saints*, 113–20.

52. Letter of May 10, 1898, TsGIA SPb, f. 2219, op. 1, d. 13a, ll. 72ob–73.

53. Ibid., d. 9a, ll. 90ob–91ob.

54. Letter of 1892 in ibid., d. 19a, ll. 23–24.

55. See mostly literate letter from Maria, ibid., d. 9d, ll. 28–28ob.

56. Undated letter and letters of September 22, 1906 and August 8, 1908, in ibid., d. 11, ll. 190, 117, 133.

57. Ibid., d. 11, ll. 117, 127, 288.
58. Ibid., d. 9a, l. 148.
59. Letter from Pavel Gozovchenko, ibid, d. 9a, ll. 32–33.
60. Ibid., d. 26, l. 2.
61. Ibid., d. 26, ll. 1, 32, 42, 82; Andrei Maylunas and Sergei Mironenko, *A Lifelong Passion: Nicholas and Alexandra, Their Own Story* (London: Weidenfeld & Nicolson, 1996), 109.
62. Robert D. Wrath, "Before Rasputin: Piety and the Occult at the Court of Nicholas II," *The Historian* 47, no. 3 (May 1985): 323–37.
63. See the discussion in Andrei Amalrik, *Raspoutine* (Paris: Seuil, 1982), 57.
64. Variations of this version appear in Robert Massie, *Nicholas and Alexandra* (London: Pan Books Ltd., 1968), 219; Colin Wilson, *Rasputin and the Fall of the Romanovs* (London: A. Barker, 1964), 51–54; Wrath, "Before Rasputin," 324; Amalrik, *Raspoutine*.
65. Massie, *Nicholas and Alexandra*, 221.
66. Amalrik, *Raspoutine*, 57, 78.
67. For such incidents, see Ioann Il'ich Sergiev, *Pis'ma o. prot. Ioanna k nastoiatel'nitse Ioanno-Predtechenskago Leushinskago pervoklassnago Monastyria Igumenii Taisii* (St. Petersburg, 1909), 14, 30, 37, 54, 72, 73.
68. The 1900 incident is reported in V. M., *Dva dnia v Kronshtadte*, 73–74.
69. The only verifiable occasion when this occurred was when the officer in question, Pavel Ivanovich Plikhankov, later became the saintly Optina elder Varsonofii. See *Zhitiia Prepodobnykh Startsev Optinoi Pustyni* (Jordanville, N.Y.: Holy Trinity Monastery, 1992), 268–300.
70. Aron Simanovich, *Rasputin i evrei: vospominaniia lichnogo sekretaria Grigoriia Rasputina* (Moscow: "Sovetskii pisatel"; Riga: "Orient," 1991), esp. 8–16; Maylunas and Mironenko, *Lifelong Passion*, entry of 1 November 1905, p. 284. But see M. V. Rodzianko, *Le Règne de Raspoutine* (Paris: Payot, 1927), 20–23; J. W. Bienstock, *Raspoutine: La Fin d'un Régime* (Paris, 1917), 96–105.
71. Wrath, "Before Rasputin," 324–30.
72. TsGIA SPb, f. 2219, op. 1, d. 26, l. 100; letter of October 20, 1893 in Maylunas and Mironenko, *Lifelong Passion*, 31. The Grand Duke was assassinated in 1905.
73. TsGIA SPb, f. 2219, op. 1, d. 13ob, l. 101.
74. Metropolitan Anthony (Khrapovitsky), *Confession: A Series of Lectures on the Mystery of Repentance* (trans. of Warsaw, 1928 ed.) (Jordanville, N.Y.: Holy Trinity Monastery, 1983), 31–32. For a hostile contemporary assessment of educated women's "excessive, morbid" religiosity, see Aleksandr Amfiteatrov, *Zhenshchina v obshchestvennykh dvizheniiakh Rossii* (Geneva, 1905), 13.
75. Letter of January 27, 1891, in TsGIA SPb, f. 2219, op. 1, d. 24, l. 30.
76. Ibid., d. 24, l. 27.
77. For a discussion of lotteries in the 1890s, see F. A. Brokgauz and I. A. Efron, *Entsiklopedicheskii slovar'*, tom XVIII (St. Petersburg, 1896), 27–29.
78. TsGIA SPb, f. 2219, op. 1, d. 24, ll. 17, 35.
79. Ibid., d. 26, l. 118.
80. Ibid., d. 26, l. 120; emphasis mine.
81. Letter of February 1903 in Ibid., d. 1, l. 20. For an examination of the uses of the potentially revolutionary content of the Bible, see Reginald E. Zelnik, "'To the Unaccustomed Eye': Religion and Irreligion in the Experience of St. Petersburg Workers in the 1870s," in Robert P. Hughes and Irina Paperno, eds., *Christianity and the Eastern Slavs*, vol. 2: *Russian Culture in Modern Times* (Berkeley and Los Angeles: University of

California Press, 1994), 49–82; for a study of workers' religious identity, see Page Herrlinger, "The Religious Identity of Workers and Peasant Migrants in St. Petersburg, 1880–1917" (Ph.D. diss., University of California at Berkeley, 1996). For "naïve monarchism" turned to the purposes of rebellion, see Daniel Field, *Rebels in the Name of the Tsar* (Boston: Houghton Mifflin, 1976).

82. Bol'shakov, *Istochnik Zhivoi Vody. Opisanie zhizni i deiatel'nosti otsa Ioanna Kronshtadtskago* (St. Petersburg, 1910; repr. Izd. "Tsarskoe Delo," 1995), 214.

83. TsGIA SPb, f. 2219, op. 1, d. 28, ll. 1–2; d. 12b, part II, l. 132.

84. See, for example, ibid., d. 28, ll. 5, 12; see also letter from Aleksandra Fidelina, ll. 45–46; emphasis mine.

85. Ibid., d. 28, l. 30.

86. Letter of November 15, 1905, in ibid., d. 28, l. 32.

87. Ibid., d. 28, l. 55.

88. Ibid., d. 24, l. 22; emphasis mine.

89. Letter of April 25, 1901, in ibid., d. 26, l. 42.

90. Sergei Hackel, ed., *The Byzantine Saint* (London: Fellowship of St. Alban and St. Sergius, 1981), 127.

91. TsGIA SPb, f. 2219, op. 1, d. 28, l. 53. For the wretched conditions on Sakhalin, see Anton Chekhov, *Ostrov Sakhalin: (Iz putevykh zapisok), Polnoe Sobranie Sochinenii i pisem, Sochineniia: v. 14–15* (Moscow: Nauka, 1978); George Kennan, *Siberia and the Exile System*, vol. 2 (New York, 1891), 548–51.

92. TsGIA SPb, f. 2219, op. 1, d. 48, l. 17.

93. Ibid., d. 48, ll. 100–102; emphases mine.

94. Ibid., d. 48, l. 27.

95. Letter of April 14, 1903, in ibid., d. 52, ll. 2–2ob.

96. Arkhimandrit Avgustin (Nikitin), *Pravoslavnyi Peterburg v Zapiskakh Inostrantsev* (St. Petersburg: too "Zhurnal NEVA," 1995), 184–89.

97. They are concentrated in TsGIA SPb, f. 2219, op. 1, dd. 12a–12d.

98. Ibid., d. 31, l. 193ob. The letter paraphrases Psalm 37, read at the beginning of Matins.

99. Ibid., d. 31, l. 250; emphasis mine.

100. See, for example, a daughter's plaint in ibid., d. 19b, l. 142.

101. Ibid., d. 15, l. 110; emphases mine. The last sentence quotes Matthew 15:27.

102. Ibid., d. 19b, l. 162. For incidents describing the salvific benefits of abandoning one's family, see "Rab Bozhii Ioann," *Dushepoleznoe Chteniie* (July–August 1904), in Pavel Novgorodskii, comp., *Raiskie tsvety s russkoi zemli* (Sergiev Posad, 1912), 78–92.

103. TsGIA SPb, f. 2219, op. 1, d. 19a, ll. 98ob–99.

104. See Brenda Meehan, *Holy Women of Russia: The Lives of Five Orthodox Women Offer Spiritual Guidance for Today* (Crestwood, N.Y.: St Vladimir's Seminary Press, 1997), 38.

105. N. A. Minenko, "Stariki v russkoi krest'ianskoi obshchine," quoted in Marina Gromyko, *Mir russkoi derevni* (Moscow: Molodaia Gvardiia, 1991), 149. The point is also made in the discussion of the Apostles' fast in Ivan Shmelev, *Leto Gospodne: Prazdniki, Radosti, Skorbi* (New York: "Put' zhizni," n.d.), 210.

106. TsGIA SPb, f. 2219, op. 1, d. 12b, part II, l. 161.

107. Ibid., d. 7g, l. 93.

108. Ibid., d. 7g, l. 439. For an analysis of the factors behind the idealization of the tsars, and the way in which this idealization was constructed and represented, see Richard S. Wortman, *Scenarios of Power: Myth and Ceremony in Russian Monarchy*, vol. 2 (Princeton: Princeton University Press, 1998).

109. TsGIA SPb, f. 2219, op. 1, d. 7g, l. 277.
110. Ibid., d. 26, ll. 87–90.
111. See Thomas Kselman, *Miracles and Prophecies in Nineteenth-Century France* (New Brunswick, N.J.: Rutgers University Press, 1983), 60–83.
112. "'Progressivnoe techenie' v akademicheskom bogoslovii. Protopresviter Ioann Ianyshev," in Metropolitan Ioann (Snychev), *Ocherki istorii Sankt-Peterburgskoi eparkhii* (St. Petersburg: "Andreev i synov'ia," 1994), 191–97.
113. Laurie Manchester, "The Secularization of the Search for Salvation: The Self-Fashioning of Orthodox Clergymen's Sons in Late Imperial Russia," *Slavic Review* 57, no. 1 (spring 1998): 50–76. Letters in TsGIA SPb, f. 2219, op. 1, d. 7b, l. 217; d. 7g, l. 270.
114. Taisiia (Nun), *Russkoe pravoslavnoe zhenskoe monashestvo XVIII–XX vekov* (Jordanville, N.Y.: Holy Trinity Monastery, 1985), 5.
115. See Jill Dubisch, "Greek Women: Sacred or Profane?" *Journal of Modern Greek Studies*, no. 1 (1983): 185–202.
116. [Protopresviter] Georgii Iv. Shavel'skii, *Vospominaniia posledniago presvitera russkoi armi i flota* (New York: Izd. Chekhova, 1954; repr. Moscow: Krutitskoe Patriarshee Podvor'e, 1996), 2: 156–75.
117. Bol'shakov, *Istochnik zhivoi vody*, 614–73. Father John sought outside funding for his convents, just as he did for the House of Industry. See his approach of Vladimir K. Sabler in *Pis'ma o. prot. Ioanna*, 38–39.
118. TsGIA SPb, f. 2219, op. 1, d. 7g, ll. 94, 98, 148.
119. For a thorough discussion of the problems, see Abbess Thaisia, *Abbess Thaisia: The Autobiography of a Spiritual Daughter of St. John of Kronstadt* (Platina, Calif.: St. Herman of Alaska Brotherhood Press, 1989), 155–58.
120. See V. Shustin, *Zapis' ob o. Ioanne Kronshtadtskom i ob Optinskikh startsakh iz lichnykh vospominanii* (Vladimirovo: tip. Iova Pochaevskago, 1929), and Nikon (Beliaev), *Dnevnik poslednego startsa Optinoi pustyni ieromonakha Nikona (Beliaeva)* (St. Petersburg: Satis, 1994), 99, 134.
121. Compare, for example, TsGIA SPb, f. 2219, op. 1, d. 7v, ll. 57–58 to d. 7v, l. 206.
122. Letter of March 29, 1905, in ibid., d. 7v, l. 241; d. 7v, l. 275; d. 7a, l. 265.
123. Letter of April 23, 1903, in ibid, d. 7a, l. 290.
124. Letter of August 13, 1897, in ibid., d. 21, l. 5.
125. Ibid., d. 41, l. 58; d. 21, ll. 12, 7.
126. Ibid., d. 21, ll. 17, 18, 25, 31, 39.
127. See, for example, the snide comment in *Poslednii samoderzhets, Ocherk zhizni i tsarstvovaniia imperatora Rossii Nikolaia II* (Berlin, 1911), 39. For photographs of Father John in sumptuous *riasas*, see Elizaveta Shelaeva and Liudmila Protsai, *Rus' pravoslavnaia* (St. Petersburg: Liki Rossii; Moscow: Dzhuliia, 1993), 202, 205.
128. May 16, 1897 letter from Nikolai Garskii, in TsGIA SPb, f. 2219, op. 1, d. 7b, l. 234. For Father John's will, see The Russian State Historical Archive (hereafter RGIA), f. 799, op. 6, d. 30 (Khoziaistvennago Upr. pri sv. Sinode, otd. I, stol I, no. 177a), ll. 2–3.
129. See an example of a sponsored memorial meal in Adele Lindenmeyr, *Poverty Is Not a Vice: Charity, Society, and the State in Imperial Russia* (Princeton: Princeton University Press, 1996), 220.
130. Letter of August 30, 1901, in TsGIA SPb, f. 2219, op. 1, d. 21, l. 19.
131. V. O. Kliuchevskii, *Tserkov' i Rossiia: Tri Lektsii* (Paris: YMCA Press, 1969), 64–65.
132. One wealthy man even reported that, when a monk asked him to donate money for a monastery, Father John told him, "You should give it to me for the poor instead." Surskii, *Otets Ioann Kronshtadtskii*, 2: 214.

133. Letter of February 18, 1904, in TsGIA SPb, f. 2219, op. 1, d. 41, ll. 19–20.
134. Letter of February 27, 1905, in ibid., d. 41, l. 21.
135. Ibid., d. 21, l. 110. Nicholas II received so many gifts that he finally decided to forbid people to present him with anything expensive. See "O prekrashchenii tsennykh podnoshenii Ikh Imperatorskikh Velichestv i zamene takovykh pozhertvovaniiami na blagotvoritel'nye i vsiakie drugiia obshchestvennyia uchrezhdeniia," *Sankt-Peterburgskii Dukhovnyi Vestnik*, no. 21 (May 23, 1897): 73.
136. The State Archive of the Russian Federation (hereafter GARF), f. 1067, op. 1, d. 26, l. 10. The potential awkwardness of such passages was not lost on others. In commenting on a similar passage, Leskov wrote, "One could hardly dream up anything more wretched and vulgar." The Russian State Archive of Literature and Art (hereafter RGALI), f. 275, op. 1, d. 830, l. 15.
137. *Prelest'*, or delusion, in the spiritual sense ought not be confused with the more conventional usage of the word (charm, fascination). See Grigorii Diachenko, comp., *Polnyi tserkovno-slavianskii slovar'*, 2 vols. (Moscow, 1899), 1:486.
138. GARF, f. 1067, op. 1, d. 26, l. 50.
139. The point is made repeatedly by the Orthodox Fathers and Mothers. See Igumen of Valamo Chariton, comp., *The Art of Prayer: An Orthodox Anthology* (London: Faber and Faber, 1973), 111–12, 116, 132–37, 261–63.
140. GARF, f. 1067, op. 1, d. 23, l. 132ob.
141. Ibid., d. 24, l. 88ob; emphasis mine.
142. Ibid., d. 24, l. 109ob.
143. See the discussion in Timothy Ware, *The Orthodox Church* (New York: Penguin Books, 1986), 283–86.
144. On the growing rates of communion, see GARF, f. 1067, op. 1, d. 24, ll. 93ob–94; d. 26, l. 18.
145. Letter dated August 28, 1900, in TsGIA SPb, f. 2219, op. 1, d. 12b, pt. II, l. 66.
146. GARF, f. 1067, op. 1, d. 26, ll. 7ob, 52ob.
147. Ibid., d. 26, l. 12.
148. Ibid., d. 26, ll. 55–55ob.
149. Ibid., d. 26, l. 26. Father John shared the Orthodox belief that sinning after having recently partaken of the divine was a profanation. See *Molitvoslov* (Kiev, 1881), 174–75.
150. GARF, f. 1067, op. 1, d. 23, l. 144ob.
151. See the description of such an encounter in V. M., *Dva dnia v Kronshtadte*, 195–97.
152. GARF, f. 1067, op. 1, d. 23, l. 146ob.
153. Ibid., d. 23, l. 155.
154. bid., d. 26, l. 9. For attitudes on corporal punishment, see Dmitrii N. Zhbankov, *Tielesnyia nakazaniia v Rossii v nastoiashchee vremia* (Moscow, 1899).
155. GARF, f. 1067, op. 1, d. 12, l. 68ob.
156. Ibid., d. 14, l. 23.
157. Ibid., d. 26, l. 9 (1892).
158. Ibid., d. 26, l. 50 (1893).
159. Ibid., d. 24, l. 126.
160. Quoted in V. M., *Dva dnia v Kronshtadte,* 209–10. An earlier trip to Kiev had gone far more smoothly. I. A. S-kii, *Otets Ioann Il'ich Sergiev Kronshtadtskii i ego prebyvanie v Kieve* (Kiev, 1893), 24–26.
161. Surskii, *Otets Ioann Kronshtadtskii*, 67.
162. GARF, f. 1067, op. 1, d. 26, l. 19.

163. See, for example, GARF, f. 1067, op. 1, d. 14, ll. 16ob, 19ob.
164. Ibid., d. 23, l. 162ob. The reference is to Jeremiah 5:27–28.
165. Ibid., d. 24, l. 54; d. 26, l. 9.
166. Ibid., d. 24, l. 92ob. Although priests' wives tended to go to church less frequently than their husbands or their children, Elizaveta Konstantinovna's sporadic attendance was exceptional.
167. R. G. Shemiakina, *Svetloi pamiati pochivshei suprugi o. Ioanna Kronshtadtskago Elizavety Konstantinovny Sergievoi* (Kronstadt, 1909), 3–12.

Chapter 5

1. "Cult" here is used in the sense of "[d]evotion or homage to a particular person, place, or thing," as in *The Compact Edition of the Oxford English Dictionary* (New York: Oxford University Press, 1985), 1: 1246.
2. *Novoe Vremia*, no. 2807 (December 20, 1883): 3.
3. V. Orlov, *Tri dukhovnykh khora* (Moscow, 1896), in V. M. [Arkhiepiskop Evdokim (Meshcherskii)], *Dva dnia v Kronshtadte, iz dnevnika studenta* (Sergiev Posad, 1902), 163.
4. For a discussion of the "Son Bogoroditsy" and "Khozhdenie Bogoroditsy" themes, see G. Fedotov, *Stikhi dukhovnye. Russkaia narodnaia vera po dukhovnym stikham* (Moscow: Progress/Gnozis, 1991), 21–23, 49–57.
5. For a discussion on battling superstition, see N. G. Petrushevskii, "O religiozno-nazidatel'nom chtenii dlia prostago naroda," *Rukovodstvo dlia sel'skikh pastyrei*, no. 30 (1883): 326–34.
6. Letter of 1890 quoted in V. M., *Dva dnia v Kronshtadte*, 451.
7. Ibid., 450–51.
8. See Eve Levin, "Supplicatory Prayers as a Source for Popular Religious Culture in Muscovite Russia," in Samuel H. Baron and Nancy Shields Kollmann, eds., *Religion and Culture in Early Modern Russia and Ukraine* (De Kalb: Northern Illinois University Press, 1997), 96–114. The requirement to pass a prayer to others is reminiscent of the St. Jude's Novena of modern Roman Catholic tradition. See Robert A. Orsi, *Thank You, Saint Jude: Women's Devotion to the Patron Saint of Hopeless Causes* (New Haven: Yale University Press, 1996), 103.
9. V. M., *Dva dnia v Kronshtadte*, 450.
10. See the discussion in Chapter 7 of the police file in The State Archive of the Russian Federation (hereafter GARF), f. 102, 4 delopr., d. 154 (I), ll. 18–50.
11. T. G. Morozova et al., eds., *V. G. Korolenko v vospominaniiakh sovremennikov* (Moscow: Goslitizdat, 1962), 458–59.
12. For examples, see Vyacheslav Mukhin, *The Church Culture of Saint Petersburg* (St. Petersburg: Ivan Fyodorov Publishers, 1994), 134, 149; for a discussion of icon decoration generally, see I. A. Sterligova, "O liturgicheskom smysle dragotsennago ubora drevnerusskoi ikony," in A. M. Lidov, ed., *Vostochnokhristianskii khram: liturgiia i iskusstvo* (St. Petersburg: Dm. Bulanin/Tsentr vostochno-khristianskoi kul'tury, 1994), 220–29.
13. For a description of Father Ioann's collection of vestments and other gifts of clothing and ornament, se V. M., *Dva dnia v Kronshtadte*, 160–63. For a representation of a "living rule," see Kathryn Hulme, *The Nun's Story* (Boston: Little, Brown, 1956), 6, 39, 128–29.
14. For a study of ex-votos, see Stephen Wilson, "Cults of Saints in the Churches of Central Paris," in Wilson, *Saints and Their Cults: Studies in Religious Sociology, Folklore,*

and History (Cambridge: Cambridge University Press, 1987), esp. 239–57; see also the discussion in A. A. Panchenko, *Issledovaniia v oblasti narodnogo pravoslaviia. Derevenskie sviatyni severo-zapada Rossii* (St. Petersburg: Izd. "Aleteia," 1998), 94–95, 155.

15. For Ars and La Salette, see Philippe Boutry and Michel Cinquin, *Deux Pelerinages au XIXe Siecle, Ars et Paray-le-Monial*, Bibliotheque Beauchesne, 8 (Paris: Editions Beauchesne, 1980); for Lourdes, Barbara Corrado Pope, "Immaculate and Powerful: The Marian Revival in the Nineteenth Centiry," in Clarissa W. Atkinson et al., eds., *Immaculate and Powerful: The Female Sacred Image and Social Reality* (Boston: Beacon Press, 1985), 55–79.

16. See a letter from one hostel-manager complaining that another woman named Evdokia Leont'ievna bribed cab-drivers with wine to drive pilgrims to her establishment, regardless of what address they gave (The Central State Historical Archive of St. Petersburg [hereafter TsGIA SPb], f. 2219, op. 1, d. 26, l. 15). For additional details, see the memoirs of (Priest) V. Il'inskii, in S. L. Firsov, comp. and ed., *Sviatoi Ioann Kronshtadtskii v vospominaniiakh sovremennikov* (Moscow: Pravoslavnyi Sviato-Tikhonovskii Bogoslovskii Institut, Bratstvo vo Imia Vsemilostivogo Spasa, 1994), 104; Aleksandr Serebrov, *Vremia i liudi: vospominaniia, 1898–1905* (Moscow: Moskovskii rabochii, 1960), 37–38, and E. K., *Vospominaniia ob otse Ioanne* (St. Petersburg, 1909), 4.

17. These "azhidatsii" were satirized in Nikolai Leskov, "Polunoshchniki," in his *Sobranie Sochinenii v odinadtsati tomakh*, vol. 9 (Moscow: Godsudarstvennoe Izdatel'stvo Khudozhestvennoi Literatury, 1958), 117–28.

18. For the tensions between hostel managers and pilgrims, see E. K., *Vospominaniia*, 11, 17.

19. A. M. Plotitsa, *O. Ioann Kronshtadtskii. Ego mnenie ob inovertsakh i inostrantsakh (iz dnevnika vracha)* (Moscow, 1915), 7, 11–14, 22–23.

20. For letters to and about Pertsova, see TsGIA SPb, f. 2219, op. 1, d. 26, ll. 11, 13, 78, et al.; and the comments of K. M. Saltykov, "M. E. Saltykov (Shchedrin) i o. Ioann Kronshtadtskii," in Firsov, *Sviatoi Ioann*, 151. Pertsova was also accused of doctoring Father John's will; see The Russian State Historical Archive (hereafter RGIA), f. 799, op. 6, d. 30, ll. 2–5; and A. I. Vitovich, "Zapiski sudebnago pristava po okhranitel'noi opisi imushchestva o. Ioanna Kronshtadtskago," *Golos minuvshago*, no. 5 (1915): 159–83.

21. Letter from Margarita Iannovmaia, in TsGIA SPb, f. 2219, op. 1, d. 26, l. 12.

22. Reminiscences of Maria Makeeva, in RGIA, f. 834, op. 4, ed. khr. 1668, ll. 9, 12. Jealousy may play a part: Pertsova is defended by Bishop Arsenii in *Vospominaniia*, 164–65.

23. See an undated letter from Evdokia, who compares herself to Judas for her sin of spending donations earmarked for Father John, even as she adds that does so because she cannot live without money. TsGIA SPb, f. 2219, op. 1, d. 26, l. 21. For the layout of the Dom, see G. Rozhalin, "Vospominaniia o Poezdke v Kronshtadt 26 Maia 1906 goda," in Firsov, *Sviatoi Ioann Kronshtadtskii*, 76–79.

24. Undated letter in TsGIA SPb, f. 2219, op. 1, d. 40, l. 20.

25. Plotitsa, *O. Ioann Kronshtadtskii*, 24.

26. See Leskov's discussion in The Russian State Archive of Literature and Art (hereafter RGALI), f. 275, op. 1, d. 830, l. 15, and E. K., *Vospominaniia*, 33.

27. For a description and reproductions of the cards, see V. M., *Dva dnia v Kronshtadte*, 75–81; Nikolai I. Bol'shakov, *Istochnik zhivoi vody. Opisanie zhizni i deiatel'nosti otsa Ioanna Kronshtadtskago* (St. Petersburg, 1910; repr. St. Petersburg: Izd. "Tsarskoe Delo," 1995), 173; V. A. Desiatnikov, comp., *Ioann Kronshtadtskii* (Moscow: "Patriot," 1992), unpaginated center insert.

28. The problem was approached from a number of perspectives. See Robert L. Nichols,

"The Icon and the Machine in Russia's Religious Renaissance, 1900–1909," in William C. Brumfield and Milos M. Velimirovic, eds., *Christianity and the Arts in Russia* (New York: Cambridge University Press, 1991), 131–44; Alevtina A. Mal'tseva, in *The Russian Icon of Late XVIII–XIX ss.* (St. Petersburg: "Kinocentre/Limbus Press," 1994), 7–8.

29. Father Ioann craved such signs of recognition, although he reproached himself for the desire. See RGIA, f. 1067, op. 1, d. 4, l. 94; d. 8, l. 63ob. For a comparison with the West, see Peter Bander van Duren, *Orders of Knighthood and of Merit: The Pontifical, Religious, and Secularised Catholic-founded Orders and their relationship to the Apostolic See* (New York: Gerrards Cross, Buckinghamshire: C. Smythe, 1995). For examples of postcards, from this period, see V. M., *Dva dnia v Kronshtadte*, 108, 142, 370, and Desiatnikov, *Ioann Kronshtadtskii*, unpaginated section of photographic reproductions.

30. See M. Didron, *Manuel d'Iconographie Chrétienne Grecque et Latine* (Paris, 1845), 455–56; A. S. Kravchenko, comp., *Ikona* (Moscow: Vek Rossii/Style A Ltd., 1993), 73–78.

31. Cover photo of Andrei Amalrik, *Raspoutine* (Paris: Seuil, 1982).

32. See the photographs of Father Ioann on the "Liubeznyi" and the "Otvazhnyi," V. M., *Dva dnia v Kronshtadte*, 207, 213.

33. Ibid., 403, 434.

34. For the Synodal decision, see RGIA, f. 796, op. 176, ed. khr. 3498, l. 1. For enamels, see Mukhin, *Church Culture*, 106, 108–9.

35. Observed at Porfiriia Kiseleva's by Aleksandr Serebrov, in Serebrov, *Vremia i liudi*, 39.

36. See Leskov's disparaging comments on the practice in L. N. Tolstoi, *Perepiska s russkimi pisateliami* (Moscow: Gosudarstvennoe Izdatel'stvo Khudozhestvennoi Literatury, 1962), 245.

37. "Ob uporiadochenii proizvodstva i prodazhy ikon i prochikh sviashchennykh izobrazhenii," *Sankt-Peterburgskii Dukhovnyi Vestnik*, no. 43 (24 October 1897), 844.

38. For the case, see RGIA, f. 796, op. 176, ed. khr. 3107, ll. 1–3.

39. One of the first such incidents occurred in 1895. See RGIA, f. 796, op. 175, ed. khr. 2017, 2 st., 3 otd., ll. 1–4.

40. For a discussion of the treatment of religion in the press from 1881 to 1895, see B. P. Valuev, *Politicheskaia reaktsiia 80kh godov XIX veka i russkaia zhurnalistika* (Moscow: Izd. Moskovskogo Universiteta, 1971), 172.

41. Nikolai Rerikh (Roerich), "Ne bolei! Listy dnevnika," in Desiatnikov, *Ioann Kronshtadtskii*, 363.

42. Nikolai Lisovoi, "Volia k spaseniiu," in Desiatnikov, *Ioann Kronshtadtskii*, 378–79; emphasis mine.

43. M. O. Menshikov, "Pamiati sviatogo pastyria," in Desiatnikov, *Ioann Kronshtadtskii*, 360–61. Menshikov has himself been recently "rehabilitated" in Russia. See the introduction by M. B. Pospelov to M. O. Menshikov, *Iz pisem k blizhnim* (Moscow: Voennoe izdatel'stvo, 1991), 3–14.

44. Vasilii Rozanov, "Russkoe Sektantstvo, kak 3 kolorita russkoi tserkovnosti," *Novoe Vremia*, no. 10594 (August 30–September 12, 1905): 4.

45. The fall of a formerly great ascetic appears regularly in the lives of the saints, but see in particular the life of "Stephana, a Man who fell into filthy Wantonness," in Ernest A. Wallis Budge, trans. and ed., *The Paradise or Garden of the Holy Fathers* (London, 1907; repr. Seattle: St. Nectarios Press, 1984), 260–62. The assessment at the end is plain: "Now the things which happened to Stephana took place because he separated himself from the brotherhoood, and because he was [unduly] exalted in his mind, and because he imagined that he was perfect."

46. Mary Jane Rossabi, "Peasants, Peddlers, and Popular Prints in Nineteenth-century Russia," in *Bulletin of Research in the Humanities* 87, no. 4 (1986–87), 418–30.

47. See Jeffrey Brooks, *When Russia Learned to Read: Literacy and Popular Literature, 1861–1917* (Princeton: Princeton University Press, 1985), esp. 306–11.

48. Contemporary scholars recognized the problems of typology and borrowing. See the discussion in Arsenii Kadlubovskii, *Ocherki po istorii drevne-russkoi literatury Zhitii Sviatykh* (Warsaw, 1902), vii–ix, 327–73.

49. I. K. Surskii, *Otets Ioann Kronshtadtskii*, 2 vols. (Belgrade, 1938–41; reprt. Forestville: St. Elias Publications, 1979–80), 1: 249–51. This argument is in line with Golubinskii's thesis in *Istoriia kanonizatsii sviatykh v russkoi tserkvi* (Moscow, 1903).

50. "Zhitie sviatogo pravednogo Ioanna, Kronshtadtskogo chudotvortsa," *Zhurnal Moskovskoi Patriarkhii*, no. 10 (1990), 58–71; Bychkov, *Zhizneopisaniia dostopamiatnykh liudei zemli russkoi X–XXvv.* (Moscow, 1992), 285–95.

51. [Arkh. Averkii, ed.] *Zhitie sviatago pravednago otsa nashego Ioanna Kronshtadtskago chudotvortsa, ko dniu proslavleniia 19 oktiabria 1964 goda* (Jordanville, N.Y.: Holy Trinity Monastery, 1964).

52. Firsov, *Sviatoi Ioann Kronshtadtskii*, 8.

53. Menshikov, in Desiatnikov, *Ioann Kronshtadtskii*, 359; Surskii, *Otets Ioann Kronshtadtskii*, 1: 83ff.

54. Archbishop Averkii, *Zhitie*, 7.

55. For these images, see Bol'shakov, *Istochnik zhivoi vody*, 45, 47, 48; Desiatnikov, *Ioann Kronshtadtskii*, unpaginated insert; V. M., *Dva dnia Kronshtadte*, 77–80, 250.

56. For the rise of travel writing in the mid-nineteenth century, see Andrew Durkin, "A Guide to Guides: Writing About Birds in 19th-Century Russia," and Christoper David Ely, "The Origins of Russian Scenery: Volga River Tourism and Russian Landscape Aesthetics," unpublished papers presented at American Association for the Advancement of Slavic Studies (AAASS) Conference, November 16, 1996.

57. Ierom. Mikhail (Semenov), *Otets Ioann Kronshtadtskii: Polnaia biografiia s illiustratsiiami* (St. Petersburg, 1903), 227, 255, 257. For an analysis of postcard subjects, see T. I. Geidor et al., *Russkii gorod na pochtovoi otkrytke kontsa XIX-nachala XX veka* (Moscow: Russkaia kniga, 1997), 6–30.

58. See the argument of Otto Boele, *The North in Russian Romantic Literature* (Amsterdam-Atlanta, Ga.: Rodopi, 1996). Earlier vitae of North Russian and Siberian saints also often include nature descriptions, however.

59. Aleksandr Semenoff-Tian-Shanskii, *Otets Ioann Kronshtadtskii* (New York: Izd. A. Chekhova, 1955), 4–5.

60. S. V. Zhivotovskii, *Na sever s otsom Ioannom Kronshtadtskim* (St. Petersburg, 1903; 2d ed., with new foreword by Metr. Antonii. [Khrapovitskii], New York: Eparkhial'noe izd., 1956), 71.

61. Boris Zaitsev, "Ioann Kronshtadtskii," in Desiatnikov, *Ioann Kronshtadtskii*, 353.

62. Ioann Il'ich (prot.), Sergiev, *Moia zhizn' vo Khriste, ili minuty dukhovnago trezveniia i sozertsaniia, blagoveinago chustva, dushevnago ispravleniia i pokoia v Boge. Izvlecheniia iz dnevnika*, 2 vols. (Moscow, 1894), 2: 43.

63. Henri Daniel-Rops, *Ces Chrétiens, Nos Frères* (Paris: Fayard, 1965), 486–87; Dom Antoine Stark, *Le Père Jean de Cronstadt, archiprêtre de l'Eglise russe, son ascétisme, sa morale. "Ma vie en Jésus-Christ,"* 2d ed. (Paris, 1902–3).

64. Mikhail, *Otets Ioann Kronshtadtskii*, 4–16; Bishop Alexander, *Father John of Kronstadt: A Life* (Crestwood, N.Y.: St. Vladimir's Seminary Press, 1979), 4–5.

65. See the discussion by G. P. Fedotov, "Tragediia drevnerusskoi sviatosti," *Put'*, in

Imperiia i svoboda (New York: Posev-ssha, 1989), 113. See also the depictions of Sergii's closeness to birds, bears, etc., in lithographs by Mikhail Gadalov, in *The Venerable Sergius of Radonezh in Works of Russian Art 15th–19th Centuries*. Catalogue, The Exhibition from the Collection of the State History and Art Museum-Reserve in Sergius Posad (Moscow, 1992), illus. nos. 68, 69–70, 77.

66. See Ivan Shmelev, *Leto Gospodne: Prazdniki, Radosti, Skorbi* (New York: "Put' zhizni," n.d.), 100–110; Marina Gromyko, ed., *Mir russkoi derevni* (Moscow: Molodaia Gvardiia, 1991), 345–60.

67. Guides to sermons contain almost exclusively examples by bishops. See M. A. Potorzhinskii, comp., *Obraztsy Russkoi Tserkovnoi Propovedi XIX veka* (Kiev, 1912).

68. Semenoff-Tian-Shanskii, *Otets Ioann Kronshtadtskii*, 3.

69. Prot. Sergii Bulgakov, *Avtobiograficheskiia zametki. Posmertnoe izdanie* (Paris: YMCA Press, 1946), 16–17.

70. I. Kniagnitskii, "Poezdka v Kronstadt," *Istoricheskii Vestnik* 80, no. 5 (1900): 632–44; emphases mine.

71. Surskii, *Otets Ioann Kronshtadtskii*, 1:39.

72. Examples of this pattern are found in N. N. Zhivotov, *P'ianitsy u o. Ioanna Kronshtadtskago* (Moscow, 1895), 8ff.

73. The contemporary Baedeker's ranked "Donon" and "Pivato" as first-class: "très bons, mais assez chers" (K. Baedeker, *La Russie, manuel du voyageur* (Leipzig, 1893), 86.

74. V. M., *dnia v Kronshtadte*, 110; emphasis mine.

75. Cf. Aleksandr Parmenov, "Proslavleniie pravednogo Ioanna," in *Zhurnal Moskovskoi Patriarkhii*, no. 10 (1990): 9.

76. V. M., *Dva dnia v Kronshtadte*, 111.

77. Ibid., 112–13.

78. See esp. Surskii, *Otets Ioann Kronshtadtskii*, 2: 30–359; Bol'shakov, *Istochnik zhivoi vody*, 350–416.

79. V. M., *Dva dnia v Kronshtadte*, p. 292.

80. *Biografiia o. Ioanna Kronshtadtskago* (St. Petersburg, 1895), 63–65.

81. V. M., *Dva dnia v Kronshtadte*, p. 123.

82. Zhivotov, *P'ianitsy*, 29.

83. Zhivotovskii, *Na sever*, 70.

84. Arkhiepiskop Nikon (Rklitskii), *Dukhovnyi oblik sv. pravednogo protoiereiia Ioanna Kronshtadtskogo chudotvortsa* (New York: All-Slavic Publishing House, 1965), 7.

85. Bishop Alexander, *Father John*, 3.

86. Zhivotovskii, *Na sever*, 71.

87. V. M., *Dva dnia v Kronshtadte*, 12–15, 19, 441.

88. Nikolai Lisovoi, "Volia k spaseniiu," in Desiatnikov, *Ioann Kronshtadtskii*, 367.

89. See, for example, the lives of Theodosius and Sergius, in Serge Zenkovsky, *Medieval Russian Epics, Chronicles, and Tales* (New York: E. P. Dutton, 1974), 116–34, 262–90.

90. This emerges particularly clearly in Konstantin [Zaitsev], *Dukhovnyi oblik prot. o. Ioanna Kronshtadtskago* (Jordanville, N.Y.: Holy Trinity Monastery, 1952), 42–43. For a discussion of patterns of clerical membership in the nineteenth century, see Manchester, "Secular Ascetics: Russian Orthodox Clergymen's Sons in Secular Society, 1861–1917," (Ph.D. diss., Columbia University, 1995), 422–28; Gregory L. Freeze, *The Parish Clergy in Nineteenth-Century Russia: Crisis, Reform, Counter-Reform* (Princeton: Princeton University Press, 1983), 144–45.

91. Arnaldo Momigliano, "The Life of Saint Macrina by Gregory of Nyssa," in his *On Pagans, Jews, and Christians* (Hanover, Conn.: Wesleyan University Press, 1987), 206–11.

92. Mikhail, *Otets Ioann Kronshtadtskii*, 4–10.
93. Konstantin, *Dukhovnyi oblik*, 43.
94. See, for example, Surskii, *Otets Ioann Kronshtadtskii*, 1:23.
95. Ibid, 22; Bol'shakov, *Istochnik zhivoi vody*, 34; Bishop Alexander, *Father John*, 7–8.
96. For a fuller discussion of trends in Russian hagiography, see Kadlubovskii, *Ocherki po istorii drevne-russkoi literatury Zhitii Sviatykh*, i–ix, 327–73.
97. Zenkovsky, *Medieval Russian Epics*, 391–99.
98. Vasilii Rozanov contributed most to the topic. See the impassioned clerical-intelligentsia debate in *Zapiski Peterburgskikh Religiozno—Filosofskikh sobranii (1902–1903 gg.)* (St. Petersburg, 1906), 50–56, 295–362.
99. For sectarian rejections of physical relations, see Chapter 6; for Solov'ev, see "Smysl liubvi," in *Smysl Liubvi: Izbrannye Proizvedeniia* (Moscow: Sovremennik, 1991), 125–82.
100. See Dyan Elliott, *Spiritual Marriage: Sexual Abstinence in Medieval Wedlock* (Princeton: Princeton University Press, 1993), 3–93. See also André Vauchez, "The Virginal Marriage of Elzéar and Delphine" and "Conjugal Chastity: A New Ideal in the Thirteenth Century," in his *The Laity in the Middle Ages: Religious Beliefs and Devotional Practices* (Notre Dame and London: University of Notre Dame Press, 1993), 185–90, 191–203.
101. See, for example, Petr Suratov, *Sviatyi pravednyi Otets Ioann, Kronshtadtskii Chudotvorets* (Petit Clamart (Seine): P. Suratov, 1965), 3; Archimandrite Panteleimon, *Zhizn', podvigi, chudesa i prorochestva sviatago pravednago otsa nashego Ioanna, Kronshtadtskago Chudotvortsa* (Jordanville, N.Y.: Holy Trinity Monastery, 1976), 5; and the official vita composed for his canonization in 1964: *Zhitie sviatago pravednago otsa nashego Ioanna, Kronshtadtskago Chudotvortsa* (Jordanville, N.Y.: Holy Trinity Monastery, 1964), 7.
102. The reference to the Apocalypse (John) 14:3–4 is made in Surskii, *Otets Ioann Kronshtadtskii*, 1: 23–24.
103. Semenoff-Tian-Shianskii, *Otets Ioann Kronshtadtskii*, 13; A. A. Sollogub, *Otets Ioann Kronshtadtskii, Zhizn', deiatel'nost', izbrannyia chudesa* (Jordanville, N.Y.: Holy Trinity Monastery, 1951), 5.
104. Sollogub, *Otets Ioann Kronshtadtskii*, 5.
105. For a sample ranging over decades, see TsGIA SPb, f. 2219, op. 1, d. 12, ll. 68, 70ob; d. 14, ll. 62ob, 67; d. 23, l. 15ob ff.
106. Different accounts of this incident appear in Surskii, *Otets Ioann Kronshtadtskii*, 1: 87–88; Bol'shakov, *Istochnik zhivoi vody*, 400–403.
107. Surskii, *Otets Ioann Kronshtadtskii*, 2: 356.
108. *Informatsionnyi Biulleten' fonda im. o. Ioanna Kronshtadtskago*, no. 10 (1963): 43.
109. Acts 13:9–11 reference in Surskii, *Otets Ioann Kronshtadtskii*, 1: 88; 1866 *Strannik* articles reprinted in *Rasskazy sel'skikh sviashchennikov o divnykh iavleniiakh milosti Bozhiei i groznykh sud'bakh Ego* (Moscow and Riga: Blagovest, 1996), 56–64, 92–96.
110. A rare example are the Bulla photographs (one is a group shot) in Elizaveta Shelaeva and Liudmila Protsai, *Rus' Pravoslavnaia* (St. Petersburg: Liki Rossii; Moscow: Dzhuliia, 1993), 203, 205.
111. "Slovo prot. o. Aleksandra Popova v pamiat' E. K. Sergievoi," in *Piatidesiatilietie*, 59–60. For the 1990 vita, see Parmenov, "Proslavleniie pravednogo Ioanna," 64.
112. See Aviad M. Kleinberg, *Prophets in Their Own Country: Living Saints and the Making of Sainthood in the Later Middle Ages* (Chicago: University of Chicago Press, 1992), 20, 40–70.

113. For the iconodule position at the Council of Nicaea, see Timothy Ware, *The Orthodox Church* (New York: Penguin Books, 1986), 40–43.

114. Cited in Konstantin, *Dukhovnyi oblik*, 60; emphases mine.

115. Ibid., 93.

116. See Leo Tolstoy, *The Gospel According to Tolstoy*, David Patterson, ed. and trans. (Tuscaloosa and London: University of Alabama Press, 1992).

117. Letter of December 27, 1901, in Sergiev, *Pis'ma o. prot. Ioanna*, 48.

118. Father John referred to Serafim in several of his early journals; see, for example, GARF, f. 1067, op. 1, d. 5, l. 11. For a discussion of Serafim's popularity, see Robert Nichols, "The Friends of God: Nicholas II and Alexandra at the Canonization of Serafim of Sarov, July 1903," in Charles E. Timberlake, ed., *Religious and Secular Forces in Late Tsarist Russia: Essays in Honor of Donald W. Treadgold* (Seattle and London: University of Washington Press, 1992), 206–29; Sapunov, "Nekotorye siuzhety russkoi ikonopisi i ikh traktovka v poreformennoe vremia," in *Kul'tura i iskusstvo Rossii XIX veka: novye materialy i issledovaniia: sbornik statei* (Leningrad: Iskusstvo, 1985), 147. But see Gregory L. Freeze, "Subversive Piety: Religion and the Political Crisis in Late Imperial Russia," *Journal of Modern History* 68 (June 1996): 314–29.

119. Nikanor, "Slovo ob o. Ioanne Kronshtadtskom," *Izvestiia po Kazanskoi Eparkhii*, no. 10 (March 8, 1909): 294.

120. Bol'shakov, *Istochnik zhivoi vody*, 148–55; Surskii, *Otets Ioann Kronshtadtskii*, 1: 26–27; Konstantin, *Dukhovnyi oblik*, 26; Bishop Alexander, *Father John*, 170.

121. See, for example, GARF, f. 1067, op. 1, d. 9, l. 20v.

122. Freeze, "Subversive Piety," 312–29.

123. Nikolai A. Rubakin, *Sredi tain i chudes* (Moscow: Politizdat, 1965), 203.

124. Quoted in Bishop Alexander, *Father John*, 6.

125. Schoolchildren in Russia began daily lessons with "The Prayer Before Education," which expressed the hope that one would would do well "for the consolation of our parents and for the benefit of our fatherland" (*Slavianskii ili Tserkovnyi bukvar'*, 28th. ed. [Kiev, 1908], 44). Father John's use of both stock phrases shows to what extent he internalized the many formulae placed at his disposal by the Orthodox Church, such as "the light of wisdom" from the Christmas troparion.

126. Surskii, *Otets Ioann Kronshtadtskii*, 1:21–22.

127. Brenda Meehan, *Holy Women of Russia: The Lives of Five Orthodox Women Offer Spiritual Guidance for Today* (Crestwood, N.Y.: St. Vladimir's Seminary Press, 1997), 4.

128. See Leskov's treatment of this mentality in "Odnodum," in vol. 6 of his *Sobranie Sochinenii*, 213. For Sergii's vision, see Zenkovsky, *Medieval Russia's Epics*, 264–65.

129. Surskii, *Otets Ioann Kronshtadtskii*, 1: 20; Abbess Thaisia, *Abbess Thaisia of Leushino: The Autobiography of a Spiritual Daughter of St. John of Kronstadt* (Platina, Calif.: St. Herman of Alaska Brotherhood Press, 1989), 38–42.

130. Earlier vitae do contain such visions. See, most notably, *The Venerable Sergius of Radonezh in Works of Russian Art 15th–19th Centuries* (Moscow, 1992), cat. no. 82.

131. Sapunov, "Nekotorye siuzhety," 148–49.

132. See Christoph Heilmann, ed., *Deutsche Romantiker: Bildthemen der Zeit von 1800 bis 1850*, catalogue, exhibition at Kunsthalle der Hypo-Kulturstiftung, June 14–September 1, 1985 (Munich: Kunsthalle der Hypo-Kulturstiftung, 1985), 141, 165, 207.

133. See the discussion of such stories, particularly the versions connected with Christmas, in Henryk Baran, "Religious Holiday Literature and Russian Modernism," in Robert P. Hughes and Irina Paperno, eds., *Christianity and the Eastern Slavs*, vol. 2: *Russian Culture in Modern Times* (Berkeley and Los Angeles: University of California Press, 1994), 201–44.

134. Father John had his first vision of Mary in his sleep on August 15, 1898, the feast of the Dormition. See Panteleimon, *Zhizn'*, 57.

135. Bishop Alexander, *Father John*, 7; Surskii, *Otets Ioann Kronshtadtskii*, 1:21–22.

136. Prot. Mikhail Pomazanskii, "Ocherk pravoslavnago mirosozertsaniia o. Ioanna Kronshtadtskago," in *Piatidesiatiletiie*, 68–70.

137. Mikhail, *Otets Ioann Kronshtadtskii*, 26; Bol'shakov, *Istochnik zhivoi vody*, 38–40; Surskii, *Otets Ioann Kronshtadtskii*, 1: 22; Alexander, *Father John*, 8.

138. See N. A. Smirnov, "Missionerskaia deiatel'nost tserkvi (Vtoraia polovina XIX v.- 1917 g.)," in A. I. Klibanov, ed., *Russkoe pravoslavie: vekhi istorii* (Moscow: Politizdat, 1989), 438–62.

139. See Paul D. Garrett, *St. Innocent: Apostle to America* (Crestwood, N.Y.: St. Vladimir's Seminary Press, 1979).

140. See Surskii, *Otets Ioann Kronshtadtskii*, 1:22.

141. Cf. his autobiography, in V. M., *Dva dnia v Kronshtadte*, 384–85.

142. Konstantin, *Dukhovnyi oblik*, 44.

143. The novella was first published as Nikolai S. Leskov, "Polunoshchniki; peizazh i zhanr," *Vestnik Evropy*, nos. 11–12 (November–December 1891), 92–137, 537–76.

144. RGALI, f. 275, op. 1, d. 830, l. 3. For a detailed study of Leskov's attitude to Father John, see Hugh McLean, "Leskov and Ioann of Kronstadt: On the Origins of *Polunoshchniki*," *American Slavic and East European Review* 12, no. 1 (February 1953): 93–108.

145. Leskov, "Polunoshchniki," 189–97.

146. Letter to Khilkov, RGALI, f. 275, op. 1, d. 830, ll. 1, 11.

147. Tolstoi, *Perepiska*, 228.

148. Ibid.

149. Letter of 6 December 1890, in ibid., 225.

150. Letter of August 1, 1890, in ibid., 246.

151. For a discussion of the phenomenon, see Peter Brown, "The Rise and Function of the Holy Man in Late Antiquity," *Journal of Roman Studies* 61 (1971), 80–101.

152. GARF, f. 1067, op. 1, d. 14, l. 40ob.

153. Ibid., d. 12, l. 68; d. 26, l. 29.

154. Konstantin, *Dukhovnyi oblik*, 25.

155. See the comments of Gregory L. Freeze in his introduction to I. S. Belliustin, *Description of the Clergy: The Memoir of a Nineteenth-Century Parish Priest*, trans. Freeze (Ithaca, N.Y.: Cornell University Press, 1985), 13–62. The Old Believer Archpriest Avvakum would be another charismatic but disruptive model.

156. Nikon, *Dukhovnyi oblik*, 51.

157. RGIA, f. 1082, op. 1, ed. khr. 37, l. 144; N. N. Esipov, comp., *Sviatitel' i Chudotvorets Arkhiepiskop Chernigovskii Feodosii Uglitskii* (St. Petersburg, 1897), 197–256.

158. *Bogoslovskii Vestnik* 2 (February 1908): 22.

159. RGIA, f. 777 (Ministry of the Interior Censorship Committee), op. 5, ed. khr. 7, ll. 3, 23; op. 4, ed. khr. 36, l. 13. This should not be pushed too far: some of the publications seem to have been banned only because of typographical errors. Even Imperial portraits were taken out of circulation if minor details were faulty.

160. See Savva's response of June 29, 1891, to the abbess of the convent of the Annunciation in Betetsk who wrote asking his blessing for Father John's visit. The Russian National Library, Otdel Rukopisei, f. 262, op. 14, d. 2, ll. 104–5. Father John took the comment to heart: on a visit to Vindava in 1900, he told the local priest that he would gladly give his flock Communion, but could not confess any of them, as they "belonged" to the priest. Reminiscences of Lieutenant-General D. A. Ozerov, in Firsov, *Sviatoi Ioann Kronshtadtskii*, 52.

161. Father John maintained that the matter, which concerned the hypostases of the

Holy Trinity, was the result of a simple typographical error. See GARF, f. 1067, op. 1, d. 26, l. 41ob.

162. See, for example, "Ob otse prot. Ioanne Il'iche Sergieve Kronshtadtskom po lichnym vospominaniiam," *Kurskie Eparkhial'nye Vedomosti*, no. 50 (December 1910): 549; Richard Batts and Viacheslav Marchenko, *Dukhovnik Tsarskoi Sem'i, sviatitel' Feofan Poltavskii (1874–1940)* (Platina, Calif.: St. Herman of Alaska Press; Moscow: Rossiiskoe otd. Valaamskago obshchestva Ameriki, 1994), 19.

163. Nikon, *Dukhovnyi oblik*, 52.

164. Quoted in Konstantin, *Dukhovnyi oblik*, 26. Although the original of this letter has not survived, Father John refers in his diaries to Feofan's recurrent criticism and his consequent antipathy for the Bishop. See GARF, f. 1067, op. 1, d. 26, l. 53, when he refers to Bishop Feofan as "a somewhat hostile and jealous person."

165. Different versions of their conversation are given in Anatolii Levitin-Krasnov, "Narodnye sviatye v Rossii, Otets Ioann Kronshtadtskii," *Cahiers du Monde russe et soviétique* 29, nos. 3–4 (July–December 1988): 455–70; Surskii, *Otets Ioann Kronshtadtskii*; and Ierom. Mikhail, *Otets Ioann Kronshtadtskii*. Pobedonostsev's objections actually stemmed from the *Novoe Vremia* publication, however, and he quickly determined that his initial suspicions of Father John were ungrounded. See his letters in A. Iu. Polunov, comp., "O. Ioann Kronshtadtskii i K. P. Pobedonostsev (1883)," *Reka Vremen*, no. 2 (1996): 88, 91.

166. Rev. Charles Mortimer Carty, *Padre Pio the Stigmatist*, 15th ed. (St. Paul, Minn.: Radio Replies Press, 1955), 14.

167. Alessandra Stanley, "Saint or No, an Old-Time Monk Mesmerizes Italy," *New York Times* (September 24, 1998), A4.

168. For a discussion of clerical perceptions of urban and rural piety, see Gregory L. Freeze, "'Going to the Intelligentsia': The Church and Its Urban Mission in Post-Reform Russia," in Edith W. Clowes, Samuel D. Kassow, and James L. West, eds., *Between Tsar and People: Educated Society and the Quest for Public Identity in Late Imperial Russia* (Princeton: Princeton University Press, 1991), 215–32. A similar argument was made by Liubov I. Emeliakh, *Antiklerikal'noe dvizhenie krestian v period pervoi russkoi revoliutsii* (Leningrad: Nauka, 1965).

169. Such phenomena were taken both by Slavophiles and subsequently by neo-Slavophiles as proof that the laity in Orthodoxy retained more of the organic role it played in early Christianity and patristic theology. Aleksei Khomiakov, for example, rejoiced at the Encyclical of the Eastern Patriarchs in 1848, which proclaimed that both the perpetuity of dogma and the purity of liturgy were entrusted not to the hierarchy alone, but to the entire people of the Church, who together made up the Body of Christ (see Edward Every, "Khomiakoff and the Encyclical of the Eastern Patriarchs in 1848," *Sobornost'*, series 3, no. 3 [summer 1948]: 102–4).

170. Surskii, *Otets Ioann Kronshtadtskii*, vol. 2, and *Piatidesiatilietie*, consist almost exclusively of lay accounts of Father John's intercession on their behalf.

171. Max Weber, *The Sociology of Religion* (Boston: Beacon Press, 1964), 47.

172. See Gustavo Gutiérrez, *A Theology of Liberation: History, Politics, and Salvation* (Maryknoll, N.Y.: Orbis Books, 1973).

Chapter 6

1. Particularly clear statements are to be found in V. F. Pustoshkin, *Tserkov' Khristova v opasnosti. Otpoved' Preosv. episkopu Filaretu, glavie Viatskoi eparkhii* (St. Petersburg,

1908); Nikolai I. Bol'shakov, *Lozhnaia zashchitnitsa pravoslaviia i "Chernye Vorony,"* supp. to no. 3 of *Kronshtadtskii Maiak* (St. Petersburg, 1908), and the journal *Kronshtadtskii Maiak*.

2. Typical of such approaches is T. I. Butkevich, *Obzor russkikh sekt i ikh tolkov* (Kharkov, 1910), 156–62. Church-connected publications also consistently drew a distinction (see *Kolokol*, no. 1054 [September 16, 1909]: 1]).

3. See, for example, *Sankt-Peterburgskie Vedomosti* (September 20, 1909): 2.

4. See, most notably, the Father Ioann selections in A. Ninov, comp. and intro., *Stikhotvornaia satira pervoi russkoi revoliutsii (1905–1907)* (Leningrad: Sovetskii pisatel', 1985), esp. 122–25.

5. For a discussion of the censorship's influence on religious publications, see G. S. Lialina, "Tsenzurnaia politika tserkvi v XIX-nachale XX veka," in A. I. Klibanov, ed., *Russkoe Pravoslavie: Vekhi Istorii* (Moscow: Nauka, 1989), 463–500.

6. Primary sources on the Ioannites survive in three main archival collections: The State Archive of the Russian Federation (hereafter GARF), f. 102 (Department of Police), 3 delopr., 3069 and 4 delopr. 1907, d. 154 ("Ob ioannitakh"); The Russian State Historical Archive (hereafter RGIA), f. 821, op. 133, ed. khr. 206 (previously Departament Dukhovnykh Del, d. 155) ("Ioannity"); and The Central State Historical Archive of St. Petersburg (hereafter TsGIA SPb), f. 569, op. 20, d. 344, sviazka 334 ("Ioannity").

7. Most such letters are in TsGIA SPb, f. 2219, op. 1, d. 38 (Perepiska ob ioannitakh, November 2, 1895–September 16, 1905).

8. For a characterization of the Church position, see statement of priest Nikolai Podosenov, TsGIA SPb, f. 569, op. 20, d. 344, sviazka 334, l. 238ob; for press statements, see "O sushchestvovanii sekty 'ioannitov,'" *Volzhsko-Kamskaia Rech'* (Kazan'), October 16, 1907, p. 5.

9. Letter of November 2, 1895, from priest Aleksii Solntsev, in TsGIA SPb, f. 2219, op. 1, d. 37, l. 1; letter of November 21, 1897, from priest Viktor Stavrov, Astrakhan gub., in ibid, d. 7g, l. 1.

10. Nikolai I. Bol'shakov, *Pravda o sekte ioannitov* (St. Petersburg: Izd. "Kronshtadtskii Maiak," 1906), 64.

11. Pustoshkin, *Tserkov' Khristova*, 16, 17. While these were articulations that were published only after the Church hierarchy had reached its conclusions, similar statements were recorded by investigators.

12. The Ioannite Prokhor Skorobogatenkov, for example, would take a *prosphora* and a chalice with wine, hold them up to a portrait of Father Ioann, and say, "Thou, O Lord, art in Father Ioann; Thou knowest and seest all; transform, then, this bread into the body of Christ and the wine into the blood of Christ." It was because the Synod finally feared such misuses of objects bearing Father Ioann's image that they declared it illegal in 1895 to make enamelled cups with an iconic representation of his face, although abuses continued. For the Synodal decision, see RGIA, f. 796, op. 176, ed. khr. 3498, l. 1; for additional testimony of the use of Father Ioann cups in "communion" ceremonies, see April 24, 1908, letter to the Gradonachalnik from priest Nikolai Podosenov, TsGIA SPb, f. 569, op. 334, d. 20, l. 237.

13. The lack of funds was the argument made by several Ioannites in response to police queries. See an investigation of October 18, 1907, in TsGIA SPb, f. 569, op. 20, d. 344, sv. 344, l. 93.

14. On the relation between submission to an elder and to the hierarchy, see S. I. Smirnov, *Dukhovnyi Otets v Drevnei Vostochnoi Tserkvi. Istoriia Dukhovnichestva na Vostoke* (Sergiev Posad, 1906), 52–64.

15. For published anticlerical statements, see Pustoshkin, *Tserkov' Khristova*, esp. 19, 25; for eyewitness testimonies, see GARF, f. 102 (Department of Police), f. 102, III otd., d. 1366 (*O Malovisherskom meshchanine Petre Trofimove, stremliashchemsia obrazovat' sektu religioznago kharaktera v Liubanskoi volosti*), ll. 5–5ob.

16. March 6, 1904, letter of Priest Pavel Vasil'ev, in TsGIA SPb, f. 2219, op. 1, d. 37, l. 6; see also April 9, 1908, clip from *Okraina* in GARF, f. 102, 4 delopr., d. 154 (I), l. 8.

17. See, for example, the obstacles encountered by Anastasiia Logacheva, in Brenda Meehan, *Holy Women of Russia: The Lives of Five Orthodox Women Offer Spiritual Guidance for Today* (Crestwood, N.Y.: St Vladimir's Seminary Press, 1997), esp. 42–50. On the other hand, this pattern was not universal: Ekaterina Vasilievna Malkova, a married laywoman, was honored for her missionary work and held up as an example to priests' wives ("Zhenshchina-missionerka i missionerskii priiut," *Sankt-Peterburgskii Dukhovnyi Vestnik*, no. 41 [October 10, 1897]: 806–9).

18. Reported in a letter from Elisaveta Zemborskaia, TsGIA SPb, f. 2219, op. 1, d. 37, l. 31.

19. See "Novoe lzheuchenie," *Strannik* 36, no. 3 (March 1895): 629.

20. This was the case with both Kondratov and Ivan Ponomarev. See "Nuzhnoe vrazumlenie," *Kostromskie Eparkhial'nye Vedomosti*, no. 12 (1902): 321–22, 549–53.

21. Letter from Zlatoustov, March 3, 1900, TsGIA SPb, f. 2219, op. 1, d. 7a, ll. 1–2.

22. Letters from Priest Sergii Dremiatskii, March 7, 1904, in ibid., d. 37, l. 8; and Priest Leonid Tomesh., d. 37, l. 14.

23. Undated letter in ibid., d. 37, l. 22.

24. Cf. a case with a peasant woman's wanting to open a religious community, claiming that Father John had given her his blessing (The Russian State Historical Archive of the City of Moscow [hereafter RGIA g. Moskvy], f. 203, op. 392, d. 3, l. 1.5ob).

25. Robert H. Davis, "19th-Century Russian Religious-Theological Journals: Structure and Access," *St. Vladimir's Theological Quarterly* 33, no. 3 (1989): 235–59.

26. For an example of this informative kind of article seeking feedback from other clergy, see sviashch. E. Ovsiannikov, "Novye obozhateli o. Ioanna Kronshtatskago v Donskoi oblasti," *Pravoslavnyi Putevoditel'* (April 1903): 489–94.

27. For such arguments, see J. Eugene Clay, "Orthodox Missionaries and 'Orthodox Heretics' in Russia, 1866–1917," in *Of Religion and Empire: Missions, Conversion, and Tolerance in Russia*, ed. Michael Khodarkovsky and Robert Geraci (Ithaca: Cornell University Press, forthcoming), 34; Protpr. Boris Nikolaev, see note 34, below.

28. Letter of March 12, 1895, in RGIA, f. 796, op. 175, ed. khr. 2017, 2 st., 3 otd., ll. 5–6.

29. Letter of 1905, in TsGIA SPb, f. 2219, op. 1, d. 37, l. 7.

30. Nikolai Volochuchin's 1899 request for such handouts was one of the first (ibid., d. 37, ll. 29–30).

31. For the akathist as a popular devotional form and its exacting demands, see Abbess Thaisia, *Abbess Thaisia of Leushino: The Autobiography of a Spiritual Daughter of St. John of Kronstadt* (Platina, Calif.: St. Herman of Alaska Brotherhood Press, 1989), 161–66. For an akathist composed before Father John's canonization, see Surskii, *Otets Ioann Kronshtadtskii*, 2: 332–44.

32. See E. Zubarev, *Ioannity prokliaty o. Ioannom Kronshtadtskim*, 2d ed. (Kostroma, 1912), 1.

33. See "Nuzhnoe vrazumlenie," 321–22.

34. This was the claim made by Prot. Boris Nikolaev, in Arkhiv Ustnoi Istorii Rossiiskogo Gosudarstvennogo Gumanitarnogo Universiteta, f. Pskovskoi ekspeditsii, interview of July 17, 1989, l. 2.

35. V. N. Terletskii, *Sekta "ioannitov"* (Poltava, 1910), 14.
36. "Strannoe prikliuchenie," *Rossiia*, no. 852 (9 September 1901): 3.
37. Ibid.
38. GARF, f. 102 (Department of Police), f. 102, d. 1366, III otd. (*O Malovisherskom meshchanine Petre Trofimove, stremliashchemsia obrazovat' sektu religioznago kharaktera v Liubanskoi volosti*), ll. 5–5ob.
39. For a discussion of the spiritual verse as a popular genre and its reception, see Georgii P. Fedotov, *Stikhi dukhovnye. Russkaia narodnaia vera po dukhovnym stikham* (Moscow: Progress/Gnozis, 1991).
40. Protocol to Police Department from the MVD of the Novgorod Governor, October 6, 1901, no. 1115; in GARF, f. 102 (Department of Police), f. 102, d. 1366, III otd., ll. 5–5ob.
41. *Spravka* of October 15, 1901, in GARF, f. 102 (Department of Police), d. 1366, III otd., ll. 5ob–7.
42. For a thorough examination of the problems of investigating the Ioannites' financial misdoings, see "Delo kantsel. Sankt-Peterburgskogo Generala-Gubernatora; obshchie rasporiazheniia po neseniia politseiskoi sluzhby," April 9, 1905, in TsGIA SPb, f. 2075, op. 1, d. 15, l. 4.
43. For a contemporary discussion of the effects of the law, see Isaac Hourwich, "Religious Sects in Russia," in *The Case of Russia: A Composite View* (New York: Fox, Duffield, and Co., 1905), 341–87. See also Andrew Blane, "Protestant Sects in Late Imperial Russia," in Andrew Blane, ed., *The Religious World of Russian Culture, Russia and Orthodoxy*, vol. 2: *Essays in Honor of Georges Florovsky* (The Hague/Paris: Mouton, 1975), 267–78.
44. In other words, although the Holy Synod was technically part of the Imperial government, and although the Orthodox faith was still the official religion of the Russian Empire, the Synod could not itself undertake the prosecution of a religious group they deemed suspicious: they had first to convince those agents and agencies whose job it was to do so.
45. For specifics on selling books from hand to hand, see Mary Jane Rossabi, "Peasants, Peddlers, and Popular Prints Prints in Nineteenth-century Russia," *Bulletin of Research in the Humanities* 87, no. 4 (1986–87): 418–30.
46. GARF, f. 102, 3 delopr. 1069, ll. 5–5ob.
47. See TsGIA SPb, f. 2219, op. 1, d. 31, l. 73.
48. GARF, f. 102, 3 delopr. 1069, l. 5ob.
49. Ibid., ll. 6, 9. For Father John's explanation of his relation to Kiseleva, see Il'ia A. Alekseev, *Razgrom ioannitov* (St. Petersburg, 1909), 30.
50. Correspondence between St. Petersburg Ministry of the Interior (stol 3, 4) and St. Petersburg Governor General, April 9–June 7, 1905, in TsGIA SPb, f. 2075, op. 1, d. 15, ll. 4–12.
51. Bol'shakov, *Pravda o sekte ioannitov*, 32, 35, 44, 47.
52. Quoted in Terletskii, *Sekta "ioannitov,"* 7.
53. TsGIA SPb, f. 2219, op. 1, d. 40, l. 40.
54. Terletskii, *Sekta "ioannitov,"* 7.
55. Aleksandr Serebrov, Serebrov, *Vremia i liudi: vospominaniia, 1898–1905* (Moscow: Moskovskii rabochii, 1960), 39. For a discussion of how a visual typology for prostitutes was created, see Laura Engelstein, *The Keys to Happiness: Sex and the Search for Modernity in Fin-de-Siècle Russia* (Ithaca: Cornell University Press, 1994), 130–52.
56. TsGIA SPb, f. 2219, op. 1, d. 40, l. 8.
57. Ibid., d. 40, l. 41; d. 65, ll. 5ff.

58. Letters of October 10, 1897, from Ferdinand de Beck to Aleksandra Ivanovna, in ibid., d. 37, l. 3; March 6, 1904, from Pavel Vasil'ev, ibid., d. 37, l. 6.

59. Letter from Iakov Dalmatov and I. Aleksandrov, March 27, 1905, in ibid., d. 37, l. 35.

60. V. V. Protopov, *Chernye Vorony, p'esa v 5 deistviiakh* (St. Petersburg, 1908).

61. See "Iz Periodicheskoi Pechati. Chernye Vorony," in *Bogoslovskii Vestnik* (December 1907): 866.

62. *Kronshtadtskii Maiak*, December 11, 1905, back cover.

63. See "Novyia meropriiatiia v oblasti bor'by s nishchestvom v Sankt-Peterburge," and "Blagotvoritel'noe obshchestvo dlia pomoshchi prikhodskim bednym pri Vladimirskoi tserkvi," *Sankt-Peterburgskii Dukhovnyi Vestnik*, no. 24 (June 13, 1897): 459–65.

64. *Novoe Vremia*, March 11, 1908, in GARF, f. 102, 4 delopr., d. 154(I), l. 7.

65. See, for example, the correspondance between Pavel Il'ianov and his father in TsGIA SPb, f. 569, op. 20, d. 344, sv. 334, ll. 26–31ob.

66. Al. Iv. Briauzova, for example (September 5, 1907; TsGIA SPb, f. 569, op. 20, d. 344, sv. 344, l. 34).

67. Form letter in TsGIA SPb, f. 2219, op. 1, d. 37, l. 28; *Russkii Palomnik*, no. 33 (1907): 526, in GARF, f. 102, 4 delopr., 1907, d. 154, ll. 2–3, and l. 58, a letter of September 29, 1907, from Upravlenie Kantseliarii Sankt Peterburgskogo Gradonachal'nika (St. Petersburg Prefect's Office Administration) to the 3d and 4th Spasskii and the 4th Petersburg precincts.

68. See, for example, "Sanitary v ioannitskikh obshchezhitiiakh/trushchobakh," GARF, f. 102, 4 delopr., d. 154, ll. 162–63. While the article claimed that there were about "ninety little girls," the police investigation listed thirteen girls from the ages of 4–13, and seventy-one people *in all*.

69. *Peterburgskaia Gazeta*, May 17, 1909, in TsGIA SPb, d. 569, op. 334, ed. khr. 20, l. 230.

70. Ibid.

71. "Ioannity," *Segodnia* (Samara), November 23, 1907, 1.

72. RGIA, f. 821, op. 133, ed. khr. 206, l. 7.

73. *Slovo*, no. 31 (April 5, 1909), 2.

74. Amfiteatrov used the word *"sretenie"* to suggest a parallel with the feast of the Meeting of Our Lord in the Temple.

75. Ninov, *Stikhotvornaia satira*, 122–23.

76. See, for example, "Bor'ba s ioannitami," *Sovremennoe Slovo*, October 15, 1909, p. 3; "Ioannitskaia agitatsiia," *Birzhevye Vedomosti*, no. 10113 (September 22, 1907): 1.

77. Police report of October 18, 1907, in TsGIA SPb, f. 569, op. 20, d. 344, sv. 344, ll. 92–93.

78. Ibid., ll. 153–54.

79. Report of November 8, 1907, to the Gradonachalnik from the Pristav of the 2d uchastok of the Petersburg chast', TsGIA SPb, ibid., ll. 168–69.

80. October 25, 1907; ibid., l. 150.

81. Report of August 11, 1907, to the Perm Dukhovnaia Konsistoriia from Priest Aleksandr Merkurov, TsGIA SPb, ibid., ll. 178–79.

82. RGIA, f. 821, op. 133, ed. khr. 206, l. 1 (*O zakrytii priiutov otkrytykh ioannitami v St.-Pb. i o vozvrashchenii vziatykh v priiutakh detei ikh roditeliam ili rodstvennikam*). In doing so, they expressed the desire for the decision to be made valid for the whole of the Empire.

83. Ibid., ed. khr. 206, ll. 2–3. The Gradonachalnik referred to article 387, v. XI, part II

of the 1893 edition of the complete codes of Russian legislation (Polnyi Svod Zakonov [PSZ]).

84. TsGIA SPb, f. 569, op. 334, d. 20, ll. 230, 376; GARF, f. 102, 3 delopr. 3069, l. 108. For letters to Stolypin, see TsGIA SPb, f. 569, op. 334, d. 20, ll. 272–73, 282.

85. Letter from Zhedenov to Privy Counselor and Senator Sergei E. Kryzhanovskii, RGIA, f. 821, op. 133, ed. khr. 206, l. 15.

86. Ibid., l. 29.

87. Ibid., ll. 50–51ob. A longer version of his letter appeared in a supplement to *Kronshtadtskii Maiak* with the title *"Uzhasnaia Mest'"* (ibid., ll. 29–30).

88. GARF, f. 102, 4 delopr, 1907, d. 154, l. 127.

89. Ibid., 3 delopr., d. 3069, l. 116; reprinted in *Sankt-Peterburgskie Vedomosti*, October 1, 1909.

90. *Zemshchina*, September 19, 1909; in ibid., 4 delopr. d. 154 (I), l. 107.

91. *Sankt-Peterburgskie Vedomosti*, September 20, 1909, p. 2.

92. *Novyi Golos*, December 13, 1908, clipping in GARF, f. 102, 4 delopr., d. 154 (I), l. 65.

93. Bol'shakov, *Lozhnaia zashchitnitsa pravoslaviia*, 3; introduction to Protopov, *Chernye Vorony*, ii.

94. Pustoshkin, *Tserkov' Khristova*, 7.

95. Quoted in *Russkoe Slovo*, May 7, 1909 (in GARF, f. 102, 4 delopr. d. 154 [I], l. 63).

96. Bol'shakov, *Lozhnaia zashchitnitsa pravoslaviia*, 2.

97. For a contemporary argument in favor of combining liberal democracy with Orthodoxy, see Vadim Voinov, "The Western Idea of Democracy Through the Prism of the Russian Religious Mind," Unpublished paper presented at the Mid-Atlantic Conference of the AAASS, March 1997, Albany, New York. For Father John's sermon on the opening of the Duma (April 27, 1906), see Ioann Il'ich Sergiev, *Propovedi otsa Ioanna Kronshtadtskago o tsarskom samoderzhavii* (St. Petersburg, 1914), 12–13.

98. Ernst Troeltsch, "Sect-type and Church-type contrasted," in his *The Social Teaching of the Christian Churches*, vol. 1 (New York: Harper & Row/Harper Torchbooks, 1960), 331–49; Georgii V. Florovsky, *Puti russkago bogosloviia* (Paris: YMCA Press, 1937), 68–69.

99. Letter of August 23, 1909, no. 5360, in RGIA, f. 821, op. 133, ed. khr. 206, l. 5.

100. "Vserossiiskii Missionerskii S'ezd," *Pribavleniia k Tserkovnym Vedomostiam*, no. 30 (1908): 1407.

101. Ibid., 1408.

102. According to *khlyst* beliefs, God did not become incarnate only once, in the person of His Son; instead, He continues to become incarnate in human beings in order to reveal additional aspects of truth and to show people the path to salvation. Such chosen righteous ones become so engulfed by God that they become living Gods to whom ordinary laws do not apply. See "Khlysty," in F. A. Brokgauz and I. A. Efron, *Entsiklopedicheskii Slovar'*, 82 vols. (St. Petersburg, 1903), 73:402–9.

103. Letter from Synod Chancellery of September 15, 1909, in RGIA, f. 821, op. 133, ed. khr. 206, l. 54.

104. Reported in *Novoe Vremia*, December 12, 1908; in GARF, f. 102, 4 delopr., d. 154 (I), l. 63.

105. Council session of December 10, 1908; in ibid., d. 154 (I), l. 64.

106. *Russkoe Slovo*, no. 176 (July 30, 1908), p. 4. Differing versions of the meeting were reported in *Russkii Narod,* August 1 and 10, 1908, nos. 360, 369; and *Golos Moskvy* July 30, 1908; see GARF, f. 102, 4 delopr., d. 154 (I), ll. 29, 37–38.

107. Reported in *Veche*, August 23, 1909, p. 2; in GARF, f. 102, 4 delopr., d. 154 (I), l. 96.

108. Ibid., 4 delopr. 1907, l. 177.

109. *Ioannovskoe Bratstvo. Ustav*, in RGIA, f. 821, op. 133, ed. khr. 206 (previously, Departament Dukhovnykh Del Inostrannykh Ispovedanii, d. 155), l. 52.

110. Letter of September 15, 1909, from Departament Dukhovnykh Del Inostrannykh Ispovedanii to St. Petersburg Gradonachalnik, in ibid., ed. khr. 206, l. 53.

111. They did so on the basis of Section I, Articles 4 and 33 of a March 4, 1906, law on unions and societies. See RGIA, f. 821, op. 133, ed. khr. 206, ll. 110, 132, 137.

112. Letter of October 9, 1909, from the Ministry of Internal Affairs to the Prefect to Gradonachalnik; in ibid, ed. khr. 206, l. 108. For the formation of the Society, see RGIA SPb, f. 2216, op. 1, d. 1, l. 17ob.

113. See, for example, cases in December 1909 in Novo-Vorontsovka and Kherson uezd; RGIA, f. 821, op. 133, ed. khr. 206, ll. 139 and 149.

114. See, for example, "Pokhod ioannitov na Kavkaz," *Tiflisskii Listok*, no. 243, October 25, 1909; in RGIA, f. 821, op. 133, ed. khr. 206, l. 119.ll. 152, 154, 174, 175, 226; GARF, f. 102, 4 delopr., 1907, d. 154, ll. 121–93.

115. Report of Kherson police, no. 9305, October 2, 1909; in GARF, f. 102, 4 delopr., 1907, d. 154, ll. 130, 135.

116. Ibid., d. 154, ll. 161–64.

117. Ibid., d. 154, l. 195.

118. Khrapovitskii, *Confession*, 44–45.

119. Telegram of December 30, 1909; RGIA, f. 821, op. 133, ed. khr. 206, l. 143.

120. See the assertion made in *Kolokol*, April 8, 1910, by "a Perm resident." When questioned by the police, the writer claimed that the Baptists in particular were spreading socialism and revolution (RGIA, f. 821, op. 133, ed. khr. 206, l. 229).

121. Ibid., ed. khr. 206, l. 166; emphases mine.

122. GARF, f. 102, 4 delopr., 1907, d. 154, l. 189.

123. Ibid., d. 154, l. 193; also reported in *Rech'*, April 14, 1912.

124. Zubarev, *Ioannity prokliaty*, 5.

125. For Russian examples of such movements, see Aleksandr I. Klibanov, *Istoriia religioznogo sektantstva v Rossii (60-e gody XIX v.-1917g.)* (Moscow: Nauka, 1965), and his *Narodnaia sotsial'naia utopiia v Rossii, XIX vek* (Moscow: Nauka, 1978).

Chapter 7

1. The uniqueness of Russia was a central Slavophile tenet. One of the most concise formulations is Ivan Kireevskii's "On the Nature of European Culture and its Relation to the Culture of Russia," in Marc Raeff, ed., *Russian Intellectual History: An Anthology* (New York: Harcourt, Brace, and World, 1966), 175–207.

2. GARF, f. 1067, op. 1, d. 13, l. 32ob.

3. Ibid, d. 12, l. 9.

4. Ibid, d. 23, l. 26.

5. Ibid, d. 23, l. 26ob.

6. Ibid., d. 23, l. 28ob.

7. Ibid.

8. S. S. Tatishchev, *Imperator Aleksandr II, ego zhizn' i tsarstvovanie* (St. Petersburg, 1903), 1: 662.

9. See Michael S. Flier, "The Church of the Savior on the Blood: Projection, Rejection, Resurrection," in Robert P. Hughes and Irina Paperno, eds., *Christianity and the Eastern*

Slavs, vol. 2: *Russian Culture in Modern Times* (Berkeley and Los Angeles: University of California Press, 1994), 2: 25–48.

10. The reference is to the selections from Isaiah (chapters 8–9) sung at Great Compline.

11. GARF, f. 1067, op. 1, d. 23, l. 28.

12. Ibid. Father John used these notes nearly verbatim in his published sermon (Ioann Il'ich Sergiev, *Slovo vo vtoruiu nedeliu posta, po povodu naglogo i derzkogo ubiistva zlodeiami blagochestiveishago Gos. Imp. Aleksandra Nikolaevicha* [Kronshtadt,] 1881), 6–7. The published text continues, "Let us cast aside luxury, which is the enemy and the scourge of society, and one to which we so readily become accustomed. Let us share willingly with the have-nots who need bread, clothing, and shelter. Forgive me for reminding you of this so often, but it is my duty to waken a sense of mercy and charity in everyone, for *only the merciful shall obtain mercy*."

13. GARF, f. 1067, op. 1, d. 24, l. 92ob.

14. His diaries show his anger toward the Holy Synod (see, in particular, ibid., d. 23, l. 31–31ob).

15. George Fedotov, for example, writes, "He [Father Ioann] was known and loved in the courts of the last two Tsars.... Only a friend of the Tsar could have been permitted to introduce such an innovation [i.e., the mass confessions] ." George P. Fedotov, *A Treasury of Russian Spirituality* (Belmont, Mass.: Norland Publishing Co., 1975), 346, 349. René Fülöp-Miller claimed that "John of Kronstadt was regarded as a saint, not only by the simple people, but also by the old Emperor himself.... In grave situations, when important decisions had to be taken or a member of the family was ill, the Emperor Alexander used to summon the holy man to the Palace and ask for his advice and help" (Fülöp-Miller, *Rasputin: The Holy Devil* [New York: Frederick Ungar Publishing Co., 1962], 113). The assertion that Father Ioann was the confessor of the Imperial family and enjoyed their exclusive favor was a staple of Soviet accounts ("The Synodal higher-ups had to stand on ceremony with his [Father Ioann's] devotees, for Ioann had the reputation of being a saint in the Emperor's palace as well," in Nikolai. M. Nikol'skii, *Istoriia Russkoi Tserkvi* [Moscow-Leningrad: Central Commitee of the Union of the Militant Godless of the USSR, 1931; 3d ed., Moscow: Politizdat, 1983], 462); and Eduard Radzinsky, *The Last Tsar* (New York: Harper & Row, 1992), 9, 172. The explanation for this ascription may lie in a later honorary designation of Father Ioann as "Spiritual Confessor to the Royal Family" (Anatolii Levitin-Krasnov, "Narodnye Sviatye v Rossii: Otets Ioann Kronshtadtskii," *Cahiers du monde russe et soviétique* 29, nos. 3–4 [July–December 1988]: 466), but this title was purely symbolic. The actual confessors of the Royal Family were Protopresbyter Ioann Ianyshev, and Archimandrite Feofan (Bystrov) (1909–10), Protoierei Nikolai Kedrinskii (1911–14), and Protoierei Aleksandr Vasil'ev (1914–17; shot 1918) (Richard Batts and Viacheslav Marchenko, *Dukhovnik Tsarskov Sem'i, sviatitel' Feofan Poltavskii. 1874–1940* [Platina, Calif.: St. Herman of Alaska Press; Moscow: Rossiiskoe otd. Valaamskago obshchestva Ameriki, 1994], 22); RGIA, f. 805, intro. to op. 1, p. xiii.

16. Ivan Zakharin-Iakunin, "Grafiniia A. Tolstaia. Lichnye vpechatleniia i vospominaniia," *Vestnik Evropy*, no. 4 (April 1905): 617.

17. (Igumen) Konstantin [Zaitsev], *Dukhovnyi oblik prot. o. Ioanna Kronshtadtskago* (Jordanville, N.Y.: Holy Trinity Monastery, 1952), 3–4; P. Sergeenko, "Tolstoi i ego sovremenniki," in *Piatidesiatiletie*, 168–69; "Dva iubeliia (Lev Tolstoi i Ioann Kronshtadtskii)," in Prot. Sergii Chetverikov, *Bog v Russkoi Dushe* (Moscow: Krutitskoe Patriarshee Podvor'e, 1998), 84–87.

18. N. A. Vel'iaminov, "Vospominaniia N. A. Veliaminova ob Imperatore Aleksandre III,'" in *Rossiikii Arkhiv* 5 (Moscow) (1994): 301, 309–10.

19. For accounts in such newspapers as *Le Monde Illustré, Deluvio Barcelona, The Christian Herald, Le Temps* et al., see RGIA, f. 834, op. 4, d. 250 (foreign newspaper clippings on Father Ioann of Kronstadt).

20. Prot. Ioann Sergiev, "Poslednie chasy zhizni Gosudaria Imperatora Aleksandra III," *Tserkovnye Vedomosti* (1894): 1656; reprinted in I. Pobedinskii, *Posledniia minuty zhizni Imperatora Aleksandra Aleksandrovicha: Pis'mo o. Ioanna Kronshtadtskago* (Moscow, 1912), p. 17.

21. Sergiev, "Poslednie chasy," 14–17.

22. The Russian National Library, Otdel Rukopisei, f. 178 (Aleksei Sergeevich Suvorin), op. 4818, d. 92, ll. 2–3ob.

23. Letter from Suvorin to Zhemchuzhnikov, November 21, 1894, in ibid., l. 1.

24. See Ioann Sergiev (Kronshtadtskii), *Slovo o blagotvornosti Tsarskago edinoderzhaviia* (St. Petersburg, 1897).

25. Sergei Fomin, comp., *Rossiia pered vtorym prishestviem: materialy k ocherku russkoi eskhatologii* (Moscow: Izd. Sviato–Troitskoi Sergievoi Lavry "Posad," 1993), 37, 39–47, 54–57, 66–67.

26. Amvrosii (Hieroschemamonk), *Sobranie pisem Blazhennoi pamiati optinskago startsa ieroskhimonakha Amvrosiia k mirskim osobam* (Sergiev Posad, 1908), 1, 21–22.

27. Metropolitan Antonii (Khrapovitskii), *Slovo ep. Antoniia (Khrapovitskago) i o. Ioanna Kronshtadtskogo po povodu nasilii khristiian s evreiami v Kishineve* (Odessa, 1903). Letter from Archbishop of June 9, 1903, in GARF, f. 102, d. 873 t4, l. 90.

28. Letter of May 22, 1903, from Tolstoy to Anatolii Step. Butkevich, in L. N. Tolstoi, *Polnoe Sobranie Sochinenii*, 90 vols. (Moscow: Gosudarstvennoe Izd. Khudozhestvennoi Literatury, 1954), 74:129.

29. GARF, f. 102 (Department of Police), 873 t4 (1903), l. 20b.

30. See in particular the letter of May 16, 1903, in ibid, ll. 51–54ob. For Father John's apology, see *Missionerskoe Obozrenie* 5 (May 1903): 1396.

31. Georgii Apollonovich Gapon, *Zapiski Georgiia Gapona (Ocherk rabochago dvizheniia v Rossii 1900-kh godov)* (Moscow, 1918), 45–56.

32. Letters of July 3, 1905, and undated, in TsGIA SPb, f. 2219, op. 1, d. 51 (letters from various persons concerning the oppression of the Orthodox by the Catholics), ll. 3–7.

33. See, for example, the letters from M. Tarasova, December 18, 1902; Elizaveta, January 24, 1907; and priest Matfei Tarentuta, March 3, 1905, in ibid., d. 55, ll. 2–3ob, 48–49, 75–76.

34. Undated letter from Natalia Ivanitskaia in TsGIA SPb, f. 2219, op. 1, d. 52, l. 72.

35. Letter of December 22, 1906, in ibid., d. 18, l. 37.

36. Honorary membership cards survive in TsGIA SPb, f. 2219, op. 1, d. 18 (correspondence with various "Black-Hundred" and monarchist societies and unions concerning the listing of I. I. Sergiev as an honorary or active member, October 16, 1885–September 26, 1908), ll. 37, 41, 49–52. Father John's exact relation with the Union of the Russian People remains unclear.

37. Letter of January 13, 1906, from Grigorii Lipatov, in ibid., d. 34, l. 17.

38. Letter of November 1, 1905 from "a citizen of the Russian land," in ibid., d. 52, l. 14.

39. Letter from Kosma Utkin, January 8, 1906, in ibid., d. 52, l. 36.

40. Undated letter from Dar'ia and Nikolai, in ibid., d. 52, l. 61.

41. Ibid., d. 52, l. 62.

42. Letter from P. Petrov, in ibid., d. 52, l. 56. Avraamii Palitsyn was the cellarer of the Trinity-Sergius Monastery at the turn of the sixteenth and seventeenth century who described the Polish attack on the monastery.

43. Letter of March 6, 1906, in ibid., d. 52, l. 42.

44. Father Ioann is referring to Hebrews 10:28 ("He that despised Moses' law died without mercy under two or three witnesses") and Romans 13:1.

45. Sermon on the day of the sacred unction and coronation of the Most Pious, Most Autocratic and Great Sovereign Emperor Nikolai Aleksandrovich. Reprinted in prot. Ioann Sergiev, *Oblichitel'nyia Propovedi otsa Ioanna Kronshtadtskago* (St. Petersburg, 1914), 5–7.

46. See Anna Geifman, *Thou Shalt Kill: Revolutionary Terrorism in Russia, 1894–1917* (Princeton: Princeton University Press, 1993).

47. "Propoved' znamenitago pastyria o. Ioanna Kronshtadtskago o iaponskoi voine i vytekaiushchikh iz neia nazidaniiakh" ("A Sermon by the Celebrated Pastor Father Ioann of Kronstadt on the Japanese War and the Edifying Lessons to be Drawn From It"), in Sergiev, *Oblichitel'nyia*, 14–16.

48. Ibid., 12–14.

49. This opposition between elite and common was made repeatedly. See Mikhail Menshikov, "Pamiati sviatogo pastyria," in V. A. Desiatnikov, *Ioann Kronshtadskii* (Moscow: "Patriot," 1992), 361–62; Sergei Chetverikov, "Dva iubileia (Lev Tolstoi I Ioann Kronshtadtskii)," in his *Bog v Russkoi Dushe* (Moscow: Krutitskoe Patriarshee Podvor'e, 1998), 84–87; and E. Lukashevskii, "Kronshtadtskii Propovednik," *Nauka I Religiia*, no. 5 (May 1990): 10–14.

50. Leo Tolstoi, "Kritika dogmaticheskago bogosloviia," in *Polnoe sobranie sochinenii zapreshchennykh v Rossii* (Christchurch, 1903). For an Orthodox critique, see N. Varzhanskii, *V chem vera L. N. Tolstago. Narodno-Populiarnyi Eskiz* (St. Petersburg, 1911), in Ioann Vostorgov et al., *Prisnopamiatnyi o. Ioann Kronshtadtskii i Lev Tolstoi* (Jordanville, N.Y.: Holy Trinity Monastery, 1960), 3–23.

51. "Suchshnost' lzheucheniia grafa L. Tolstogo, Slovo v nedeliu dvadtsat' piatuiu po piatidesiatnitse [The essence of the false teaching of Count L. Tolstoy: Sermon on the twenty-fifth week after Pentecost], 1896," in I. I. Sergiev [Kronshtadtskii], *Protiv grafa L. N. Tolstogo, drugikh eretikov i sektantov nashego vremeni i raskol'nikov* (St. Petersburg, 1902), 17–18.

52. Ibid., 27–28.

53. See his review of Father John's "Response by a Church Pastor to Lev Tolstoy's 'Address to the Clergy,'" in Russian State Library, Manuscript Section, op. 369, ch. 71 (Bonch-Bruevich), d. 12, ll. 1–3.

54. Letter of July 17, 1908, in GARF, f. 102, 4 delopr., d. 154 (I), l. 22.

55. Nikolai Bol'shakov, who had printed the text in the May 4, 1908 (no. 18) issue of *Kronshtadtskii Maiak* (p. 3), claimed that he had gotten the text from *Sozertsatel'noe podvizhnichestvo, Vypiski iz dnevniki 1906–1907 prot. Ioanna Il'icha Sergieva*. See GARF, f. 102, 4 delopr., d. 154 (I), l. 48.

56. See the dismay of the writer Vladimir Korolenko, in V. G. Korolenko, *Polnoe Sobranie Sochinenii* (St. Petersburg, 1914), 1: 318.

57. The vaguely left *New Voice* even argued that under the old censorship restrictions, most social phenomena could not be evaluated objectively, while one could honestly report only good things about Father Ioann. Newspapers therefore "fell over their feet" in their hurry to report Father John's miracles (*Novyi Golos*, December 13, 1908, p. 65). For the treatment of religion in the press from 1881 to 1895, see B. P. Valuev, *Politicheskaia reaktsiia 80kh godov XIX veka i russkaia zhurnalistika* (Moscow: Izd. Moskovskogo Universiteta, 1971), 172.

58. "Zver' v riase," *Novaia Mysl'*, no. 22, January 27, 1907, p. 3.

59. *Mysl'*, no. 8, June 28–July 11, 1906, p. 3.
60. "'Piat' chasov s Iliodorom," *Grazhdanin*, no. 20 (March 15, 1907): 2.
61. *Tovarishch*, no. 42 (August 23–September 5, 1906): 2.
62. *Novaia Mysl'*, no. 10 (January 13, 1907): 4.
63. *Perelom*, no. 110 (December 7, 1906): 2.
64. See the exhortations of Prot. G. S. Debol'skii, *O liubvi k otechestvu i trudie po slovu Bozhiiu*, 4th ed. (repr. Moscow: Izd. "Pravilo Very," 1996); see also the inclusion of URP medals in *Pravoslavie, armiia i flot Rossii* [exhibition catalogue] (St. Petersburg: izd. "Ego," 1996), item 111.
65. For examples of Soviet labeling from different periods, see Naum Rostov, *Dukhovenstvo i russkaia kontr-revoliutsiia* (Moscow: Ateist, 1930), 29ff; N. S. Gordienko, ed., *Pravoslavie: slovar' ateista* (Moscow: Politizdat, 1988), 94–95.
66. See the descriptions of their activity in *Grazhdanin*, nos. 31–32 (May 3, 1907): 6; and nos. 41–41 (June 1, 1907): 22.
67. On Father John's health, see RGIA, f. 796, op. 189, d. 515, l. 10 (letter from Father Ioann pleading illness to the Holy Synod dated September 24, 1908); and op. 188, d. 619, 2a stol, I otd. (letter from Father John pleading same, January 8, 1908); Ioann Il'ich Sergiev, *Pis'ma o. prot. Ioann k nastoiatel'nitse Ioanno-Predtechenskago Leushinskago Pervoklassnago Monastyria Igumenii Taisii* (St. Petersburg, 1909), 96. (Father Ioann wrote on January 22, 1908: "I have not been at a single session of the Holy Synod—I am sick, and blind too, what use would I be?"). On declining audiences, see E. K., *Vospominaniia ob otse Ioanne* (St. Petersburg, 1909), 34.
68. *Strely*, no. 2 (November 5, 1905), cover; "Iskhod iz Kronshtadta," *Pulemet* no. 1 (1905): 11.
69. A. Ninov, comp., *Stikhotvornaia satira pervoi russkoi revoliutsii (1905–1907)* (Leningrad: Sovetskii pisatel', 1985), 217.
70. Ibid., 396–97; emphasis mine.
71. *Sankt-Peterburgskie Vedomosti*, no. 251 (October 29–November 11, 1905): 6.
72. Asssertion of November 1, 1905, quoted in A. L. Sidorova et al., eds., *Revoliutsiia 1905–07 gg. v Rossii, Dokumenty i materialy* (Moscow: Izd. Akad. Nauk, 1955), 1:202.
73. Leon Trotsky, *1905* (New York: Random House, 1971), 119.
74. *Novyi Put'*, no. 14 (January 19, 1906): 4. Because of incomplete records, it is impossible to determine whether donations to Father Ioann dropped off after 1905. See TsGIA SPb, f. 2219, op. 1, d. 58.
75. Mikhail O. Menshikov, "Pis'ma k blizhnim. Kronshtadtskii Bunt. Pastyr' dobryi," in *Novoe Vremia*, no. 10646 (October 30 [November 12], 1905): 4.
76. See, for example, the reminiscences of the worker K. Mironov, in *Vestnik russkoi revoliutsii*, no. 3 (March 1903) (repr. Moscow, 1906), pp. 25–56; and Semen Kanatchikov, *A Radical Worker in Tsarist Russia: The Autobiography of Semën Ivanovich Kanatchikov*, Reginald E. Zelnik ed. (Stanford: Stanford University Press, 1986), 29.
77. Letters of October 31 and November 26, 1906, in Sergiev, *Pis'ma o. prot. Ioanna k nastoiatel'nitse*, 87–88.
78. For more liberal varieties of Orthodox opinions on politics, see Bernice Glatzer Rosenthal and Martha Bohachevsky-Chomiak, eds., *A Revolution of the Spirit: Crisis of Value in Russia, 1890–1924* (New York: Fordham University Press, 1990).
79. TsGIA SPb, f. 2219, op. 1. d. 32 (letters from various persons in response to the sermon of Ioann Sergiev against Lev Tolstoi), ll. 1–2ob.
80. Letter dated March 12, 1903, in TsGIA SPb, f. 2219, op. 1, d. 32, l. 15. In the selection, Father John is quoted as saying: "Do not give in to a dark or hostile disposition of

your heart towards your neighbor, but master them and uproot them through the power of faith and the light of good sense—and you will be good-spirited" (l. 16).

81. Quoted in Liubimov's letter of March 28, 1906, in TsGIA SPb, f. 2219, op. 1, d. 32, ll. 27–28ob.

82. Ibid., d. 32, ll. 28–28ob.

83. Ronald H. Carpenter, *Father Charles E. Coughlin: Surrogate Spokesman for the Dissaffected* (Westport, Conn.: Greenwood Press, 1998).

84. This letter is also anonymous and undated, signed only "Kievan women who are truly dedicated to you." TsGIA SPb, f. 2219, op. 1, d. 32, ll. 44–44ob.

Chapter 8

1. "Blazhennaia konchina o. Ioanna," in *Pastyrskii venok dorogomu batiushke o. Ioannu Kronshtadtskomu* (St. Petersburg, 1911), 201–12.

2. For a discussion of the hymn, see A. V. Motorin, "Obraz Ierusalima v russkom romantizme," in V. A. Kotel'nikov, ed., *Khristianstvo i Russkaia Literatura* (St. Petersburg: "Nauka," 1996), 83–84.

3. One *versta* is 1.06km, or 3500 feet. For the importance of chapels in devotional practice, see E. Poselianin, *Russkaia Tserkov' i Russkie Podvizhniki 18-go veka* (St. Petersburg, 1905), 18–20.

4. For the importance of saints' relics and their locations, see Wilson, *Saints and Their Cults: Studies in Religious Sociology, Folklore, and History* (Cambridge: Cambridge University Press, 1987), 4–5, 9–11.

5. See Nikolai I. Bol'shakov, *Istochnik zhivoi vody. Opisanie zhizni i deiatel'nosti otsa Ioanna Kronshtadtskago* (St. Petersburg, 1910; repr. St. Petersburg: Izd. "Tsarskoe Delo," 1995), 832; A. I. Vitovich, "Zapiski sudebnago pristava po okhranitel'noi opisi imushchestva o. Ioanna Kronshtadtskago," *Golos minuvshago*, no. 5 (1915): 183.

6. Compare earlier versions of Father John's wills, in The Russian State Historical Archive (hereafter RGIA), f. 799, op. 6, d. 30 (Economic Administration of the Holy Synod), otd. I, stol 1, no. 177a, ll. 4, 5. For an account of the police investigation, see Vitovich, "Zapiski."

7. Vitovich, "Zapiski," 177, 182–83; A. Trifonov, "Vynos tela i pogrebenie Elizavety Konstantinovny Sergievoi," in R. G. Shemiakina, *Svietloi Pamiati Pochivshei suprugi otsa Ioanna Kronshtadtskago Elizavety K. Sergievoi* (Kronstadt, 1909), 13–15. For the celebration of Father John's forty-day funeral anniversary services at Fedora Vlas'evna's crypt, see Bol'shakov, *Istochnik zhivoi vody*, 242.

8. See, for example, the collection of healing miracles and exorcisms in *Pastyrskii venok dorogomu batiushke o. Ioannu Kronshtadtskomu* (St. Petersburg, 1911; repr. Utica, N.Y., 1965), 252–300.

9. Orthodox Christians commemorate with special prayers the nine-day, forty-day, and annual anniversaries of their dead.

10. For the text of the rescript of January 12, 1909, see *Pastyrskii venok*, 226–29; for the Synodal resolutions of January 19, 1909, see *Pastyrskii venok*, 230–36, and RGIA, f. 802, op. 10, ed. khr. 677, l. 1.

11. See, for example, the request of the Shablykinskoe school in Omsk diocese, in RGIA, f. 796, op. 180, ed. khr. 1441, I stol, 2 otd., ll. 14.

12. RGIA, f. 802, op. 10, ed. khr. 677, l. 6. For the classification of Synodal-era monasteries, see Igor Smolitsch, *Russisches Mönchtum: Entstehung, Entwicklung und Wesen, 988–1917* (Würzburg: Augustinus-Verlag, 1953), 383–469.

13. *Pastyrskii venok*, 122.
14. See "Chem dorog nam o. Ioann Kronshtadtskii?," in *Pastyrskii venok*, 143.
15. "Istinnyi missioner," in *Pastyrskii venok*, 80–81. For parish reform projects and debates, see A. G. Boldovskii, *Vozrozhdenie tserkovnago prikhoda. Obzor mnenii pechati* (St. Petersburg, 1903).
16. S. L. Firsov, comp. and ed., *Sviatoi Ioann Kronshtadtskii v vospominaniiakh sovremennikov* (Moscow: Pravoslavnyi Sviato-Tikhonovskii Bogoslovskii Institut, Bratstvo vo Imia Vsemilostivogo Spasa, 1994), consists of some of these memoirs.
17. Ibid., p. 61; emphases mine; *Muzhichki* and *soldatiki* in the original.
18. See *Piatidesiatiletie*, 175–76; "Zhitie sviatogo pravednogo Ioanna Kronshtadtskogo chudotvortsa," *Zhurnal Moskovskoi Patriarkhii*, no. 10 (1990): 67.
19. See Gregory L. Freeze, "'Going to the Intelligentsia': The Church and Its Urban Mission in Post-Reform Russia," in Edith W. Clowes, Samuel D. Kassow, and James L. West, eds., *Between Tsar and People: Educated Society and the Quest for Public Identity in Late Imperial Russia* (Princeton: Princeton University Press, 1991), 215–32.
20. See Pope, "Immaculate and Powerful," 174–76; Ann Douglas, *The Feminization of American Culture* (New York: Knopf, 1977), 6–13.
21. Aleksei Makushinskii, "Vospominanie byvshago pevchago Kronshtadtskago Andreevskago Sobora," in *Piatidesiatilietie*, 42.
22. Memoirs of Priest V. Il'inskii, in Firsov, *Sviatoi Ioann Kronshtadtskii*, 113.
23. Prot. P. Al'bitskii, "O. Ioann Kronshtadtskii, kak pastyr' i obshchestvennyi deiatel'," in *Pastyrskii Venok*, 92.
24. See René Fülöp-Miller, *Raspoutine et les femmes* (Paris: Payot, 1928), 320.
25. See the 1927–28 Sofia lectures by Protopresviter G. I. Shavel'skii in *Pravoslavnoe Pastyrstvo* (St. Petersburg: Russkii Khristianskii Gumanitarnyi Institut, 1996), 510–15; Arkhimandrit Konstantin, "K chemu zovet nas sviatost' o. Ioanna Kronshtadtskogo," in his *Chudo russkoi istorii. Sbornik statei, raskryvaiushchikh promyslitel'noe znachenie Istoricheskoi Rossii* (Jordanville, N.Y.: Holy Trinity Monastery, 1970), 224–33.
26. "Dukhovnaia sviaz' mezhdu pravednom otsom Ioannom Kronshtadtskim i startsem Varsonofiem," in I. M. Kontsevich, *Optina Pustyn' i eia vremia* (Jordanville, N.Y.: Holy Trinity Monastery, 1970; repr. Moscow, 1995), 359–65.
27. See St. John of Kronstadt Memorial Fund, Inc., Financial Report of 1995, 2.
28. John Meyendorff, *St. Gregory Palamas and Orthodox Spirituality* (Crestwood, N.Y.: St. Vladimir's Seminary Press, 1974), 168–70; Georgii V. Florovskii, *Puti russkago bogosloviia* (Paris: YMCA Press, 1937), 400–401; 432.
29. Archbishop Averkii, *Otets Ioann Kronshtadtskii, kak Prorok Bozhii, poslannyi Rossii dlia vrazumleniia* (Jordanville, N.Y.: Holy Trinity Monastery, 1963); see also I. K. Surskii, *Otets Ioann Kronshtadtskii*, 2 vols. (Belgrade, 1938–41; reprt. Forestville: St. Elias Publications, 1979–80), 2: 335–44.
30. Surskii, *Otets Ioann Kronshtadtskii*, 2: 220.
31. In Arkhimandrit Konstantin, *Chudo russkoi istorii*, see "K chemu zovet nas sviatost' o. Ioanna," 232–33; "Pamiat' sv. pravednago o. Ioanna Kronshtadtskago k chemu nas zovet?" (*IBFISPOIK*, no. 15 [1967]), 234–35; "Otets Ioann Kronshtadtskii," (*IBFISPOIK*, no. 8 [1961]), 314–15.
32. *St. John of Kronstadt: Life, Service, and Akathist Hymn* (Liberty, Tenn.: St. John of Kronstadt Press, n.d.), 45.
33. English translation is from *St. John of Kronstadt*, 43–45; emphases mine. For the troparion text, see pp. 15–16.
34. Father John is not the only saint to be "translated" geographically and temporally.

The same brochure about Saint Xenia was published first in Shanghai, China, in 1948; in Jordanville, New York, in 1964 and 1971; in London, Canada, in 1986; and finally in St. Petersburg after 1988 (S. D. Chechuga, ed., *Raba Bozhiia Blazhennaia Kseniia* (St. Petersburg: "Revers," n.d.).

35. "Son otsa Ioanna Kronshtadtskago," circulated by hand in the 1920s and 1930s; reprinted in *Grad-Kitezh* 2, no. 7 (1992): 12–14.

36. G. K. Tsimbal, "Manifest pravoslavnykh khristiian," quoted in Aleksei Moskalenko, *Ideologiia i deiatel'nost' khristianskikh sekt* (Novosibirsk: Nauka, 1978), 288.

37. Information on his relics is contradictory. See The Russian Federation State Archive of St. Petersburg (hereafter GARF SPb), f. 1001, d. 46 (Correspondence concerning the Karpovka convent; November 21, 1923–October 20, 1926), esp. ll. 1–32, 39–54.

38. Letter in *IBFISPOIK*, no. 10 (October 1963): 49.

39. Quoted in *V chest' dorogogo batiushki otsa Ioanna Kronshtadtskogo, vospominaniia ochevidtsev* (Moscow, 1995), 5–10.

40. Arkhim. Panteleimon, comp., *Zhizn', podvigi, chudesa i prorochestva sv. prav. otsa nashego Ioann, Kronshtadtskago Chudotvortsa* (Jordanville, N.Y.: Holy Trinity Monastery, 1976), 183–208.

41. Panteleimon, *Zhizn', podvigi, chudesa*, 201.

42. For the cult of wells, see Francis Jones, *The Holy Wells of Wales* (Cardiff: University of Wales Press, 1954). See also the careful discussion in A. A. Panchenko, *Issledovaniia v oblasti narodnogo pravoslaviia. Derevenskie sviatyni severo-zapada Rossii* (St. Petersburg: Izd. "Aleteia," 1998), 40–45, 61–65, 113–23.

43. Panteleimon, *Zhizn', podvigi, chudesa*, 201; Panchenko, *Issledovaniia*, 77. See the discussion of NEP-era omens and signs in Lynne Viola, *Peasant Rebels Under Stalin* (New York: Oxford University Press, 1996), 53–55.

44. Panteleimon, *Zhizn', podvigi, chudesa*, 198–200.

45. Ibid., 201–2. For Soviet-era revenge stories not connected with Father John, see Panchenko, *Issledovaniia*, 124–26.

46. Some of these have been collected in Sergei Fomin, *Rossia pered vtorym prishestviem: materialy k ocherku russkoi eskhatologii* (Sergiev Posad: Izd. Sviato–Troitskoi Sergievoi Lavry "Posad," 1993).

47. Panteleimon, *Zhizn', podvigi, chudesa*, 203–4.

48. Mikhail Bulgakov, *Master i Margarita* (Frankfurt am Main: Possev Verlag, 1969), 78. Some claim that the Griboedov House in the novel, which houses a Soviet literary organization, is a parody of Father John's House of Industry. See Boris Sokolov, *Entsiklopediia Bulgakovskaia* (Moscow: Lokid-Mif, 1996), 193.

49. Nikol'skii, *Istoriia russkoi tserkvi*, 462; N. P. Krasnikov, *Sotsial'no-eticheskie vozzreniia russkogo pravoslaviia v XX veke* (Kiev: "Vyssha shkola," 1988), 30; N. S. Gordienko, ed., *Pravoslavie: slovar' ateista* (Moscow: Politizdat, 1988), 94–95.

50. See, most notably, the apocryphal "Videnie otsa Ioanna Kronshtadtskago," circulated by hand in the 1920s and 1930s (Institut Istorii AN SSSR, f. Tambovskoi eksp. 1959 g., d. 53, l. 54) and reprinted in *Nash Sovremennik*, no. 9 (1991): 42–49, and *Pravoslavnaia Rus'*, no. 517 (October 15 [October 28], 1952): 2–5.

51. A. Iurin, "Ioannity," *Bezbozhnik* 5, no. 668 (February 12, 1939), 2.

52. See "Protokol doznaniia pristava Usmanskogo uezda o propagande sredi krest'ian sela Zaval'nogo ucheniia ioannitov," in *Voprosy istorii religii i ateizma* 9 (Moscow, 1961), 110.

53. Moskalenko, *Ideologiia i deiatel'nost' khristianskikh sekt*, 287, 304. Bishop John of San Francisco was canonized by the Russian Orthodox Church Outside Russia in 1994.

54. Gordienko, *Pravoslavie,* 95.
55. Eugene Clay, "Orthodox Missionaries and Orthodox Heretics," in Russia, 1886–1917," in Khodarkovsky and Geraci, *Religion and Identity;* Kolarz, *Religion in the Soviet Union,* 346–68; Christel Lane, *Christian Religion in the Soviet Union: A sociological study* (Albany: State University of New York, 1978), 80–81; Dimitry Pospielovsky, *Soviet Studies on the Church and the Believer's Response to Atheism,* vol. 3: *A History of Soviet Atheism in Theory and Practice, and the Believer* (London: Macmillan, 1988), 205–6.
56. *St. John of Kronstadt,* 15.
57. Service to Father John, in *Sviatoi pravednyi Ioann, Kronshtadtskii chudotvorets* (St. Petersburg: Satis, 1997), 96; emphases mine.
58. Nikolai K. Simakov, *Pravoslavnaia tserkov'. Sovremennye eresi i sekty v Rossii,* 2d ed. (St. Petersburg: Izd. Sankt-Peterburgskoi mitropolii "Pravoslavnaia Rus'," 1995), 237–38.
59. *V chest' dorogogo batiushki,* 3. In the 1990s, the late Metropolitan Ioann (Snychev) of St. Petersburg and Ladoga was a rare exception.
60. N. S. Gordienko, *Kto takoi Ioann Kronshtadtskii* (St. Petersburg: Znanie, 1991).
61. For documentation of the transfer, see GARF Spb, f. 1001, op. 9, d. 46, ll. 1–12 (correspondence concerening the closing of the Karpovka convent). For assertions to the contrary, see A. V. Kobak and Iu. M. Piriutko, comps., *Istoricheskiie kladbishcha Peterburga* (St. Petersburg, 1993), 537; M. V. Shkarovskii, *Sviato-Ioannovskii Stavropigial'nyi Zhenskii Monastyr': Istoriia Obiteli* (St. Petersburg, 1998), 144–50.
62. For the association with St. Petersburg, see *Molitvy sviatym, vo grade sviatogo Petra osobo pochitaemym* (Leningrad, 1991); the anniversary moleben is described in Avgustin, *Pravoslavnyi Peterburg,* 64; and the verses on the praises in *Sviatoi pravednyi Ioann Kronshtadtskii chudotvorets,* 98.
63. See the discussion of the iconographic categories of physician, singer, poet, warrior, and good musician in M. Didron, *Manuel d' iconographie Chrétienne Grecque et Latine* (Paris, 1844), 311, 320, 322–23, 339.
64. November 1, 1991, lecture given in St. Petersburg at the opening of "Otets" (Selicheva, 1991). For accounts of assault and battery, see Surskii, *Otets Ioann Kronshtadtskii,* 1: 122–23.
65. "Zhitiie sviatogo pravednogo Ioanna," 64.
66. Bol'shakov, *Istochnik zhivoi vody,* 148–88, 350–95, 799.

Bibliography

Archival and Manuscript Sources

Arkhiv Ustnoi Istorii Rossiiskogo Gosudarstvennogo Gumanitarnogo Universiteta, f. Pskovskoi ekspeditsii.
Bakhmeteff Archive, Rare Book and Manuscript Library, Columbia University, New York. Protopresbyter Georgii Shavel'skii, letter of June 12, 1939.
The Central State Archive of Cine- and Photo-Documents (TsGAKFD).
The Central State Historical Archive of St. Petersburg (Tsentral'nyi Gosudarstvennyi Istoricheskii Arkhiv Sankt-Peterburga [TsGIA Spb]).
   f. 569, op. 20, d. 344. On the episteme of the Ioannite sect.
   f. 2219. Sergiev, Ioann Kronshtadskii. 1856–1908. There are seventy-three individual *dela* that cover virtually all of Father Ioann's surviving correspondence. This is the largest single archival source on him.
The Russian Federation State Archive of St. Petersburg (Gosudarstvennyi Arkhiv Rossiiskoi Federatsii Sankt-Peterburga [GARF SPb]).
   f. 1001, d. 46. Correspondence concerning the Karpovka convent; November 21, 1923–October 20, 1926.
The Russian State Archive of Literature and Art (Rossiiskii Gosudarstvennyi Arkhiv Literatury I Iskusstva [RGALI]).
   f. 275, op. 1, d. 830. Leskov on Ioann Kronshtadtskii.

Bibliography

f. 402, op. 1, d. 284. Correspondence with S. I. Ponomarev.
f. 525, op. 1, d. 414. K. M. Fofanov's Reminiscences.
f. 1009, op. 1, d. 13. Correspondence with N. M. Anichkov.
f. 1345, op. 2, d. 83. Ioann Kronshtadtskii's miscellaneous manuscripts.

The Russian State Historical Archive (Rossiiskii Gosudarstvennyi Istoricheskii Arkhiv [RGIA], formerly).

f. 728, op. 1, d. 38. Correspondence with Tertii Ivanovich Filippov.
f. 777, op. 5, d. 7. Ministry of the Interior—St. Petersburg Censorship Committee.
f. 796. Synodal Archives. Those pertaining to Father Ioann are as follows:
—op. 173, d. 789. On establishing a foundation in his name.
—op. 174, d. 743. On his commemoration in church schools.
—op. 174, d. 521. On creating a scholarship in his name.
—op. 175, d. 2017. On a false doctrine worshipping him propagated by Kabanova.
—op. 175, d. 3107. On the right to officially stamp his portraits.
—op. 176, d. 3498. On the dissemination of a deliberately iconlike portrait.
—op. 177, d. 29. On his philanthropy.
f. 797, op. 23. Correspondance with Father John.
f. 799. Synodal Economic Administration.
f. 805, Chancellery of the Court Clergy Administration.
f. 821, op. 133, d. 206. On the Ioannite sect.
f. 834, op. 2, no. 1701, fol. 2. Condemnation of *iurodstvo*.
—op. 4, op. 2, no. 1701, fol. 2. Synodal condemnation of *iurodstvo*.
—op. 4, d. 250. Foreign newspaper clippings on Father Ioann of Kronstadt.
—op. 4, d. 1668. Reminiscences of a devotee.
f. 1082, op. 1, d. 21. Correspondence with K. P. Shabel'skii.
f. 1111, op. 1, d. 5. Miscellaneous correspondence with I. Sergiev.
f. 1120. Miscellaneous manuscripts and photographs pertaining to I. Sergiev.
f. 1405, op. 539, d. 502. Information on the circumstances of Kronshtadtskii's death.
f. 1574, op. 2, d. 708. K. P. Pobedonostsev.

The Russian State Historical Archive of the City of Moscow (Rossiiskii Gosudarstvennyi Istoricheskii Arkhiv [RGIA]) g. Moskvy.

f. 203. Moscow Religious Consistory, op. 392, d. 3. Rejection of a Father John–sponsored request to open a women's religious community.

Russian State Humanities University Oral History Archive.

The Russian State Library (Rossiiskaia Gosudarstvennaia Biblioteka) (formerly Lenin Library), Otdel Rukopisei.

f. 178, Aleksei Sergeevich (Suvorin).
f. 253, S. A. Romanov.
f. 262, op. 14, d. 2. Savva (Tikhomirov).
f. 369, Bonch-Bruevich.

The State Archive of the Russian Federation (Gosudarstvennyi Arkhiv Rossiiskii Federatsii [GARF]).

f. 1067, op. 1, d. 1–34. Ioann Kronshtadtskii's diaries from 1856–1904; some correspondence.

Bibliography

f. 102. Department of Police
—d. 154. Material on the Ioannite sect (in two parts).
—d. 873. On Kronshtadtskii's involvement with the Kishinev pogroms.
—d. 1366. On attempts to form a new sect.
The State Museum of Ethnography (Gosudarstvennyi Muzei Etnografii) (GME), Tenishev Archive, f. 7, op. 1.

Published Sources

Agursky, Michail. "Caught in a Cross Fire: The Russian Church between Holy Sinod and Radical Right. 1905–1908." *Orientalia Christiana Periodica* 50 (1984): 163–96.
Alekseev, Il'ia A. *Razgrom ioannitov*. St. Petersburg, 1909.
Alexander, Bishop. *See* Aleksandr Semenoff-Tian-Shanskii
Almazov, A. I. *Apokrificheskiia molitvy, zaklinaniia, i zagovory*. Odessa, 1901.
———. *Tainaia ispoved' v pravoslavnoi vostochnoi tserkvi: opyt vneshnei istorii*, 3 vols. Odessa, 1894–95.
Amalrik, Andrei. *Raspoutine*. Paris: Seuil, 1982.
Amand, Dom David. *L'Ascèse Monastique de Saint Basile, Essai Historique*. Maredsous: Editions de Maredsous, 1948.
Amfiteatrov, Aleksandr. *Zhenshchina v obshchestvennykh dvizheniiakh Rossii*. Geneva, 1905.
Amvrosii, Hieroschemamonk. *Sobranie pisem Blazhennoi pamiati optinskogo startsa ieroskhimonakha Amvrosiia k mirskim osobam*. Sergiev Posad, 1908.
Anthony [Khrapovitsky], Metropolitan. *See* Antonii Khrapovitskii.
Antonov, V. V., and A. V. Kobak. *Sviatyni Sankt-Peterburga, Istoriko-tserkovnaia entsiklopediia v trekh tomakh*. 3 vols. St. Petersburg: Izd. Chernysheva, 1996.
Apostol. St. Petersburg, 1860.
Arapova, D. A. *Life of Father John of Kronstadt: Related for Children and Youth*, trans. C. Aleeff. San Francisco: Russian Convent of Our Lady of Vladimir, Inc. 1958.
Ariès, Philippe. *The Hour of Our Death*. New York: Random House, 1982.
Arsenii, Bishop. *See* Zhadanovskii, Arsenii (Bishop).
Atkinson, Clarissa W., et al. *Immaculate and Powerful: The Female Sacred Image and Social Reality*. Boston: Beacon Press, 1985.
Auxentios (Bishop). Response to letter in *Orthodox Tradition*, 11, no. 3 (1994): 69.
Averkii, Archbishop. *Otets Ioann Kronshtadtskii, kak Prorok Bozhii, poslannyi Rossii dlia vrazumleniia*. Jordanville, N.Y.: Holy Trinity Monastery, 1963.
Avgustin, Arkhimandrit (Nikitin). *Pravoslavnyi Peterburg v Zapiskakh Inostrantsev*. St. Petersburg: too "Zhurnal NEVA," 1995.
Badone, Ellen, ed. *Religious Orthodoxy and Popular Faith in European Society*. Princeton: Princeton University Press, 1990.
Baedeker, K. *La Russie, manuel du voyageur*. Leipzig, 1893.
Bakunin, Mikhail. *God and the State*. New York: Dover Publications, 1970.
Balzer, Marjorie Mandelstam, ed. *Russian Traditional Culture: Religion, Gender, and Customary Law*. Armonk, N.Y.: M. E. Sharpe, 1992.

Bibliography

Bander van Duren, Peter. *Orders of Knighthood and of Merit: The Pontifical, Religious, and Secularised Catholic-founded Orders and their relationship to the Apostolic See*. New York: Gerrards Cross, Buckinghamshire: C. Smythe, 1995.

Baran, Henryk. "Religious Holiday Literature and Russian Modernism," in Robert P. Hughes and Irina Paperno, eds., *Christianity and the Eastern Slavs*, vol. 2: *Russian Culture in Modern Times*. Berkeley and Los Angeles: University of California Press, 1994.

Baring, Maurice. *A Year in Russia*. New York: Dutton, 1917; repr. Westport: Hyperion, 1981.

Bartenev, I. A., and V. N. Batazhkova. *Russkii inter'er XIX veka*. Leningrad: Iskusstvo, 1984.

Batalden, Stephen K., et al. *Seeking God: The Recovery of Religious Identity in Orthodox Russia, Ukraine, and Georgia*. DeKalb: Northern Illinois University Press, 1993.

Batts, Richard, and Viacheslav Marchenko. *Dukhovnik Tsarskoi Sem'i, sviatitel' Feofan Poltavskii. 1874–1940*. Platina, Calif.: St. Herman of Alaska Press; Moscow: Rossiiskoe otd. Valaamskago obshchestva Ameriki, 1994.

Behr-Sigel, E. "Notes sur l'idée russe de sainteté d'apres les saints canonisés de l'Eglise russe." *Revue de l'Histoire et de la Philosophie Religieuse* 13 (1933): 537–54.

———. *Prière et sainteté dans l'Eglise russe suivi d'un essai sur le role du monachisme dans la vie spirituelle du peuple russe*. Paris: Editions du Cerf, 1950.

Belliustin, I. S. *Description of the Clergy in Rural Russia The Memoir of a Nineteenth-Century Parish Priest*, trans. Gregory Freeze. Ithaca: Cornell University Press, 1985.

Belting, Hans. *Likeness and Presence: A History of the Image Before the Era of Art*. Chicago: University of Chicago Press, 1994.

Biografiia o. Ioanna Kronshtadtskago. St. Petersburg, 1895.

Birkbeck, W. J., ed. *Russia and the English Church During the Last Fifty Years*, vol. 1. London: Rivington, Percival & Co., 1895.

Blagovidov, F. V. *Deiatel'nost' russkogo dukhovenstva v otnosshenii k narodnomu obrazovaniiu v tsarstvovanie imp. Aleksandra II*. Kazan, 1891.

Blane, Andrew. "Protestant Sects in Late Imperial Russia," in Andrew Blane, ed., *The Religious World of Russian Culture, Russia and Orthodoxy*, vol. 2: *Essays in Honor of Georges Florovsky*. The Hague and Paris: Mouton, 1975.

Bloch, Marc. *Les Rois thaumaturges, Etude sur le caractère surnaturel attribué à la puissance royale particulièrement en France et en Angleterre*. Strasbourg and Paris: Librairie Istra, 1924.

Boele, Otto. *The North in Russian Romantic Literature*. Amsterdam and Atlanta: Rodopi, 1996.

Bogdanovich, E. *Otkrytoe pis'mo starosty Isaakievskago Sobora g. Pashkovu*. St. Petersburg, 1883.

Boldovskii, A. G. *Vozrozhdenie tserkovnago prikhoda. Obzor mnenii pechati*. St. Petersburg, 1903.

Bol'shakov, Nikolai I. *Istochnik zhivoi vody. Opisanie zhizni i deiatel'nosti otsa Ioanna Kronshtadtskago*. St. Petersburg, 1910; repr. St. Petersburg: Izd. "Tsarskoe Delo," 1995.

Bibliography

———. *Lozhnaia zashchitnitsa pravoslaviia i "Chernye Vorony,"* supp. to no. 3 of *Kronshtadtskii Maiak*. St. Petersburg, 1908.
———. *Pravda o sekte ioannitov*. St. Petersburg: Izd. "Kronshtadtskii Maiak," 1906.
Bossy, John. "The Counter-Reformation and the People of Catholic Europe." *Past and Present*, no. 47 (May 1970): 51–70.
Boutry, Philippe, and Michel Cinquin. *Deux Pelérinages au XIXe Siècle, Ars et Paray-le-Monial*, Bibliothèque Beauchesne, 8. Paris: Editions Beauchesne, 1980.
Boyle, Leonard. "Popular Piety in the Middle Ages: What Is Popular?" *Florilegium* 4 (1982): 184–89.
Brianchianinov, Bishop Ignatii. *The Arena: An Offering to Contemporary Monasticism*. Jordanville, N.Y.: St. Job of Pochaev Press, 1983.
Brokgauz, F. A., and I. A. Efron. *Entsiklopedicheskii Slovar'*. 82 vols., with 4 supp. vols. St. Petersburg, 1890–1907.
Brooks, Jeffrey. *When Russia Learned to Read: Literacy and Popular Literature, 1861–1917*. Princeton: Princeton University Press, 1985.
Brown, Peter. *The Body and Society: Men, Women, and Sexual Renunciation in Early Christianity*. New York: Columbia University Press, 1988.
———. *The Cult of Saints: Its Rise and Function in Latin Christianity*. Chicago: University of Chicago Press, 1982.
———. "The Rise and Function of the Holy Man in Late Antiquity." *Journal of Roman Studies* 61 (1971): 80–101.
———. *Society and the Holy in Late Antiquity*. Berkeley and Los Angeles: University of California Press, 1982.
Brundage, James A. "Carnal Delight: Canonistic Theories of Sexuality." *Proceedings of the Fifth International Congress of Medieval Canon Law, Salamanca, 21–25 September 1965*, p. 375–88.
Budge, Ernest A. Wallis, trans. and ed. *The Paradise or Garden of the Holy Fathers, vol. I, containing the Life of St. Anthony, by Athanasius, Archbishop of Alexandria*.... London, 1907; repr. Seattle: St. Nectarios Press, 1994.
Bulgakov, Mikhail. *Master i Margarita*. Frankfurt and Main: Possev Verlag, 1969.
Bulgakov, (Archpriest) Sergii. *Avtobiograficheskiia zamietki. Posmertnoe izdanie*. Paris: YMCA Press, 1946.
Bulgakov, S. V. *Nastol'naia Kniga dlia sviashchenno—tserkovno sluzhitelei. Sbornik svedenii, kasaiushchikhsia preimushchestvenno prakticheskoi deiatel'nosti otechestvennago dukhovenstva*. 2d ed., 2 vols. Kharkov, 1900.
Bushkovitch, Paul. "The Limits of Hesychasm: Some Notes on Monastic Spirituality in Russia, 1350–1500." *Forschungen zur osteuropäischen Geschichte* 38 (Berlin, 1986): 97–109.
Butkevich, T. I. *Obzor russkikh sekt i ikh tolkov*. Kharkov, 1910.
Bychkov, S. S., comp. *Zhizneopisaniia dostopamiatnykh liudei zemli russkoi, X–XXvv*. Moscow: Moskovskii rabochii, 1992.
Bystrov, Nikolai. "Religiozno—nravstvennye sobesedovaniia v Il'inskoi tserkvi pogosta Muraveina, Ostrovskago uezda." *Pskovskie Eparkhial'nye Vedomosti*, no. 22 (November 15, 1896): 388.

Bibliography

Bynum, Caroline Walker. *Holy Feast and Holy Fast: The Religious Significance of Food to Medieval Women.* Berkeley and Los Angeles: University of California Press, 1987.

———. *Jesus as Mother: Studies in the Spirituality of the High Middle Ages.* Berkeley and Los Angeles: University of California Press, 1982.

Carroll, Michael P. *Catholic Cults and Devotions: A Psychological Inquiry.* Kingston and Montreal: McGill-Queen's University Press, 1989.

———. *Veiled Threats: The Logic of Popular Catholicism in Italy.* Baltimore: Johns Hopkins University Press, 1996.

Carty, Rev. Charles Mortimer. *Padre Pio the Stigmatist*, 15th ed. St. Paul, Minn.: Radio Replies Press, 1955.

The Case of Russia: A Composite View. New York: Fox, Duffield, and Co., 1905.

Chadwick, Owen. *The Secularization of the European Mind in the Nineteenth Century: The Gifford Lectures in the University of Edinburgh for 1973-74.* Cambridge: Cambridge University Press, 1975.

Chariton, Igumen of Valamo, comp. *The Art of Prayer: An Orthodox Anthology.* London: Faber and Faber, 1973.

Chekhov, Anton. *Ostrov Sakhalin: (Iz putevykh zapisok), Polnoe Sobranie Sochinenii i pisem, Sochineniia: v. 14–15.* Moscow: Nauka, 1978.

Chernovskii, A., comp., and Viktorov, V. P., ed. *Soiuz russkogo naroda po materialam chrezvychainoi sledstvennoi komissii vremennogo pravitel'stva 1917 g.* Moscow and Leningrad, Gosudarstvennoe izd., 1929.

Chetverikov, (Archpriest) Sergii. *Bog v russkoi dushe.* Moscow: Krutitskoe Patriarshee Podvor'e, 1998.

———. *Dukhovnyi oblik o. Ioanna Kronshtadtskago i ego pastyrskie zavety.* Jordanville, N.Y.: Holy Trinity Monastery, 1958.

———. *Optina Pustyn'*, 2d ed. Paris: YMCA Press, 1988.

———. "Optinskii Starets Ieroskhimonakh Amvrosii." *Vechnoe/L'Eternel*, no. 122 (February 1958): 28–54.

Chizhov, P. M., ed. *Otets Ioann Kronshtadtskii, Zhizn', deiatel'nost', izbrannye chudesa.* Jordanville, N.Y.: Holy Trinity Monastery, 1958.

Christian, William A., Jr. *Local Religion in Sixteenth-Century Spain.* Princeton: Princeton University Press, 1981.

———. *Visionaries: The Spanish Republic and the Reign of Christ.* Berkeley and Los Angeles: University of California Press, 1996.

———. "Holy People in Peasant Europe." *Comparative Studies in Society and History* 15 (1973): 106–14.

Clay, J. Eugene. "Orthodox Missionaries and 'Orthodox Heretics' in Russia, 1866–1917," in *Religion and Identity*, ed. Michael Khodarkovsky and Robert Geraci.

Clowes, Edith W., Samuel D. Kassow, and James L. West, eds. *Between Tsar and People: Educated Society and the Quest for Public Identity in Late Imperial Russia.* Princeton: Princeton University Press, 1991.

Cracraft, James A. *The Church Reform of Peter the Great.* Stanford: Stanford University Press, 1971.

Crummey, Robert O. "Old Belief as Popular Religion: New Approaches." *Slavic Review* 52, no. 4 (winter 1993): 700–712.

Bibliography

———. *The Old Believers and the World of Anti-Christ*. Madison: University of Wisconsin, 1970.
Curtiss, John L. *Church and State in Imperial Russia*. New York: Columbia University Press, 1948.
Dal', Vladimir I. *Poslovitsy russkago naroda: sbornik poslovits, pogovorok, rechenii, prislovii, chistogovorok, pribautok, zagadok, poverii, i proch.* 2 vols. Moscow, 1862.
Daniel-Rops, Henri. *Ces Chrétiens, Nos Frères*. Paris: Fayard, 1965.
Davis, Natalie Zemon. "Some Tasks and Themes in the Study of Popular Religion," in Charles Trinkhaus, ed., *The Pursuit of Holiness in Late Medieval and Renaissance Religion*, Papers from the University of Michigan Conference on Late Medieval and Renaissance Religion. Leiden: Brill, 1974.
Davis, Robert H. "19th-Century Russian Religious-Theological Journals: Structure and Access." *St. Vladimir's Theological Quarterly* 33, no. 3 (1989): 235–59.
Debol'skii, (Archpriest) G. S. *O liubvi k otechestvu i trudie po slovu Bozhiiu*, 4th ed. repr. Moscow: Izd. "Pravilo Very," 1996.
Delooz, Pierre. *Sociologie et canonisations*. Liège: Faculté de droit, 1969.
Desiatnikov, V. A., comp. *Ioann Kronshtadtskii*. Moscow: "Patriot," 1992.
Diachenko, Grigorii. *Khristianskiia utesheniia neschastnykh i skorbiashchikh, ispytyvaiushchikh bednost', bolezni, poteri rodnykh i blizkikh serdtsu, zhiteiskiia neudachi....* 3 parts. Moscow, 1898.
———. *Polnyi tserkovno-slavianskii slovar'*, 2 vols. Moscow, 1899.
———. *V podarok detiam. Iskra Bozhiia. Sbornik razskazov i stikhotvorenii, prisposoblennykh k chteniiu v khristianskoi i shkole dlia devochek sredniago vozrasta*. Moscow, 1903.
Didron, M. *Manuel d'iconographie Chrétienne Grecque et Latine*. Paris, 1845.
Dimitrii. Episkop. *Domashnii molitvoslov dlia userdstvuiushikh*. Kharbin: Bratstvo sv. Ioanna Bogoslova, 1943.
Di Tota, Mia. "Saint Cults and Political Alignments in Southern Italy." *Dialectical Anthropology* 5 (1981): 317–29.
Dix, Dom Gregory. *The Shape of the Liturgy*, 2d ed. London: Adam & Charles Black, 1975.
Dixon, Simon. "The Church's Social Role in St. Petersburg, 1880–1914," in Geoffrey A. Hosking, ed., *Church, Nation and State in Russia and Ukraine*, 178–92. London: Macmillan, 1991.
Dobroliubov, Nikolai. *Selected Philosophical Essays*. Moscow: Foreign Languages Publishing House, 1948.
Dobrotoliubiie, tom pervyi. Repr. of unspecified prerevolutionary edition, by Sergiev Posad: Sviato-Troitskaia Sergieva Lavra, 1993.
Dobryi pastyr': biografiia o. Ioanna Kronshtadtskogo, pis'ma k batiushke i vospominaniia o nem. St. Petersburg: Izd. Aleksandro-Nevskoi Lavry, 1994.
Dooley, Eugene A. *Church Law on Sacred Relics*. Washington, D.C., 1931. Catholic University of America Canon Law Studies 70: 10–19.
Dörner, Klaus, ed., *Madmen and the Bourgeoisie: A Social History of Insanity and Psychiatry*. Oxford: Blackwell, 1981.
Dostoyevsky [Dostoevskii], Fedor. *Brat'ia Karamazovy, roman v chetyrekh chastiakh s epilogom*. Moscow: Pravda, 1980.

Bibliography

Doucet, Catherine Bortoli. Personal documents.
Douglas, Ann. *The Feminization of American Culture*. New York: Knopf, 1977.
Dubisch, Jill. "Culture Enters through the Kitchen: Women, Food, and Social Boundaries in Rural Greece," in her *Gender and Power in Rural Greece*. Princeton: Princeton University Press, 1986.
———. "Greek Women: Sacred or Profane?" *Journal of Modern Greek Studies* 1 (1983): 185–202.
Duffy, Eamon. *Stripping the Altars: Traditional Religion in England circa 1400 to circa 1580*. New Haven: Yale University Press, 1992.
Dukhonina, E. *Iz moikh vospominanii ob o. Ioannie Kronshtadtskom*. St. Petersburg, 1907
———. *Kak postavil menia na put' spaseniia otets Ioann Kronshtadtskii. Dnevnik dukhovnoi docheri*. St. Petersburg, 1911; repr. Moscow: Izd. Otchii dom, 1998.
Dumskii, F. I. *Zolotyia slova; sbornik propovedei russkikh tserkovnykh vitii*. St. Petersburg, 1905.
Dushepoleznoe chteniie: Ukazatel' statei, pomieshchennykh v Duzhepoleznom chtenii v techenie desiati liet, ot nachala v 1860 do 1869 goda. Moscow: tip. V. Got'e, 1870.
Dushepoleznyi Sobesednik za 1889 g. Moscow: Izd. Russkago Panteleimonskago Monastyrie na Afone/tip. I. Efimova, 1902.
Efimenko, Aleksandra. *Izsledovaniia Narodnoi Zhizni*. Moscow, 1884.
Efremov, Prot. Luka Vasil'evich. *Dobryi Pastyr. Kratkoe opisanie zhizni otsa Ioanna Borisovicha, sviashchennika Preobrazhenskoi tserkvi goroda El'tsa. 1750–1824*. Voronezh, 1893.
Eklof, Ben. *Russian Peasant Schools: Officialdom, Village Culture, and Popular Pedagogy, 1861–1914*. Berkeley and Los Angeles: University of California Press, 1986.
Elagin, N. V. *Chto nado zhelat' dlia nashei tserkvi*. St. Petersburg, 1882–85.
Elliott, Dyan. *Spiritual Marriage: Sexual Abstinence in Medieval Wedlock*. Princeton: Princeton University Press, 1993.
Emeliakh, Liubov I. *Antiklerikal'noe dvizhenie krestian v period pervoi russkoi revoliutsii*. Leningrad: Nauka, 1965.
Engel, Barbara Alpern. *Between the Fields and the City: Women, Work, and Family in Russia, 1861–1914*. Cambridge: Cambridge University Press, 1994.
Engelstein, Laura. *The Keys to Happiness: Sex and the Search for Modernity in Fin-de-Siècle Russia*. Ithaca: Cornell University Press, 1994.
Esipov, N. N., comp. *Sviatitel' i Chudotvorets Arkhiepiskop Chernigovskii Feodosii Uglitskii*. St. Petersburg, 1897.
Evans, J. M. *Paradise Lost and the Genesis Tradition*. Oxford: Oxford University Press, 1968.
Every, Edward. "Khomiakoff and the Encyclical of the Eastern Patriarchs in 1848." *Sobornost'*, series 3, no. 3(summer 1948): 102–10.
Evlogii, (Metropolitan). *Vospominaniia*. Paris: YMCA Press, 1957.
Evstratii [Golovanskii], (Hieromonk). *Tysiacha dvesti voprosov sel'skikh prikhozhan o raznykh dushepoleznykh predmetakh s otvetami na onye byvshago prikhodskago ikh sviashchennika*, 2d ed. Kiev, 1869.
Farnsworth, Beatrice, and Lynne Viola, eds. *Russian Peasant Women*. New York: Oxford University Press, 1991.

Bibliography

Fedotov, George P. *Imperiia i Svoboda*. New York: Possev-SSha, 1989.

———. *The Russian Religious Mind*, vol. 1: *Kievan Christianity, The 10th to the 13th Centuries*. Cambridge, Mass.: Harvard University Press, 1946.

———. *The Russian Religious Mind*, vol. 2: *The Middle Ages, the 13th to the 15th Centuries*. Belmont, Mass: Nordland, 1975.

———. *Stikhi dukhovnye. Russkaia narodnaia vera po dukhovnym stikham*. Moscow: Progress/Gnozis, 1991.

———. *A Treasury of Russian Spirituality*. Belmont, Mass.: Nordland Publishing Co., 1975.

Felmy, Karl Christian. *Predigt im orthodoxen Rußland, Untersuchungen zu Inhalt und Eigenart der russischen Predigt in der zweiten Hälfte des 19. Jahrhunderts*. Göttingen: Vandenhoek & Ruprecht, 1972.

Feofan [Govorov], (Archbishop). *Chto est' dukhovnaia zhizn' i kak na nee nastroitsia? Pis'ma Episkopa Feofana*. Moscow, 1914.

———. *Pis'ma k raznym litsam o raznykh predmetakh viery i zhizni*, 2d ed. Moscow, 1892.

———. *Primery zapisyvaniia dobrykh myslei, prikhodiashchikh vo vremia bogomysliia i molitvy....* Moscow, 1903; repr. Saratov: Blagovest, 1997.

Field, Daniel. *The End of Serfdom*. Cambridge, Mass.: Harvard University Press, 1976.

———. *Rebels in the Name of the Tsar*. Boston: Houghton Mifflin, 1976.

Filaret, Drozdov (Metropolitan). *Khristianskoe uchenie o Tsarskoi vlasti iz propovedei Filareta, mitropolita Moskovskogo*. Moscow, 1901.

Firsov, S. L., comp. and ed. *Sviatoi Ioann Kronshtadtskii v vospominaniiakh sovremennikov*. Moscow: Pravoslavnyi Sviato-Tikhonovskii Bogoslovskii Institut, Bratstvo vo Imia Vsemilostivogo Spasa, 1994.

Flier, Michael S. "The Church of the Savior on the Blood: Projection, Rejection, Resurrection," in Robert P. Hughes and Irina Paperno, eds., *Christianity and the Eastern Slavs*, vol. 2: *Russian Culture in Modern Times*. Berkeley and Los Angeles: University of California Press, 1994.

Florovskii, Georgii V. *Puti russkago bogosloviia*. Paris: YMCA Press, 1937.

Fomin, Sergei, comp. *Rossiia pered vtorym prishestviem: materialy k ocherku russkoi eskhatologii*. Moscow: Izd. Sviato–Troitskoi Sergievoi Lavry "Posad," 1993.

Freeze, Gregory L. *The Parish Clergy in Nineteenth-Century Russia: Crisis, Reform, Counter-Reform*. Princeton: Princeton University Press, 1983.

———. *The Russian Levites: Parish Clergy in the Eighteenth Century*. Cambridge, Mass.: Harvard University Press, 1977.

———. "'Going to the Intelligentsia': The Church and Its Urban Mission in Post-Reform Russia," in Edith W. Clowes, Samuel D. Kassow, and James L. West, eds., *Between Tsar and People: Educated Society and the Quest for Public Identity in Late Imperial Russia*. Princeton: Princeton University Press, 1991.

———. "The Wages of Sin: The Decline of Public Penance in Imperial Russia," in Stephen K. Batalden, ed., *Seeking God: The Recovery of Religious Identity in Orthodox Russia, Ukraine, and Georgia*. DeKalb: Northern Illinois University Press, 1993.

———. "A Case of Stunted Anticlericalism: Clergy and Society in Imperial Russia." *European Studies Review* (SAGE) 13 (1983): 179–91.

Bibliography

———. "Handmaiden of the State? The Church in Imperial Russia Reconsidered." *Journal of Ecclesiastical History* 30, no. 1 (January 1985): 82–102.

———. "The Orthodox Church and Serfdom in Prereform Russia." *Slavic Review* 48 (1989): 376–98.

———. "The Rechristianization of Russia: The Church and Popular Religion, 1750–1850." *Studia Slavica Finlandensia* 7 (1990): 101–36.

———. "Subversive Piety: Religion and the Political Crisis in Late Imperial Russia." *Journal of Modern History* 68 (June 1996): 308–50.

Fülöp-Miller, René. *Raspoutine et les femmes*. Paris: Payot, 1928.

———. *Rasputin: The Holy Devil*. New York: Frederick Ungar Publishing Co., 1962.

Gagarin, Father, S.J. *The Russian Clergy*. New York: AMS Press, 1970; repr. of London, 1872.

Galavaris, George. *The Icon in the Life of the Church: Doctrine, Liturgy, Devotion*. Leiden: Brill, 1981.

Gal'kovskii, N. M. *Bor'ba Khristianstva s ostatkami iazychestva v drevnei Rusi*. Kharkov, 1916.

Gannushkin, P. B. "Sladostrastie, zhestokost' i religiia," in *Izbrannye trudy*. Moscow: Politizdat, 1964.

Gapon, Georgii Apollonovich. *Zapiski Georgiia Gapona (Ocherk rabochago dvizheniia v Rossii 1900-kh godov)*. Moscow, 1918.

Gardner, Johann von. *Bogosluzhebnoe penie Russkoi Pravoslavnoi Tserkvi: Sistema, sushchnost', istoriia*, 2 vols. Jordanville, N.Y.: Holy Trinity Monastery, 1980–82.

Garrett, Paul D. *St. Innocent: Apostle to America*. Crestwood, N.Y.: St. Vladimir's Seminary Press, 1979.

Gellner, E., and J. Waterbury, eds. *Patrons and Clients in Mediterranean Societies*. London: Duckworth, 1977.

Geidor, T. I., et al. *Russkii gorod na pochtovoi otkrytke kontsa XIX-nachala XX veka*. Moscow: Russkaia kniga, 1997.

Geifman, Anna. *Thou Shalt Kill: Revolutionary Terrorism in Russia, 1894–1917*. Princeton: Princeton University Press, 1993.

Genicot, Leopold. "Sur l'interêt des textes hagiographiques." *Academie Royale de Belgique, Bulletin de la Classe des Lettres et de Sciences Morales et Politiques*, 5th series, 5 (1965): 65–75.

Giliarov-Platonov, Nikita P. *Iz perezhitago: avtobiograficheskie vospominaniia*, 2 vols. Moscow, 1886–87.

Gippius, Zinaida. *Zhivye Litsa*. Leningrad: Iskusstvo, 1991.

Gleason, Abbott. *European and Muscovite: Ivan Kireevsky and the Origins of Slavophilism*. Cambridge, Mass.: Harvard University Press, 1972.

Glizhinskii, K., *Iz ob'iatii umiraiushchei bursy v gornilo zhizni. Ocherki poslednikh dnei bursy i sovremennago razvala tserkovno-prikhodskoi zhizni*. Ekaterinburg, 1912.

Goldstein, Darra. "Domestic Porkbarreling in Nineteenth-Century Russia, or Who Holds the Keys to the Larder?" in Helena Goscilo and Beth Holmgren, eds. *Russia, Women, Culture*. Bloomington: Indiana University Press, 1996.

Bibliography

Goloshchapov, S. *Galliutsinatsii i religioznye videniia*. Kazan: "Tan," 1992; repr. Kharkov, 1915.
Golubinskii, Evgenii. *Istoriia kanonizatsii sviatykh v russkoi tserkvi*. Moscow, 1903.
———. *Istoriia russkoi tserkvi*. 4 vols. Moscow, 1880–1907.
Golovanskii, Evstratii. *See* Evstratii (Golovanskii)
Gordienko, N. S. *Kto takoi Ioann Kronshtadtskii*. St. Petersburg: Znanie, 1991.
———. *Novye pravoslavnye sviatye*. Kiev: Izd. "Ukraina," 1991.
———, ed. *Pravoslavie: slovar' ateista*. Moscow: Politizdat, 1988.
Gorodetzky, Nadejda. *Saint Tikhon of Zadonsk: Inspirer of Dostoyevsky*. Crestwood, N.Y.: St. Vladimir's Seminary Press, 1976.
Goscilo, Helena. "Keeping A-Breast of the Waist-land: Women's Fashion in Early-Nineteenth-Century Russia," in Helena Goscilo and Beth Holmgren, eds., *Russia, Women, Culture*.Bloomington: Indiana University Press, 1996.
Graham, Stephen. *With the Russian Pilgrims to Jerusalem*. London: Macmillan, 1913.
Grant-Duff, F. "A Psycho-Analytical Study of a Phantasy of St Thérèse de l'Enfant Jésus." *British Journal of Medical Psychology* 5 (1925): 345–53.
Gromyko, Marina. *Mir russkoi derevni*. Moscow: Molodaia Gvardiia, 1991.
Grundmann, Herbert. *Religious Movements in the Middle Ages: The Historical Links between Heresy, the Mendicant Orders, and the Women's Religious Movement in the Twelfth and Thirteenth Centuries*. Notre Dame: University of Notre Dame Press, 1995.
Günter, Heinrich. *Psychologie der Legende, Studien zu einer wissenschaftlichen Heiligen-Geschichte*. Freiburg: Herder, 1949.
Gutiérrez, Gustavo. *A Theology of Liberation: History, Politics, and Salvation*. Maryknoll, N.Y.: Orbis Books, 1973.
Hackel, Sergei, ed., *The Byzantine Saint*. London: Fellowship of St. Alban and St. Sergius, 1981.
Hall, David, ed. *Lived Religion in America: Towards a History of Practice*. Princeton: Princeton University Press, 1997.
Hapgood, Isabel, comp. *Service Book of the Holy Orthodox-Catholic Apostolic Church*. Englewood, N.J.: Antiochian Orthodox Christian Archdiocese, 1975.
Harline, Craig. "Official Religion–Popular Religion in Recent Historiography of the Catholic Reformation." *Archive for Reformation History* 81 (1990): 239–62.
Harris, Robin. "On Trial Again." *The Catholic World Report*, August–September 1998, 41–43.
Hauptmann, Peter. "Johann von Kronstadt, 'Der Große Hirte des Russischen Landes.'" *Kirche im Osten*, Bd. 3: 33–71. Stuttgart: Evangelisches Verlagswerk, 1960.
Heier, Edmund. *Religious Schism in the Russian Aristocracy, 1860–1900*. The Hague: Nijhoff, 1970.
Heller, Wolfgang. "Johannes von Kronstadt," in *Biographisch-Bibliographisches Kirchenlexikon*, Bd. 3: 448–51. Herzberg: T. Bautz, 1992.
Heretz, Leonid. "The Practice and Significance of Fasting in Russian Peasant Culture at the Turn of the Century," in Musya Glants and Joyce Toomre, eds., *Food in Russian History and Culture*. Bloomington: Indiana University Press, 1997.

Hirschon, Renée. "Women, the Aged, and Religious Activity: Oppositions and Complementarity in an Urban Locality." *Journal of Modern Greek Studies* 1 (1983): 113–30.

Hilton, Alison. "Piety and Pragmatism: Orthodox Saints and Slavic Nature Gods in Russian Folk Art," in William C. Brumfield and Milos M. Velimirovich, eds., *Christianity and the Arts in Russia*. New York: Cambridge University Press, 1991.

Hosking, Geoffrey A., ed. *Church, Nation and State in Russia and Ukraine*. London: Macmillan; New York: St. Martin's Press, 1991.

Hourwich, Isaac. "Religious Sects in Russia," in *The Case of Russia: A Composite View*. New York: Fox, Duffield, and Co., 1905.

Hubbs, Joanna. *Mother Russia: The Feminine Myth in Russian Culture*. Bloomington: Indiana University Press, 1988.

Hulme, Kathryn. *The Nun's Story*. Boston: Little, Brown, 1956.

Hutchinson, John. *Politics and Public Health in Revolutionary Russia, 1890–1918*. Baltimore: Johns Hopkins University Press, 1990.

Iakov (Archimandrite). *Pastyr' v otnoshenii k sebie i pastvie*. St. Petersburg, Lebedeva, 1880.

Iarygina, I. V., comp. *The Russian Icon of Late XVIII–XIX ss.* St. Petersburg: "Kinocentre/Limbus Press," 1994.

Ignatov, F. "Vospominaniia ob o. Ioannie Kronshtadtskom." *Volynskie Eparkhial'nye Vedomosti* no. 6 (1914): 151–54.

Informatsionnyi Biulleten' fonda im. o. Ioanna Kronshtadtskago, no. 10, 1963. Utica, N.Y.

Ioann (of the Ladder). *Prepodobnago otsa nashego Ioanna, igumena Sinaiiskoi gory, Lestvitsa*, 7th ed. Sergiev Posad, 1908.

Ioann [Sokolov] (Bishop of Smolensk). *O Monashestvie Episkopov*. Pochaev, 1904.

Ioasaf (Hieromonk.) *Kratkiia svedeniia o sv. ugodnikakh Bozhiikh i mestno chtimykh podvizhnikakh blagochestiia....* Vladimir, 1860.

Isaac le Syrien. *Oeuvres spirituels, les 86 discours ascétiques*. Paris: Desclée de Brouwers, 1993.

Iuriev and Vladimirskii, comp. *Pravila svetskoi zhizni i etiketa. Khoroshii Ton*. St. Petersburg, 1889.

Ivanits, Linda J. *Russian Folk Belief*. Armonk, N.Y.: M. E. Sharpe, Inc., 1989.

Ivanka, Endre von. *Aufsatze zur byzantinischen Kultur*. Amsterdam: Hakkert, 1984.

Ivanov, M. "Vospominaniia o protoiereie o. Ioanne Sergieve–Kronshtadtskom." *Izvestiia po Kazanskoi Eparkhii*, no. 8 (1909) 249–53.

Iz zapisnoi knizhki sviashchennika. Moscow: Blagovest, 1996.

Jackson, David. "Icons in 19th Century Russia," in his *Icons 88: An Exhibition of Russian Icons in Ireland*. Dublin: The National Gallery of Ireland/Veritas Publications, 1988.

John Chrysostom. *The Divine Liturgy*, trans. Monk Laurence. Jordanville, N.Y.: St. Job of Pochaev Press, n.d.

"John of Cronstadt Dies in Poverty." *The New York Times*, January 3, 1909.

Jonas, Hans. *The Gnostic Religion: The Message of the Alien God and the Beginnings of Christianity*. Boston: Beacon, 1963.

Jones, Francis. *The Holy Wells of Wales*. Cardiff: University of Wales Press, 1954.

Just, Roger. "Anti-Clericism and National Identity: Attitudes Towards the Orthodox Church in Greece," in W. James and D. Johnson, eds., *Vernacular Christianity: Essays in the Social Anthropology of Religion Presented to Godfrey Lienhardt*. Oxford: JASO, 1988.

E. K. *Vospominaniia ob otse Ioanne*. St. Petersburg, 1909.

Kanatchikov, Semen. *A Radical Worker in Tsarist Russia: The Autobiography of Semën Ivanovich Kanatchikov*, Reginald E. Zelnik ed. Stanford: Stanford University Press, 1986.

Kadlubovskii, Arsenii. *Ocherki po istorii drevne-russkoi literatury Zhitii Sviatykh*. Warsaw, 1902.

Kadson, I. Z. "Anti-tserkovnaia bor'ba narodnykh mass v Rossii v trudakh sovetskikh istorikov." *Voprosy istorii*, no. 3 (1969): 151–57.

Kantorowicz, Ernst. *The King's Two Bodies: A Study in Mediaeval Political Theology*. Princeton: Princeton University Press, 1957.

Karpov, P. I. *Bytovoe Emotsional'noe Tvorchestvo v Drevne—Russkom Iskusstve*. Moscow: Izdanie Gosud. Istor. Muzeiia, 1928.

Kartashev, A. V. *Vozsozdanie Sv. Rusi*. Paris, Izd. Osobago Komiteta..., 1956.

Katanskii, Lev Efimovich. *Dukhovnik sv. Rusi*. St. Petersburg, 1907.

Kharalampovich, Konstantin V. *Malorossiiskoe vliianie na velikorusskoiu tserkovnuiu zhizn'*. Kazan, 1914.

Khrapovitskii, (Metropolitan) Antonii. *Confession: A Series of Lectures on the Mystery of Repentance*, trans. of Warsaw, 1928 ed. Jordanville, N.Y.: Holy Trinity Monastery, 1983.

———. *Slovo ep. Antoniia. Khrapovitskago i o. Ioanna Kronshtadtskogo po povodu nasilii khristian s evreiami v Kishineve*. Odessa, 1903.

———. *Uchenie o Pastyre, Pastyrstve i ob Ispovedi*. New York: Izd. Severo-Amerikanskoi i Kanadskoi eparkhii, 1966.

Khrisanf (Bishop). *Ot Seula do Vladivostoka. Putevyia zapiski missionera*. Moscow, 1905.

Kleinberg, Aviad M. *Prophets in Their Own Country: Living Saints and the Making of Sainthood in the Later Middle Ages*. Chicago: University of Chicago Press, 1992.

Kleist, James A., ed. *The Epistles of St. Clement of Rome and St. Ignatius of Antioch*. London: Longmans, Green, and Co., 1962.

Klibanov, A. I., ed. *Istoriia religioznogo sektantstva v Rossii (60—e gody XIX v.-1917g.)*. Moscow: Nauka, 1965.

———. *Russkoe pravoslavie: vekhi istorii*. Moscow: Politizdat, 1989.

———. *Narodnaia sotsial'naia utopiia v Rossii, XIX vek*. Moscow: Nauka, 1978.

Kliuchevskii, Vasilii O. *Drevnerusskia zhitiia sviatykh kak istoricheskii istochnik*. Moscow, 1871.

———. *Tserkov' i Rossiia: Tri Lektsii*. Paris: YMCA Press, 1969.

Kniagnitskii, I. "Poiezdka v Kronstadt." *Istoricheskii Vestnik* 80, no. 5 (1900): 632–44.

Kolarz, Walter. *Religion in the Soviet Union*. London: Macmillan & Co. Ltd, 1961.

Kolesnichenko, D. "K 90-lietiiu konchiny sviatogo pravednago otsa Ioanna Kronshtadtskago chudotvortsa," *Pravoslavnaia Zhizn'*, no. 3 (591), March 1999, pp. 1–29.

Konstantin [Zaitsev], (Hegumen). *Dukhovnyi oblik prot. o. Ioanna Kronshtadtskago*. Jordanville, N.Y.: Holy Trinity Monastery, 1952.

———, (Archimandrite). *Chudo russkoi istorii. Sbornik statei, raskryvaiushchikh promyslitel'noe znachenie Istoricheskoi Rossii.* Jordanville, N.Y.: Holy Trinity Monastery, 1970.

Kontsevich, I. M. *Optina Pustyn' i eia vremia.* Jordanville, N.Y.: Holy Trinity Monastery, 1970; repr. Moscow, 1995.

Korolenko, V. G. *Polnoe Sobranie Sochinenii,* vol. 1. St. Petersburg, 1914.

Korshunova, T. T. *Kostium v Rossii XVIII-nachala XX veka: iz sobraniia Gosudarstvennogo Ermitazha.* Leningrad: Khudozhnik RSFSR, 1979.

Kostomarov, N., ed. *Pamiatniki starinnoi russkoi literatury.* 4 vols. Moscow, 1862.

Kotel'nikov, V. A., ed. *Khristianstvo i Russkaia Literatura.* St. Petersburg: "Nauka," 1996.

Krasnikov, Nikolai P. *Sotsial'no-eticheskie vozzreniia russkogo pravoslaviia v XX veke.* Kiev: "Vyssha shkola," 1988.

Kravchenko, A. S., and A. P. Utkin, comps. *Ikona.* Sekrety Remesla series. Moscow: Vek Rossii/Style A Ltd., 1993.

Kronshtadtskii, Ioann. *See* Ioann Il'ich Sergiev

Kselman, Thomas. *Miracles and Prophecies in Nineteenth-Century France.* New Brunswick, N.J.: Rutgers University Press, 1983.

Kuntsevich, G. "Podlinnyi spisok o novykh chudotvortsakh." *IORIaS* 15 (1910): 252–57.

Kurganovskii, (Hieromonk) Gerontii. *Metod Bogosluzhebnykh Vozglasov Polozhennykh na Noty s Ustavnym Ukazaniem v Posobie Sviashchennosluzhiteliam pri Bogosluzhenii.* Moscow, 1897.

Laiou-Thomadakis, Angeliki. "Saints and Society in the Late Byzantine Empire," in A. Laiou-Thomadakis, ed., *Charanis Studies: Essays in Honor of Peter Charanis.* New Brunswick, N.J.: Rutgers University Press, 1980.

Lane, Christel. *Christian Religion in the Soviet Union: A Sociological Study.* Albany: State University of New York Press, 1978.

Laqueur, Walter. *Black Hundred: The Rise of the Extreme Right in Russia.* New York: HarperCollins, 1993.

Lassus, Louis-Albert. "Jean de Cronstadt, prêtre de Dieu—ami des hommes." *Contacts,* no. 94 (1976): 143–54.

Lebedev, Vladimir E. "Moe vospominaniie o poiezdke k o. Ioannu v Kronshtadt." *Pskovskie Eparkhial'nye Vedomosti,* nos. 21–24, (November 1–December 15, 1896): 359–62, 381–84, 405–8, 431–33.

Leont'ev, Konstantin. *Otets Kliment Zedergol'm: Ieromonakh Optinoi Pustyni.* Paris: YMCA Press, 1978.

Leskov, Nikolai S. *Sobranie sochinenii v odinadtsati tomakh.* 11 vols. Moscow: Gosudarstvennoe Izdatel'stvo Khudozhestvennoi Literatury, 1956–58.

———. "Polunoshchniki," in vol. 9 of *Sobranie sochinenii v odinadtsati tomakh* (1958). First published as Nikolai S. Leskov, "Polunoshchniki; peizazh i zhanr," *Vestnik Evropy,* nos. 11–12 (November–December 1891).

———. *Soboriane.* New York: Izd. Im. Chekhova, 1952.

———. *Velikosvetskii raskol: Lord Redstok, ego uchenie i propoved': ocherk sovremennago religioznago dvizheniia v Petersburgskom obshchestvie.* Moscow, 1877.

Levin, Eve. *Sex and Society in the World of the Orthodox Slavs, 900–1700.* Ithaca: Cornell University Press, 1989.

Bibliography

———. "Supplicatory Prayers as a Source for Popular Religious Culture in Muscovite Russia," in Samuel H. Baron and Nancy Shields Kollmann, eds., *Religion and Culture in Early Modern Russia and Ukraine*. De Kalb: Northern Illinois University Press, 1997.

Levitin-Krasnov, Anatolii. "Narodnye sviatye v Rossii: Otets Ioann Kronshtadtskii." *Cahiers du Monde russe et soviétique* 29, nos. 3–4 (July–December 1988): 455–70.

Levitskii, P. P. Prot. *Ioann Il'ich Sergiev Kronshtadtskii: Nekotorye cherty iz ego zhizni*. Petrograd, 1916.

The Limonarion. London: Faber and Faber, 1976.

Lindenmeyr, Adele. *Poverty Is Not a Vice: Charity, Society, and the State in Imperial Russia*. Princeton: Princeton University Press, 1996.

Lisavtsev, E. I. *Kritika burzhuaznoi fal'sifikatsii polozheniia religii v SSSR*, 2d ed. Moscow: "Mysl," 1975.

Litvak, Boris G. "Russkoe pravoslavie v XIX veke," in A. I. Klibanov, ed., *Russkoe Pravoslavie: vekhi istorii*. Moscow: Politizdat, 1989.

Liubomudrov, Aleksei, ed. and comp. *Svetil'nik Very i Blagochestiia—Sv. Prav. Ioann, Kronshtadtskii Chudotvorets. Zhitiie i Novye Chudesa*. St. Petersburg: Svetoslov/Sv. Ioannovskii Stavropigial'nyi Zhenskii Monastyr', 1996.

Lopez-Ginisty, Claude. *A Dictionary of Orthodox Intercessions*. Liberty, Tenn.: St. John of Kronstadt Press, 1997.

Lukashevskii, Evgenii. "Kronshtadtskii propovednik," *Nauka i religiia*, no. 5 (1990): 10–14.

L'vov, Fedor. *O penii v Rossii*. St. Petersburg, 1834.

V. M. (Archbishop Evdokim [Meshcherskii]). *Dva dnia v Kronshtadte, iz dnevnika studenta*. Sergiev Posad, 1902.

Maksimov, Sergei V. *Nechistaia, nevedomaia i krestnaia sila*. St. Petersburg, 1903.

Manchester, Laurie. "The Secularization of the Search for Salvation: The Self-Fashioning of Orthodox Clergymen's Sons in Late Imperial Russia." *Slavic Review* 57, no. 1 (spring 1998): 50–76.

Marsh, Rosalind, ed. *Women in Russia and Ukraine*. Cambridge: Cambridge University Press, 1996.

Massie, Robert. *Nicholas and Alexandra*. London: Pan Books Ltd., 1968.

Maylunas, Andrei, and Sergei Mironenko. *A Lifelong Passion: Nicholas and Alexandra, Their Own Story*. London: Weidenfeld & Nicolson, 1996.

Mazo, Margarita. "'We Don't Summon Spring in Summer': Traditional Music and Beliefs in the Contemporary Russian Village," in William C. Brumfield and Milos M. Velimirovic, eds., *Christianity and the Arts in Russia*. Cambridge: Cambridge University Press, 1991.

McCarthy, Kathleen, ed. *Lady Bountiful Revisited: Women, Philanthropy, and Power*. New Brunswick, N.J.: Rutgers University Press, 1990.

McLean, Hugh. "Leskov and Ioann of Kronstadt: On the Origins of *Polunoščniki*." *American Slavic and East European Review* 12, no. 1 (February 1953): 93–108.

———. *Nikolai Leskov: The Man and His Art*. Cambridge, Mass.: Harvard University Press, 1977.

Bibliography

Meck, Galina von. *As I Remember Them.* London: Dennis Dobson, 1973.
Meehan, Brenda. *Holy Women of Russia: The Lives of Five Orthodox Women Offer Spiritual Guidance for Today.* Crestwood, N.Y.: St Vladimir's Seminary Press, 1997.
———."From Contemplative Practice to Charitable Activity: Russian Women's Religious Communities and the Development of Charitable Work," in Kathleen McCarthy, ed., *Lady Bountiful Revisited: Women, Philanthropy, and Power.* New Brunswick, N.J.: Rutgers University Press, 1990.
——— [Meehan-Waters]. "Popular Piety, Local Initiative, and the Founding of Women's Religious Communities in Russia, 1764–1917." *St. Vladimir's Theological Quarterly* 25 (1986): 117–42.
———. "To Save Oneself: Russian Peasant Women and the Development of Women's Religious Communities in Pre-Revolutionary Russia," in Beatrice Farnsworth and Lynne Viola, eds., *Russian Peasant Women.* New York: Oxford University Press, 1992.
Mefodii (Archimandrite). *Otets Ioann Il'ich Sergiev.* Sofia: Mashinopis', 1957.
Meinardus, Otto. "A Study of the Relics of Saints of the Greek Orthodox Church." *Oriens Christianus* 54 (1970): 130–278.
Menshikov, Mikhail O. *Iz pisem k blizhnim* (Moscow, 1991).
———. "Pis'ma k blizhnim. Kronshtadtskii Bunt. Pastyr' dobryi." *Novoe Vremia,* no. 10646 (October 30 [November 12], 1905): 4.
Mernissi, Fatima. "Women, Saints, and Sanctuaries." *Signs* 3 (1977): 101–12.
Meyendorff, John. "Monastic Theology," in his *Byzantine Theology: Historical Trends and Doctrinal Themes.* New York: Fordham University Press, 1987.
———. *St. Gregory Palamas and Orthodox Spirituality.* Crestwood, N.Y.: St. Vladimir's Seminary Press, 1974.
Mikhail [Semenov], (Hieromonk). *Otets Ioann Kronshtadtskii: Polnaia biografiia s illustratsiiami.* St. Petersburg: Sinodal'naia tip, 1903.
Mironov, K. *Vestnik russkoi revoliutsii,* no. 3 (March 1903): 255–56; repr. in Moscow: Izd. Vestnik russkoi revoliutsii, 1906.
Mitrofan (Monk). *Kak zhivut nashi umershie i kak budem zhit' i my po smerti,* 6th ed. St. Petersburg, 1897.
Moessner, Eugenio. *Sviatoi pravednyi otets Ioann Kronshtadtskii.* Buenos Aires: n.p., 1973.
Molitvoslov. Kiev, 1881; Moscow, 1904.
Molitvy sviatym, vo grade sviatogo Petra osobo pochitaemym. Leningrad: Izd. Leningradskoi Dukhovnoi Akademii, 1991.
Molokhovets, Elena. *Classic Russian Cooking: Elena Molokhovets' "A Gift to Young Housewives,"* Joyce Toomre, trans. Bloomington: Indiana University Press, 1993.
Mols, R. "Une Approche Sociographique de la Sainteté." *Nouvelle Revue Théologique* 95 (1973): 748–63.
Momigliano, Arnaldo. *On Pagans, Jews, and Christians.* Hanover, Conn.: Wesleyan University Press, 1993.
"Monashestvo i sovremennye o nem tolki." *Obshchestvo istorii i drevnostei Rossiiskikh pri Moskovskom Universitete: Chteniia,* vol. 89, sec. 5, part 11, pp. 76–112.
Morosan, Vladimir. *Choral Performance in Pre-Revolutionary Russia.* Ann Arbor: UMI Research Press, 1986.

Bibliography

Morozova, T. G., et al. *V. G. Korolenko v vospominaniiakh sovremennikov*. Moscow: Goslitizdat, 1962.

Morris, Rosemary. "The Political Saint of the Eleventh Century," and Evelyne Patlagean, "Sainteté et pouvoir," in Sergei Hackel, ed., *The Byzantine Saint*. London: Fellowship of St. Alban and St. Sergius, 1981. University of Birmingham Fourteenth Spring Symposium of Byzantine Studies, Supplement to *Sobornost'*.

Moses, Monk. *Married Saints of the Church*. Wildwood, Calif.: St. Xenia Skete, 1991.

Moskalenko, Aleksei. *Ideologiia i deiatel'nost' khristianskikh sekt*. Novosibirsk: Nauka, 1978.

Motorin, A. V. "Obraz Ierusalima v russkom romantizme," in V. A. Kotel'nikov, ed., *Khristianstvo i Russkaia Literatura*. St. Petersburg: "Nauka," 1996.

Mukhin, Vyacheslav. *The Church Culture of Saint Petersburg*. St. Petersburg: Ivan Fyodorov Publishers, 1994.

Murav'ev, A. N. *Zhitii sviatykh rossiiskoi tserkvi, takzhe Iverskikh i Slavianskikh i mestno chtimykh podvizhnikov blagochestiia*. St. Petersburg, 1855–58.

Nakhimovsky, Alexander D., and Alice Stone Nakhimovsky, eds. *The Semiotics of Russian Cultural History*. Ithaca: Cornell University Press, 1985.

Nartsizova, A. F. *Poezdka v Goritskiie kinovii i vstrecha s o. Ioannom Kronshtadtskim*. St. Petersburg, 1892.

Neel, Carol. "The Origins of the Beguines." *Signs* 4, no. 2 (winter 1989): 321–41.

Nichols, Robert L. "The Icon and the Machine in Russia's Religious Renaissance, 1900–1909," in William C. Brumfield and Milos M. Velimirovic, eds., *Christianity and the Arts in Russia*. Cambridge: Cambridge University Press, 1991.

———, and Theofanis Stavrou, eds. *Russian Orthodoxy Under the Old Regime*. Minneapolis: University of Minnesota Press, 1978.

Nikanor (Archbishop). "Slovo ob o. Ioanne Kronshtadtskom." *Izvestiia po Kazanskoi Eparkhii*, no. 10 (March 8, 1909): 294.

Nikitin [Fokagitov], Admiral D. V. *Na beregu i v morie*. San Francisco: Morskoe Izd., 1937.

Nikodim (Hieromonk). *Arkhangel'skii Paterik. Istoricheskiie ocherki o zhizni i podvigakh Russkikh sviatykh i nekotorykh prisnopamiatnykh muzhei, podvizavshikhsia v predelakh Arkhangel'skoi eparkhii*. St. Petersburg, 1901.

Nikolaevskii, A. *Velikii pastyr' zemli russkoi*. Munich: Izd. V. Prostetovskii, 1948.

Nikol'skii, Nikolai M. *Istoriia russkoi tserkvi*. Moscow-Leningrad: Central Commitee of the Union of the Militant Godless of the USSR, 1931; 3d ed., Moscow: Politizdat, 1983.

Nikon [Beliaev], (Hieromonk). *Dnevnik poslednego startsa Optinoi pustyni ieromonakha Nikona (Beliaeva)*. St. Petersburg: Satis, 1994.

Nikon [Rklitskii], (Archbishop). *Dukhovnyk oblik sv. pravednogo protoiereiia Ioanna Kronshtadtskogo chudotvortsa*. New York: All-Slavic Publishing House, 1965.

Ninov, A., comp. *Stikhotvornaia satira pervoi russkoi revoliutsii (1905–1907)*. Leningrad: Sovetskii pisatel', 1985.

Novgorodskii, Pavel, comp. *Raiskie tsvety s russkoi zemli*. Sergiev Posad, 1912.

O'Shea, James. *Priest, Politics, and Society in Post-Famine Ireland*. Dublin: Wolfhound Press, 1983.

O Reformakh v Nashem Bogosluzhenii. St. Petersburg, 1906.

Obolensky, Dimitri. *The Bogomils: A Study in Balkan Neo-Manichaeism.* Cambridge: Cambridge University Press, 1948.

———. "Popular Religion in Medieval Russia," in Andrew Blane, ed., *The Religious World of Russian Culture*, vol. 2: *Russia and Orthodoxy.* The Hague: Mouton, 1975.

Orsi, Robert A. *Thank You, Saint Jude: Women's Devotion to the Patron Saint of Hopeless Causes.* New Haven: Yale University Press, 1996.

Otkrovennye rasskazy strannika dukhovnomu svoemu otsu. Paris: YMCA Press, 1948.

Otzyvy eparkhial'nykh arkhiereev po voprosu o tserkovnoi reformie. St. Petersburg, 1906.

Ouspensky, Leonid, and Vladimir Lossky. *The Meaning of Icons.* Crestwood, N.Y.: St. Vladimir's Seminary Press, 1983.

Panchenko, A. A. *Issledovaniia v oblasti narodnogo pravoslaviia. Derevenskie sviatyni severo-zapada Rossii.* St. Petersburg: Izd. "Aleteia," 1998.

Panteleimon (Archimandrite). *Zhizn', podvigi, chudesa i prorochestva sviatago pravednago otsa nashego Ioanna, Kronshtadtskago Chudotvortsa.* Jordanville, N.Y.: Holy Trinity Monastery, 1976.

Paozerskii, (Priest) M. "Vpechatleniia pervago sosluzheniia o. Ioanna Sergieva (Kronshtadtskago) na bozhestvennoi liturgii." *Santkt-Peterburgskii Dukhovnyi Vestnik*, no. 32 (August 8, 1897): 619–21.

Parmenov, Aleksandr. "Proslavleniie pravednogo Ioanna," in *Zhurnal Moskovskoi Patriarkhii*, no. 10 (1990).

Pastyrskii venok dorogomu batiushke o. Ioannu Kronshtadtskomu. St. Petersburg, 1911; repr. Utica, N.Y., 1965.

Patlagean, Evelyne. *See* Morris, Rosemary.

Pavlov, Aleksei S. *Kurs tserkovnago prava.* Moscow, 1902.

Pecherskaia, N. A., comp. *Pravoslavnoe Bogoslovie i Blagovroritel'nost' (diakoniia), Sbornik statei.* St. Petersburg: Vysshaia religiozno-filosofskaia shkola, 1996.

Peeters, P. "La Canonisation des Saints dans l'Eglise Russe." *Analecta Bollandiana* 33 (1914): 380–420.

Pelikan, Jaroslav. *The Christian Tradition, A History of the Development of Doctrine*, vol. 2: *The Spirit of Eastern Christendom, 600–1700.* London and Chicago: University of Chicago Press, 1974.

Perrie, Maureen. "Folklore as Evidence of Peasant *Mentalité*: Social Attitudes and Values in Russian Popular Culture." *Russian Review* 48, no. 2 (1989): 119–43.

Petrushevskii, N. G. "O religiozno-nazidatel'nom chtenii dlia prostago naroda," *Rukovodstvo dlia sel'skikh pastyrei*, no. 30 (1883): 326–34.

Philokalia. Writings from the Philokalia on Prayer of the Heart. London: Fernhill, 1951–52.

Piatidesiatilietie prestavleniia prisnopamiatnago otsa Ioanna Kronshtadtskago, iubeleinyi sbornik. New York: All-Slavic Pub., 1958.

Pipes, Richard. *Russia under the Old Regime*, 2d ed. New York: Macmillan, 1992.

Plotitsa, A. M. *O. Ioann Kronshtadtskii. Ego mnenie ob inovertsakh i inostrantsakh (iz dnevnika vracha).* Moscow, 1915.

Pobedinskii, I. *Posledniia minuty zhizni Imperatora Aleksandra Aleksandrovicha: Pis'mo o. Ioanna Kronshtadtskago.* Moscow, 1912.

Bibliography

Podol'skii, V. M., and N. E. Akopova, eds. *V chest' dorogogo batiushki o. Ioanna Kronshtadtskogo: vospominaniia ochevidtsev.* Moscow: too Rarog, 1995.
Polnoe Sobranie Postanovlenii i Rasporiazhenii po Vedomstvu Pravoslavnago Ispovedaniia. St. Petersburg, 1879–1915.
Polunov, A. Iu., comp. "O. Ioann Kronshtadtskii i K. P. Pobedonostsev (1883)." *Reka Vremen*, no. 2 (1996): 86–92.
Pomazansky, Protopresbyter Michael. *Orthodox Dogmatic Theology: A Concise Exposition.* Platina, Calif.: St. Herman of Alaska Brotherhood, 1984.
——— [Mikhail Pomazanskii]. "Ocherk pravoslavnago mirosozertsaniia o. Ioanna Kronshtadtskago," in *Piatidesiatilietie prestavleniia prisnopamiatnago otsa Ioanna Kronshtadtskago, iubeleinyi sbornik* (New York: All Slavic Publishers, 1958), 66–82.
Pope, Barbara Corrado. "Immaculate and Powerful: The Marian Revival in the Nineteenth Century," in Clarissa W. Atkinson et al., eds., *Immaculate and Powerful: The Female Sacred Image and Social Reality.* Boston: Beacon Press, 1985.
Popov, Evgenii. *Grigorii Rasputin v svete istoricheskoi pravdy.* São Paulo: n.p., 1960.
Popov, (Archpriest) I. *Nezabvennoi pamiati dorogogo batiushki o. Ioanna Kronshtadtskago.* St. Petersburg, 1909.
Poselianin, E., "K. N. Leont'ev v Optinoi Pustyni," in *Pamiati Konstantina Nikolaevicha Leont'eva, † 1891 g., literaturnyi sbornik.* St. Petersburg, 1911.
———. *Russkaia Tserkov' i Russkie Podvizhniki 18-go veka.* St. Petersburg, 1905.
Poslednii samoderzhets, Ocherk zhizni i tsarstvovaniia imperatora Rossii Nikolaia II. Berlin, 1911.
Pospielovsky, Dimitry. *Soviet Studies on the Church and the Believer's Response to Atheism.* 3 vols. London: Macmillan, 1988.
Potorzhinskii, (Priest) M. A., comp. *Obraztsy russkoi tserkovnoi propovedi XIX veka*, 3d ed. Kiev, 1912.
Pravila sviatykh apostol, sviatykh soborov vselenskikh i pomiestnykh i sviatykh otets s tolkovaniiami, 4th ed. Moscow, 1912.
Pravila sviatykh otets s tolkovaniiami. Moscow, 1884.
Pravilo Molitvennoe Gotoviashchimsia ko Sviatomu Prichashcheniiu i Ezhednevnoe Vechernee i Utrennee. Vladimirova: tip. prep. Iova Pochaevskago, 1948.
Pravoslavie, armiia i flot Rossii. Exhibition catalogue. St. Petersburg: izd. "Ego," 1996.
Preobrazhenskii, (Archpriest) Aleksandr. *O Bogosluzhenii Pravoslavnoi Tserkvi s Podrobnym Ob'iasneniem Vsenoshchnago Bdeniia i Liturgii.* St. Petersburg, 1884.
Preobrazhenskii, Antonin. *Kul'tovaia muzyka v Rossii.* Leningrad: Akademiia, 1924.
Preobrazhenskii, I. V. *Novyi i traditsionnyi: dukhovnye oratory oo. Grigorii Petrov i Ioann Sergiev (Kronshtadtskii). Kriticheskii etiud.* St. Petersburg, 1902.
Pretty, Dave. "The Saints of the Revolution: Political Activists in 1890s Ivanovo-Voznesensk and the Path of Most Resistance," *Slavic Review* 54, no. 2 (summer 1995): 276–304.
Protopov, V. V. *Chernye Vorony, p'esa v 5 deistviiakh.* St. Petersburg, 1908.
Punin, Andrei L'vovich. *Arkhitektura Peterburga serediny XIX veka.* Leningrad: Lenizdat, 1990.

Bibliography

Pustoshkin, V. F. *Tserkov' Khristova v opasnosti. Otpoved' Preosv. episkopu Filaretu, glavie Viatskoi eparkhii*. St. Petersburg, 1908.

Pypin, Aleksandr N. *Izsledovaniia i stat'i po epokhu Aleksandra Pervogo*. Petrograd, 1916–17.

———. Review of P. Znamenskii, *Istoriia Kazanskoi Dukhovnoi Akademii za Pervyi (Do-Reformennyi) Period Eia Sushchestvovaniia (1842–1870)* (Kazan, 1891–92). In an offprint from *Vestnik Evropy* [n.d.], 710–11, 732.

P. R. "Vazhnoe znachenie dnevnika dlia prikhodskogo sviashchennika." *Rukovodstvo dlia sel'skikh pastyrei*, no. 16 (1876): 475–88.

Radzinsky, Eduard. *The Last Tsar*. New York: Harper & Row, 1992.

Raeff, Marc, ed. *Russian Intellectual History: An Anthology*. New York: Harcourt, Brace, and World, 1966.

Ramet, Pedro, ed. *Eastern Christianity and Politics in the Twentieth Century*. Durham and London: Duke University Press, 1988.

Rasskazy sel'skikh sviashchennikov o divnykh iavleniiakh milosti Bozhiei i groznykh sud'bakh Ego. Moscow and Riga: Blagovest, 1996.

Ripa, Yannick. *Women and Madness: The Incarceration of Women in Nineteenth-Century France*. Minneapolis: University of Minnesota Press, 1990.

Rivelli, Marco Aurelio. *Le génocide occulté, état indépendant de Croatie 1941–1945*. Paris: L'Age d'Homme, 1998.

Robson, Roy R. "Liturgy and Community Among Old Believers, 1905–1917." *Slavic Review* 52, no. 4 (winter 1993): 713–24.

Rodzianko, Mikhail V. *Le Règne de Raspoutine*. Paris: Payot, 1927.

Rosenthal, Bernice Glatzer, ed. *The Occult in Russian and Soviet Culture*. Ithaca: Cornell University Press, 1997.

———. "The Search for a Russian Orthodox Work Ethic," in Edith W. Clowes et al., eds., *Between Tsar and People: Educated Society and the Quest for Public Identity in Late Imperial Russia*. Princeton: Princeton University Press, 1991.

———, and Martha Bohachevsky-Chomiak, eds. *A Revolution of the Spirit: Crisis of Value in Russia, 1890–1924*. New York: Fordham University Press, 1990.

Rossabi, Mary Jane. "Peasants, Peddlers, and Popular Prints in Nineteenth-century Russia." *Bulletin of Research in the Humanities* 87, no. 4 (1986–87): 418–30.

Rostislavov, D. I. *Ob ustroistve dukhovnykh uchilishch v Rossii*, 2 vols. Leipzig, 1863.

Rostov, Naum. *Dukhovenstvo i russkaia kontr-revoliutsiia*. Moscow: Ateist, 1930.

Rozhnov, Vasilii E. *Proroki i chudotvortsy: etiudy o mistitsizme*. Moscow: Politizdat, 1977.

Rozanov, Vasilii. "Russkoe Sektantstvo, kak 3 kolorita russkoi tserkovnosti." *Novoe Vremia*, no. 10594 (August 3 [September 12], 1905): 4.

Rubakin, Nikolai A. *Sredi tain i chudes*. Moscow: Politizdat, 1965.

Ruud, C. A. "The Russian Empire's New Censorship Law of 1865." *Canadian-American Slavic Studies* 3 (1969): 77–93.

St. John of Kronstadt: Life, Service, and Akathist Hymn, comp. I. V. Iarygina. Liberty, Tenn.: St. John of Kronstadt Press, n.d.

Saltykov, K. M. *Intimnyi Shchedrin*. Moscow-Petrograd: Gosudarstvennoe Izdatel'stvo, 1923.

Bibliography

Sapunov, B. V. "Nekotorye siuzhety russkoi ikonopisi i ikh traktovka v poreformennoe vremia," in G. A. Printseva, ed., *Kul'tura i iskusstvo Rossii XIX veka: novye materialy i issledovaniia: sbornik statei.* Leningrad: Iskusstvo, 1985.

Selawry, Alla. *Johannes von Kronstadt, Starez Rußlands.* Basel: Verlag die Pforte, 1981.

Semenoff-Tian-Shanskii, Aleksandr. *Otets Ioann Kronshtadtskii.* New York: Izd. A. Chekhova, 1955.

——— [Bishop Alexander]. *Father John of Kronstadt: A Life.* Crestwood, N.Y.: St. Vladimir's Seminary Press, 1979.

Serafim [Chichagov], (Archimandrite). *Letopis' Serafimo-Diveevskago Monastyria.* 2d ed. St. Petersburg, 1903.

Serebrov, Aleksandr. *Vremia i liudi: vospominaniia, 1898–1905.* Moscow: Moskovskii rabochii, 1960.

Sergiev, (Archpriest) Ioann Il'ich. *Besedy sviatago pravednago Ioanna Kronshtadtskogo s igumeniei Taisiei.* Moscow: Palomnik, 1995.

———. *Gor'kaia pravda o sovremennykh devushkakh i zhenshchinakh.* St. Petersburg, 1903.

———. *"Imeiushchie ushi, slushaite!" Slovo protiv p'ianstva.* St. Petersburg, 1902; repr. 1996.

———. *Iz dnevnika o. Ioanna Kronshtadtskago v oblichenie lzheucheniia grafa L. Tolstogo.* St. Petersburg, 1910.

———. *Khristianskaia filosofiia.* St. Petersburg, 1902.

———. *Moia zhizn' vo Khriste, ili minuty dukhovnago trezveniia i sozertsaniia, blagogoveinago chustva, dushevnago ispravleniia i pokoia v Boge. Izvlecheniia iz dnevnika,* 2 vols. Moscow, 1894; repr. Utica, N.Y.: Memorial Fund of Father John of Kronstadt, 1957.

———. *Mysli khristianina o pokaianii i sv. prichashchenii.* Moscow: Obsh. sv. Vasiliia Velikogo "Palomnik," 1997.

———. *Mysli moi po povodu nasilii khristian s evreiami v Kishineve.* Kishinev, 1903.

———. [Ioann Kronshtadtskii] *Neizdannyi dnevnik; vospominaniia Episkopa Arseniia ob otse Ioanne Kronshtadtskom.* Moscow: Pravoslavnoe Blagotvoritel'noe bratstvo vo imia vsemilostivogo Spasa, 1992.

———. *Novye Groznye Slova o Strashnom Poistine Sude Bozhiem....* Moscow: "Skit," 1993.

———. *O dushepagubnom p'ianstve, maternom slove, i tabakokurenii.* St. Petersburg, 1915; repr. 1995.

———. *O svetskoi zhizni: urok blagodatnoi zhizni po rukovodstvu o. Ioanna Kronshtadtskago.* Moscow, 1894.

———. *Oblichitel'nyia Propovedi otsa Ioanna Kronshtadtskago.* St. Petersburg, 1914.

———. *Otets Ioann Kronshtadtskii o p'ianstve.* Moscow: tip. sv. Sinoda, 1991.

———. *Pis'ma o. prot. Ioanna k nastoiatel'nitse Ioanno-Predtechenskago Leushinskago Pervoklassnago Monastyria Igumenii Taisii.* St. Petersburg, 1909.

———. *Pochemu Bog dopuskaet voiny?.* Petrograd, 1914.

———. *Polnoe sobraniie sochinenii pravednika Bozhiia Ioanna Kronshtadtskago,* 2 vols. St. Petersburg, 1911.

Bibliography

———. *Polnyi krug pouchenii.* Moscow: "Rodnik," 1997.
———. *Prizyv na zashchitu rodiny.* Moscow, 1905.
———. *Probudites' pianitsy! i plach'te, vse p'iushchie vino!* St. Petersburg, 1910.
———. *Propovedi otsa Ioanna Kronshtadtskago o tsarskom samoderzhavii.* St. Petersburg, 1914.
———. [Kronshtadtskii]. *Protiv grafa L. N. Tolstogo, drugikh eretikov i sektantov nashego vremeni i raskol'nikov.* St. Petersburg, 1902.
———. *Slova i poucheniia,* 3 vols. St. Petersburg, 1897–99.
———. *Slovo vo vtoruiu nedeli posta, po povodu naglogo i derzkogo ubiistva zlodeiami blagochestiveishago Gos. Imp. Aleksandra Nikolaevicha.* [Kronshtadt], 1881.
——— [Kronshtadtskii]. *Slovo o blagotvornosti Tsarskago edinoderzhaviia.* St. Petersburg, 1897.
———. *V mirie molitvy.* New York: Komitet russkoi pravoslavnoi molodezhi zagranitsei, 1988; repr. Moscow: Otdel religioznogo obrazovaniia i katekhizatsii Moskovskogo Patriarkhata, 1994.
———. *Zhivoi kolos s dukhovnoi nivy protoiereiia Ioanna Il'icha Sergieva-Kronshtadtskago. Vypiski iz dnevnika za 1907–1908 g.g.* St. Petersburg, 1909.
Shamaro, Aleksandr. *Delo Igumenii Mitrofanii.* Leningrad: Lenizdat, 1990.
Shavel'skii, (Protopresbyter) Georgii Iv. *Vospominaniia posledniago presvitera russkoi armi i flota.* 2 vols. New York: Izd. Chekhova, 1954; repr. Moscow: Krutitskoe Patriarshee Podvor'e, 1996.
———. *Pravoslavnoe Pastyrstvo.* St. Petersburg: Russkii Khristianskii Gumanitarnyi Institut, 1996.
Shelaeva, Elizaveta, and Liudmila Protsai. *Rus' pravoslavnaia.* St. Petersburg: Liki Rossii; Moscow: Dzhuliia, 1993.
Shevzov, Vera. "Chapels and the Ecclesial World of Prerevolutionary Russian Peasants." *Slavic Review* 55, no. 3 (fall 1996): 585–613.
Shmelev, Ivan. *Lieto Gospodne: Prazdniki, Radosti, Skorbi.* New York: "Put' zhizni," n.d.
Shkarovskii. *Sviato-Ioannovskii Stavropigial'nyi Zhenskii Monastyr': Istoriia Obiteli.* St. Petersburg: "LOGOS," 1998.
Shmeman, (Protopresbyter) A. *Evkharistiia: Tainstvo Tsarstva.* Paris: YMCA Press, 1984.
Shustin, V. *Zapis' ob o. Ioanne Kronshtadtskom i ob Optinskikh startsakh, iz lichnykh vospominanii.* Belaia Tserkov: Pravoslavno-missionerskoe Kn-vo, 1929.
Sidorova, A. L., et al., eds. *Revoliutsiia 1905–07 gg. v Rossii, Dokumenty i materialy,* vol. 1: *Vyshii pod'em revoliutsii, vooruzhennye vostaniia noiabria-dekabria 1905.* Moscow: Izd. Akad. Nauk, 1955.
"Sikh zhe pamiat' prebyvaet vo veki (Memorial'nyi aspekt v kul'ture russkogo pravoslaviia)," Materialy nauchnoi konferentsii, 29–30 noiabria 1997 g. St. Petersburg: Rossiiskaia Natsional'naia Biblioteka/Fond po izuchenii istorii pravslavnoi tserkvi vo imia Svt. Dmitriia Rostovskogo, 1997.
Silvianova, I. V. *Sovremennaia meditsina i pravoslavie.* Moscow: Moskovskoe podvor'e Troitskoi-Sergievoi Lavry, 1998.
Simakov, Nikolai K. *Pravoslavnaia tserkov'. Sovremennye eresi i sekty v Rossii,* 2d ed. St. Petersburg: Izd. Sankt-Peterburgskoi mitropolii "Pravoslavnaia Rus'," 1995.

Bibliography

Simanovich, Aron. *Rasputin i evrei: vospominaniia lichnogo sekretaria Grigoriia Rasputina.* Moscow: "Sovetskii pisatel"; Riga: "Orient," 1991.
Skaballanovich, Mikhail. *Tolkovyi Tipikon. Ob'iasnitel'noe izlozhenie Tipikona s istoricheskim vvedeniem.* Kiev, 1910.
S-kii, I. A. *Otets Ioann Il'ich Sergiev Kronshtadtskii i ego prebyvanie v Kieve.* Kiev, 1893.
Skrobucha, Heinz. *The Patrons of the Doctors.* Recklinghausen: Aurel Bongers, 1967.
Skvortsov, I. V. *V zashchitu belogo dukhovenstva. Po povodu knigi N. Elagina 'Beloe dukhovenstvo i ego interesy.'* St. Petersburg, 1881.
Slavianskii ili Tserkovnyi bukvar', 28th. ed. Kiev, 1908.
Smirnov, Evgenii K. *A Short Account of the Historical Development and Present of Russian Orthodox Missions.* London, 1903; repr. Liberty, Tenn.: St. John of Kronstadt Press, 1998.
Smirnov, N. A., ed., *Tserkov' v istorii Rossii (IXv.–1917 g.): Kriticheskie ocherki.* Moscow: Nauka, 1967.
Smirnov, S. I. "Baby bogomerzkiia," in *Sbornik statei, posviashchennykh Vasiliiu Osipovichu Kliuchevskomu...*, ed. Ia. L. Barskov. Moscow, 1909.
———. *Drevne-russkii dukhovnik. Izsledovanie po istorii tserkovnago byta.* Moscow, 1913.
———. *Dukhovnyi Otets v Drevnei Vostochnoi Tserkvi. Istoriia Dukhovnichestva na Vostoke.* Sergiev Posad, 1906.
Smolitsch, Igor. *Geschichte der russischen Kirche*, 2 vols. Leiden and Wiesbaden: Brill, 1964.
———. *Russisches Mönchtum: Entstehung, Entwicklung und Wesen, 988–1917.* Würzburg: Augustinus-Verlag, 1953.
Sokolof, (Archpriest) D., comp. *A Manual of the Orthodox Church's Divine Services.* Repr. Jordanville, N.Y.: Holy Trinity Monastery, 1975.
Sokolov, Boris. *Entsiklopediia Bulgakovskaia.* Moscow: Lokid-Mif, 1996.
Sokolov, (Archpriest Dimitrii), comp. *Zakon Bozhii, Nachal'noe nastavlenie v pravoslavnoi khristianskoi vere*, 102d ed., St. Petersburg, 1914; repr. Montreal: Monastery Press, 1974.
Sokolova, T. A., comp. and ed. *Sviatoi Pravednyi Ioann Kronshtadtskii—Sbornik.* Moscow: Novator, 1998. Series: ROSS—Russkie sud'by: Zhizneopisaniia, Fakty i Gipotezy, Portrety i Dokumenty v 30 Knigakh.
Sollogub, A. A. *Otets Ioann Kronshtadtskii, Zhizn', deiatel'nost', izbrannyia chudesa.* Jordanville, N.Y.: Holy Trinity Monastery, 1951.
Solov'ev, (Hieromonk) Aleksei. *Istoricheskoe razsuzhdenie o postakh Pravoslavnoi Tserkvi.* Moscow, 1837.
Solov'ev, N. I. *Pravoslavnoe dukhovenstvo: ocherki, povesti, i razskazy iz zhizni prikhodskogo dukhovenstva.* St. Petersburg, 1902.
Soloviev, Vs. S. "Otets Ioann," *Sever*, no. 49 (1888): 14–15.
Sperber, Jonathan. *Popular Catholicism in Nineteenth-Century Germany.* Princeton: Princeton University Press, 1984.
Speranskii, (Priest) Aristarkh. "Vstrecha s o. Ioannom Kronshtadtskim." *Izvestiia po Kazanskoi Eparkhii*, no. 8 (February 22, 1909): 300–304.

Bibliography

Spiridovitch, Alexandre. *Raspoutine, 1863–1916, d'après les documents russes et les archives privées de l'auteur.* Paris: Payot, 1935.
Stanley, Alessandra. "Saint or No, an Old-Time Monk Mesmerizes Italy." *New York Times* (September 24, 1998): A4.
Starets Makarii Optinskii. Kharbin: Bratstvo im. s. Ioanna Bogoslova, 1940.
Stark, Dom Antoine. *Le Père Jean de Cronstadt, archiprêtre de l'Eglise russe, son ascétisme, sa morale. "Ma vie en Jésus–Christ,"* 2d ed. Paris, 1902–3.
Sterligova, I. A. "O liturgicheskom smysle dragotsennogo ubora drevnerusskoi ikony," in A. M. Lidov, ed., *Vostochnokhristianskii khram: liturgiia i iskusstvo.* St. Petersburg: Dm. Bulanin/Tsentr vostochno-khristianskoi kul'tury, 1994.
Stewart, Charles. *Demons and the Devil: Moral Imagination in Modern Greek Culture.* Princeton: Princeton University Press, 1991.
Stites, Richard. *The Women's Liberation Movement in Russia: Feminism, Nihilism, and Bolshevism, 1860–1930.* Princeton: Princeton University Press, 1978.
Strizhev, Aleksandr Nikolaevich, comp. and ed., *Sviatoi Pravednyi Ioann Kronshtadtskii v Vospominaniiakh Samovidtsev.* Moscow: Izd. Otchii dom, 1997.
Sumarokov, E. N. "Starchestvo i pervye Optinskie startsy," in *Starets Makarii Optinskii.* Kharbin: Bratstvo im. s. Ioanna Bogoslova, 1940.
Suratov, Petr. *Sviatyi pravednyi Otets Ioann, Kronshtadtskii Chudotvorets.* Petit Clamart (Seine): P. Suratov, 1965.
Surovetsky, N. V. *Vospominaniia ob otse Ioanne Kronshtadtskom.* St. Petersburg, 1902.
Surskii, I. K. *Otets Ioann Kronshtadtskii,* 2 vols. Belgrade, 1938–41; reprt. Forestville: St. Elias Publications, 1979–80.
Suslova, A. V., and A. V. Superanskaia. *O russkikh imenakh.* Leningrad: Lenizdat, 1991.
Suvorov, N. "Zametki o kanonizatsii sviatykh." *Zhurnal Ministerstva narodnago Prosvieshcheniia* 348 (1903): 263–308.
Sviatoi pravednyi Ioann, Kronshtadtskii chudotvorets. St. Petersburg: Satis, 1997.
Sv. Prav. Ioann Kronshtadtskii v Vospominaniiakh Sovremennikov. Moscow: Sretenskii Monastyr', "Novaia Kniga," "Kovcheg," 1998.
Sventitsky, (Archpriest) Valentin. *Six Lectures on the History of the Mystery of Repentance: Against General Confession.* Jordanville, N.Y.: Printshop of St. Job of Pochaev/Holy Trinity Monastery, 1996.
Svod Zakonov Rossiiskoi Imperii Poveleniem Gosudaria Imperatora Nikolaia Pervogo Sostavlennym. St. Petersburg, 1833.
Symeon the New Theologian. *The Discourses.* New York: Paulist Press, 1980.
Taisiia (Nun). *Russkoe pravoslavnoe zhenskoe monashestvo XVIII–XX vekov.* Jordanville, N.Y.: Holy Trinity Monastery, 1985.
Talbot, Alice-Mary, ed. *Holy Women of Byzantium: Ten Saints' Lives in English Translation.* Washington, D.C.: Dumbarton Oaks Research Library and Collection, 1996.
Tarasov, I. F. "Ob otse Prot. Ioanne Il'iche Sergieve Kronshtadskom po lichnym vospominaniiam." *Kurskie eparkhial'nye vedomosti,* no. 49 (December 3, 1910): 541–42.
Tatishchev, S. S. *Imperator Aleksandr II, ego zhizn' i tsarstvovanie.* 2 vols. St. Petersburg, 1903.
Tentler, Thomas N. *Sin and Confession on the Eve of the Reformation.* Princeton: Princeton University Press, 1977.

Bibliography

Terletskii, V. N. *Sekta "ioannitov."* Poltava, 1910.
Thaisia, Abbess. *Abbess Thaisia of Leushino: The Autobiography of a Spiritual Daughter of St. John of Kronstadt*. Platina, Calif.: St. Herman of Alaska Brotherhood Press, 1989.
Tikhon (Archbishop of Zadonsk). *Tvoreniia sviat. Tikhona Zadonskago*. St. Petersburg, 1836.
────── [Zadonskii]. *Sochineniia*. 15 vols. St. Petersburg: tip. Ivana Glazunova, 1825–26.
Timberlake, Charles E., ed. *Religious and Secular Forces in Late Tsarist Russia: Essays in Honor of Donald W. Treadgold*. Seattle and London: University of Washington Press, 1992.
Tipikon, siest' izobrazhenie china tserkovnago, iazhe zovetsia Ustav. Moscow, 1885.
Tokarev, S. A. *Religioznye verovaniia vostochno-slavianskikh narodov XIX-nachala XX vv.* Moscow: Izd. Akademii Nauk SSSR, 1957.
Tolstaja, S. "The Worshipping of Saints and its Transformation in Slavic Folk Belief/Traditional Folk Belief Today." Conference dedicated to the 90th anniversary of Oskar Loorits. Tartu: Folklore Department of the Literary Museum of Estonian Academy of Sciences, 1990.
Tolstaia, Sof'ia. *Dnevniki Sof'i Andreevny Tolstoi, 1860–1891*. Leningrad: Izd. M. i S. Sabashnikovykh, 1928.
Tolstoy, Leo. *The Gospel According to Tolstoy*, David Patterson ed. and trans. Tuscaloosa and London: University of Alabama Press, 1992.
────── [L. N. Tolstoi]. *Perepiska s russkimi pisateliami*. Moscow: Gosudarstvennoe Izdatel'stvo Khudozhestvennoi Literatury, 1962.
────── [L. N. Tolstoi]. *Polnoe Sobranie Sochinenii*. 90 vols. Moscow: Gosudarstvennoe Izd. Khudozhestvennoi Literatury, 1954.
──────. *Soedinenie, perevod i izsledovanie chetyrekh Evangelii*, vol. 3 in *Polnoe sobranie sochnineii zapreshchennykh v Rossii*. Christchurch, England, 1906.
Toomre, Joyce, trans. and ed., *Classic Russian Cooking: Elena Molokhovets' "A Gift to Young Housewives."* Bloomington: Indiana University Press, 1993.
Treadgold, Donald W. "The Peasant and Religion," in Wayne S. Vucinich, ed., *The Peasant in Nineteenth-Century Russia*. Stanford: Stanford University Press, 1968.
Trinkhaus, Charles, ed. *The Pursuit of Holiness in Late Medieval and Renaissance Religion*. Papers from the University of Michigan Conference on Late Medieval and Renaissance Religion. Leiden: Brill, 1974.
Troeltsch, Ernst. *The Social Teaching of the Christian Churches*, vol. 1. New York: Harper & Row/Harper Torchbooks, 1960.
Trotsky, Leon. *1905*. New York: Random House, 1971.
Tsurikov, Catherine. "Der heilige Ioann Kronshtadtskii: Die Beteiligung der Kirche an den sozialen Aufgaben," in *1000 Jahre Christliches Russland, Zur Geschichte der Russischen Orthodoxen Kirche*, ed. Thomas Meyer. Recklinghausen: A. Bongers, 1988.
Turgenev, Ivan. *Literary Reminiscences and Autobiographical Fragments*, David Magarshack, trans. New York: Farrar, Straus, and Cudahy, 1958.
Turner, Victor, and Edith Turner. *Image and Pilgrimage in Christian Culture: Anthropological Perspectives*. New York: Columbia University Press, 1978.
Ukazatel' statei, Pomieshchennykh v Dushepoleznom chtenii v techenie desiati liet, ot nachala izdaniia v 1860 do 1869 goda. Moscow: tip. V. Got'e, 1870.

Bibliography

Ukhanova, I. N., ed. *Khudozhestvennoe Ubranstvo Russkogo Inter'era XIX Veka: Ocherk-Putevoditel'*. Leningrad: Iskusstvo, 1986.
V chest' dorogogo batiushki otsa Ioanna Kronshtadtskogo, vospominaniia ochevidtsev. Moscow: too Rarog, 1995.
Valuev, B. P., *Politicheskaia reaktsiia 80kh godov XIX veka i russkaia zhurnalistika*. Moscow: Izd. Moskovskogo Universiteta, 1971.
Varzhanskii, N. *V chem vera L. N. Tolstogo. Narodno-Populiarnyi Eskiz*. St. Petersburg, 1911.
Vauchez, André. *The Laity in the Middle Ages: Religious Beliefs and Devotional Practices*. Notre Dame and London: University of Notre Dame Press, 1993.
——. *La sainteté en occident aux derniers siècles du Moyen Age d'après les procès de canonisation et les documents hagiographiques*. Bibliothèque des écoles françaises d'Athènes et de Rome, fasc. 241. Rome: Ecole française de Rome, 1981.
Vel'iaminov, N. A. "Vospominaniia N. A. Veliaminova ob Imperatore Aleksandre III." *Rossiikii Arkhiv* 5 (Moscow: Studia "Trite" Nikity Mikhalkova) (1994): 301, 309–10.
Velikii Sbornik. Chast' Tret'ia iz Triodi Tsvetnoi. Jordanville, N.Y.: Holy Trinity Monastery, 1956.
Velikii sbornik v trekh chastiakh, chast' pervaia: chasoslov, voskresnyi oktoikh i obshchaia mineia, 2d ed. Jordanville, N.Y.: Holy Trinity Monastery, 1951.
The Venerable Sergius of Radonezh in Works of Russian Art 15th–19th Centuries. Catalogue no. 82, The Exhibition from the Collection of the State History and Art Museum-Reserve in Sergius Posad. Moscow: "Posad," 1992.
Verkhovtseva, V. T. *Vospominaniia ob o. Ioanne Kronshtadtskom ego dukhovnoi docheri*. Sergiev Posad, 1916.
Viola, Lynne. *Peasant Rebels Under Stalin: Collectivization and the Culture of Peasant Resistance*. New York: Oxford University Press, 1996.
Vitovich, A. I. "Zapiski sudebnago pristava po okhranitel'noi opisi imushchestva o. Ioanna Kronshtadtskago." *Golos minuvshago*, no. 5 (1915): 159–83.
Vlasov, V. G. "Khristianizatsiia russkhikh krest'ian." *Sovetskaia etnografiia*, no. 3 (1988): 15–21.
Vostorgov, Ioann, et al. *Prisnopamiatnyi otets Ioann Kronshtadtskii i Lev Tolstoi*. Jordanville, N.Y.: Holy Trinity Monastery, 1960.
Vovelle, Michel. *Idéologies et Mentalités*. Paris: Lib. François Maspero, 1982.
Ward, Benedicta, trans. and ed. *The Sayings of the Desert Fathers, The Alphabetical Collection*. Kalamazoo, Mich.: Cistercian Publications, Inc., 1984.
Ware, Timothy. *The Orthodox Church*. New York: Penguin Books, 1986.
Warner, Marina. *Alone of All Her Sex: The Myth and the Cult of the Virgin Mary*. New York: Vintage Books, 1983.
Weber, Max. *The Sociology of Religion*. Boston: Beacon Press, 1964.
Whyte, Alexander. *Father John of the Greek Church: An Appreciation*. New York, 1898.
Wilson, Colin. *Rasputin and the Fall of the Romanovs*. London: A. Barker, 1964.
Wilson, Stephen, ed. *Saints and Their Cults: Studies in Religious Sociology, Folklore, and History*. Cambridge: Cambridge University Press, 1987.
Worobec, Christine. "Witchcraft Beliefs and Practices in Prerevolutionary Russian and Ukrainian Villages." *The Russian Review* 54 (April 1995): 165–87.

Bibliography

Wortman, Richard A. *The Development of a Russian Legal Consciousness.* Chicago: University of Chicago Press, 1976.

——. *Scenarios of Power: Myth and Ceremony in Russian Monarchy,* 2 vols. Princeton: Princeton University Press, 1995, 1999.

Wrath, Robert D. "Before Rasputin: Piety and the Occult at the Court of Nicholas II." *The Historian* 47, no. 3 (May 1985): 323–37.

Zakharin-Iakunin, Ivan. "Grafiniia A. Tolstaia. Lichnye vpechatleniia i vospominaniia." *Vestnik Evropy,* no. 4 (April 1905): 611–17.

Zapiski Peterburgskikh Religiozno—Filosofskikh sobranii. 1902–1903 gg. St. Petersburg, 1906.

Zaitsev, Konstantin. *See* Konstantin, (Hegumen, Archimandrite).

Zasosov, Dmitrii A., and Vladimir I. Pyzin. *Iz zhizni Peterburga 1890–1910x godov.* Leningrad: Lenizdat, 1991.

Zelenin, D. *Ocherki russkoi mifologii,* vol. 1: *Umershie neestestvennoiu smert'iu i rusalki.* Petrograd, 1916.

Zelnik, Reginald E. *Labor and Society in Tsarist Russia: The Factory Workers of St. Petersburg, 1855–1870.* Stanford: Stanford University Press, 1971.

——. "'To the Unaccustomed Eye': Religion and Irreligion in the Experience of St. Petersburg Workers in the 1870s," in Robert P. Hughes and Irina Paperno, eds., *Christianity and the Eastern Slavs,* vol. 2: *Russian Culture in Modern Times.* Berkeley and Los Angeles: University of California Press, 1994.

Zenkovsky, Serge. *Medieval Russia's Epics, Chronicles, and Tales.* New York: E. P. Dutton, 1974.

Zernov, Nicolas. *The Russian Religious Renaissance of the Twentieth Century.* New York: Harper & Row, 1963.

Zertsalova, Anna Ivanovna. *Podvizhnik Very i Blagochestiia. Protoierei Valentin Amfiteatrov.* Repr. Moscow: Pravoslavnyi Sviato-Tikhonovskii Bogoslovskii Institut, 1995.

Zhadanovskii, Arsenii (Bishop). *Vospominaniia.* Moscow: Izd. Pravoslavnogo Sviato-Tikhonovskogo Bogoslovskogo Instituta, 1995.

Zhbankov, Dmitrii N. *Tielesnyia nakazaniia v Rossii v nastoiashchee vremia.* Moscow,. 1899.

Zhevakhov, N. D. *Vospominaniia Tovarishcha Ober-Prokurora Sv. Sinoda Kniazia N. D. Zhevakhova.* Munich: Vinberg, 1923.

Zhitie i pisaniia moldavskago startsa Paisiia Velichkovskago. Moscow, 1847.

Zhitie startsa Serafima. St. Petersburg, 1863.

Zhitie sviatago pravednago otsa nashego Ioanna Kronshtadtskago Chudotvortsa, ko dniu proslavleniia 19 oktiabria 1964 goda. Jordanville, N.Y.: Holy Trinity Monastery, 1964.

Zhitiia Prepodobnykh Startsev Optinoi Pustyni. Jordanville, N.Y.: Holy Trinity Monastery, 1992.

Zhivotov, N. N. *P'ianitsy u o. Ioanna Kronshtadtskago.* Moscow, 1895.

Zhivotovskii, S. V. *Na sever s otsom Ioannom Kronshtadtskim.* St. Petersburg, 1903; 2d ed., with new foreword by Metr. Antonii. (Khrapovitskii), New York: Eparkhial'noe izd., 1956.

Zhuk, Vladimir. *Mat' i Ditia. Gigiena v obshchedostupnom izlozhenii*, 9th ed. St. Petersburg, 1911.
Zinin, S. I. *Vvedenie v russkuiu antroponimiiu*. Tashkent: izd. Tashkentskogo un-ta, 1972.
Znamenskii, P. *Istoriia Kazanskoi Dukhovnoi Akademii za Pervyi (Do-Reformennyi) Period Eia Sushchestvovaniia (1842–1870)*. Kazan, 1891–92.
Zubarev, E. *Ioannity prokliaty o. Ioannom Kronshtadtskim*, 2d ed. Kostroma, 1912.
Zuzek, Ivan. *Kormchaia Kniga: Studies on the Chief Code of the Russian Canon Law*, Orientalia Christiana Analecta. Rome: Pont. Institutum Orientalium Studiorum, 1964.
Zybin, A. A., comp. *Ioann Il'ich Sergiev. Protoierei, kliuchar' Kronshtadtskago Andreevskago Sobora. Ocherk zhizni i deiatel'nosti*. Petrograd, 1891.

Unpublished Dissertations and Conference Papers

Bouteneff, Peter. "The History, Hagiography, and Humor of the Fools for Christ." Crestwood, N.Y.: St. Vladimir's Orthodox Theological Seminary, 1990.
Durkin, Andrew. "A Guide to Guides: Writing About Birds in 19th-Century Russia." Unpublished paper presented at conference of American Association for the Advancement of Slavic Studies, November 16, 1996.
Ely, Christoper David. "The Origins of Russian Scenery: Volga River Tourism and Russian Landscape Aesthetics." Unpublished paper presented at conference of American Association for the Advancement of Slavic Studies, November 16, 1996.
Geraci, Robert. "Window on the East: Ethnography, Orthodoxy, and Russian Nationality in Kazan, 1870–1914." Ph.D. diss., University of California at Berkeley, 1995.
Hedda, Jennifer Elaine. "Good Shepherds: The St. Petersburg Pastorate and the Emergence of Social Activism in the Russian Orthodox Church, 1855–1917." Ph.D. diss., Harvard University, 1998.
Herrlinger, Page. "The Religious Identity of Workers and Peasant Migrants in St. Petersburg, 1880–1917." Ph.D. diss., University of California at Berkeley, 1996.
Kizenko, Nadieszda. "The Making of a Modern Saint: Ioann of Kronstadt and the Russian People, 1855–1917." Ph.D. diss., Columbia University, 1995.
Manchester, Laurie. "Secular Ascetics: The Mentality of Orthodox Clergymen's Sons in Late Imperial Russia." Ph.D. diss., Columbia University, 1995.
Shevzov, Vera. "Popular Orthodoxy in Late Imperial Rural Russia." Ph.D. diss., Yale University, 1994.
Voinov, Vadim. "The Western Idea of Democracy Through the Prism of the Russian Religious Mind," paper presented at the Mid-Atlantic Conference of the American Association for the Advancement of Slavic Studies, March 1997. Albany, New York.

Russian Journals and Other Periodicals

Birzhevye Vedomosti, 1899–1912
Bogoslovskii Vestnik, December 1907

Bibliography

Dushepoleznoe chtenie, January–March 1870
Dushepoleznyi Sobesednik, 1880–1917
Grazhdanin, 1904–8
Informatsionnyi Biulleten' fonda im. o. Ioanna Kronshtadtskago, 1958–68
IORIaS, 1910
Istoricheskii Vestnik, 1900–18
Izvestiia po Kazanskoi Eparkhii, 1900–1910
Kurskie Eparkhial'nye Vedomosti, 1900–1910
Mysl', 1906
Nash Sovremennik, 1991
Nasha Zhizn', 1905–8
Nauka i Religiia, 1990
Novaia Mysl', 1906–7
Novoe Vremia, 1888–1914
Pchela, 1906
Perelom, 1906
Permskie Eparkhial'nye Vedomosti, 1893
Pravoslavnaia Rus', 1952
Pravoslavnaia Zhizn', 1958–99
Pskovskie Eparkhial'nye Vedomosti, 1896–1917
Pulemet, 1905
Reka Vremen, 1996
Rossiikii Arkhiv, 1994
Rukovodstvo dlia sel'skikh pastyrei, 1875–1909
Russkii Vestnik, 1881
Sankt-Peterburgskie Vedomosti, 1905
Sankt-Peterburgskii Dukhovnyi Vestnik, 1890–1912
Sever, 1888
Strely, 1905
Tovarishch, 1906
Tverskiie Eparkhial'nye Vedomosti, 1908–9
Vechnoe/L'Eternel, 1958
Vestnik Evropy, 1891, 1905–7
Volynskie Eparkhial'nye Vedomosti, 1910–14
Voprosy istorii, 1969
Zhurnal Ministerstva Narodnago Prosveshcheniia, 1903
Zhurnal Moskovskoi Patriarkhii, 1990

Index

Abdraimov, Magomet Rakhim, 125
Adam, 27, 35
Adventist, 230
Afanas'evskii, Pavel, 109
akathist, 155, 205, 206, 269
Aksakov, Konstantin, 1
Aksakov, Sergei, 166
Alaska, 126, 187
Albania, 134
alcohol, 105, 106, 133, 157, 171–76, 277, 285
Aleksandra Iosifovna, Grand Duchess, 237
Aleksii, Bishop of Taurida, 265
Alexander II, 10, 71, 78, 87, 132, 233–37, 241, 243, 284
Alexander III, 2, 114–16, 138, 235, 237–38, 241, 283
Alexander Nevsky, Saint, 229, 277
Alexandra, Empress, 114–16
Alexis (Romanov), 31
Alger, Horatio, 168, 171
All-Russian Kiev Missionary Convention, 226, 230–31
America, 5, 131, 268, 270. *See also* United States
Amfiteatrov, Aleksandr, 6, 220–21
Amirov, Akhmet, 125
Amvrosii, elder of Optina, 90, 242
Andrei, Bishop of Mamadysh, 227
angel, angels, 19, 28, 41, 44, 46, 57, 95, 149, 161, 172, 186–87, 200, 246, 284
Angelina, Abbess, 263
Anglican, 55, 126
Anna Karenina, 180
Anthony the Great, Saint, 13
anti-Semitism, 2, 228, 232, 243
Antichrist, 202, 207, 230, 236, 242, 249, 259, 271
Antonii (Metropolitan), Khrapovitskii, 51, 60, 66, 243
Apocalypse, 180, 231, 242, 271, 274

Index

apostles, 16, 20, 41, 43, 44, 45, 159, 209, 225, 276, 282
apparitions, 270, 272, 274, 285
Apraksin, 114
Arian heresy, 198
aristocracy, 113, 114
Arius, 183
Arkhangelsk, 2, 12, 166, 167, 251, 265
Armenia, 78, 125
Ars, 59, 65, 84, 154, 283, 285
Arsen'ev, Nadezhda, 116
Arsenii (Minin), 229
Arts Academy, 72
ascetic, asceticism, 7, 13, 19–27, 35, 38–40, 43, 66–67, 72, 85, 133, 149, 164, 177, 179, 181, 184, 192–93, 249, 278, 280–81
Astrakhan, 156
atheism, 3, 88, 110, 261, 272
Athos, Mount, 134, 163, 269
Augustine, 8, 178
autocracy, 87, 188, 198, 228, 234, 237, 242, 250, 257, 261, 283, 284
Avvakum, Archpriest, 8

Babel, Tower of, 15
Bacchus, 171
Bagration, 114
Bakunin, Mikhail, 71
Baptist, 200, 229–30
Barbara, Saint, 112, 159
Bari, Italy, 263
Bariatinskii, 114, 131
Barskov, Pavel and Elizaveta, 123–24
Basil the Great, Saint, 21, 41, 178
Beacon, Kronstadt, 199, 215–16, 227–28, 280
Bear, The, 172
bee(s), 47, 74, 138
Belgrade, Serbia, 7, 268
Belinskii, Vissarion, 42
Bell, The, 225, 228
Benjamin, Walter, 158
Bernard, Saint, 184
Bezbryzhii, Colonel, 125
Bible, 13, 17, 34, 242
bishops, 10, 29, 30, 44–45, 70, 73, 86, 94, 162, 168, 179, 191–93, 196–97, 203, 210, 225, 241, 265, 280, 283
Black Hundred, 220, 252, 256, 274

Black Ravens, 157, 215, 220, 225
body, bodies, 5, 10, 13, 15, 23–26, 28–29, 32, 35, 38–39, 43, 45–48, 50, 62, 66, 74, 92, 97, 98, 100, 102–5, 110, 118, 128, 167, 178, 206, 216, 217, 219, 228, 262, 265, 281
Bogoliubov, Dmitrii, 227
Bogoslovskoe cemetery, 277
Bol'shakov, Nikolai, 181, 216, 226, 229–30, 278
Bolshevik, 271, 284
Bonch-Bruevich, V. D., 250
Boniface, Saint, 105
Botkin, S. P. (Dr.), 110
Boule, 158
Bourse Gazette, The, 217, 229
Break, The (Perelom), 252
Brilinskii, Avgust, 124
Brothers Karamazov, The, 61, 250
Bulgakov, Mikhail, 273
Bulgakov, Sergei, 168
Burachek, Stepan, 180
Butkevich, Anatolii, 328 n. 28
Byzantium, 45, 177, 234

Cabasilas, Nicholas, 269
canonical, 1, 54, 62, 64, 201, 231
canonization, 1, 6, 7, 10, 108, 122, 154, 158, 160, 162, 164, 173–74, 176–77, 183–84, 187, 192, 194, 196, 215, 261, 262, 265–66, 268–70, 274–75, 277–78, 280, 285
Catholic, Roman, 2, 10, 18, 27, 34, 44, 51, 55–56, 65, 104, 122, 125, 136, 140, 154, 186, 194, 196, 223, 226, 243–44, 282, 285
chain letter, 152
chalice, 2, 49, 56, 64, 66, 107, 110, 114–15
chapel, 262, 264–65, 272
charisma, 3, 6, 10, 59, 60, 64, 66, 107, 122, 125, 150, 190, 191, 192, 194, 195, 197, 198, 201, 281, 282
charity, 4, 39, 66–71, 73, 76, 87, 96–97, 127, 132, 136–37, 141–43, 145, 234, 268, 282–83
Cheka, 271
Cherkass, 114
Chernyi, Sasha, 254
Chernyshevsky, Nikolai, 42, 74
Chertkov, Vladimir, 159

Index

Cherubic hymn, 53, 57, 107
child, 12, 19, 34, 48, 58, 63, 77, 79, 99, 104, 120, 130, 140, 149, 179, 219, 220
children, 27, 32, 34, 47, 61, 69, 76, 99, 104–6, 112, 114, 117, 119, 120–21, 124, 127, 129–30, 135, 140–41, 148, 149, 163, 168, 171–74, 186, 189, 216–24, 244, 248, 256, 269, 276
Christ, 16–18, 32, 34, 36–37, 46–48, 50, 52–53, 56–57, 59, 62, 72, 74, 84, 94, 118, 121, 124, 126, 145, 148, 153, 159, 161, 172, 182–4, 192, 200, 202, 204–5, 211–12, 214–15, 225–26, 235–36, 244, 249–50, 252, 265, 267, 276. *See also* Jesus
Christopher, Saint, 2
Chrysostom, John, Saint, 12–13, 19, 43, 268
Church Fathers, 12, 34, 225
Church Slavonic, 54, 93, 128, 189
Chursikov, 230
Civil War, 261, 267, 269, 284
class, social, 3–5, 57, 62, 67, 70–71, 81, 83, 86, 88, 93–95, 107, 109, 114, 119, 149, 179, 192, 201, 247, 251, 256, 266–67
clothing, 20, 63, 71–72, 75, 77, 83, 95, 117, 136, 161, 218, 220–21
collective farm, 272
collectivization, 271
collector, 21
communion, 10–11, 26, 29–30, 34, 47–51, 54–56, 58–60, 64–66, 77, 85, 95, 107–9, 115, 118–19, 135, 140–42, 148, 152, 154, 171, 173, 175, 181, 193, 200–201, 212, 239, 246, 259. *See also* Eucharist
Communist, 256, 261, 272–73, 275
confession, 2, 28–29, 58–66, 81, 85–86, 95, 108–9, 119, 127, 134, 140, 173, 175, 193–94, 200, 202, 209, 246, 283
Consistory, Spiritual, 62, 211
Constantine, Saint (Emperor), 45
Constantinople, 39
constitution, 242, 260
Content, 172
Corinthians, 28
Cosmas and Damian, Saints, 194
Cossack, 103, 108, 247
Council of Ministers, 227
Crime and Punishment, 61

cross, 24, 34, 37, 51–52, 56, 80, 108, 118, 120, 130, 149, 158, 172, 186, 216, 235
culture, 36, 82–84, 89, 130, 149, 174, 177, 186, 258, 267, 285
curse, 93, 103–4, 106, 130, 206
Cyril of Jerusalem, Saint, 10

Dal', Vladimir, 159
Daniel, Prophet, 42, 271
David, Prophet, 17–18, 47, 83
death, 3, 7, 16, 59, 84, 102, 105–6, 115, 119, 137, 152–53, 158, 160–61, 163–64, 167, 194, 199, 235–37, 239, 241, 248, 250–52, 256, 259, 261–63, 265–68, 272–73, 282, 284
Decembrist revolt, 86–87
Department of Spiritual Matters of Foreign Confessions, 210, 226, 230
desert fathers, 7, 15, 21, 22, 39, 81
devil, 18, 22, 25, 28, 33, 46, 52, 58, 106, 132, 189, 271
devotio moderna, 18
diary, diaries, 7, 8, 13, 15–17, 20, 29, 30–31, 33–34, 38, 47, 51, 57, 68–69, 71, 99, 138, 141, 143–44, 146, 149, 180, 191, 234, 283
Dmitriev, Nazarii, 213, 231, 280
Dmitrii of Rostov, Bishop, 43
Dobroliubov, Nikolai, 42, 74, 90
Dom Trudoliubiia. See House of Industry
Donon, 172
Doré, Gustav, 186
Dormition, 103, 110, 192, 228
Dorn, Gustav, 126
Dorpat, 238, 249. *See also* Iuriev
Dostoyevsky, Feodor, 40, 61, 224, 250, 267
Dowager Empress, 114. *See also* Maria Feodorovna
dream, 13, 22, 23, 31, 44, 130, 152–53, 170–71, 174, 176
Duma, 75, 77, 79, 225–26, 245–46, 252
dushevnobol'nye, 106
Dvina, 166

Ecumenical Council, Sixth, 294 n. 83
Edison, Thomas Alva, 126
education, 11–12, 36–37, 45, 48, 59, 63, 67, 74, 81–83, 85–88, 95–96, 104, 111, 117, 131–32, 163, 168, 172, 179, 181, 197, 207, 222, 229, 244, 249, 266

367

Index

Elijah, Prophet, 20, 42, 181, 200
Elisaveta Feodorovna, Grand Duchess, 116
Elisha, Prophet, 42
Elizaveta Konstantinovna, 13, 29, 30–35, 146, 148–49, 181, 278. *See also* wife
Elvira, Council of, 29
Elymas, 181
Emancipation, 60, 69, 93, 132, 186
émigré, 3, 152, 163, 261, 266–71, 273–75, 277
emperor, 2, 45, 78, 80, 121–22, 125, 229, 235, 237–39, 247, 283. *See also* tsar; sovereign
Empire, 11, 78, 100, 124–26, 131, 198, 233, 236, 260, 278, 283
employment, 2, 70, 91, 121, 123, 171, 179, 219
Ephesians, 295 n. 96
Ephraim the Syrian, Saint, 19
eschatology, 132, 197, 201, 207, 224, 242, 271, 274–75
Eucharist, 10, 21, 29, 46–52, 56, 59, 60, 65–66, 74, 115, 139, 140, 167, 250, 281. *See also* communion
Europe, 2, 5, 9, 127, 188, 238, 241–42, 250, 268, 270, 272, 281–82, 285
Evdokiia, eldress, 131
Eve, 27, 34–35
Evfimiia, eldress, 96
Evgeniia, secretary, 155
exodus, 48, 253
exorcism, 44, 184, 230, 331 n. 8
Ezekiel, Prophet, 18, 226

Family Happiness, 180
family, 2, 12, 28–31, 33–34, 36
far right, 3, 244, 250, 270. *See also* radical right
Farrar, Frederic William, 229
fasting, 24–25, 35, 58, 66, 130–31
fasts, 25, 35, 131, 149, 161
Father John as a Prophet Sent by God to Bring Russia to its Senses, 269
"Father John's Dream," 271
Fedora Vlas'evna, 12, 37. *See also* mother
Fedoristy, 275
feminist, 5, 72, 107, 129–30, 211, 267
Feodosii of Chernigov, Saint, 112, 192
Feodosii of Kievo-Pecherskaia Lavra, Saint, 39

Feofan (Bystrov), Archimandrite, 327 n. 15
Feofan (the Recluse) (Govorov), Bishop, 30, 41, 115, 133, 134, 193, 215
Filaret (Drozdov), Metropolitan of Moscow, 11–12, 19, 30, 161, 242
fin-de-siècle, 163
Five-Year Plan, 271, 284
flesh, 23, 25–26, 34–35, 43–44, 48–49, 53, 145, 161, 200–271
Fofanov, Konstantin, 52
food, 17, 22, 24–27, 32, 35, 48, 69–71, 75–76, 91, 94, 96, 137, 140, 173, 212, 222, 282
fool, holy, 10, 40, 63, 116, 194, 220
France, 11, 65, 106–7, 132, 196, 241, 267, 285
Francis of Assisi, 167, 194
Frankfurt, 153, 250
Freemason, 229
Friedman, Theodore, 159

Gagarin, 114
Galaction and Episteme, Saints, 294 n. 80
Gapon, Georgii (Priest), 76, 243
Gehenna, 63, 85, 127
gender, 3–5, 201, 267
Genesis, 15
George the Dragon-Slayer, Saint, 1, 125, 272
Georgii, recluse of Zadonsk, 136
Germany, 285
Gippius, Zinaida, 6
Giverny, 264
God, 5, 15–24, 26, 28, 31–34, 41, 43–50, 52, 54–57, 60–62, 68–77, 82, 84–89, 91, 92, 94–95, 98–100, 102–5, 107–19, 121, 124, 127, 128–31, 137–44, 148–53, 156, 161–63, 167, 168, 175, 177–78, 180–83, 185–87, 200, 202–9, 211, 215–16, 225–26, 229, 231, 234–38, 245–50, 252, 256–59, 261, 270, 272, 277, 282–83
Gog, 226
Gogol, Nikolai, 86, 166
Golitsyn, 114, 120
Gordienko, Nikolai, 277
Gospel, 24, 52, 68, 70, 79, 80, 121, 128, 134, 171, 183, 187, 223, 230, 246, 250, 282

Great October Socialist Revolution, 274.
  See also revolution of 1917
Great Reforms, 2, 10, 71, 80–81, 93
Gregory of Nyssa, Saint, 19, 294 nn. 76, 77
Gregory of Tours, Saint, 178
Gregory the Theologian (of Nazianzen),
  Saint, 178, 268
Griboedov House, 333 n. 48
Gurii, Archbishop of Novgorod, 210
Guseva, Maria, 215

hagiography, 3, 6, 7, 29, 98, 100, 163–64,
  166, 176–81, 184, 188, 277–78
Halloween, 268
healing, 2, 3, 8, 43, 46, 59, 65–66, 82,
  97–100, 102–3, 105, 108–14, 116–17,
  126, 128, 139, 149–50, 152, 154, 172,
  175, 184, 189, 193–96, 230, 239, 256,
  265, 269, 273, 276, 280, 282, 285
heaven, 10, 15, 17, 19, 44, 46, 51, 57, 68,
  73, 82, 105, 121–22, 131, 140, 161, 173,
  186, 205, 220, 234, 276
Hebrews, 329 n. 44
Helsinki, 107, 268
Hermione, abbess, 136
hermit, 21, 39, 43, 161, 164, 182, 184
hesychasm, 268
hierarch, 1, 5, 10–12, 44, 51, 56, 60, 85,
  100, 112, 121–22, 127, 133, 151–52,
  159–60, 162, 184, 190–95, 198, 201, 203,
  206, 210, 225, 237, 241, 251, 269, 273,
  275–78, 282–85
Hoffmeister Court, 231
holiness, 3, 8, 13, 28, 97, 100, 111, 118,
  132, 134, 138–39, 141, 143, 146, 149,
  150, 161, 164, 183, 195, 199, 206, 228,
  251, 257, 270, 278, 281–85
Holy Land, 163
holy spirit, 24, 50, 61, 94, 128
Holy Trinity Monastery, 7
holy, 7, 10, 13, 16, 19, 21–23, 28, 32, 36,
  40–41, 44, 47–54, 57–58, 63, 66, 73, 77,
  83, 85
House of Industry *(Dom Trudoliubiia)*,
  75–78, 96, 115, 137, 143, 156, 171, 201,
  217, 229, 333 n. 48
humility, 12, 36, 164, 206, 276

Ianyshev, Ioann (Protopresbyter), 114, 116

icon, 1, 9–10, 21, 36, 55–56, 80, 91, 99, 103,
  109, 112, 114, 122, 130–31, 143, 154–60,
  163, 168, 173, 176, 181, 186, 188, 190,
  194, 200, 204–5, 211–12, 224, 246,
  272–74, 281
Ignatiev, Countess, 115
Ignatii (Brianchianinov), Bishop, 22, 241
Ignatius, Saint, 45
Il'iashevich, 7. *See also* Surskii
Iliodor, Monk, 251–52
imiaslavtsy, 275
industry, 95, 100, 171, 283, 285
Innocent of Alaska, Saint, 187
Innokentevtsy, 275
Ioann (Snychev), Metropolitan of St.
  Petersburg and Ladoga, 280
Ioannites, 155, 157, 160, 190, 196,
  198–202, 204, 206, 211–32, 266, 273–78
  280
Ioannov Brotherhood, 229
Iosifites, 275
Isaiah, Prophet, 15, 42
Isidor, Metropolitan of St. Petersburg, 90,
  180, 191, 193
Israel, 89, 248
istinno-pravoslavnaia tser'kov (IPTs), 275
istinno-pravoslavnye khristiane (IPKh),
  275
Iuriev, 238, 249, 258. *See also* Dorpat
Ivanov brothers, 230
Izvestiia, 272

Japan, 131, 249, 266
Jeremiah, Prophet, 42, 225
Jerusalem, 10, 205, 241
Jesus, 18, 204, 282, 283. *See also* Christ
Jesus Prayer, 8, 133
Jew(s), 74, 125–26, 198, 217–19, 223, 229,
  243. *See also* anti-Semitism
Job, 18
John (Maximovich), Bishop, Saint, 275
John Climacus (of the Ladder), Saint, 20
John of Ryla (Ioann Ryl'skii), Saint, 157,
  181–83
John the Baptist, Saint, 283
John the Theologian, Saint, 213, 242, 297
  nn. 31, 34
Jordanville, New York, 7
Joy of All Who Sorrow, 154

Index

Judaizer, 198
Judas, 49, 225, 243, 313 n. 23
Jude, Saint, 312 n. 8
Judgment, 80, 82, 85, 89, 94, 229
Julian and Basilissa, Saints, 294 n. 80

Kabanova, Pelagiia, 204
Karamzin, Nikolai, 83
Karpovka, 219, 222, 262–65, 271, 277
Kazan, 11, 131, 136, 154, 184, 190, 193, 244
Kaznakov, Admiral, 159
Kedrinskii, Nikolai (Protoierei), 327 n. 15
Kharanbaev, Usendbai, 125
Kharkov, 145, 244
Khilkov, Dimitrii, Prince, 189
khlyst, 62, 108, 227, 231, 325 n. 102
Khodynka, 157
Khomiakov, Aleksei, 40, 320 n. 169
Khrapovitskii. *See* Antonii (Metropolitan)
Kiev, 40, 103, 124, 228, 230–31, 259, 311 n. 160
Kirghiz, 125
Kirill, Hieromonk, 134–35
Kiseleva, Porfiriia, 201, 205, 213–15, 280
Kishinev, 243
Kislovodsk, 230
klikushy, 106
Klipikova, 202
Kliuchegorsk, 136
Kliuchevskii, Vasilii, 73, 100
Kochubei, 124
Koloskov, 230
Komsomol, 272
Konashkina, Aleksandra, 106
Kondratov, Vasilii, 202
Koni, Anatolii, 52
Konstantin (Zaitsev), Archimandrite, 178, 188
Konstantin Konstantinovich, Grand Duke, 79
kontakion, 44, 269, 276
Korchacheva, Elizaveta, 213
Kornilii, elder, 131
Kotlin, 153
Kovrigina, Paraskeva, 98, 184, 280
Kreuzer Sonata, 84, 180, 283
Kronstadt, 2, 3, 6, 13, 25, 30, 39–42, 59–60, 64–66, 69, 72, 75, 76–78, 85, 88, 114, 122–23, 135, 141–42, 145–46, 151–61, 167, 173, 184, 188, 190, 193, 196, 200, 202, 205, 207, 209, 211–20, 222, 227–28, 231, 238, 245, 251–57, 262–63, 266–67, 272–77, 280–81, 285
Kronstadt Pastor, 266
Kropotkin, 114
Kuban, 108
Kulomzin, 114
Kutuzov, 114

Lanskii, Special Inspector, 221
Lanskoi, 114
Latin America, 110
lay, laity, 10–11, 12, 30, 41, 45, 66, 93, 99, 132, 134–35, 162, 176, 192, 195–96, 204, 216, 241, 270, 282.
Lebedeva, Aleksandra, 156
Lenin, Vladimir, 271
Lent, 21, 24, 26, 35, 61, 65, 91, 149, 155, 221
Lermontov, Mikhail, 88, 177
Leskov, Nikolai, 93, 188–90, 259, 311 n. 136
Leushin, 57, 134, 186
Liberty, Tennessee, 268
Lieven, Baroness, 112
Lipatov, Grigorii, 328 n. 37
Lisovoi, Nikolai, 177
liturgy, liturgical. 1–4, 10–11, 16–21, 29–30, 36, 39, 44–45, 51–58, 61, 66–67, 70, 80–81, 83, 90–91, 94–95, 97, 113, 136–37, 139, 141–42, 149–50, 154, 158–59, 167–68, 176–77, 187, 205, 235, 246, 262, 269, 275–76, 282
Litvintsev, Polikarp, 103
Liubimov, Aleksandr (Priest), 258
Livadia, 116, 238, 241
lived religion, 4–6, 271–72
Lives of Remarkable People, 163, 185
Living Church, 271
Lobanov-Rostovskii, 114
Lobodin, Fedor, 230
Lomonosov, Mikhail, 177
lottery, 8, 118–19
Lourdes, 154, 194
Lukullian, 131
Lutheran, 55, 126, 223
Lvov, 57

Index

Macarius of Egypt, Saint, 293 n. 48
Machine-Gun (Pulemet), 253
Maitov, Aleksei, 137
Makarii of Optina, Saint, 90
Makarov, Admiral, 262
Makushinskii, Aleksei, 267
Malkova, Ekaterina, 322 n. 17
Manichean, 198
Marcian and Pulcheria, Saints, 294 n. 80
Mardi Gras, 304 n. 82
Maria Feodorovna, Empress, 239
Mark, Evangelist, 71
Marks, atlas publisher, 189
marriage, 27–8, 30–31, 33, 36, 38, 46, 122, 146, 179, 192, 202, 230, 248
Marx, Karl, 79, 123
Mary Magdalene, Saint, 214
Mary, 122, 125, 186, 250. *See also* Mother of God, Queen of Heaven
Maslenitsa. *See* Mardi Gras
Master and Margarita, 273
Matthew, Evangelist, 34, 43
Mayakovsky, Vladimir, 3
media, 3, 282
medicine, 11, 69, 99, 100, 109–10, 230
Meissner, Julia, 131
Melania and Valerian, Saints, 294 n. 80
memory, 7, 11, 78, 82, 183, 229–30, 265–66, 268, 274, 282
Mendeleev, Dmitrii, 267
Menshikov, Mikhail, 160–61, 255–56
menstruation, 34, 55–56, 102
meshchane, 63, 74–76, 84, 211
Meshkov, Evdokim, 138
Michael, Archangel, 213, 229, 244, 272, 283–84
millennium, 3, 41
Ministry of Finance, 77
Ministry of Interior, 131, 193, 207, 210, 226, 229
Ministry of Justice, 213, 223
Minsk, 230
miracles, 11, 43–44, 47–50, 100, 154, 175, 180–85, 188, 194–95, 200, 220, 223–24, 255–56, 258, 261, 265–66, 268, 273, 276, 285
missionary, 11, 54, 65, 126, 187–88, 215, 225–31, 243, 268, 278
Mitrofan of Voronezh, Saint, 112

modern, 2–3, 5–8, 54, 60, 95, 195, 198, 218, 225, 228, 231, 281, 282–85
molchalniki, 275
moleben, 54, 65–66, 95, 98–99, 110, 119, 142, 150, 156, 173
monarchist, 3, 121, 228, 236, 242, 249, 273–74
monastic, monastism, 4, 9, 13, 15, 20, 24, 27, 28, 41, 46, 132–34, 150, 179, 187, 188, 193, 270, 278. *See also* monk
Monet, Edouard, 264
monk, 9, 10–13, 15, 21–24, 27, 30, 41, 55, 132–35, 177, 179, 184, 187, 191–95, 217, 229, 251–52, 269, 277–78, 281. *See also* monastic, monasticism
Montenegrin princesses, 115
Moscow, 12, 77, 111, 138, 193, 211, 213, 230, 236, 242, 245, 257, 273
Moscow Patriarchate, 173, 262, 270, 275–78, 280, 285
Moses, 3, 42, 49, 248, 252
mother, 12, 19, 33–37, 48, 95, 103–9, 117, 119, 120, 127–29, 141, 149, 153, 166, 178, 189, 212, 218, 250, 264
Mother of God, 36, 52, 94, 103, 112, 130–31, 152, 154, 172, 201, 205, 211–15
Mtsensk, 136
Murav'eva-Amurskaia, Olga, 109
Muslim, 74, 125, 134
My Life in Christ, 152, 167, 268–69
Mysteries, Holy, 26, 47, 49–50, 57, 59, 77, 118, 135, 139–40, 142, 182, 276. *See also* communion; Eucharist
Mystical Supper, 48

Nesvitskii, Konstantin (Protoierei), 13, 30
New martyrs and confessors of Russia, 285
New Path (Novyi Put'), 238
New Testament, 16, 187
New Thought (Novaia Mysl'), 251
New Time (Novoe Vremia), 2, 102, 110, 152, 160, 189, 191, 240–41, 255
newspaper, 2, 102, 145, 152–53, 162, 191–92, 195, 207, 213, 217, 219, 221–22, 228, 230, 235–36, 238, 245, 250–52, 255, 257, 259, 272–73, 282–83
Nicaea, Council of, 318 n. 113
Nicholas I, 32

371

Index

Nicholas II, 114, 122, 138, 184, 192, 230, 261, 265, 271, 284, 285
Nicholas, Saint, 112, 115–16, 159, 168, 174, 181, 183, 194, 263
Nikanor, Archbishop of Kazan, 184
Nikolai, Bishop of Alaska, 126
Nikon, Patriarch, 291 n. 17
Nina of Georgia, Saint, 214
Niva, 189
Novatians, 198
Novikov, Nikolai, 87
nun, 8, 23–24, 27, 46, 57, 132–34, 154, 179, 193, 265–66, 277, 281

Ober-Procurator, 52, 77, 123, 155, 191, 194, 204, 210, 226, 242, 283
Obolenskii, 114
October Revolution, 7, 271
Odessa, 134, 243
Ol'denburgskii, 114
Old Believer, 8, 54, 57, 107, 197, 226
Old Testament, 81, 248
Olonets, 166
Onegin, Eugene, 177
Optina monastery, 15, 90, 100, 133, 190, 241, 242, 268
Oranienbaum, 151, 213–14, 219, 262
ordination, 7, 13, 18, 24, 27, 69, 179
Origen, 294 n. 77
Ornatskii, Filosof (Priest), 203
Orthodox Church, 2–3, 29, 35, 45, 53–55, 61, 81, 105, 108, 122, 158, 162, 177, 181, 187, 194–95, 198–99, 215, 217, 226–28, 231–32, 242, 250–51, 260–62, 268–69, 274–65, 282, 284
Orthodoxy, 44, 55, 57, 59–60, 81, 83–84, 86–87, 109, 112, 116, 125–26, 136, 152, 154, 188, 190, 196–99, 201, 203, 218, 220–21, 224–29, 231–32, 234, 241–42, 247–48, 250, 258, 260, 271, 274–78, 281–84
Otets, 277
Our Father, 86, 173, 234
Ozerov, David, 266

Pachomius, Hiero-Schemamonk, 269
Pachomius, Saint, 41
Padre Pio, 194, 282
Palitsyn, Avraamii, 246

Panteleimon, Saint, 112–13, 134
Paozerskii, Mikhail (Priest), 53
parish, 2, 4–5, 10–12, 30, 57, 61, 65, 78, 122, 132, 135, 137, 142, 149, 168, 175, 181, 192–93, 195, 202, 219, 233, 239, 256, 265–66, 281
Paschal, 18, 148
Pashkovites, 200, 229
Paul I, 304 n. 75
Paul the Simple, Saint, 145
Paul, Apostle, 28, 43, 159, 181
peasant, 4, 21, 57, 84, 102–4, 108, 111, 115, 130–31, 135, 138, 149, 166–68, 179, 192, 202, 204–5, 209–11, 215, 217, 222, 230, 243–46, 266, 284
Pechorin, 177
Penny (Kopeika), 217
Pentecost, 168, 212
People's Will, 88
perestroika, 3, 262, 270
Perm, 222
Pertsova, Vera, 155–56
Peter I, 9, 192, 234
Peter, apostle, 43, 159, 277
Petersburg, 2, 7–8, 12, 40, 55, 59, 69, 72, 78, 85, 88, 90, 92, 113, 122–23, 141–42, 151, 154, 156, 171, 179, 180, 182, 191, 193, 209, 213, 218–19, 221–22, 227, 229–30, 244, 261–63, 277
Petrine, 73, 282
Petrov, Georgii (Priest), 78–79
Philippe, Nizier Anthelme, 115
photograph, 158–60, 166, 181, 200, 211–12, 214, 218, 280
Piatigorsk, 230
pilgrimage, 2, 9, 11, 65–66, 103, 109, 151, 154, 157, 163, 196, 212, 256, 262, 264, 283
Pivato, 172
Plikhakov, Pavel, 308 n. 69. *See also* Varsonofii, Saint
Pobedonostsev, Konstantin, 77, 194, 210, 238
Podgorny, Stefan, 230
pogrom, 243, 246, 252
police, 7, 117, 144, 146, 198, 206–7, 209–11, 213, 216, 218–22, 229–30, 243, 246, 254, 257, 274
Polish, 243

politics, 1–8, 67, 74–75, 78–79, 87, 96, 100, 121, 132, 154, 163, 188, 196, 198, 200, 225–27, 229, 233–34, 237, 241–46, 248–53, 255–57, 260–62, 266–71, 274–77, 281, 283–85
Polunoshchniki. See *Vigil-aunties*
Ponomarev, Ivan, 205–6
poor, 2, 12, 20–21, 30, 36, 37, 42, 63, 68–79, 81–82, 87, 91, 94–97, 111, 113, 130–31, 133, 135–37, 140, 142–46, 157, 164, 168, 171, 186, 189, 200–201, 212, 217, 222, 237, 250, 257, 260, 281, 285
popular piety, 4, 214
portrait, 121, 138, 154, 157, 159, 200, 202, 204, 265, 273–74
postcard, 2, 151, 154, 157, 282–83
prayer, 2–3, 11–13, 23–25, 31, 36, 39, 46–48, 51–59, 62, 66, 69, 73, 80–81, 92–94, 97–99, 102–3, 105, 107, 109–16, 118, 120, 122, 123, 125–27, 130–31, 137, 139, 141–43, 148–55, 159, 167, 173, 175–76, 187, 200, 209, 211–12, 214, 217, 235–36, 239, 244–45, 250, 256, 264, 271, 278, 282
preach, 11, 20, 58, 67, 85, 96, 194–95, 200–202, 206, 218, 227, 229–30, 247, 276, 281, 284
Prefect, 219, 223
priest, 3, 5, 7–13, 18, 20, 23, 26–30, 37–48, 50–67, 69–70, 75–82, 85, 89–93, 95–100, 105, 108–9, 111–12, 115, 122, 125–26, 132–36, 138, 142–43, 145, 149–50, 158, 160–61, 164, 167–68, 177–79, 184, 187–88, 190–95, 200, 202–7, 219, 222, 225, 233–34, 239, 243, 247, 251, 255–56, 258, 265, 267, 272, 281–82
proletarian, 4
prophet, 3, 20, 81, 89, 164, 181, 184, 195, 200, 220, 230, 233, 259, 269, 276–78, 282, 284
prostitution, 76, 214
Protestant, 2, 49, 53–55, 61, 81, 136, 283
Protopov, V. V., 215, 220, 225
psalm, 12, 17, 18, 51, 83, 130, 173, 176, 178, 209, 253
Psalter, 187
punishment, corporal, 9, 144
purgatory, 303 n. 65
purge, 271

Pushkin, Aleksandr, 88, 159, 177, 183, 187
Pustoshkin, Vasilii, 215–16, 226, 231

Queen of Heaven, 111, 118, 130, 211

radical right, 197, 224, 229, 234, 244, 246, 284. *See also* far right
Ramennikov, Georgii, 153
Raskolnikov, 61
Raspopov, Vasilii and Paraskeva, 129
Rasputin, 114–16, 158, 267
recluse, 9, 41, 133–34, 136, 161, 193, 215–16, 255
Red Cross, 78–79
relics, 9–10, 99, 107, 146, 161, 194, 220, 263–64, 281
Reminiscences about Tsarskoe Selo, 177
Repin, Il'ya, 159
Reshmin pustyn', 184
Resurrection, 250
revolution of 1905, 132, 188, 225, 233, 244, 246–48, 252, 260
revolution of 1917, 3, 6, 9, 266–67, 269–70, 274–75, 284–85
revolutionary movement, 3, 7, 85, 200, 217, 224–25, 229, 233, 237, 241–42, 244, 247–48, 260, 269–71, 274, 278, 284–85
Rimsky-Korsakov, Lidiia, 76, 114
Roerich, Nikolai, 160
Romanov, 238, 240
Romans, 329 n. 44
Romantic, 19, 166, 186
Rozanov, Vasilii, 160–2, 190
Rudin, 177
Russian Banner (Russkoe Znamia), 228
Russian Gathering (Russkoe Sobranie), 244
Russian Liberation Army, 269. *See also* Vlasov, Audrei
Russian Orthodox Church Abroad, 269, 274, 284
Russian Patriotic Society, 244
Russian Pilgrim (Russkii Palomnik), 218

Sabaoth, 200
Sabler, Vladimir, 123, 204
sacrament, 5, 10, 37, 45–47, 51, 55–57, 59–61, 64, 66, 89–90, 94–95, 115, 126, 142, 148, 155, 188, 190, 195, 200, 202, 227, 237, 250, 260, 282–83

Index

saint, 1–8, 10, 18, 21–22, 24, 28–29, 31, 38, 46, 52, 55, 59, 90, 98, 100, 103, 108–9, 112, 117–18, 122, 124, 127, 129–30, 139, 144, 150, 152, 157, 159, 160–63, 166, 171, 174, 177–80, 182–86, 188, 190, 194–95, 205, 214, 220, 251, 257, 261–65, 267, 272, 277–78, 282–83, 285
Sakhalin, 125
Saltykov-Shchedrin, Mikhail, 110
salvation, 5, 7, 13, 28, 31–33, 37–38, 40–42, 44–47, 73, 84, 92, 112, 128, 178, 182–83, 195, 200–201, 203, 235
Samara, 202, 230
Samokhin, Averkii, 110
Samoyed, 37
Samuel, Prophet, 42
Sarapul, 98
Saratov, 156, 230, 245
Satan, 26, 49, 52, 83, 205, 225, 256, 272–73, 284. *See also* devil
Satz, Lazar, 126
Savva (Tikhomirov), Bishop, 133, 193
Savva of Solovki, Saint, 20
Schmidt, Lieutenant, 253
scripture, 8, 11, 13, 15–18, 33, 44, 67, 79, 102, 121, 163, 175, 201, 225, 250
Second World War, 268, 269
sect, 3, 55, 62, 107–8, 157, 160, 179, 196–203, 210–11, 220, 223, 226–28, 230, 231, 239, 275–76
secular, 3, 6, 44, 83–84, 94, 105, 177, 186, 191, 195, 198, 207, 224, 229, 231, 234, 242, 260
seminary, 2, 12, 19, 86, 185, 193, 265, 281
Serafim, Saint, 1, 41, 90, 107, 181, 184, 192, 241, 268, 271
Serebrov, Aleksandr, 63, 154, 214
Sergei Aleksandrovich, Grand Duke, 116, 121
Sergiev, Il'ia Mikhailovich, 12
Sergieva, Elizaveta. *See* Elizaveta Konstantinovna
Sergii of Radonezh, Saint, 43, 167, 185–86, 271
sermon, 15, 34, 56, 67, 71, 76, 85, 88, 90, 92, 105, 167, 168, 177, 183, 202, 215–16, 229, 241, 243–44, 247, 250, 257, 259, 269
sexual, 23, 26–29, 32, 34–35, 88, 108, 128, 135, 217, 223

Shakhovskoi, 114, 119, 120
Shanshiev, Nikolai, 125–26
Shavel'skii, Georgii (Protopresbyter), 133, 289 n. 16
shelter, 75–77, 83, 137, 199, 216–17, 219, 221–22, 224, 267
Shemiakin, Ruth, 146, 148
Shenarii, Nikolai, 102
Sheremetev, 114
Shkliarevich, Varvara, 300–301 n. 3
shrine, 9, 99, 103, 120, 194, 212, 264, 285
Silaev, 271
Silent Ones (molchal'niki), 275
Simanovich, Aron, 115
Sinai, Mount, 3, 248
Skobelev, 267
Skorobogatenkov, Prokhor, 321 n. 12
Slavophile, 40, 74, 177, 234
snokhachestvo, 108
sobornost, 40
Society for the Care of Poor and Sick Children, 223
Society for the Prevention of Cruelty to Animals, 78, 244
Socrates, 33
Solovki, 179
soul, 13, 15, 17, 19, 23–25, 32, 40, 42, 49–51, 54, 56, 58–59, 62–64, 68, 84–86, 89, 100, 102–7, 116, 118, 126–28, 137, 140, 153, 161, 167, 173, 178, 183, 185, 216, 218–19, 256, 276
Source of Living Water, 278
souvenir, 2, 138, 151, 157, 283
sovereign, 77, 80, 131, 138, 235, 239–40, 245, 247, 269. *See also* tsar; emperor
Soviet, 3, 5, 7, 64, 72, 100, 107, 110, 123, 152, 184, 186, 199, 252, 270–76, 278
sovkhoz, 272, 274
Spain, 285
Speranskii, Nikolai, 122
spiritual verse, 193, 209, 216, 323 n. 39
St. Andrew's Cathedral, 13, 30, 60, 78, 81, 90–91, 142, 155–56, 218, 255, 257, 262, 267, 271
St. John of Kronstadt Press, 7, 268
State, 2–3, 5–6, 11, 45, 78–80, 158, 177, 201, 216–17, 224–25, 234, 242, 245, 250, 269–70
Stephana, 314 n. 45

Stepinac, Alojzije, Cardinal, 287 n. 1
Stolypin, Petr, 223–27
Storm (Groza), 229
Strigolniki, 198
Strugglers of Piety (Podvizhniki blagochestiia), 163
Studion, 39
suicide, 88, 106
Sukhanova, Nataliia, 211–13
Sura, 2, 12, 115, 166
Surskii (Il'iashevich), I. K., 7, 163, 181, 268
Sus'tie, 207
Suvorin, Aleksei, 189, 240–41
Suvorov, Field Marshal Alexander, 267
Sventitsky, Valentin (Priest), 64
Sviatopolk-Mirskii, 114
symphony, 45, 234, 269–70, 284
Synod, Holy, 40, 77, 86, 123, 155, 159, 160–61, 191, 194, 198, 201, 205, 209–11, 213, 224–27, 229, 231, 234, 242, 252, 261–62, 265, 275, 278, 283

Taisiia, Abbess, 134, 184, 256
Taneev, 114
Tarentuta, Matfei (Priest), 328 n. 33
Tatar, 5, 37, 154
Tatishchev, Vasilii, 114, 236
Tchaikovsky, Peter, 88–89, 267
tears, 17, 19, 22, 24, 45, 52, 62, 73, 118, 170, 173, 191
teetotaler, 230
temperance, 2, 26, 78
temptation, 17, 23, 25–26, 35, 92, 94, 133–34, 155, 189, 193, 245
Teresa of Avila, 8
terrorism, 3, 88, 100, 132, 235, 247–48
thaumaturge, 194, 282
Thecla, Saint, 214
Theological Academy, 2, 11–12, 78, 179, 187
Third Rome, 269
Tian-Shanskii, Alexander (Bishop), 7, 65, 166
Tiesenhausen, 114
Tifiaeva, 189
Tikhomirov, Savva (Bishop), 133, 193
Tikhon of Zadonsk, Saint, 30, 43–44, 70, 87, 90, 271

Tikhon, Patriarch, 275, 278, 285
Tikhvin, 112, 143
Tobolsk, 231
Tolstoy, Lev, 78, 84–85, 87–89, 92, 96, 114, 153, 166, 174, 180, 183, 188–90, 230, 233, 235, 238, 241–43, 249–50, 252, 257–59, 283
Tolstoy, Sophia, 31
Tomsk, 136, 231
Torzhok, 112
transubstantiation, 50
travel writing, 163, 166, 315 n. 52
Trinity, 32, 163, 192, 200, 205, 234
Trofimov, Petr, 209–11
troparion, 183, 269, 276, 277, 318 n. 125
Trotsky, Lev, 255
Trubetskoi, 114
tsar, 3, 6, 78, 114, 120–22, 131, 138, 154, 177, 225–26, 233, 236–39, 241, 244, 248–49, 254, 260, 269, 271, 278, 284. *See also* emperor; sovereign
Tübingen, 160
Turgenev, Ivan, 166, 177
Tver, 138, 274
Typicon, 53

ugodnik, 149–50
Ukhtomski, 114
Ukraine, 230
Ul'iana Lazarevskaia, Saint, 179, 295 n. 87
Uniate, 226, 244
Union of the Russian People, 3, 223, 227–28, 251–52, 284
United States, 2, 126, 239, 267–68. *See also* America
Ustasha, 287 n. 1
Ustiug, 166
Utica, New York, 7, 268
Utkin, Kos'ma, 328 n. 39
Uvarov, Count Sergei, 242

Varsonofii, elder of Optina, Saint, 268
Vasil'ev, Aleksandr (Protoierei), 327 n. 15
Vasil'ev, B. A., 229
Vatican II, 51
Vaulov, 228
Vel'iaminov, Nikolai, 238
Vereshchagin, Vasilii, 189
Veselitsk, 188

Index

vestments, 20–21, 61, 90, 136, 154, 158, 168
Vianney, Jean-Marie, 59, 65, 196, 282
Victoria, Queen, 138, 186
Vigil-aunties, 188
Vilna Students' Mutual Aid Society, 244
virgin, 27, 33, 122, 153, 180, 214, 224, 250, 277
virginity, 9, 27, 28, 29, 31, 179, 192, 202, 282
Vissarion, Bishop, 204–5
Vladimir, 230, 277
Vlasov, Andrei, General, 269
vodka, 26, 80, 106, 136, 172
Volkonsk, 114
Vologda, 230, 245
Voronezh, 136, 230
Vostorgov, Ioann (Priest), 252

"white" clergy, 304 n. 69
wanderer, 9, 21, 24, 43, 55, 167, 195, 202, 212, 272
warrior, 10, 179, 277
wells, 271, 272
What is Art?, 283
wife, 27, 29–35, 38, 40, 53, 146, 148–49, 156, 178–81, 191, 278

wine, 10, 26, 46, 48, 50, 94, 136–37, 164, 172
Witte, Sergei, 92, 154, 230, 250
women, 3–5, 31–32, 34, 41, 44, 46, 55–6, 59, 69, 76, 94, 102, 106–7, 109, 111, 117, 119, 127, 129–30, 132–33, 135–36, 145–46, 148, 156, 163, 166, 179, 184, 190, 201–2, 204, 207, 211–13, 216, 218, 221, 258–59, 266–67, 281–82
workers, 4, 76, 120, 122, 247, 256

Xanthippe, 33
Xenia, Blessed, Saint, 1, 277, 333 n. 34

Yahweh, 49

Zaccheus, 80, 302 n. 45
Zaitsev, Boris, 167
zastupnik, 150
Zelenova, Aleksandra, 127–29
Zemshchina, 224
Zhedenov, Nikolai, 223, 228–29
Zhemchuzhnikov, Aleksei, 240
Zhitomir, 265
Zhivotovskii, 166, 176
Zlatoustov, Aleksei (Priest), 202
Zosima of Optina, Saint, 61

Studies of the Harriman Institute
Selected Titles in Russian Literature and History

Richard S. Wortman, *Scenarios of Power: Myth and Ceremony in Russian Monarchy,* vol. 1 (Princeton University Press, 1995).

Deborah A. Martinsen, ed., *Literary Journals in Imperial Russia* (Cambridge University Press, 1997).

David L. Hoffman, *Peasant Metropolis: Social Identities in Moscow, 1929–1941* (Cornell University Press, 1994).

Robert A. Maguire, *Exploring Gogol* (Stanford University Press, 1994).

Theodore H. Friedgut, *Iuzovka and Revolution,* 2 vols. (Princeton University Press, 1989–94).

Olga Meerson, *Dostoevsky's Taboos* (Dresden University Press, 1998).

Catherine Theimer Nepomnyashchy, *Abram Tertz and the Poetics of Crime* (Yale University Press, 1995).

Hilary L. Fink, *Bergson and Russian Moderism, 1900–1930* (Northwestern University Press, 1998).

Cathy Popkin, *The Pragmatics of Insignificance: Chekhov, Zoshchenko, Gogol* (Stanford University Press, 1993).

Mark von Hagen, *Soldiers in the Proletarian Dictatorship* (Cornell University Press, 1990).

Michael David-Fox, *Revolution of the Mind: Higher Learning Among the Bolsheviks, 1918–1929* (Cornell University Press, 1997).

www.ingramcontent.com/pod-product-compliance
Lightning Source LLC
Chambersburg PA
CBHW031542300426
44111CB00006BA/145